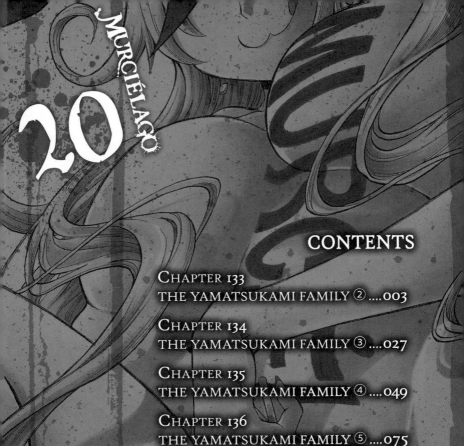

MURCIÉLAGO

20

CONTENTS

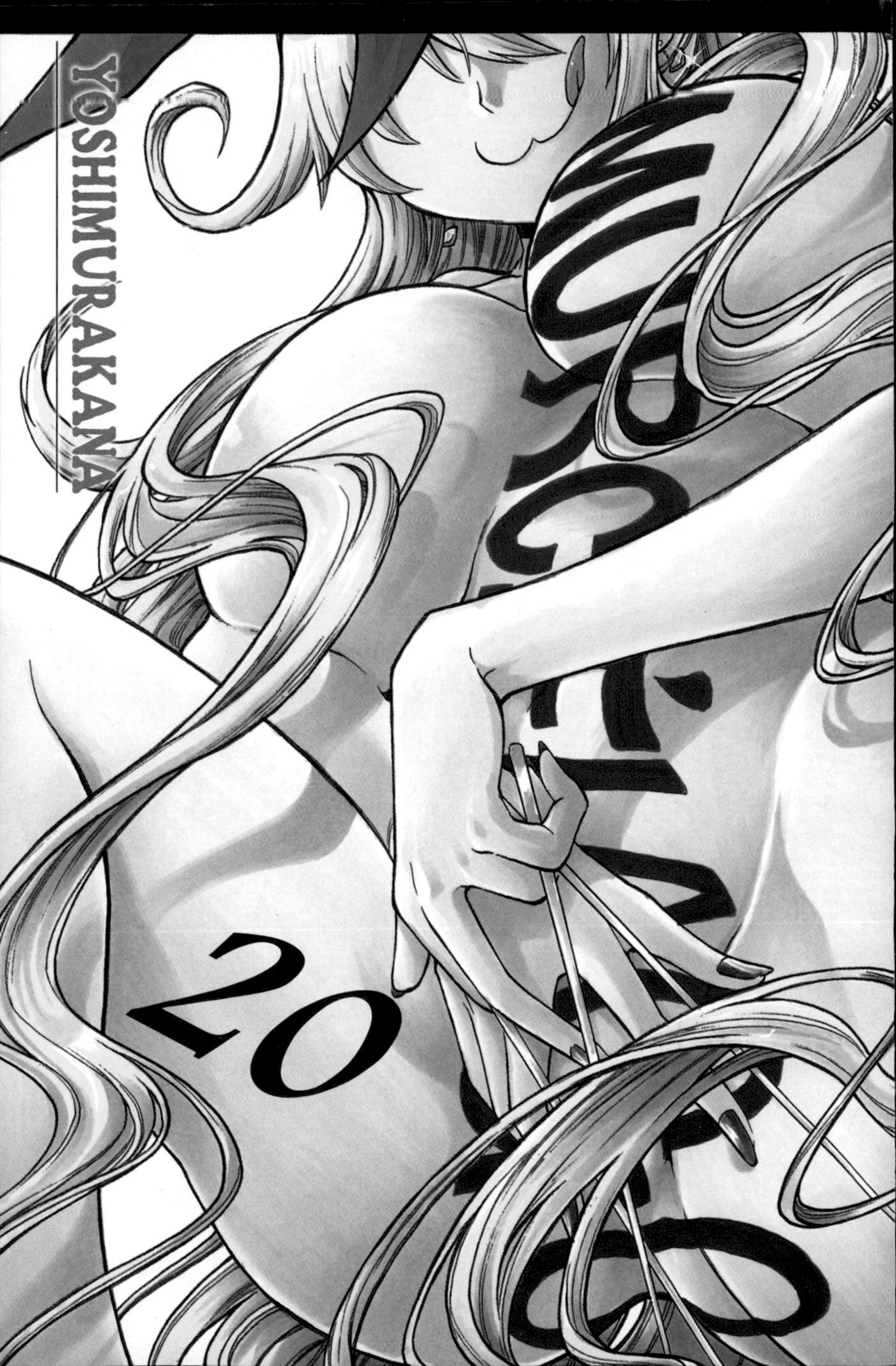
YOSHIMURAKANA
20

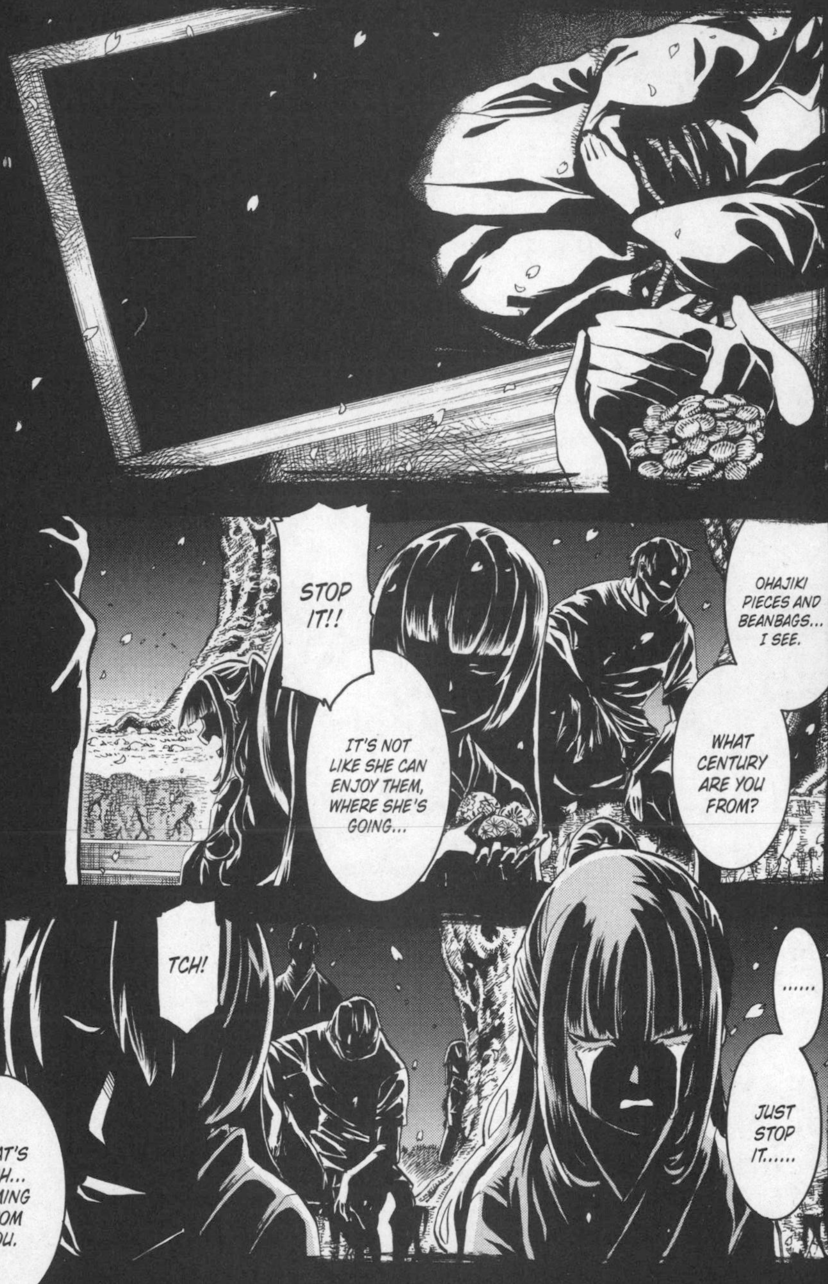
OHAJIKI PIECES AND BEANBAGS... I SEE.
WHAT CENTURY ARE YOU FROM?
IT'S NOT LIKE SHE CAN ENJOY THEM, WHERE SHE'S GOING...
STOP IT!!
......
JUST STOP IT......
TCH!
THAT'S RICH... COMING FROM YOU.

MURCIÉLAGO

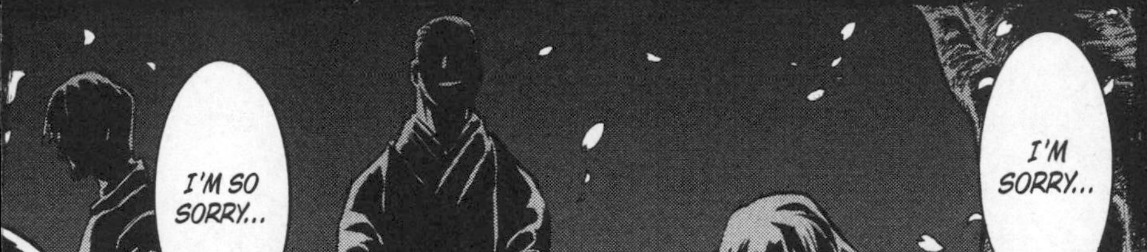
I'M SORRY...
I'M SO SORRY...
... AYAKO ...

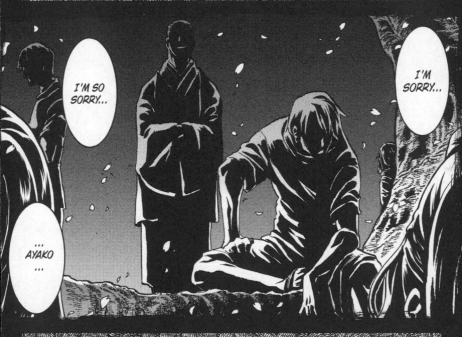

Chapter 133
The Yamatsukami Family ②

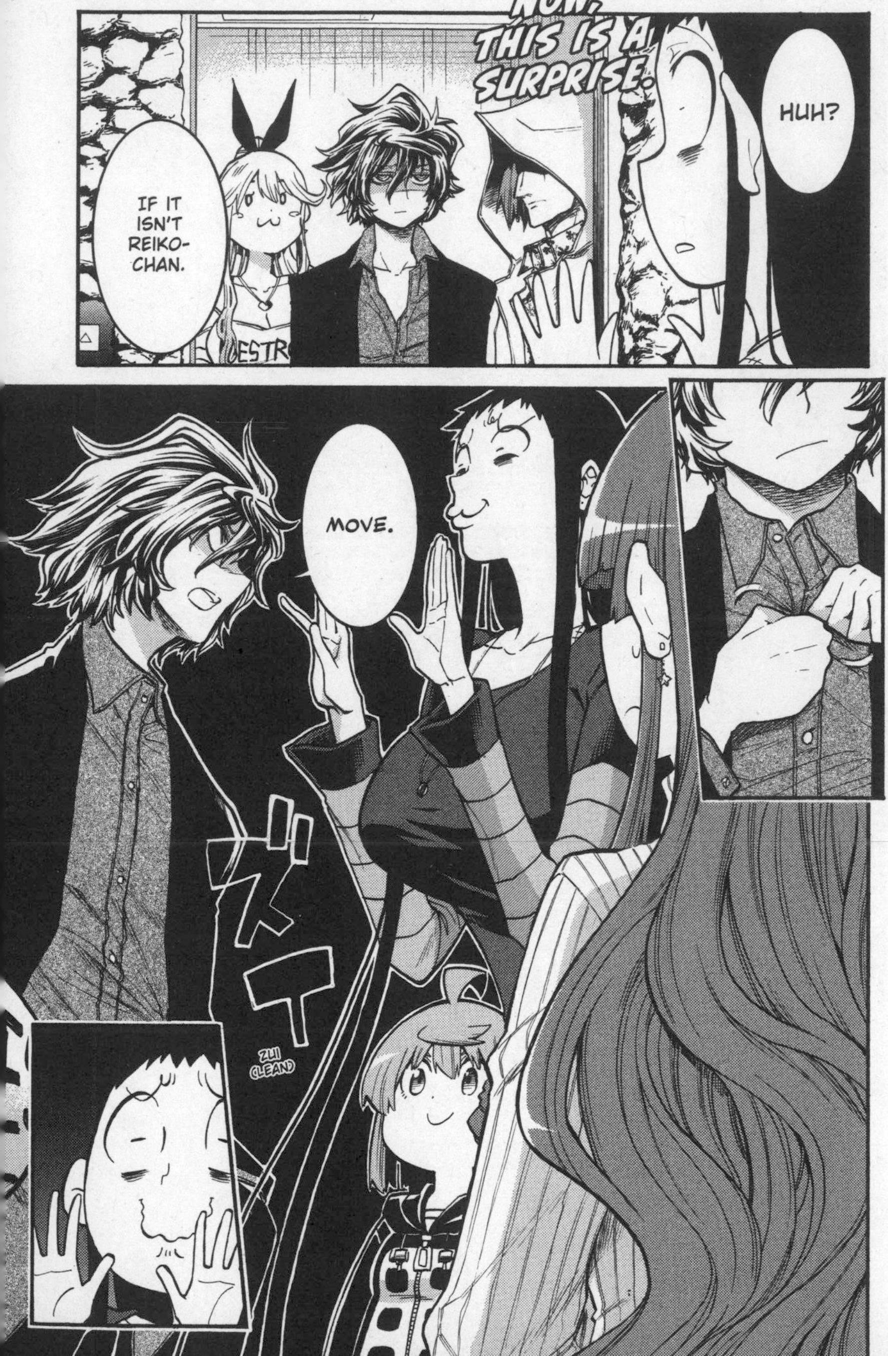
HUH?
NOW, THIS IS A SURPRISE.
IF IT ISN'T REIKO-CHAN.
MOVE.
ZUI (LEAN)

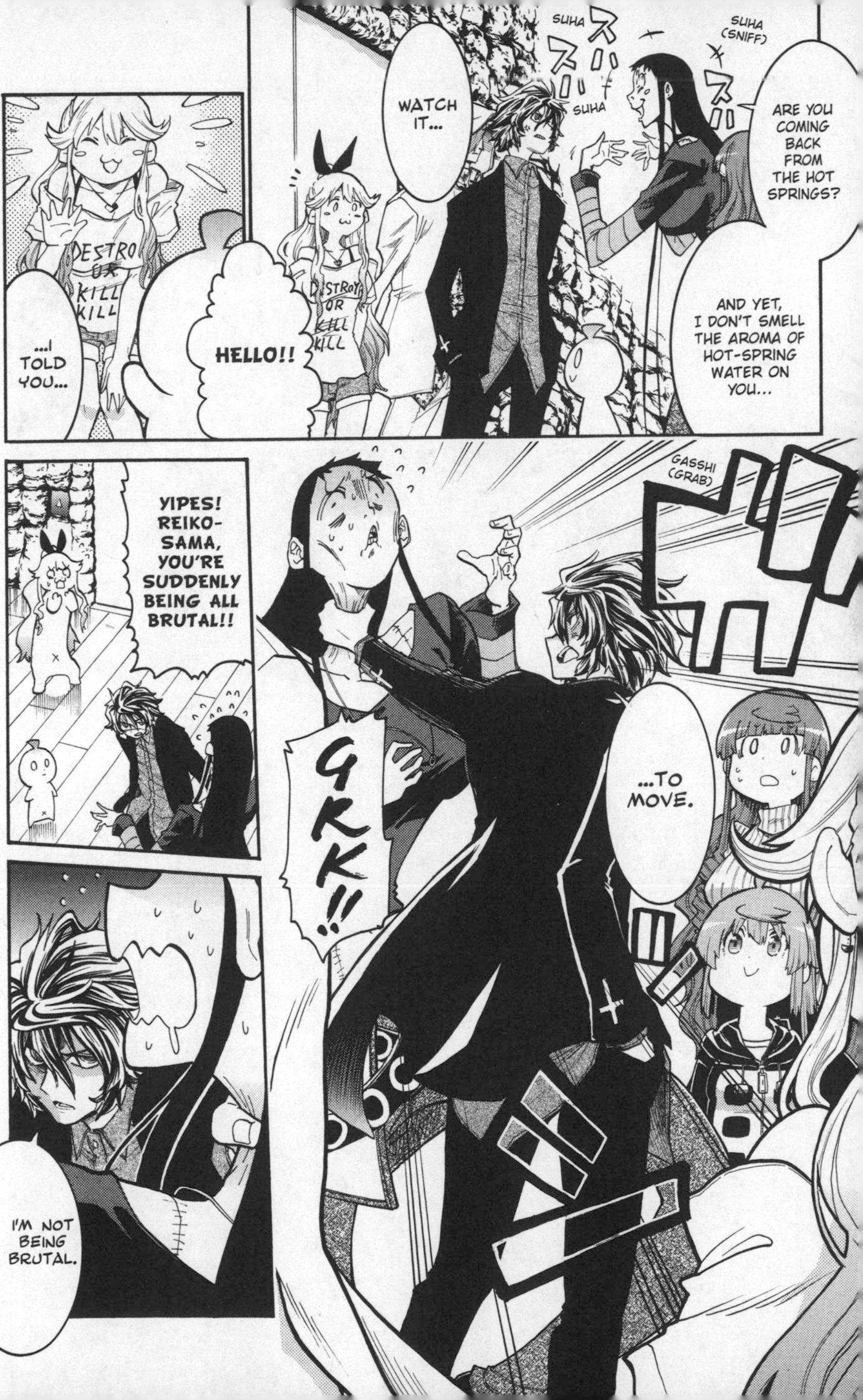
SUHA (SNIFF)
ARE YOU COMING BACK FROM THE HOT SPRINGS?
SUHA
SUHA
AND YET, I DON'T SMELL THE AROMA OF HOT-SPRING WATER ON YOU...
WATCH IT...
HELLO!!
...I TOLD YOU...
GASSHI (GRAB)
...TO MOVE.
GRK!!
YIPES! REIKO-SAMA, YOU'RE SUDDENLY BEING ALL BRUTAL!!
I'M NOT BEING BRUTAL.

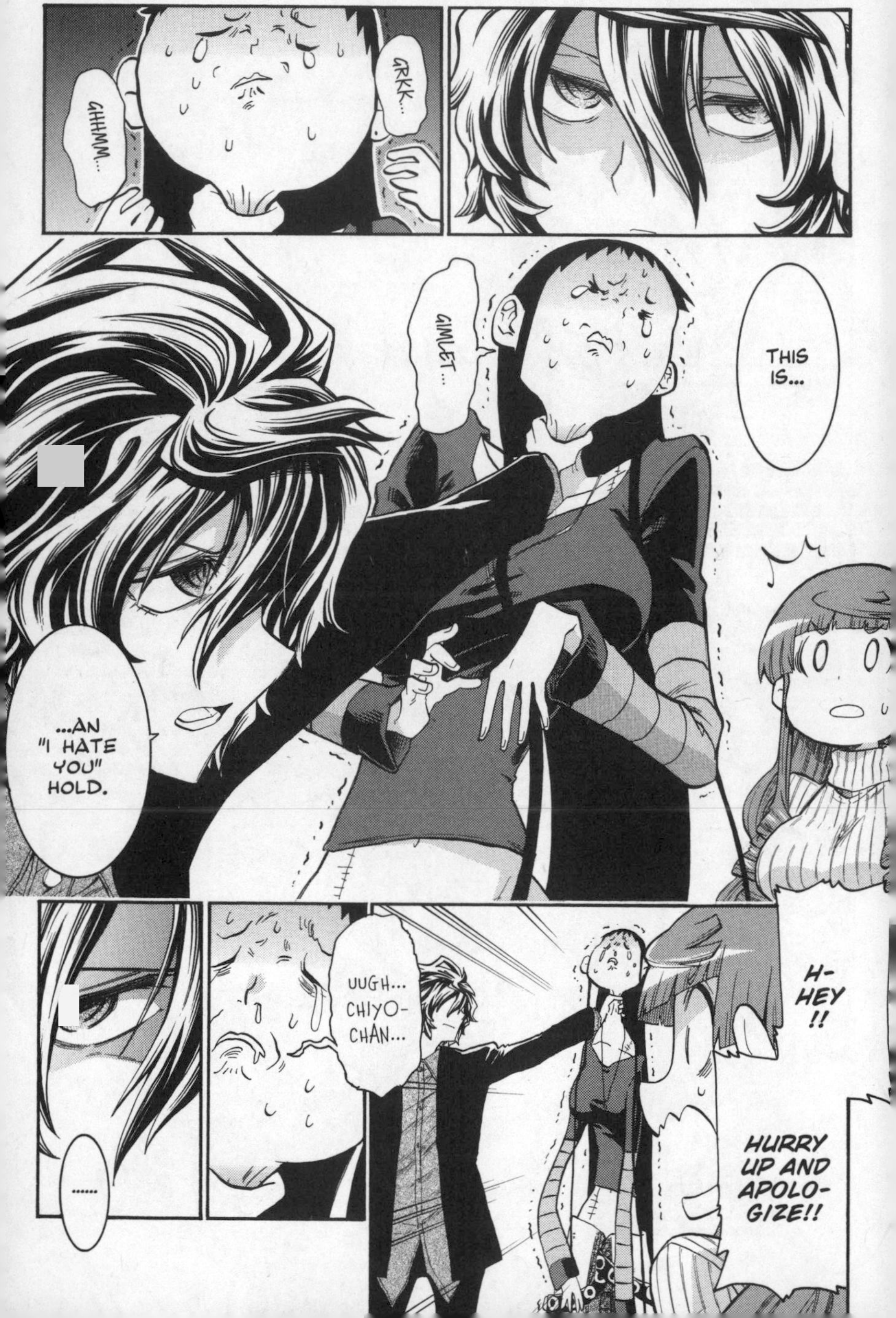
GRKK...
GHMM...
THIS IS...
GIMLET...
...AN "I HATE YOU" HOLD.
H-HEY!!
HURRY UP AND APOLOGIZE!!
UUGH... CHIYO-CHAN...
......

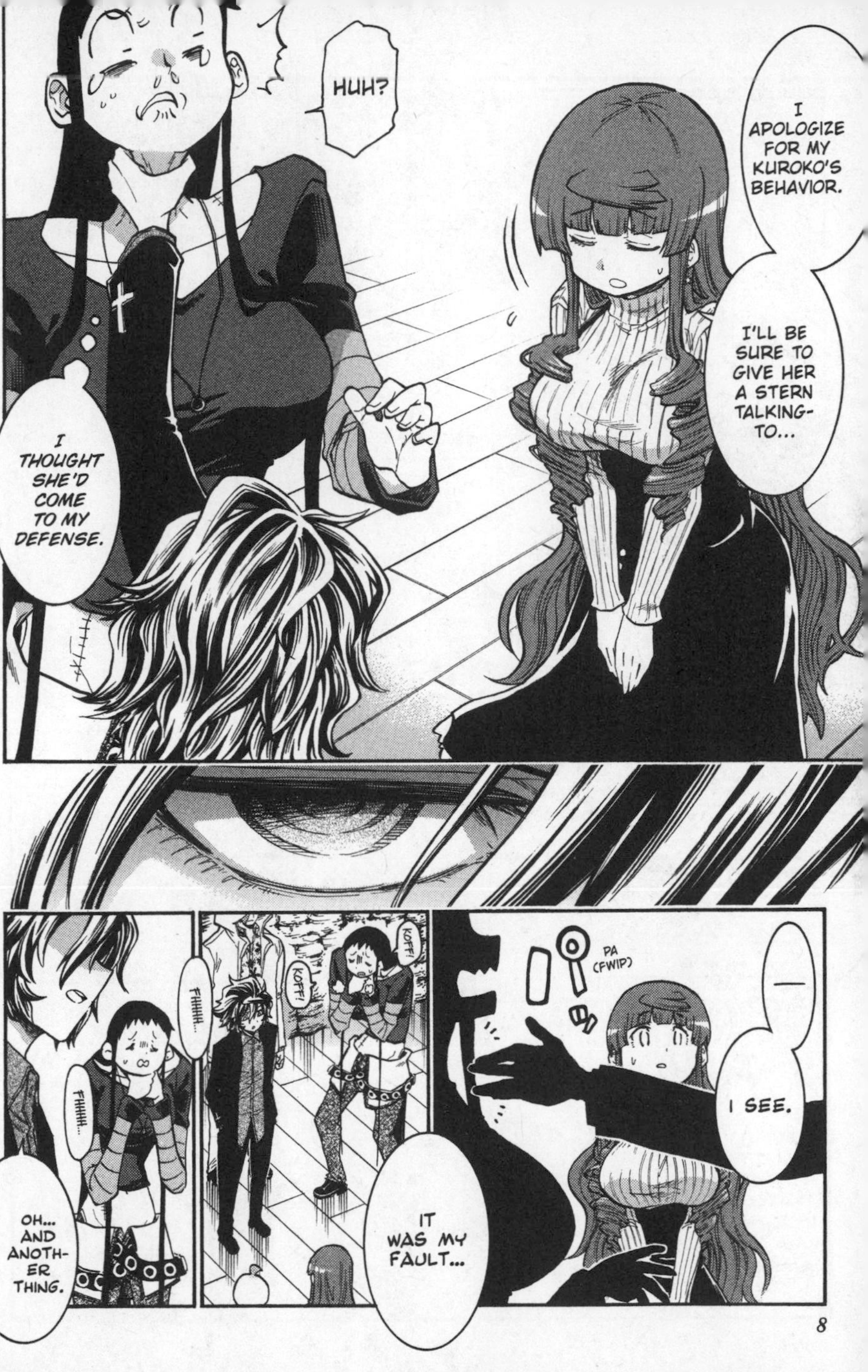
I APOLOGIZE FOR MY KUROKO'S BEHAVIOR.
I'LL BE SURE TO GIVE HER A STERN TALKING-TO...
HUH?
I THOUGHT SHE'D COME TO MY DEFENSE.
PA (FWIP)
—
I SEE.
KOFF!
KOFF!
IT WAS MY FAULT...
FHHHHH...
FHHHHH...
OH... AND ANOTHER THING.

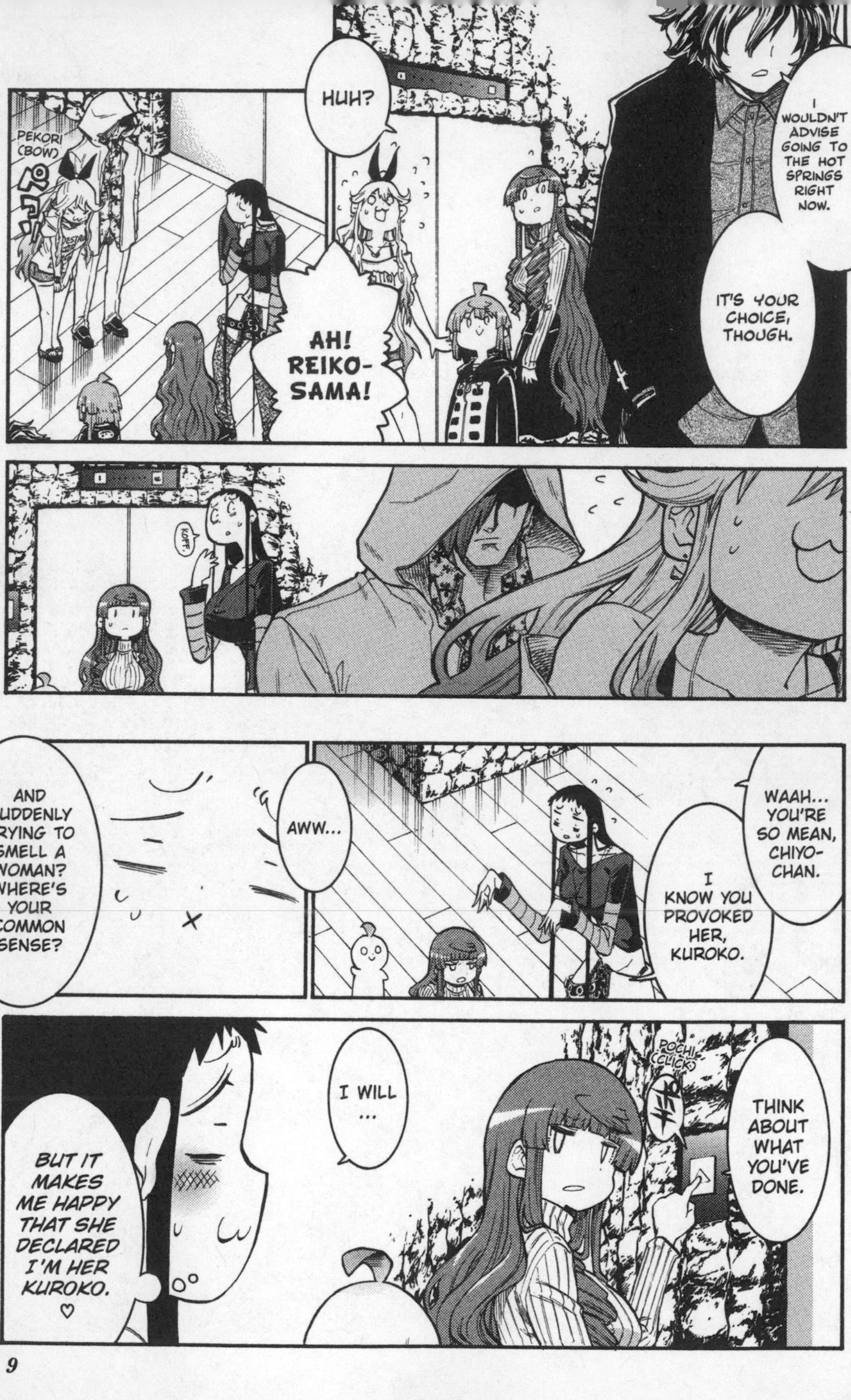
I WOULDN'T ADVISE GOING TO THE HOT SPRINGS RIGHT NOW.
IT'S YOUR CHOICE, THOUGH.
HUH?
AH! REIKO-SAMA!
PEKORI (BOW)
KOFF.
WAAH... YOU'RE SO MEAN, CHIYO-CHAN.
I KNOW YOU PROVOKED HER, KUROKO.
AWW...
AND SUDDENLY TRYING TO SMELL A WOMAN? WHERE'S YOUR COMMON SENSE?
THINK ABOUT WHAT YOU'VE DONE.
POCHI (CLICK)
I WILL ...
BUT IT MAKES ME HAPPY THAT SHE DECLARED I'M HER KUROKO. ♡

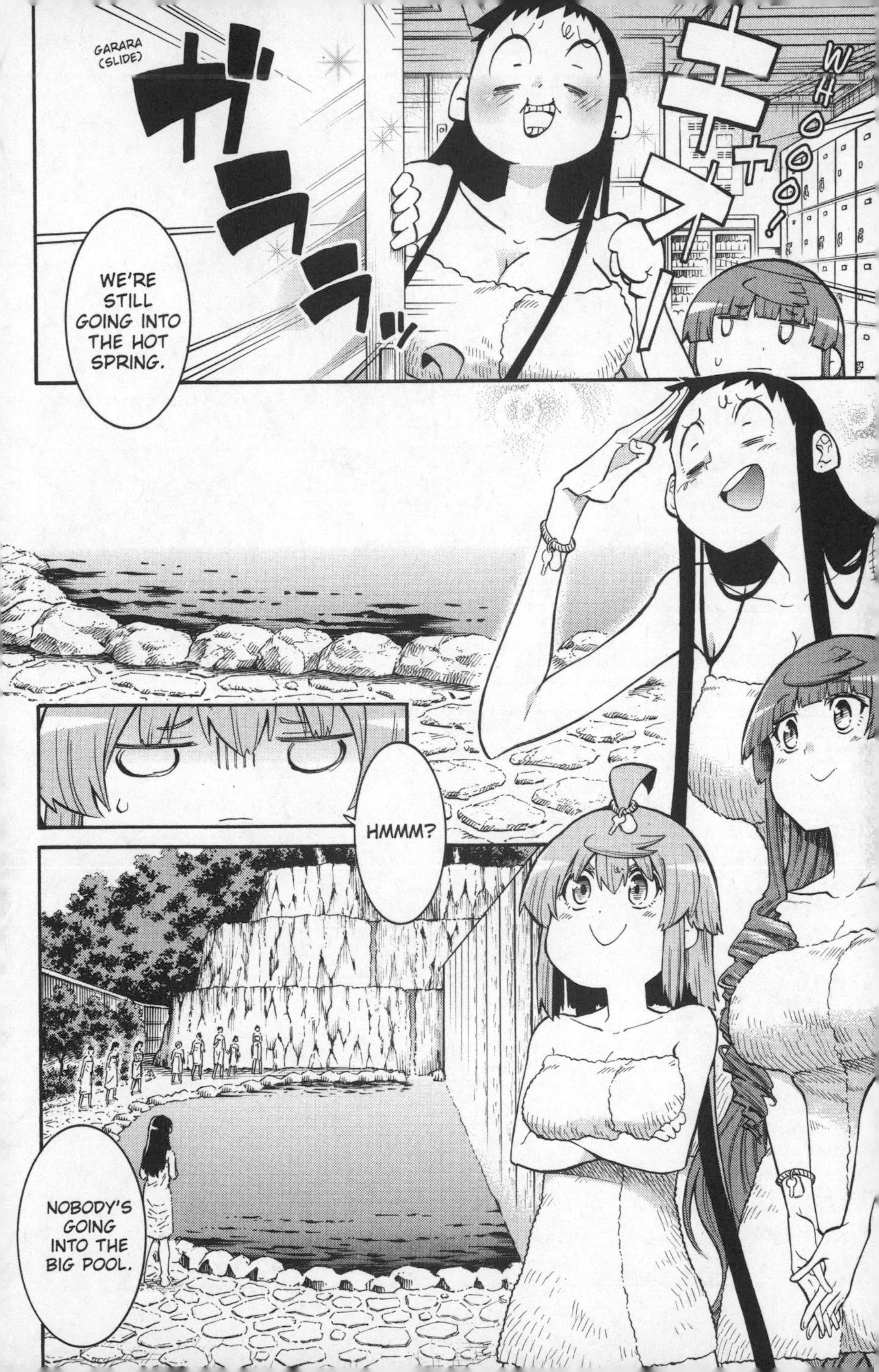
WHOOOO!
GARARA (SLIDE)
WE'RE STILL GOING INTO THE HOT SPRING.
HMMM?
NOBODY'S GOING INTO THE BIG POOL.

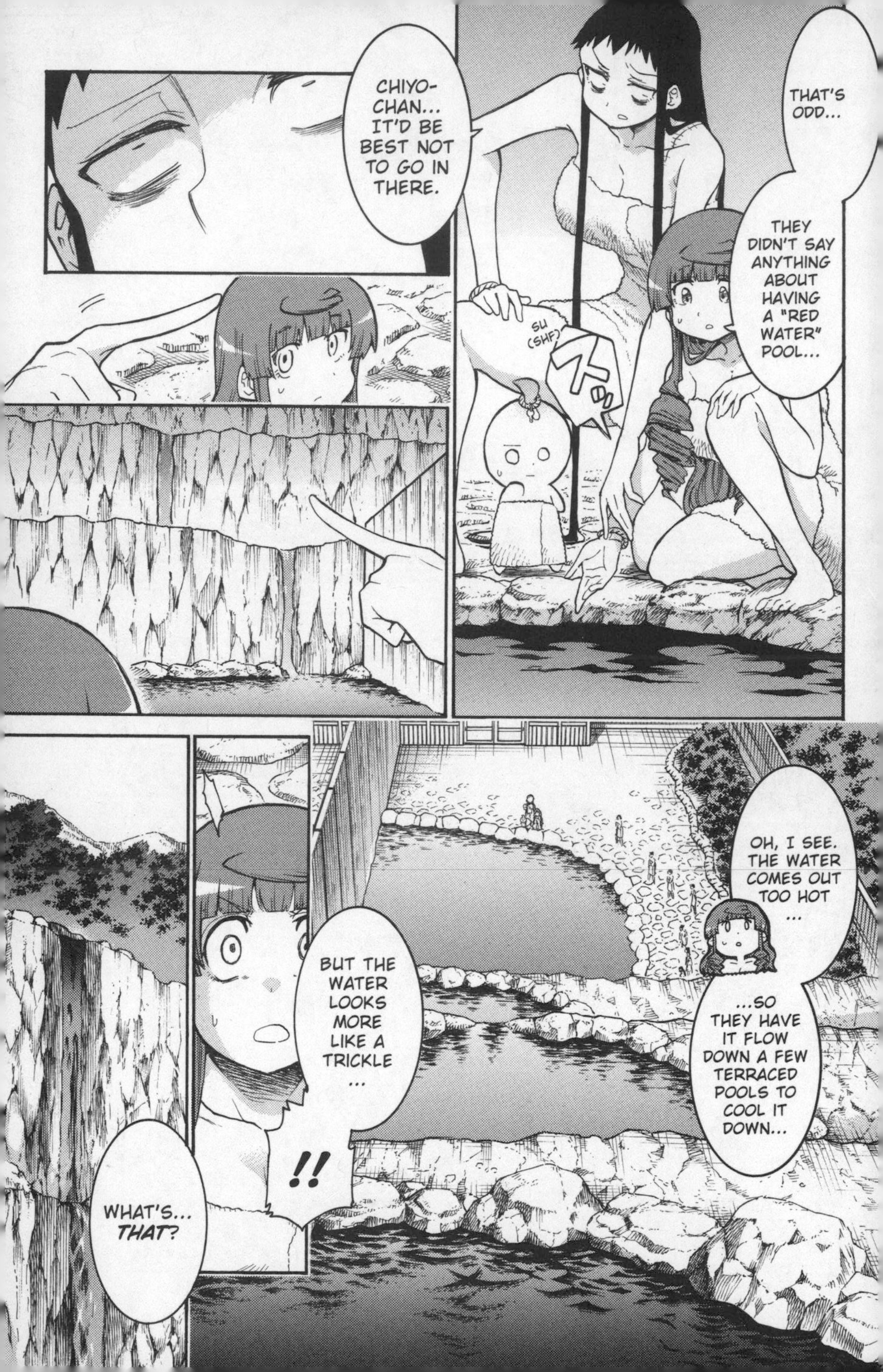
THAT'S ODD...
THEY DIDN'T SAY ANYTHING ABOUT HAVING A "RED WATER" POOL...
SU (SHF)
CHIYO-CHAN... IT'D BE BEST NOT TO GO IN THERE.
OH, I SEE. THE WATER COMES OUT TOO HOT ...
...SO THEY HAVE IT FLOW DOWN A FEW TERRACED POOLS TO COOL IT DOWN...
BUT THE WATER LOOKS MORE LIKE A TRICKLE ...
!!
WHAT'S... *THAT*?

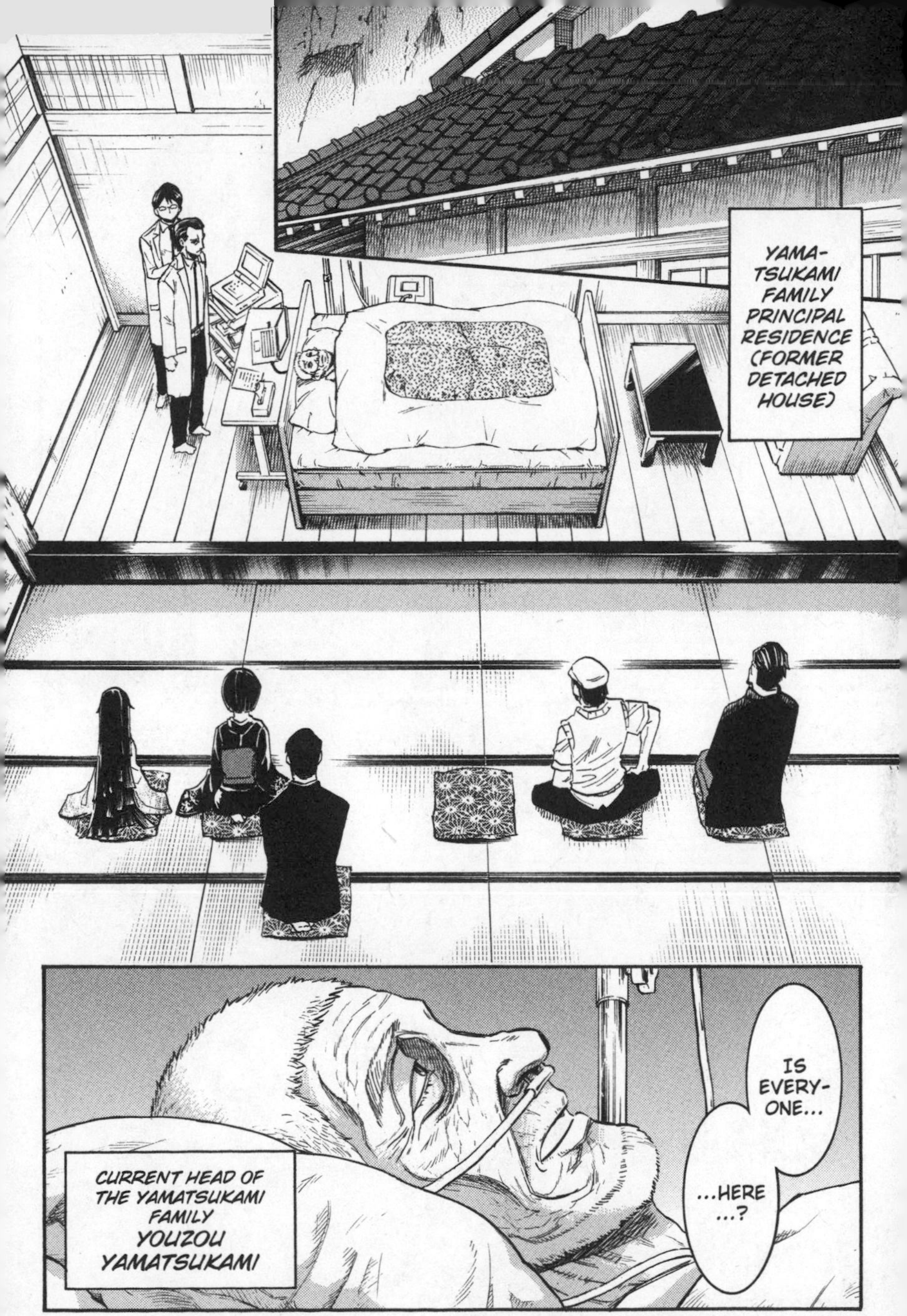
YAMA-TSUKAMI FAMILY PRINCIPAL RESIDENCE (FORMER DETACHED HOUSE)
IS EVERY-ONE...
...HERE ...?
CURRENT HEAD OF THE YAMATSUKAMI FAMILY YOUZOU YAMATSUKAMI

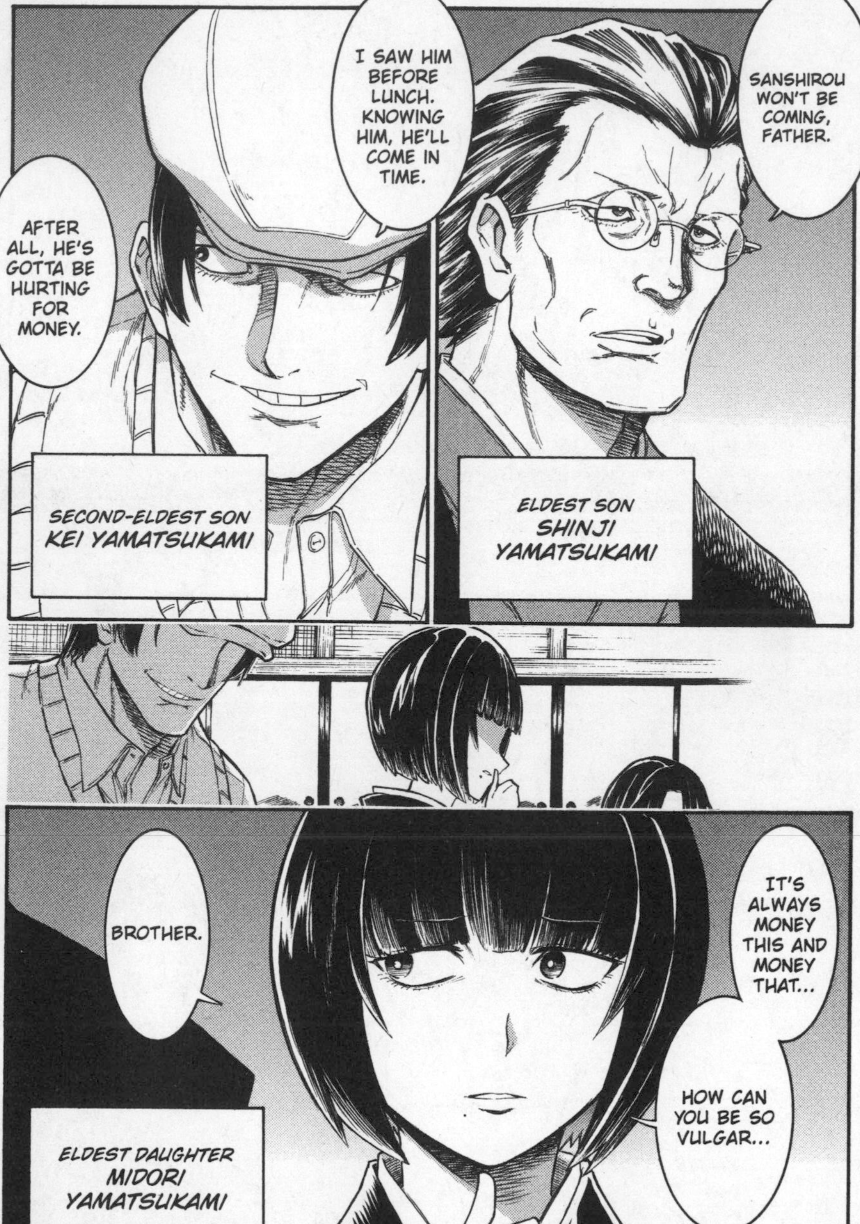
SANSHIROU WON'T BE COMING, FATHER.
ELDEST SON SHINJI YAMATSUKAMI
I SAW HIM BEFORE LUNCH. KNOWING HIM, HE'LL COME IN TIME.
AFTER ALL, HE'S GOTTA BE HURTING FOR MONEY.
SECOND-ELDEST SON KEI YAMATSUKAMI
IT'S ALWAYS MONEY THIS AND MONEY THAT...
HOW CAN YOU BE SO VULGAR...
BROTHER.
ELDEST DAUGHTER MIDORI YAMATSUKAMI

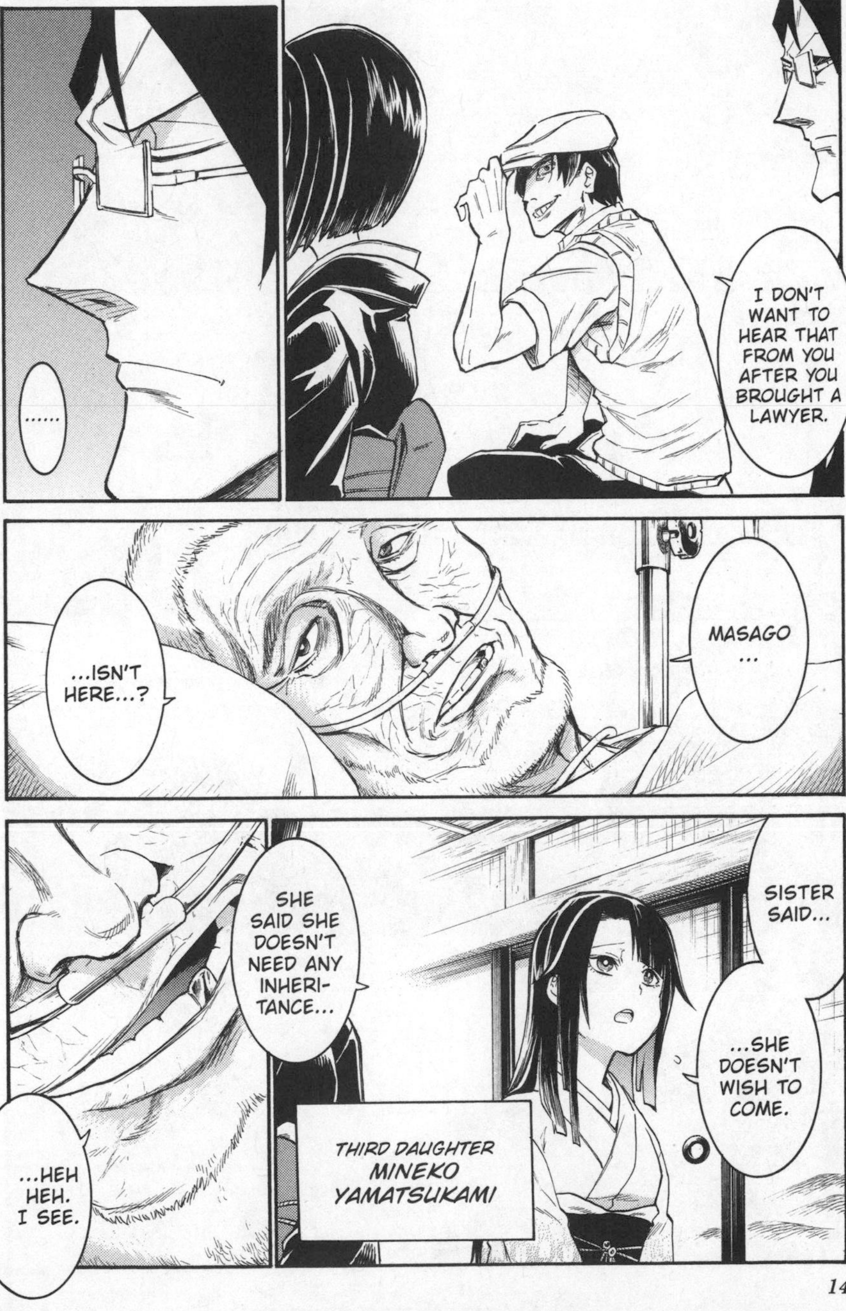
I DON'T WANT TO HEAR THAT FROM YOU AFTER YOU BROUGHT A LAWYER.
......
MASAGO ...
...ISN'T HERE...?
SISTER SAID...
...SHE DOESN'T WISH TO COME.
THIRD DAUGHTER MINEKO YAMATSUKAMI
SHE SAID SHE DOESN'T NEED ANY INHERI-TANCE...
...HEH HEH. I SEE.

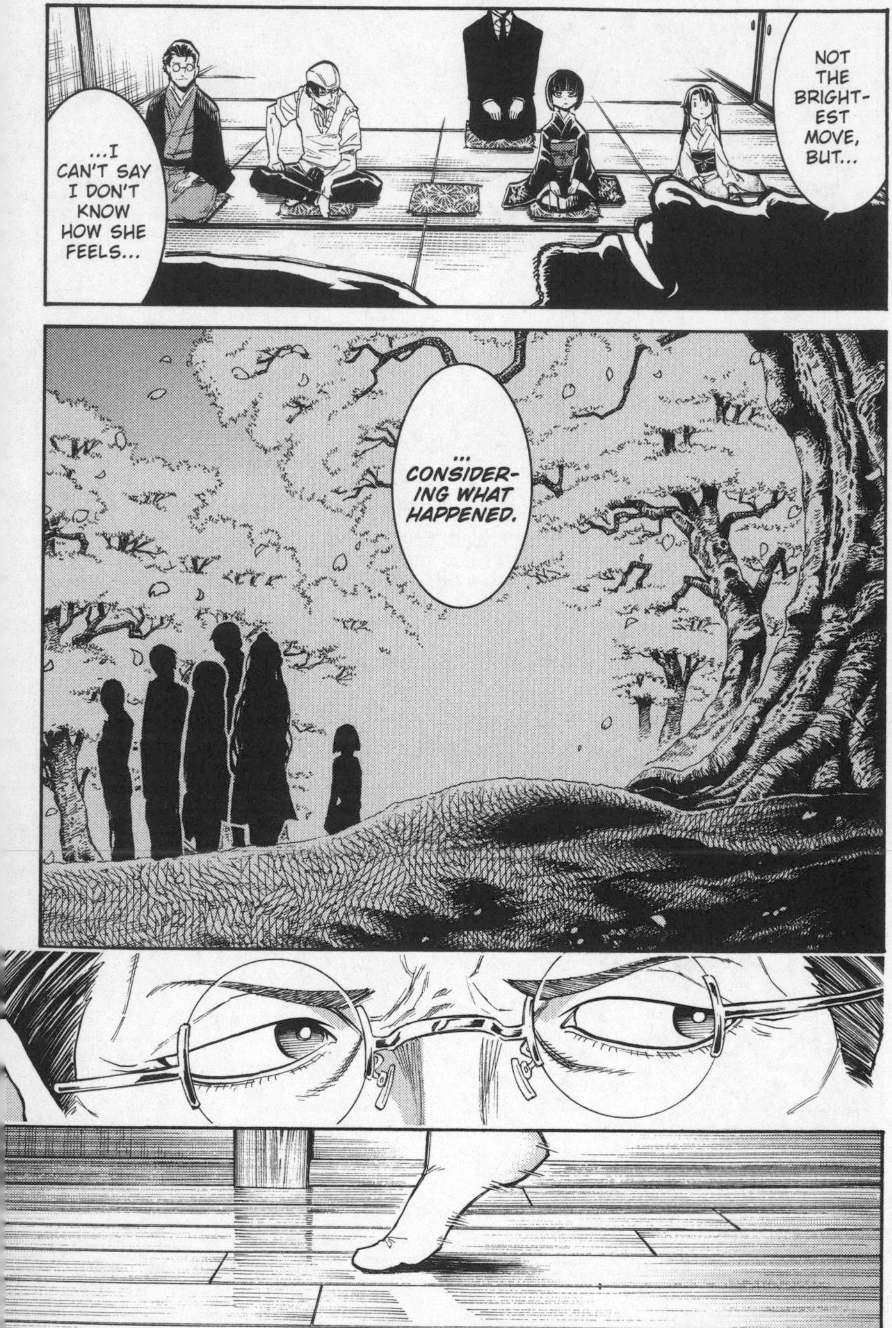
NOT THE BRIGHT-EST MOVE, BUT...
...I CAN'T SAY I DON'T KNOW HOW SHE FEELS...
...CONSIDER-ING WHAT HAPPENED.

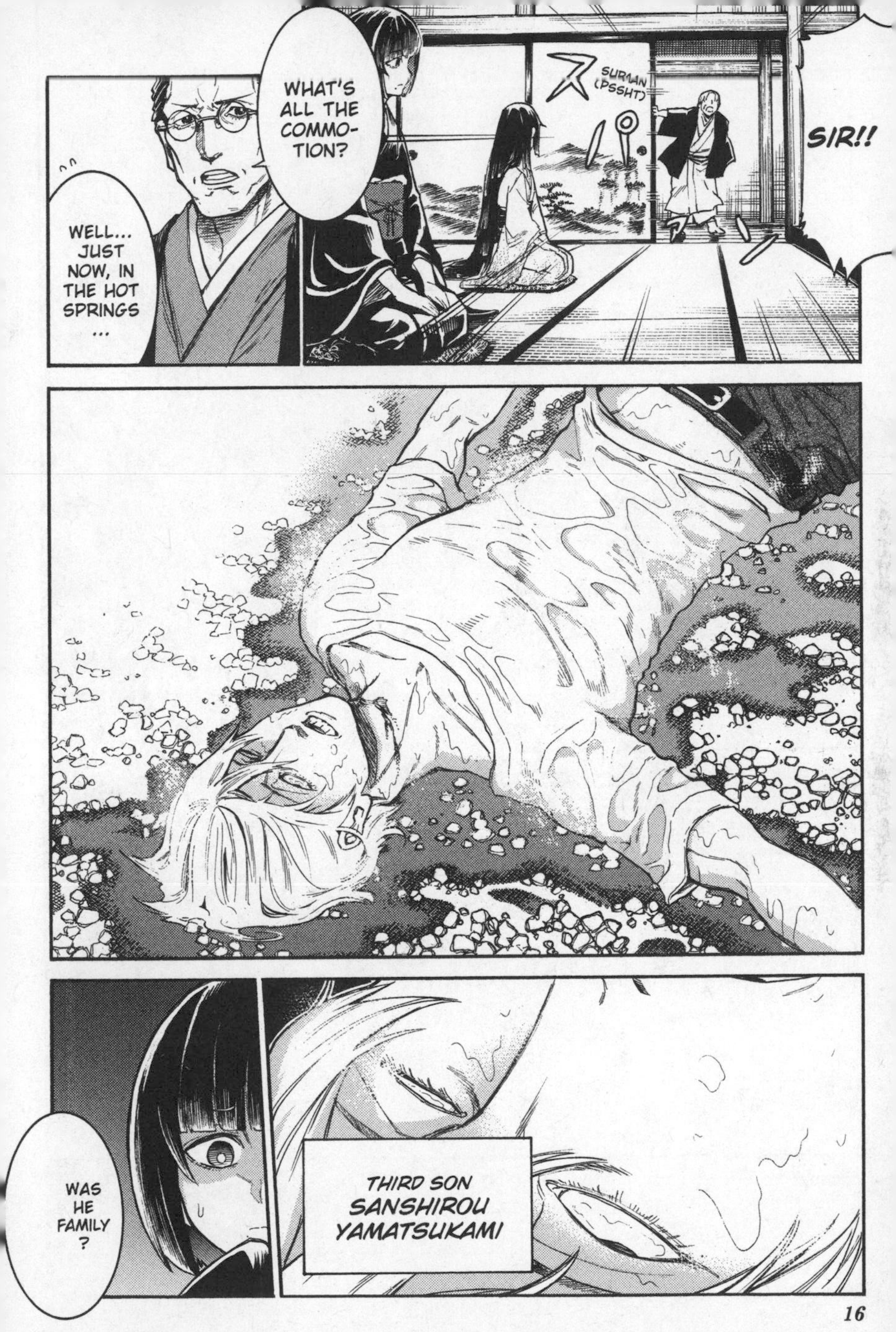
SIR!!
SURAAN (PSSHT)
WHAT'S ALL THE COMMOTION?
WELL... JUST NOW, IN THE HOT SPRINGS...
THIRD SON SANSHIROU YAMATSUKAMI
WAS HE FAMILY?

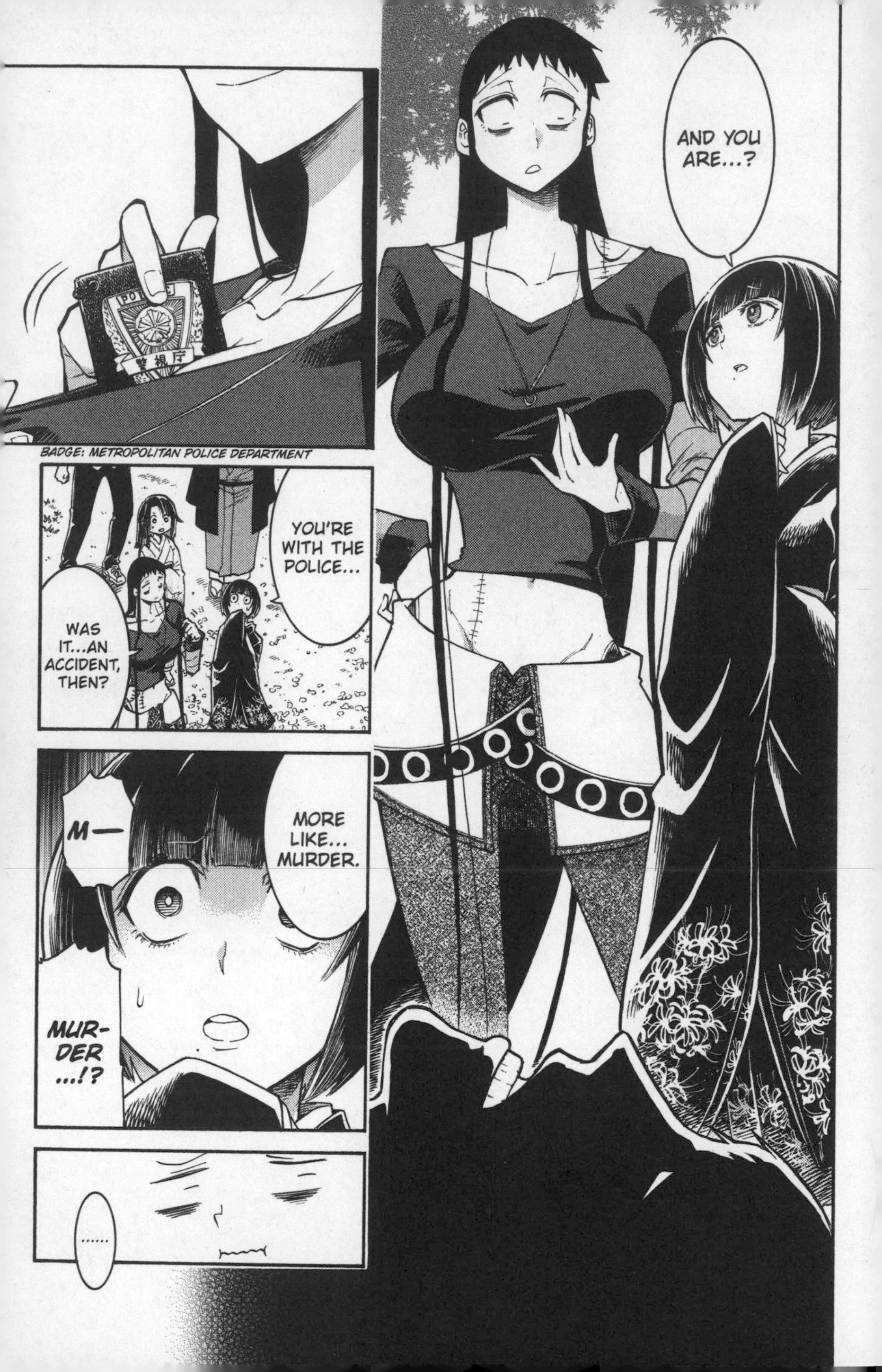
AND YOU ARE...?
警視庁
BADGE: METROPOLITAN POLICE DEPARTMENT
YOU'RE WITH THE POLICE...
WAS IT...AN ACCIDENT, THEN?
MORE LIKE... MURDER.
M—
MUR-DER...!?
......

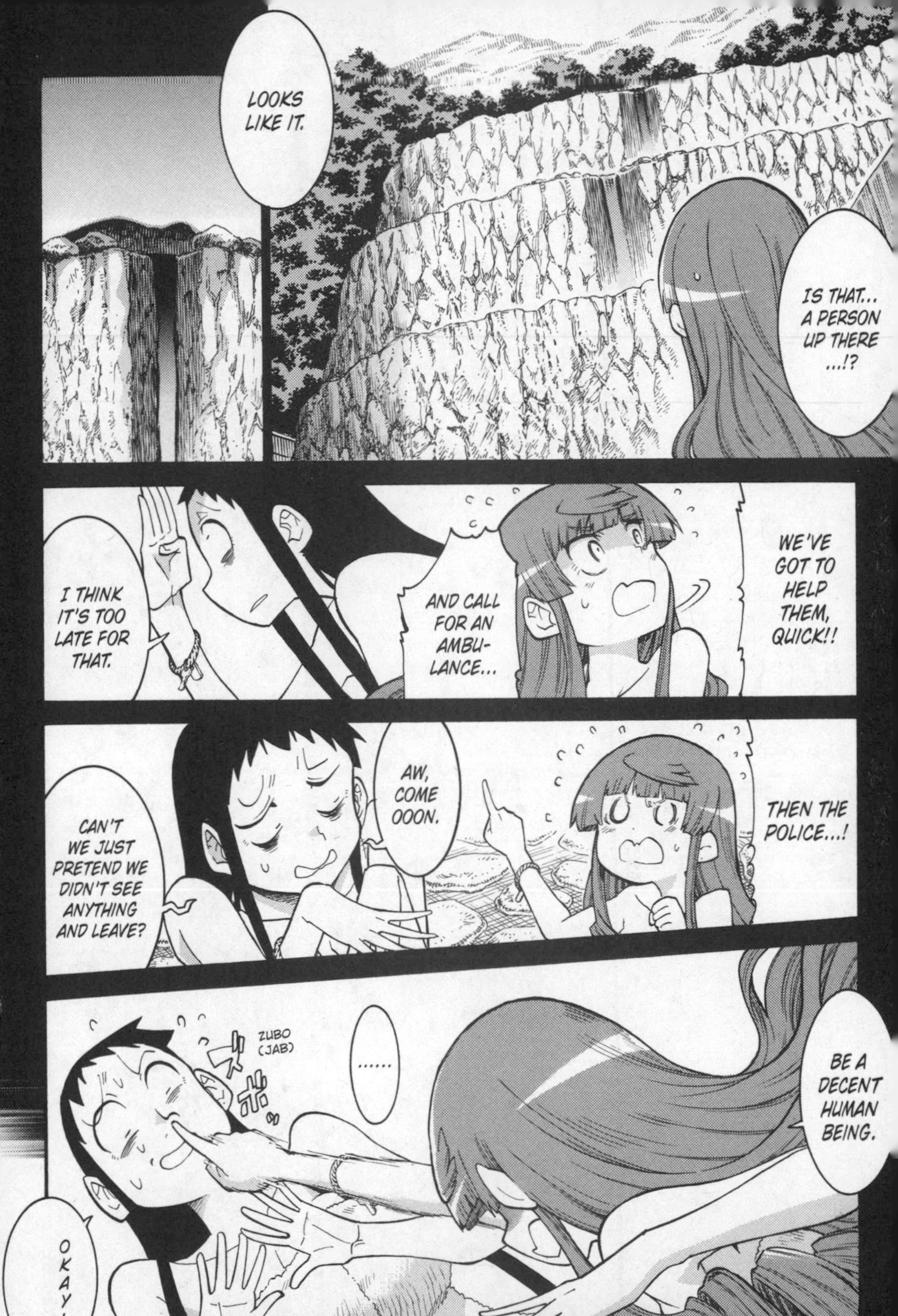
IS THAT... A PERSON UP THERE ...!?
LOOKS LIKE IT.
WE'VE GOT TO HELP THEM, QUICK!!
AND CALL FOR AN AMBU-LANCE...
I THINK IT'S TOO LATE FOR THAT.
THEN THE POLICE...!
AW, COME OOON.
CAN'T WE JUST PRETEND WE DIDN'T SEE ANYTHING AND LEAVE?
BE A DECENT HUMAN BEING.
......
ZUBO (JAB)
OKAY.

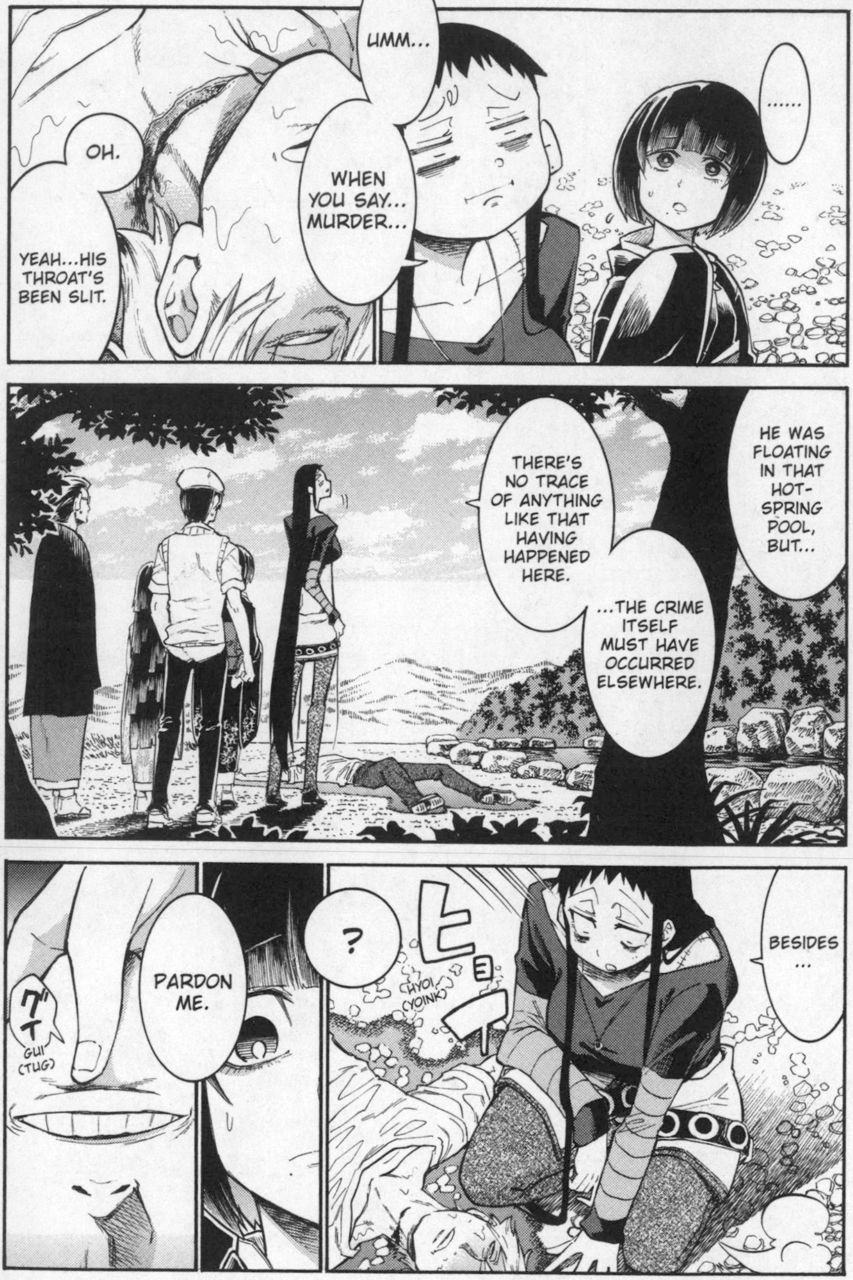
......
UMM...
WHEN YOU SAY... MURDER...
OH.
YEAH...HIS THROAT'S BEEN SLIT.
HE WAS FLOATING IN THAT HOT-SPRING POOL, BUT...
THERE'S NO TRACE OF ANYTHING LIKE THAT HAVING HAPPENED HERE.
...THE CRIME ITSELF MUST HAVE OCCURRED ELSEWHERE.
BESIDES ...
ヒョイ
(HYOI) (YOINK)
?
PARDON ME.
グイ
GUI (TUG)

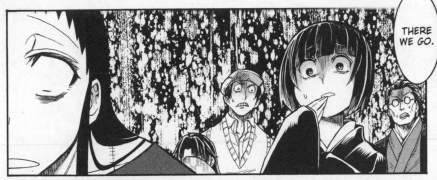

THERE WE GO.

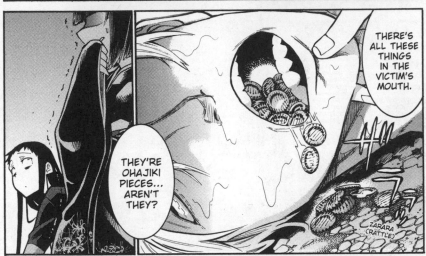

THERE'S ALL THESE THINGS IN THE VICTIM'S MOUTH.

THEY'RE OHAJIKI PIECES... AREN'T THEY?

ZARARA (RATTLE)

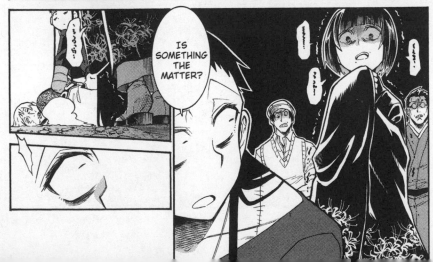

IS SOMETHING THE MATTER?

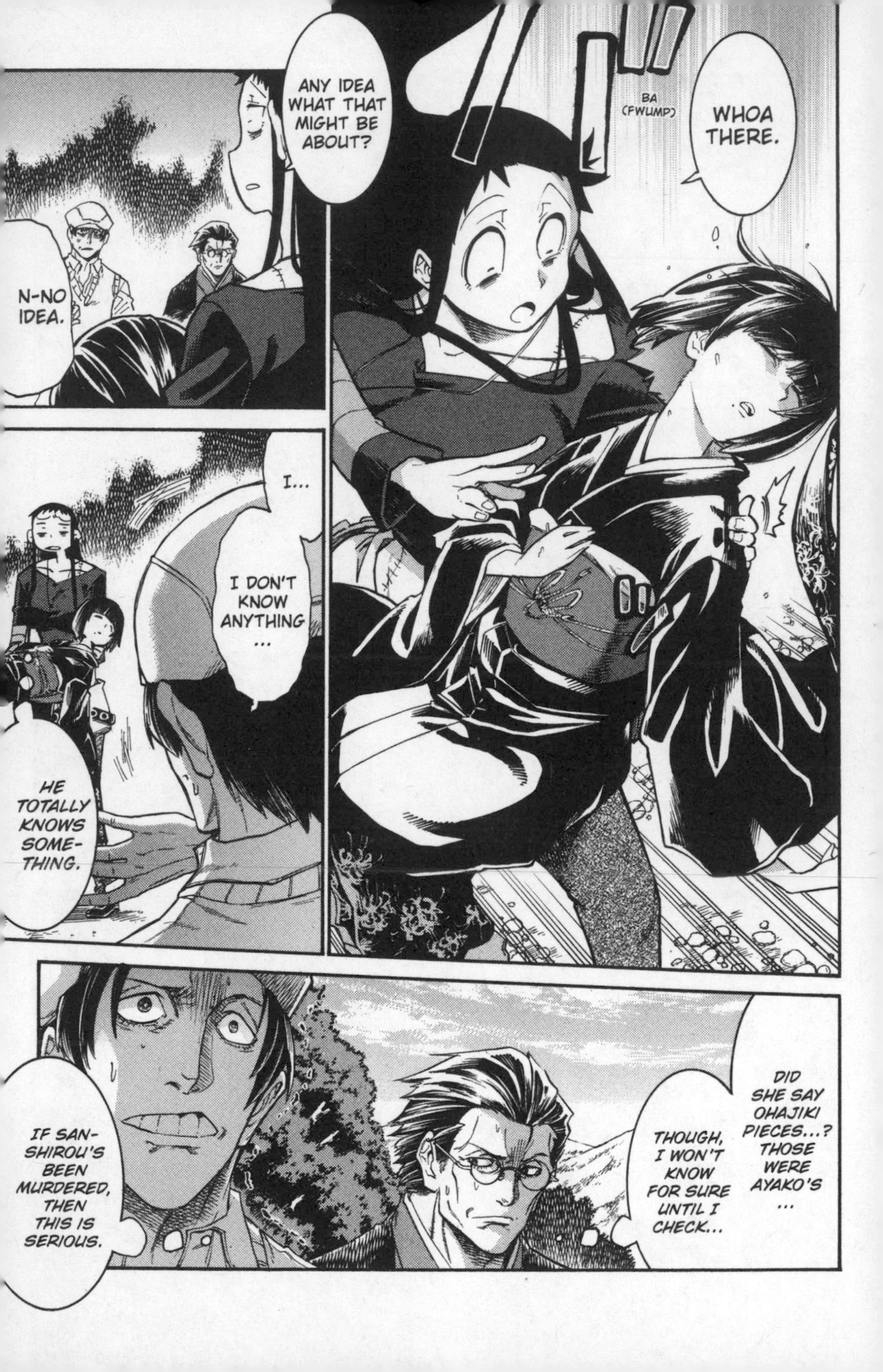
WHOA THERE.
BA (FWUMP)
ANY IDEA WHAT THAT MIGHT BE ABOUT?
N-NO IDEA.
I...
I DON'T KNOW ANYTHING ...
HE TOTALLY KNOWS SOME-THING.
DID SHE SAY OHAJIKI PIECES...? THOSE WERE AYAKO'S ...
THOUGH, I WON'T KNOW FOR SURE UNTIL I CHECK...
IF SAN-SHIROU'S BEEN MURDERED, THEN THIS IS SERIOUS.

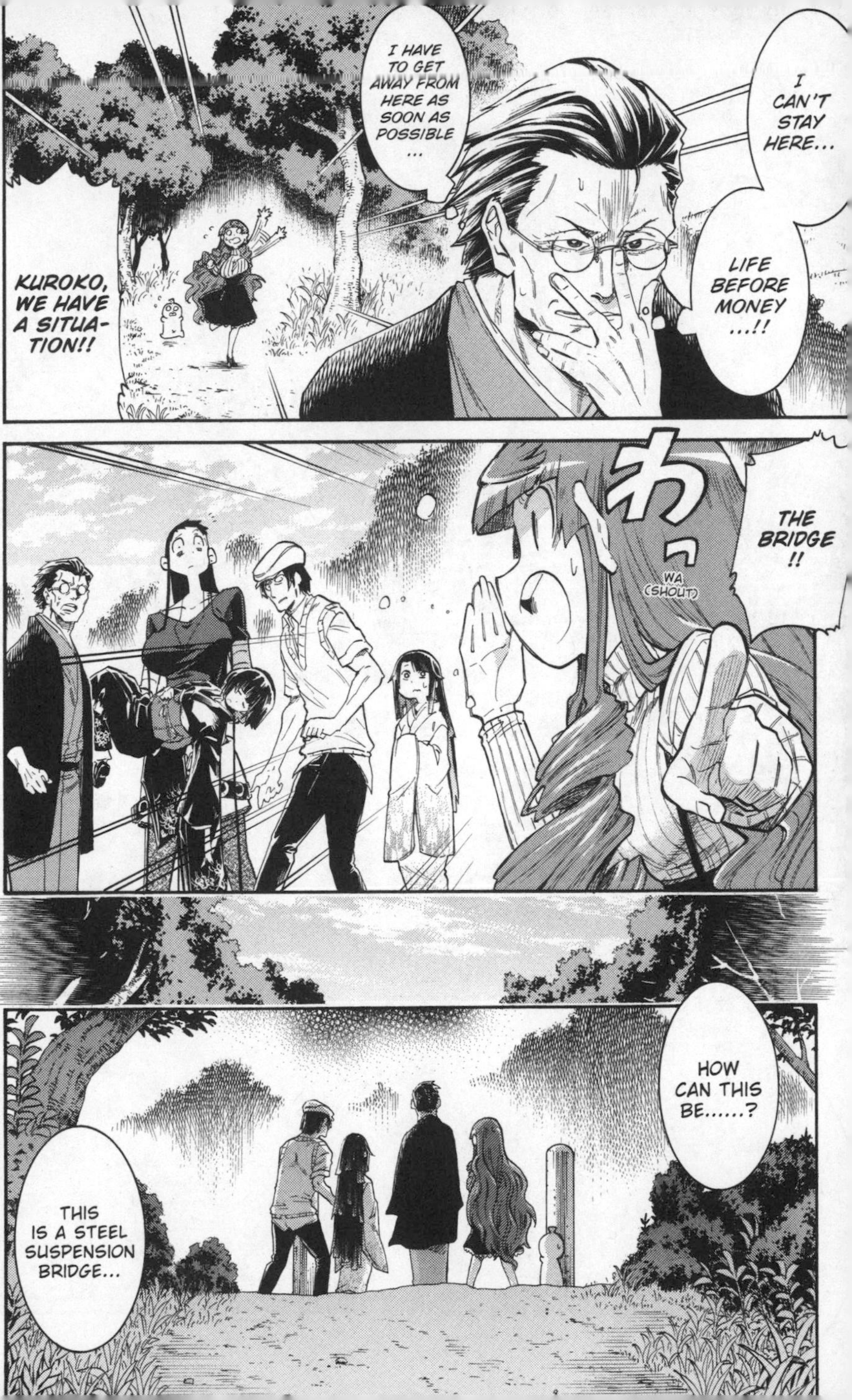
I CAN'T STAY HERE...
LIFE BEFORE MONEY ...!!
I HAVE TO GET AWAY FROM HERE AS SOON AS POSSIBLE ...
KUROKO, WE HAVE A SITUATION!!
THE BRIDGE !!
わっ
WA (SHOUT)
HOW CAN THIS BE......?
THIS IS A STEEL SUSPENSION BRIDGE...

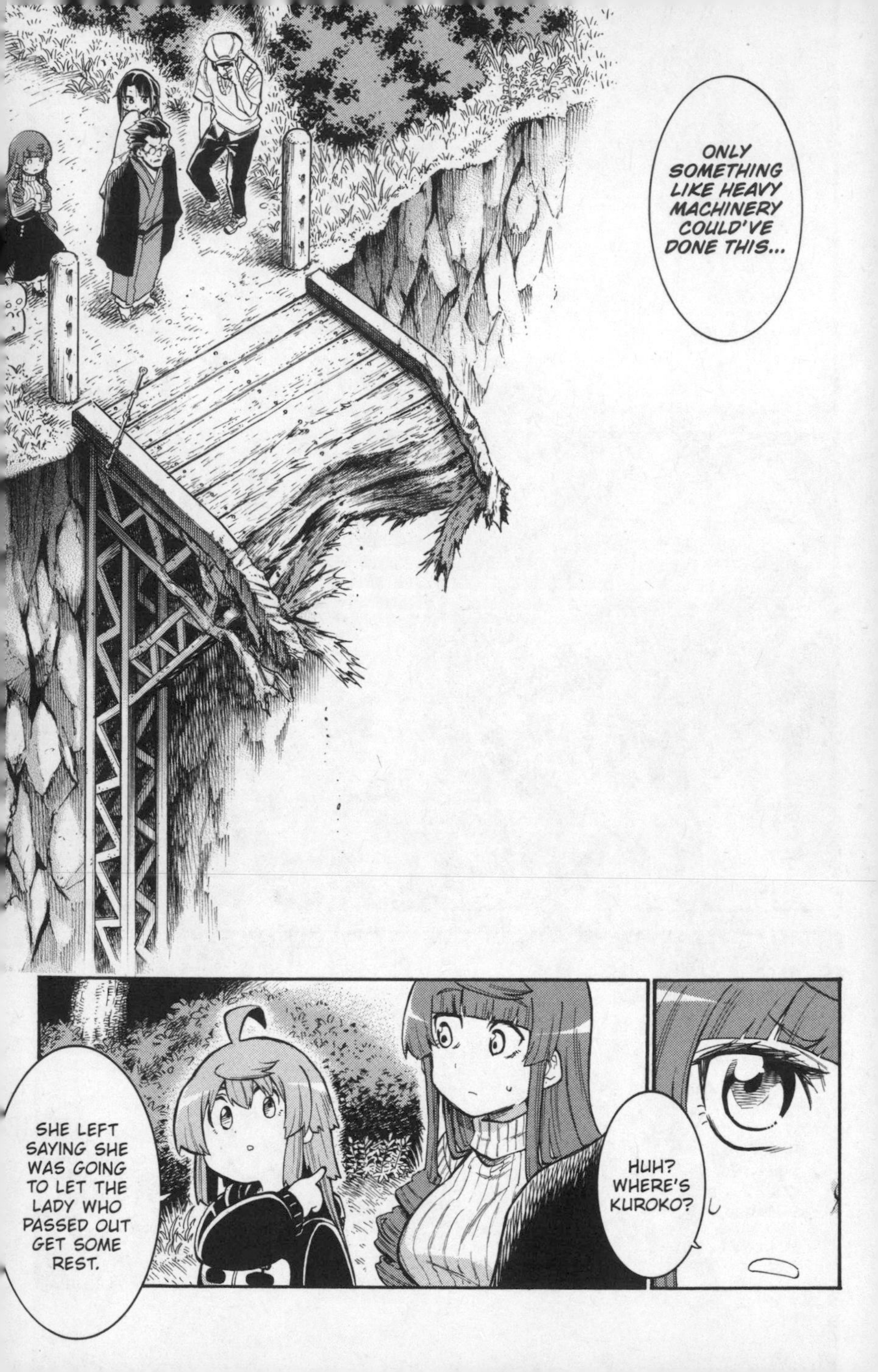
ONLY SOMETHING LIKE HEAVY MACHINERY COULD'VE DONE THIS...
HUH? WHERE'S KUROKO?
SHE LEFT SAYING SHE WAS GOING TO LET THE LADY WHO PASSED OUT GET SOME REST.

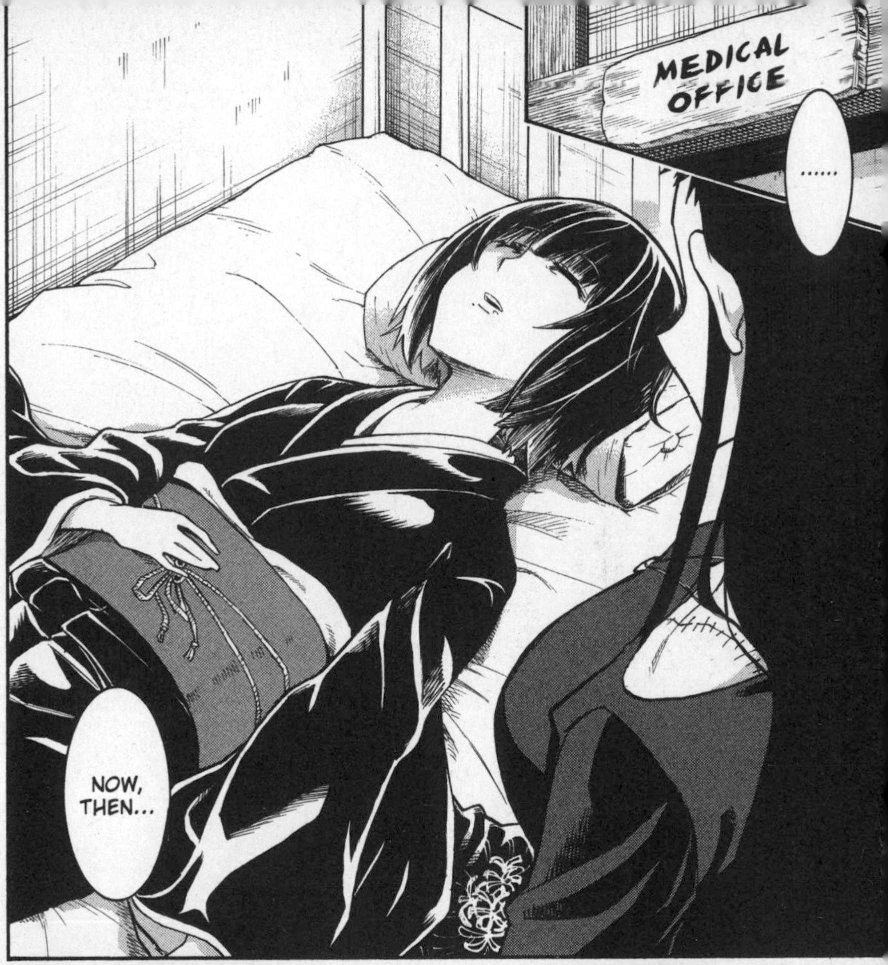
MEDICAL OFFICE
......
NOW, THEN...

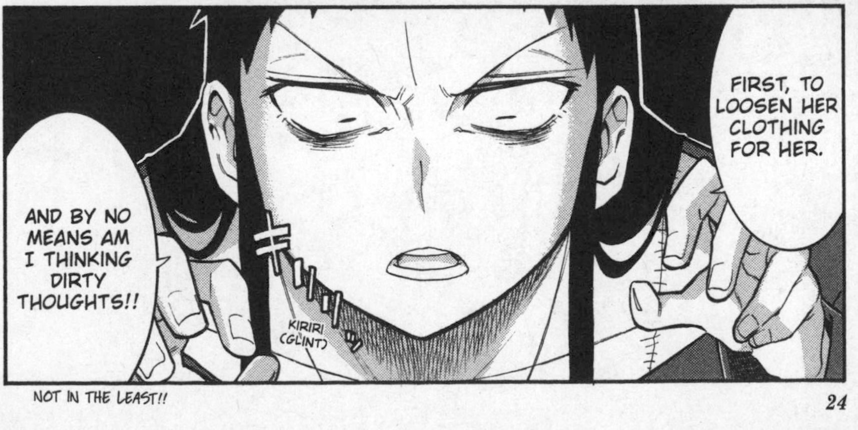
FIRST, TO LOOSEN HER CLOTHING FOR HER.
AND BY NO MEANS AM I THINKING DIRTY THOUGHTS!!
KIRIRI (GLINT)

NOT IN THE LEAST!!

MURCIÉLAGO

MURCIÉLAGO

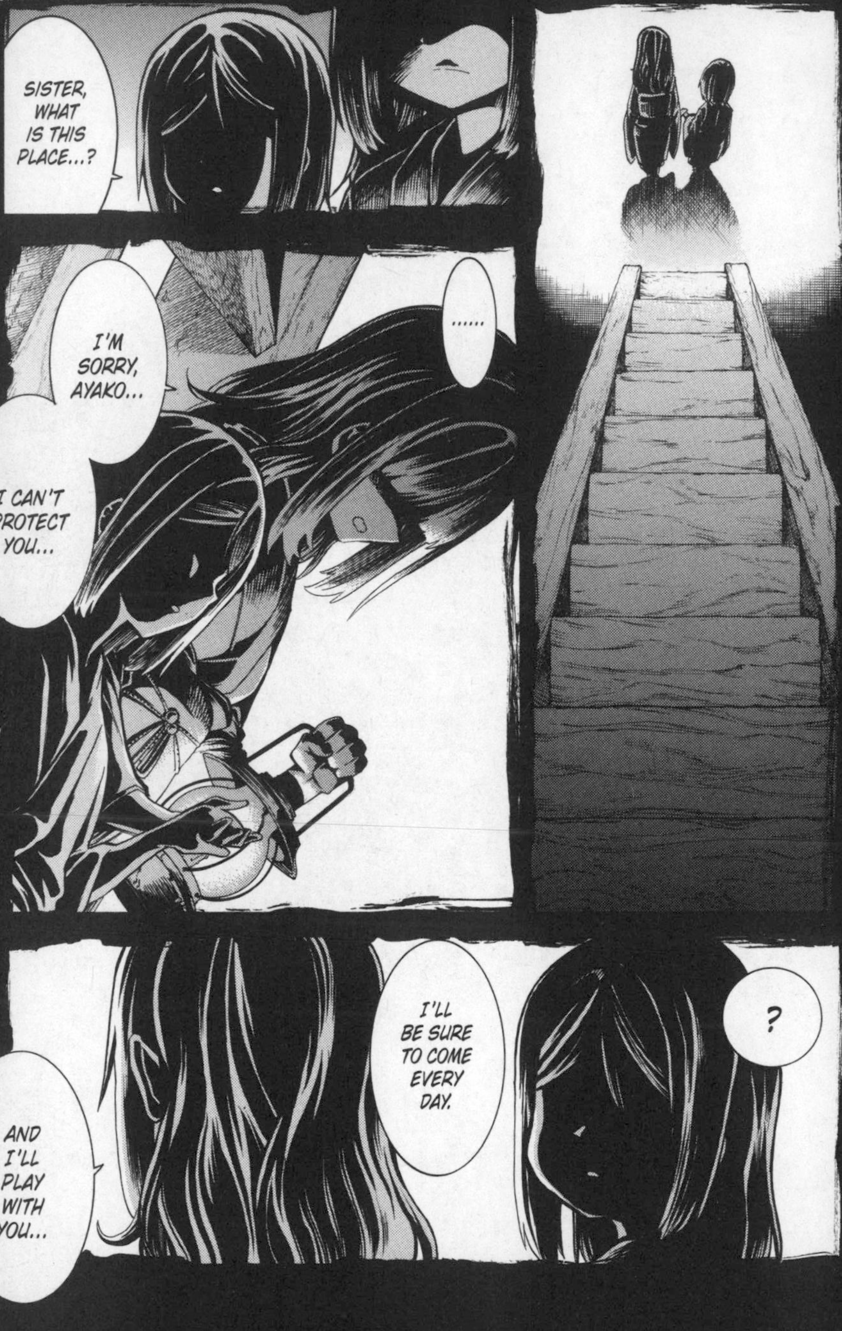
SISTER, WHAT IS THIS PLACE...?
......
I'M SORRY, AYAKO...
I CAN'T PROTECT YOU...
?
I'LL BE SURE TO COME EVERY DAY.
AND I'LL PLAY WITH YOU...

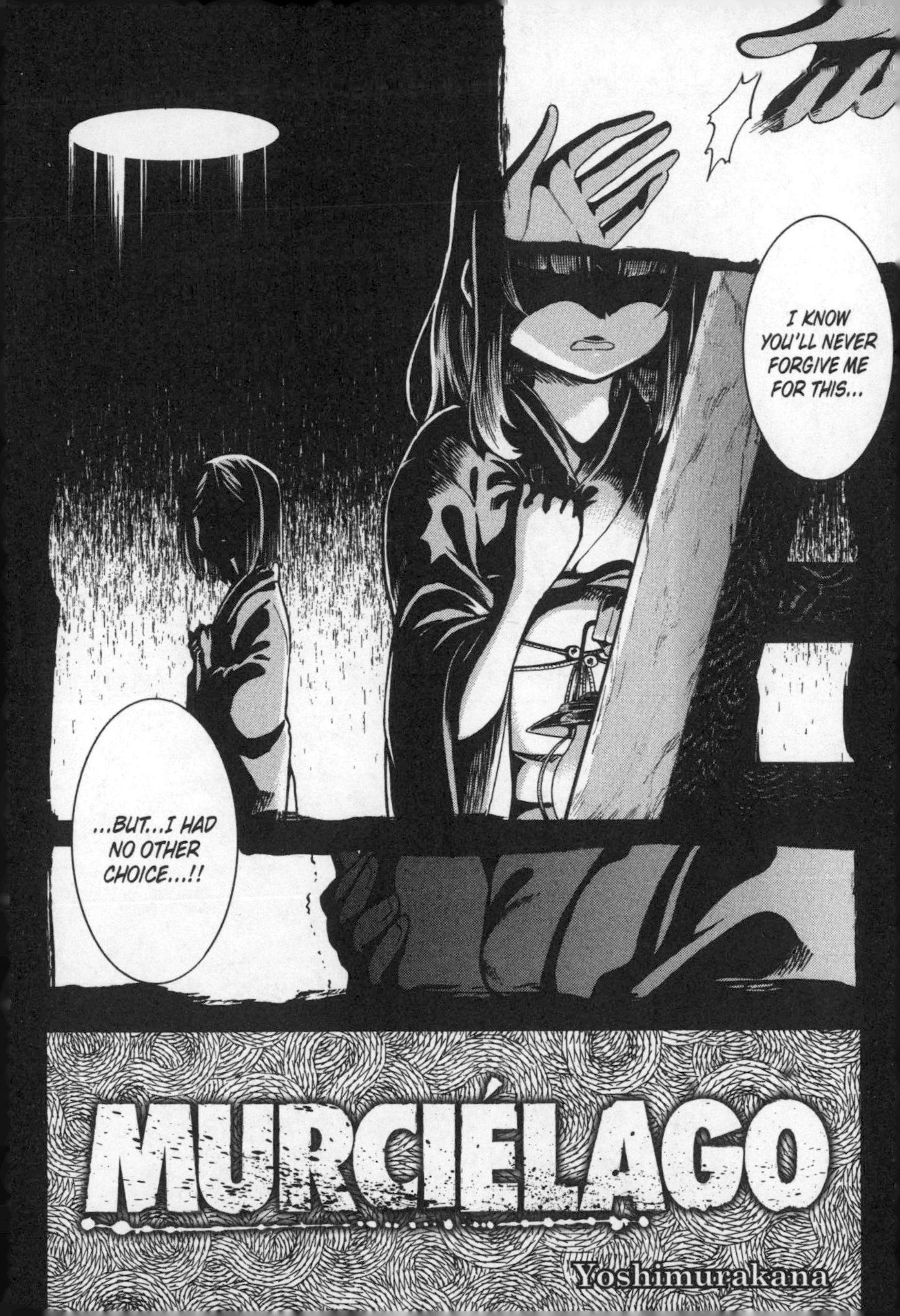
I KNOW YOU'LL NEVER FORGIVE ME FOR THIS...
...BUT...I HAD NO OTHER CHOICE...!!
MURCIÉLAGO
Yoshimurakana

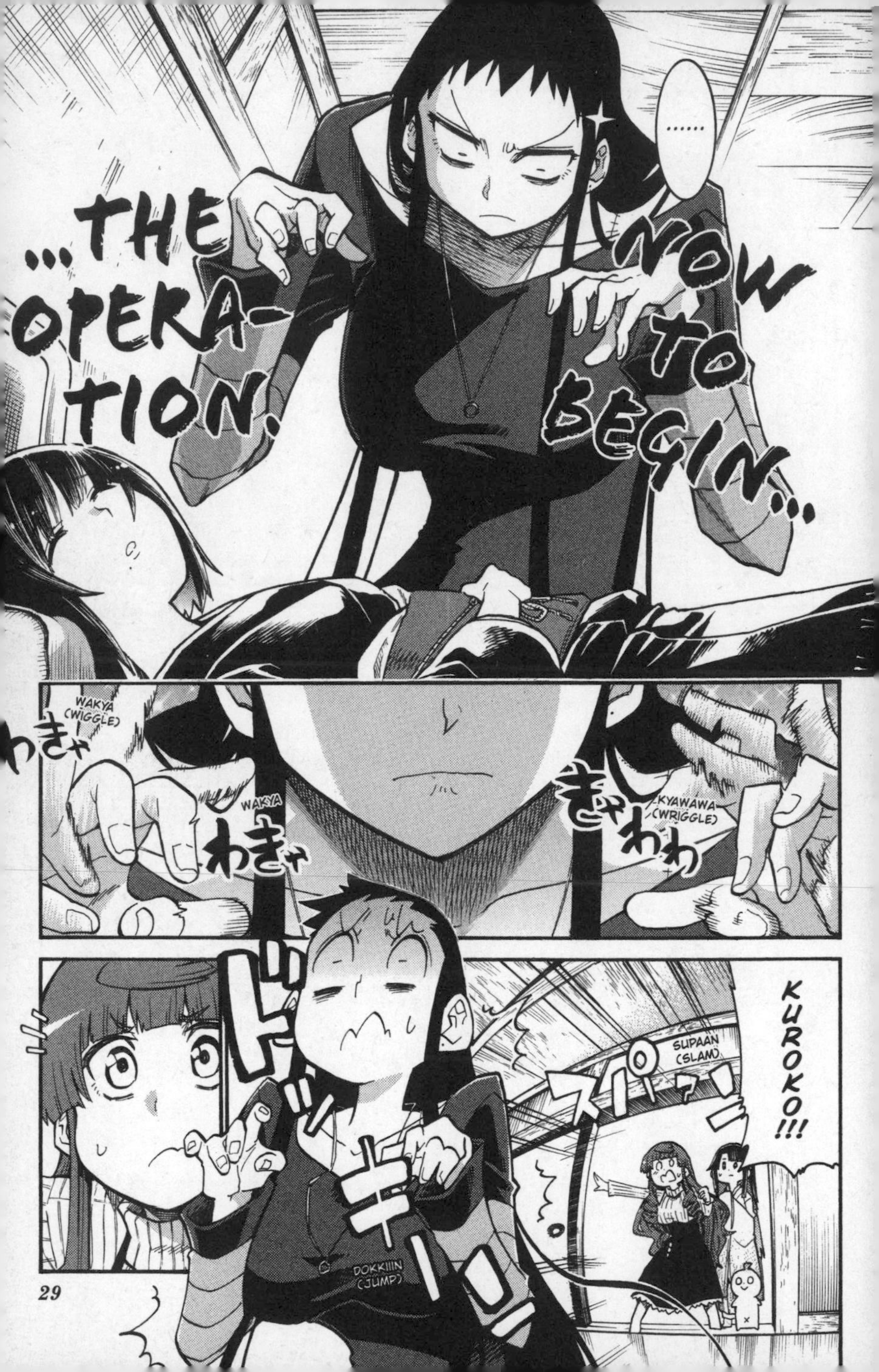
......
NOW TO BEGIN...
...THE OPERATION.
KYAWAWA (WRIGGLE)
WAKYA
WAKYA (WIGGLE)
KUROKO!!!
SUPAAN (SLAM)
DOKKIIN (JUMP)

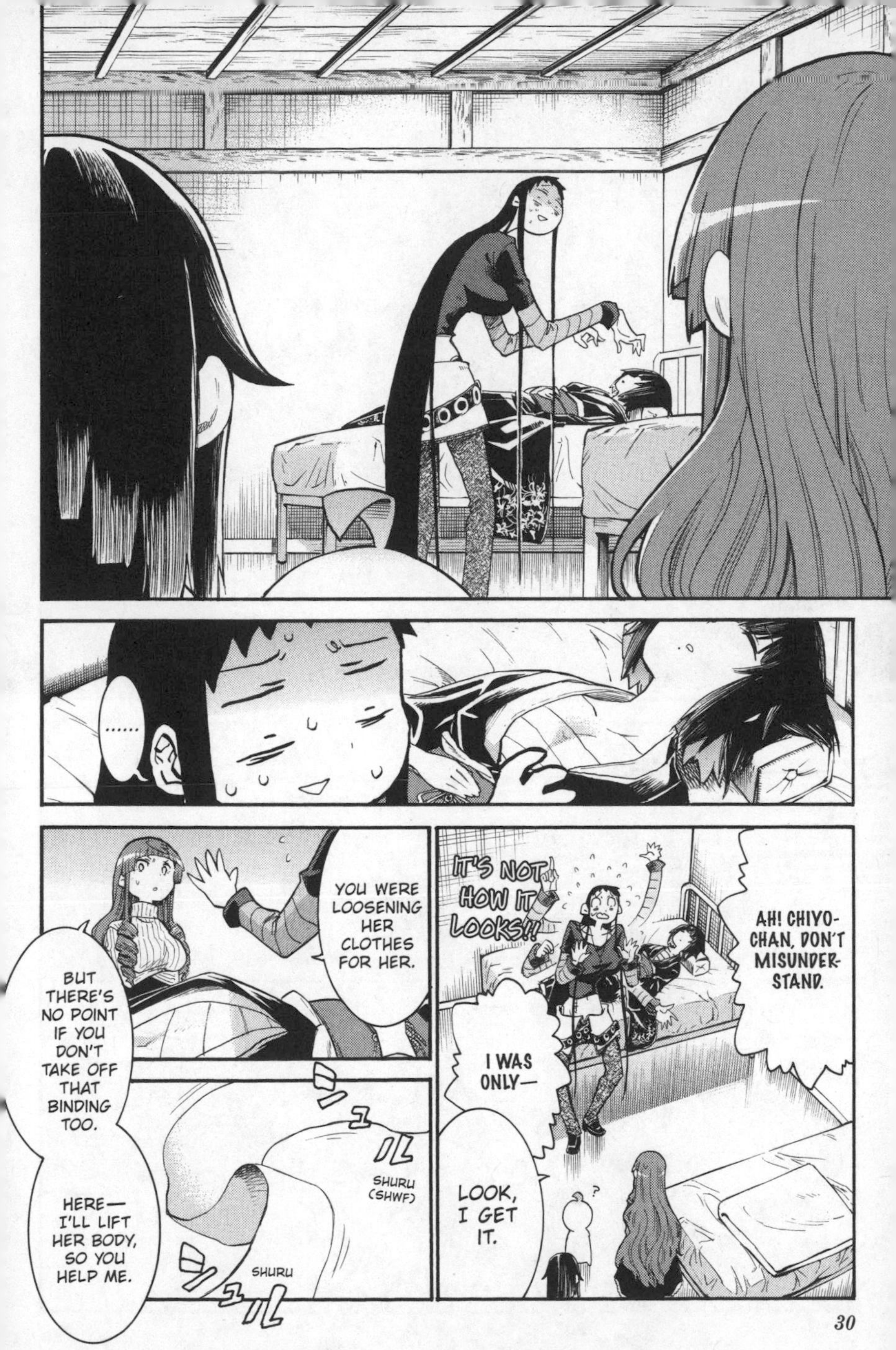
......
AH! CHIYO-CHAN, DON'T MISUNDERSTAND.
IT'S NOT HOW IT LOOKS!!
I WAS ONLY—
LOOK, I GET IT.
YOU WERE LOOSENING HER CLOTHES FOR HER.
BUT THERE'S NO POINT IF YOU DON'T TAKE OFF THAT BINDING TOO.
SHURU (SHWF)
HERE— I'LL LIFT HER BODY, SO YOU HELP ME.
SHURU

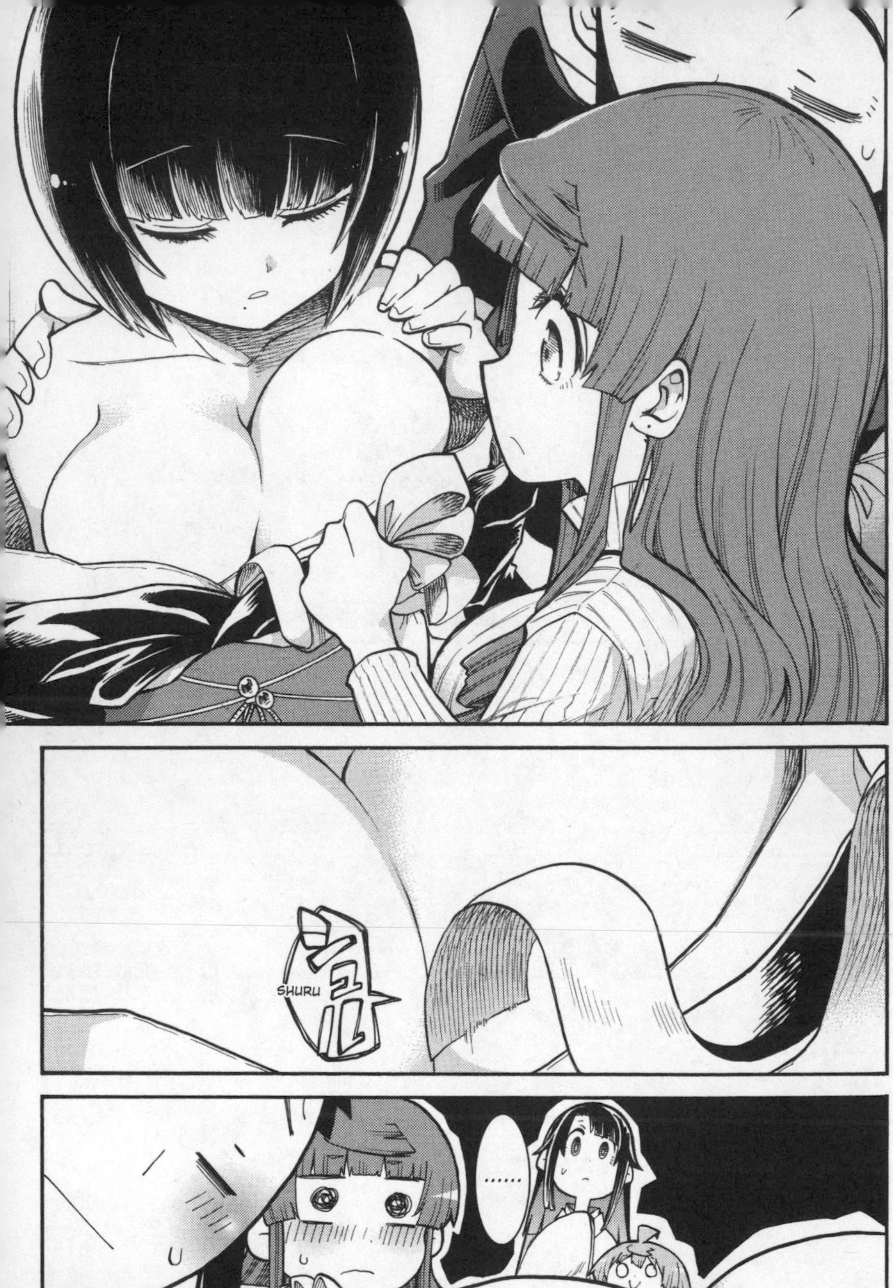
シュル
SHURU
......

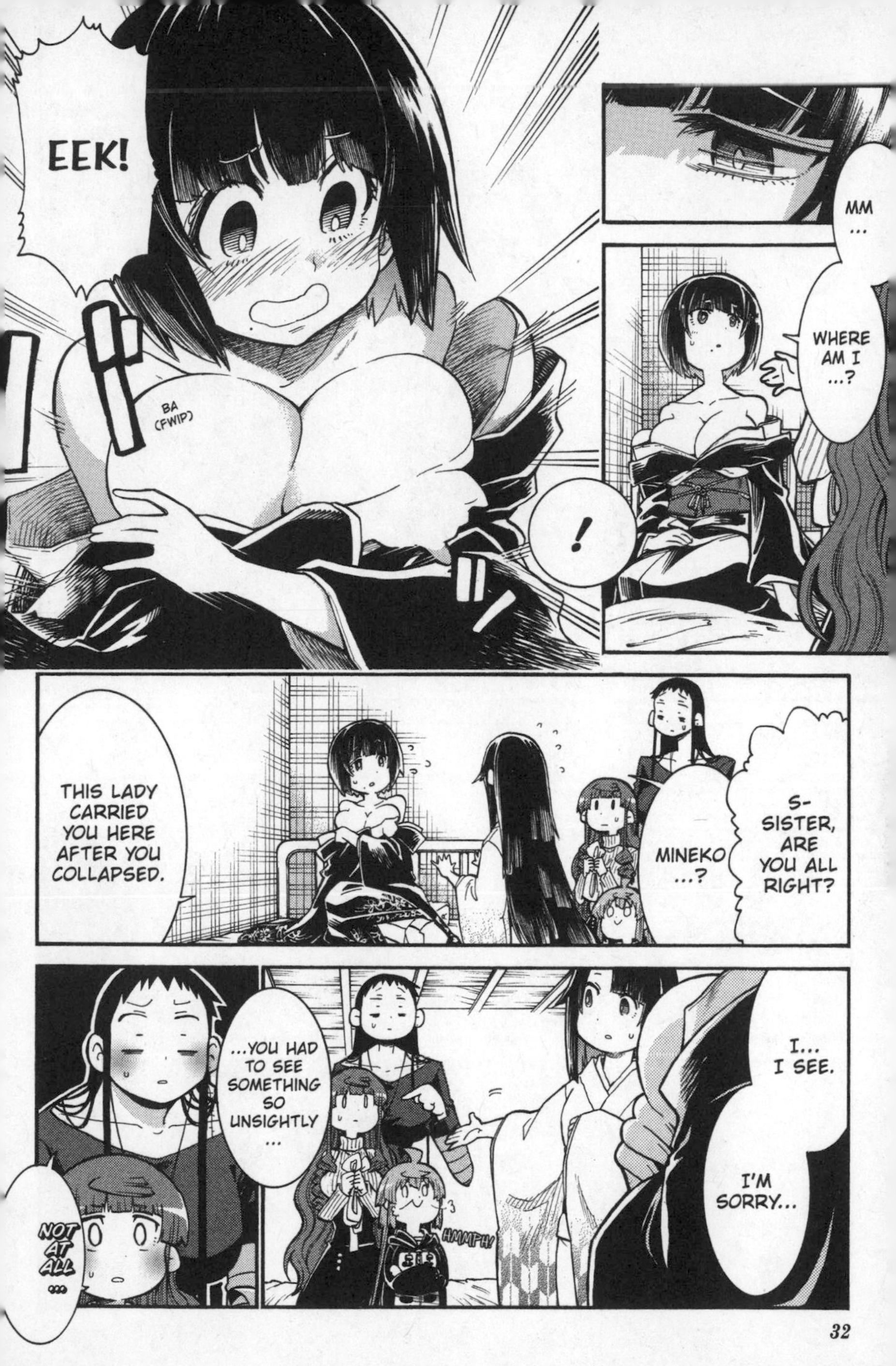
MM ...
WHERE AM I ...?
!
EEK!
BA (FWIP)
S-SISTER, ARE YOU ALL RIGHT?
MINEKO ...?
THIS LADY CARRIED YOU HERE AFTER YOU COLLAPSED.
I... I SEE.
I'M SORRY...
...YOU HAD TO SEE SOMETHING SO UNSIGHTLY ...
HMMPH!
NOT AT ALL ...

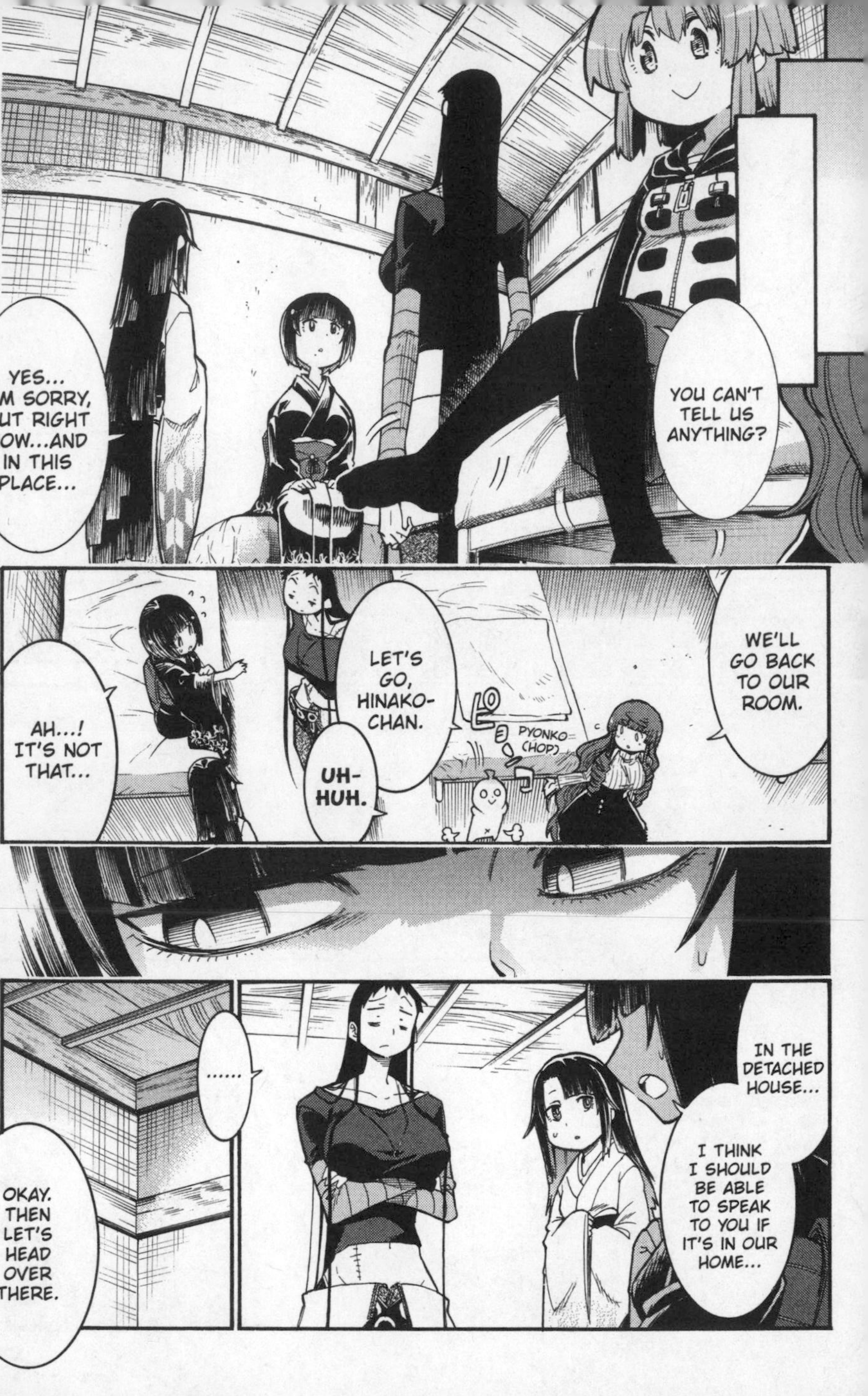
YOU CAN'T TELL US ANYTHING?
YES... I'M SORRY, BUT RIGHT NOW...AND IN THIS PLACE...
WE'LL GO BACK TO OUR ROOM.
PYONKO (HOP)
LET'S GO, HINAKO-CHAN.
UH-HUH.
AH...! IT'S NOT THAT...
IN THE DETACHED HOUSE...
I THINK I SHOULD BE ABLE TO SPEAK TO YOU IF IT'S IN OUR HOME...
......
OKAY. THEN LET'S HEAD OVER THERE.

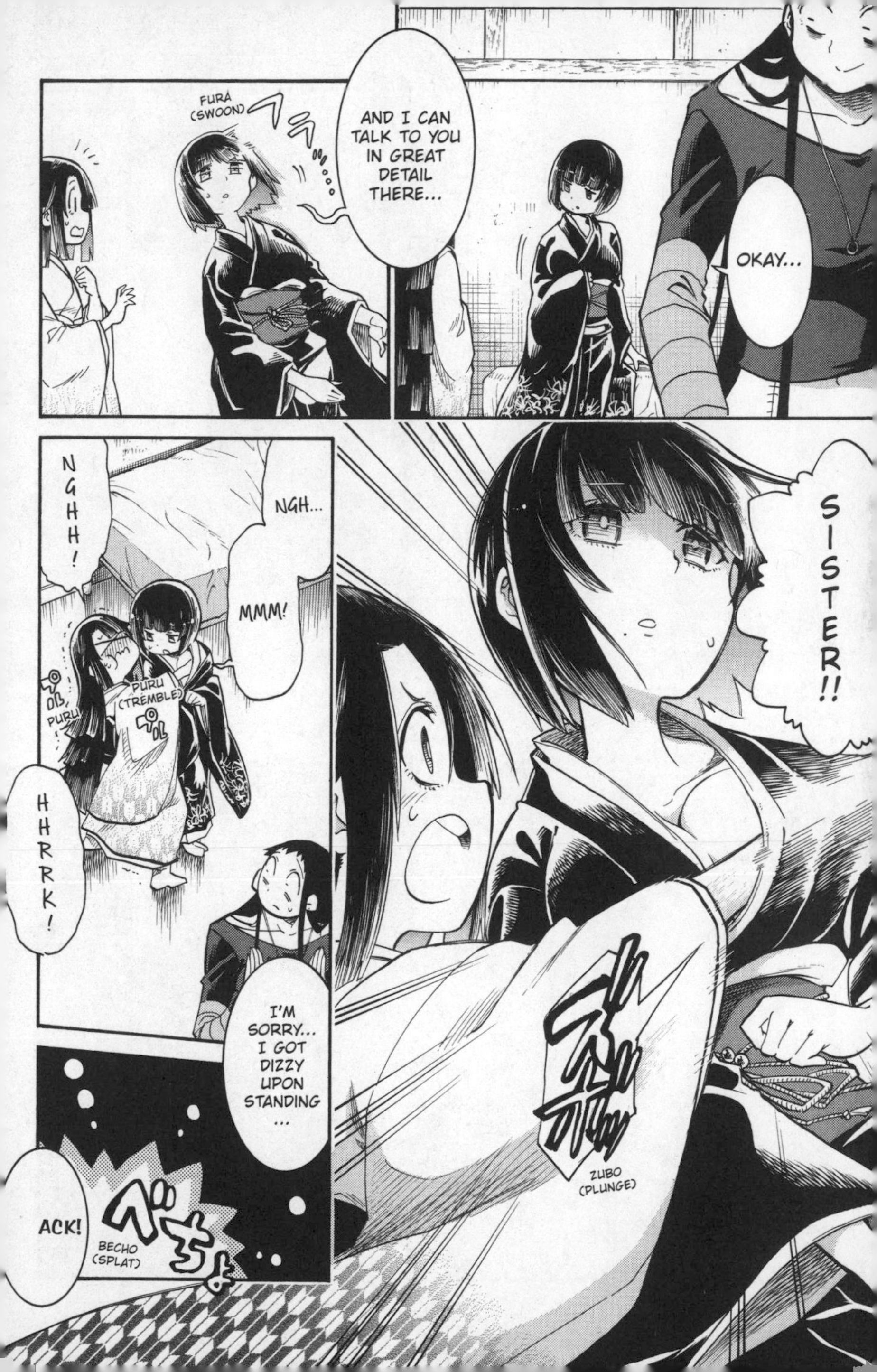
AND I CAN TALK TO YOU IN GREAT DETAIL THERE...
OKAY...
FURA (SWOON)
SISTER!!
ZUBO (PLUNGE)
NGH...
MMM!
NGHH!
PURU (TREMBLE)
PURU
HHRRK!
I'M SORRY... I GOT DIZZY UPON STANDING...
BECHO (SPLAT)
ACK!

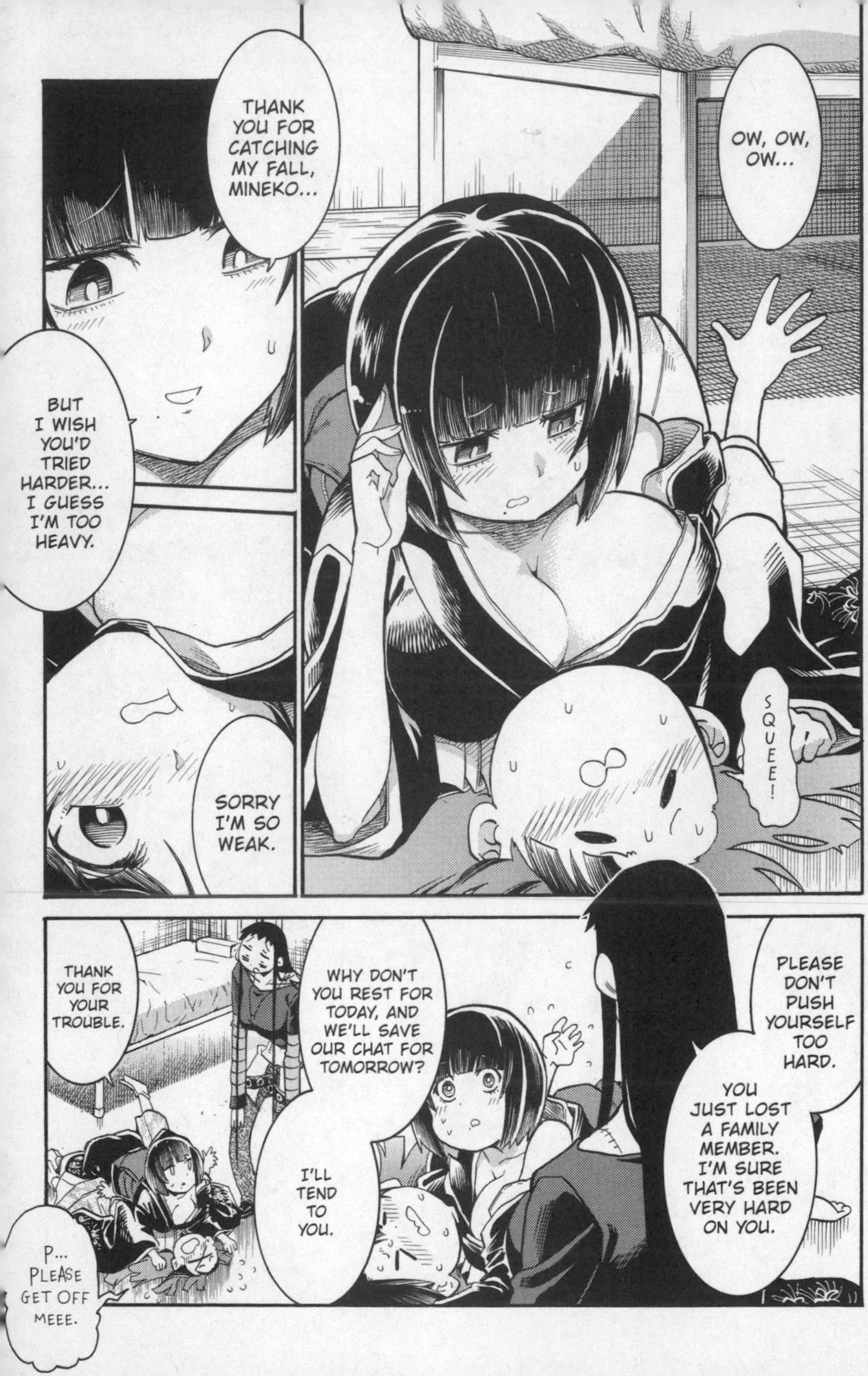
OW, OW, OW...
SQUEEE!
THANK YOU FOR CATCHING MY FALL, MINEKO...
BUT I WISH YOU'D TRIED HARDER... I GUESS I'M TOO HEAVY.
SORRY I'M SO WEAK.
PLEASE DON'T PUSH YOURSELF TOO HARD.
YOU JUST LOST A FAMILY MEMBER. I'M SURE THAT'S BEEN VERY HARD ON YOU.
WHY DON'T YOU REST FOR TODAY, AND WE'LL SAVE OUR CHAT FOR TOMORROW?
I'LL TEND TO YOU.
THANK YOU FOR YOUR TROUBLE.
P... PLEASE GET OFF MEEE.

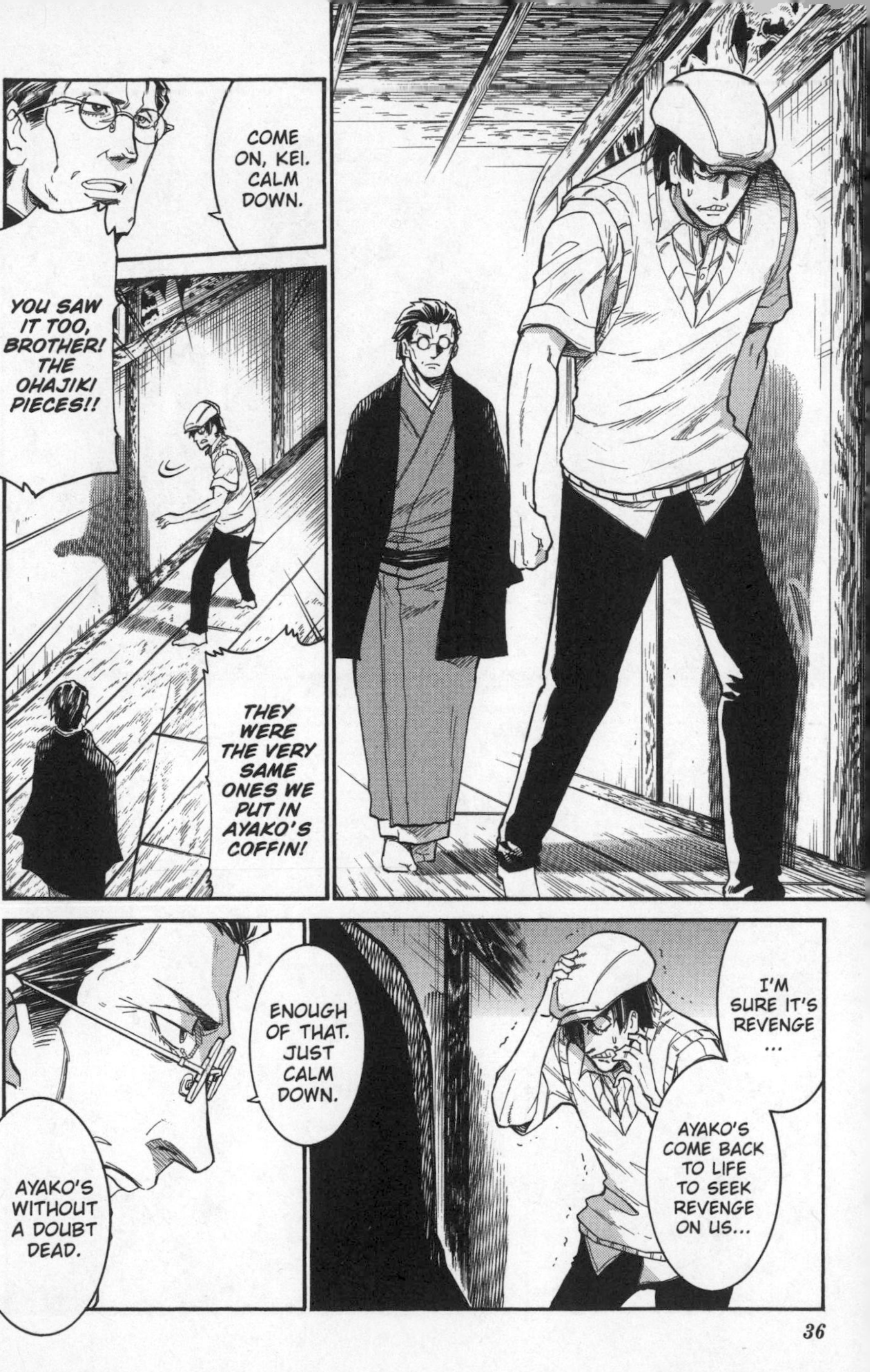
COME ON, KEI. CALM DOWN.
YOU SAW IT TOO, BROTHER! THE OHAJIKI PIECES!!
THEY WERE THE VERY SAME ONES WE PUT IN AYAKO'S COFFIN!
I'M SURE IT'S REVENGE...
AYAKO'S COME BACK TO LIFE TO SEEK REVENGE ON US...
ENOUGH OF THAT. JUST CALM DOWN.
AYAKO'S WITHOUT A DOUBT DEAD.

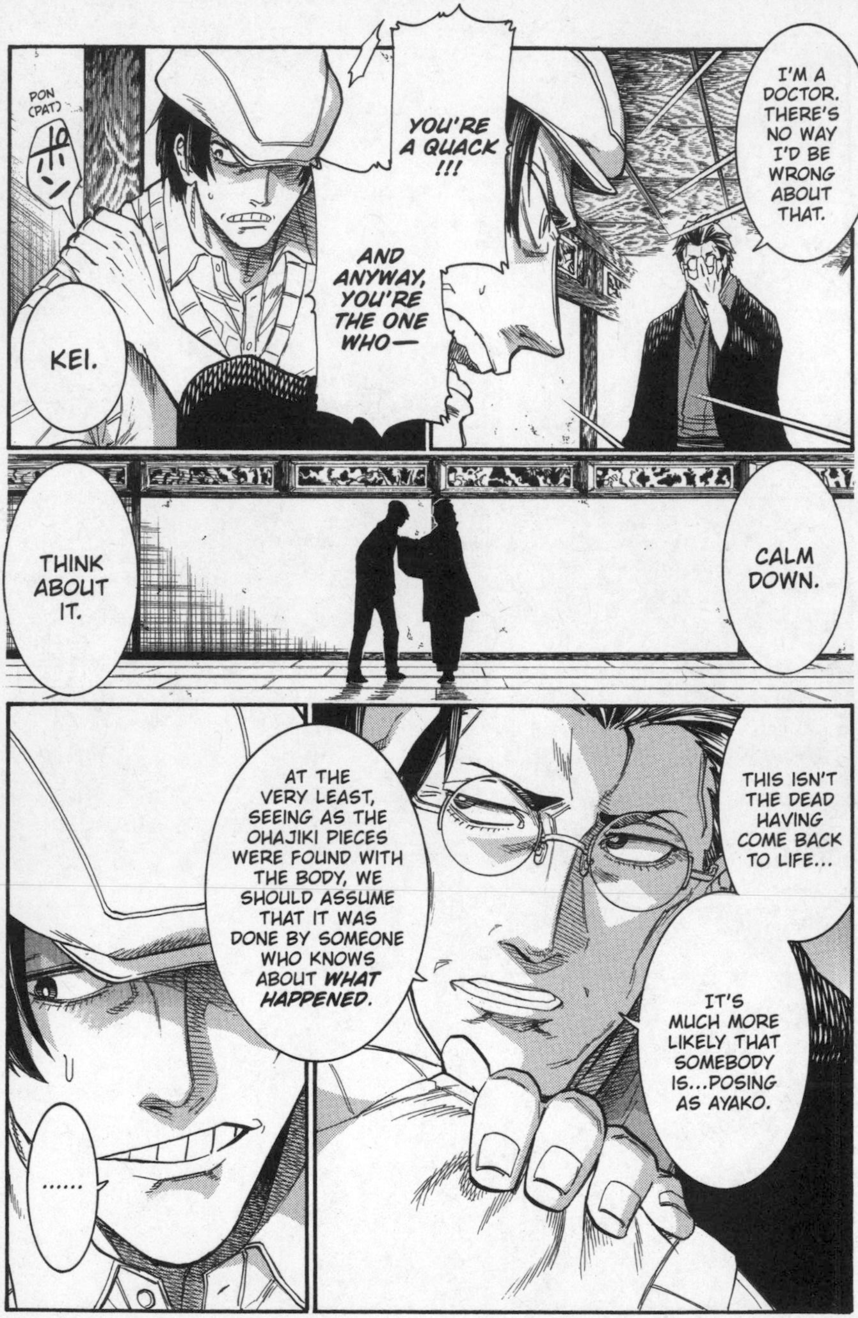

I'M A DOCTOR. THERE'S NO WAY I'D BE WRONG ABOUT THAT.
YOU'RE A QUACK !!!
AND ANYWAY, YOU'RE THE ONE WHO—
PON (PAT)
KEI.
CALM DOWN.
THINK ABOUT IT.
THIS ISN'T THE DEAD HAVING COME BACK TO LIFE...
IT'S MUCH MORE LIKELY THAT SOMEBODY IS...POSING AS AYAKO.
AT THE VERY LEAST, SEEING AS THE OHAJIKI PIECES WERE FOUND WITH THE BODY, WE SHOULD ASSUME THAT IT WAS DONE BY SOMEONE WHO KNOWS ABOUT *WHAT HAPPENED*.
......

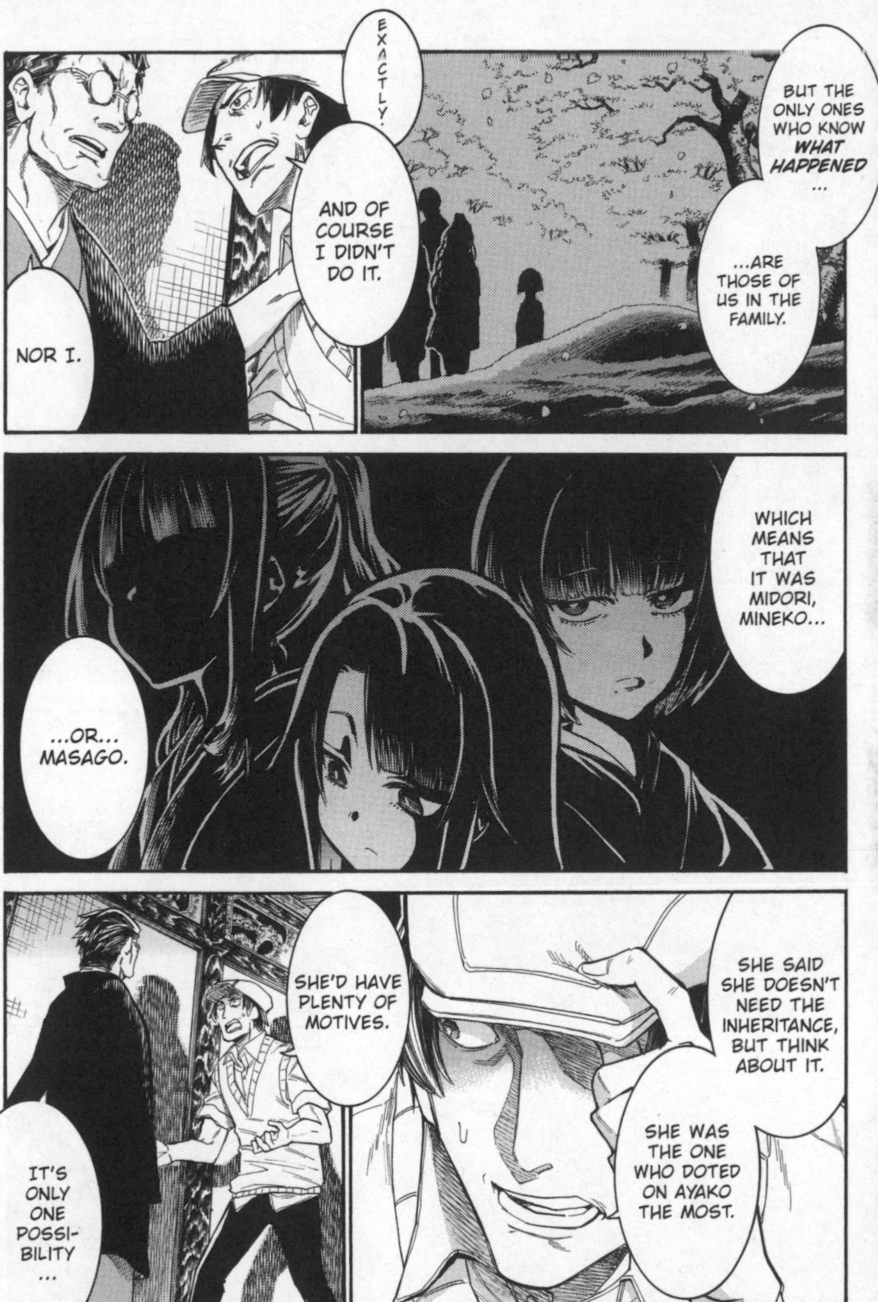
BUT THE ONLY ONES WHO KNOW ***WHAT HAPPENED***...
...ARE THOSE OF US IN THE FAMILY.
EXACTLY!
AND OF COURSE I DIDN'T DO IT.
NOR I.
WHICH MEANS THAT IT WAS MIDORI, MINEKO...
...OR... MASAGO.
SHE SAID SHE DOESN'T NEED THE INHERITANCE, BUT THINK ABOUT IT.
SHE WAS THE ONE WHO DOTED ON AYAKO THE MOST.
SHE'D HAVE PLENTY OF MOTIVES.
IT'S ONLY ONE POSSIBILITY...

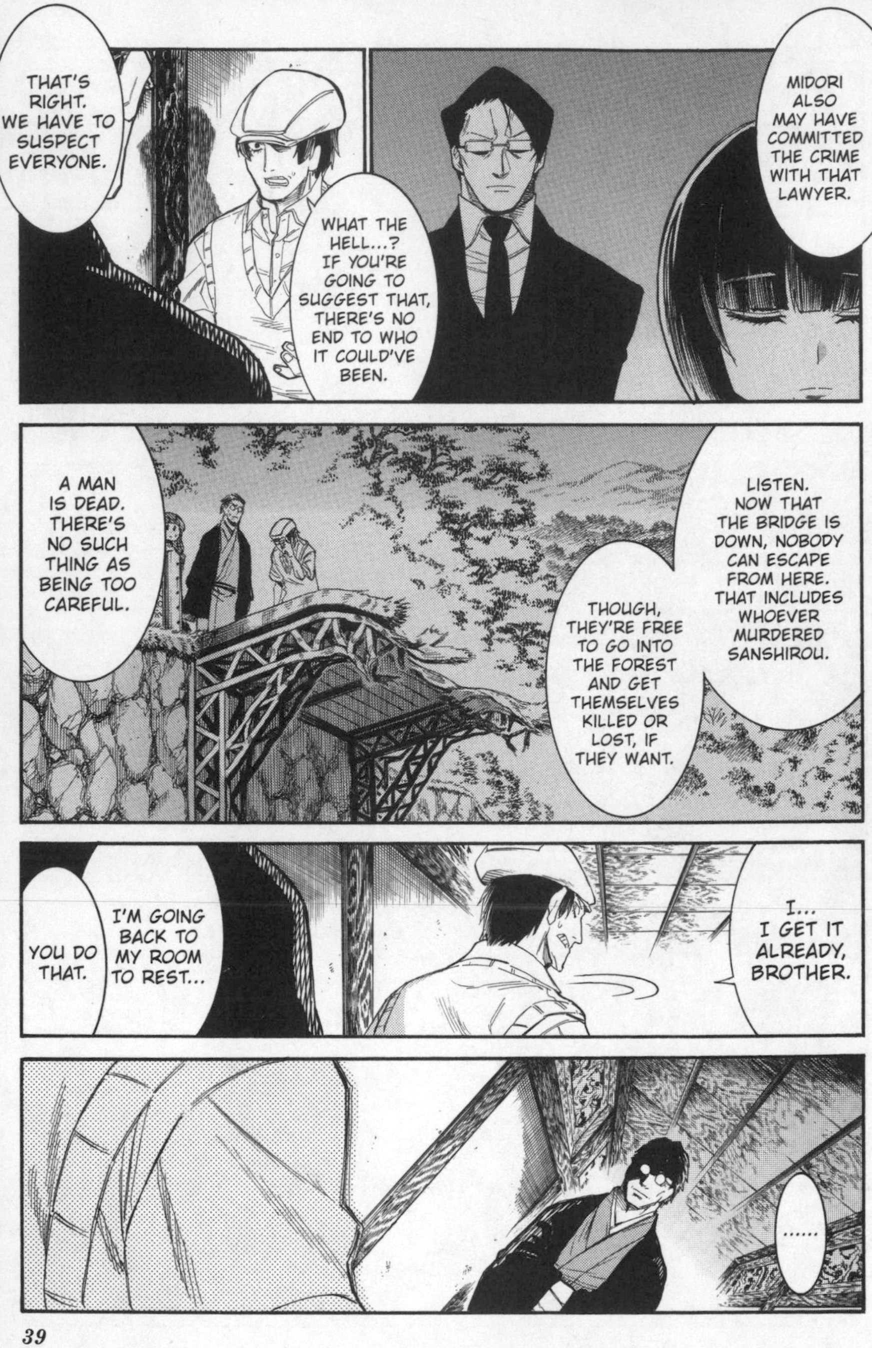
MIDORI ALSO MAY HAVE COMMITTED THE CRIME WITH THAT LAWYER.
WHAT THE HELL...? IF YOU'RE GOING TO SUGGEST THAT, THERE'S NO END TO WHO IT COULD'VE BEEN.
THAT'S RIGHT. WE HAVE TO SUSPECT EVERYONE.
LISTEN. NOW THAT THE BRIDGE IS DOWN, NOBODY CAN ESCAPE FROM HERE. THAT INCLUDES WHOEVER MURDERED SANSHIROU.
THOUGH, THEY'RE FREE TO GO INTO THE FOREST AND GET THEMSELVES KILLED OR LOST, IF THEY WANT.
A MAN IS DEAD. THERE'S NO SUCH THING AS BEING TOO CAREFUL.
I... I GET IT ALREADY, BROTHER.
I'M GOING BACK TO MY ROOM TO REST...
YOU DO THAT.
......

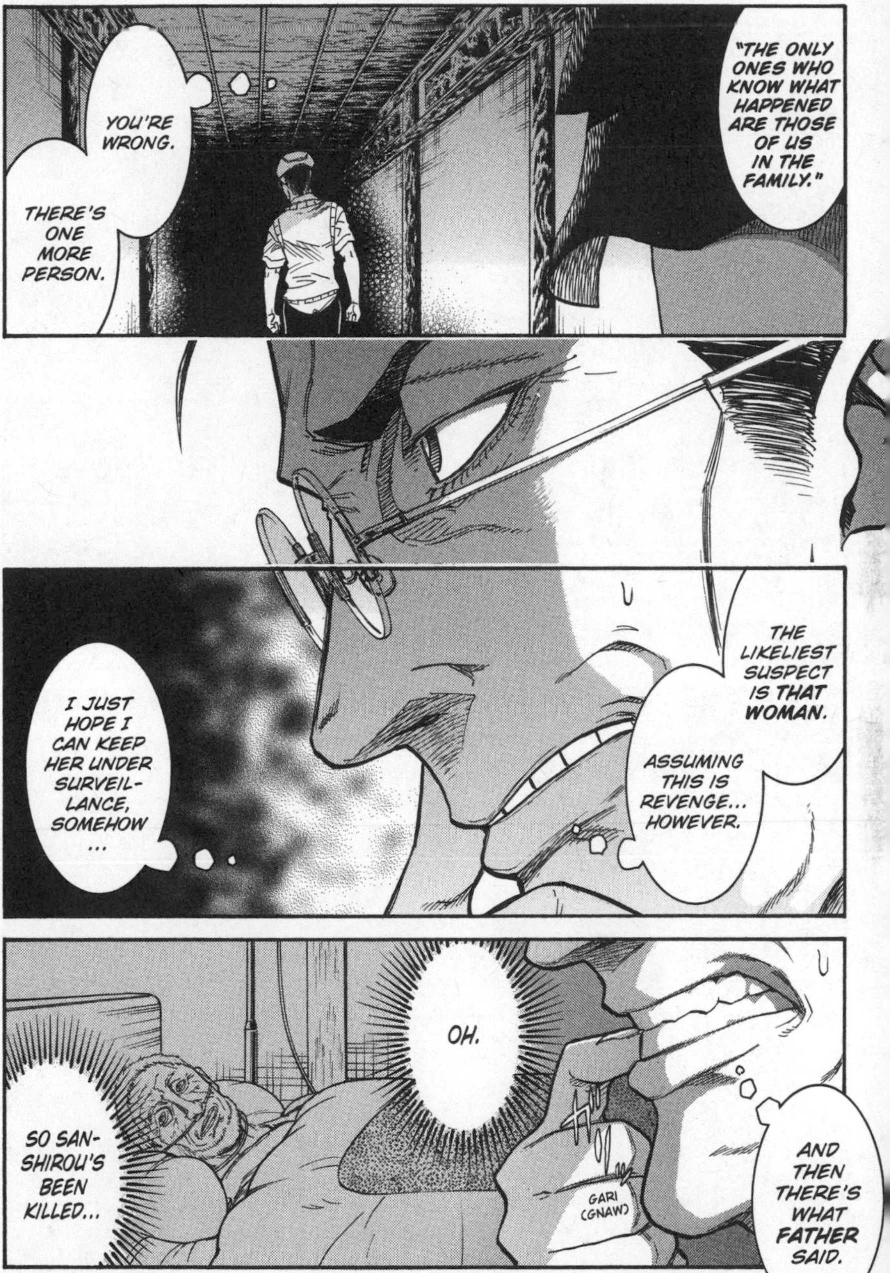
"THE ONLY ONES WHO KNOW WHAT HAPPENED ARE THOSE OF US IN THE FAMILY."
YOU'RE WRONG.
THERE'S ONE MORE PERSON.
THE LIKELIEST SUSPECT IS THAT WOMAN.
ASSUMING THIS IS REVENGE... HOWEVER.
I JUST HOPE I CAN KEEP HER UNDER SURVEIL-
LANCE, SOMEHOW...
AND THEN THERE'S WHAT FATHER SAID.
GARI
(GNAW)
OH.
SO SAN-
SHIROU'S BEEN KILLED...

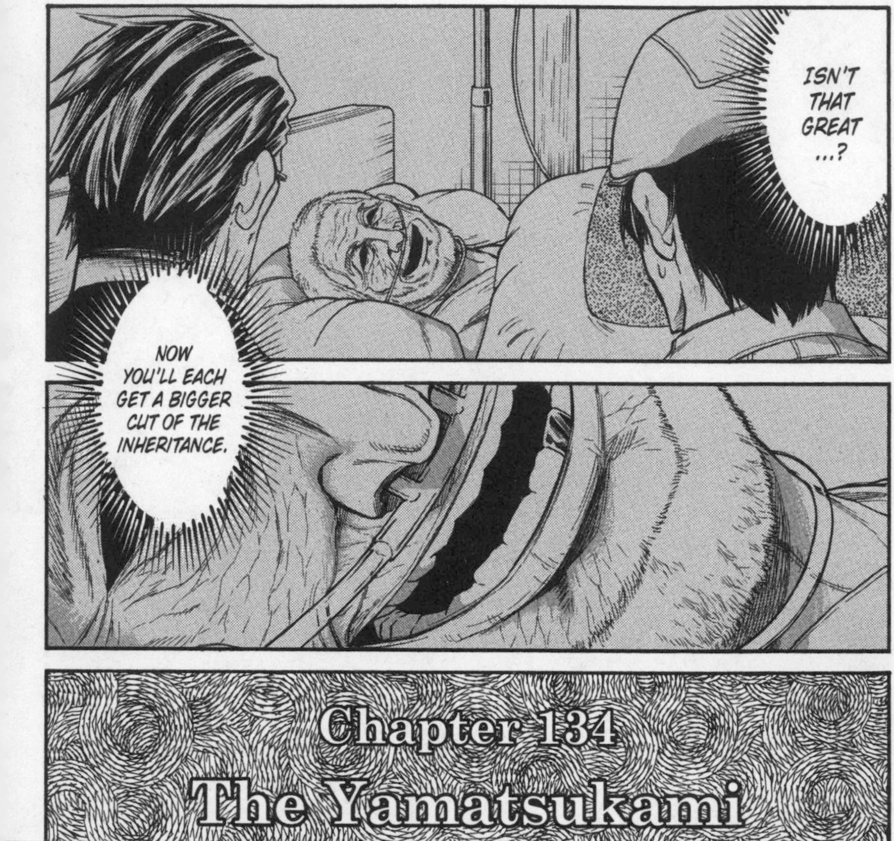
ISN'T THAT GREAT ...?
NOW YOU'LL EACH GET A BIGGER CUT OF THE INHERITANCE.

Chapter 134
The Yamatsukami Family ③

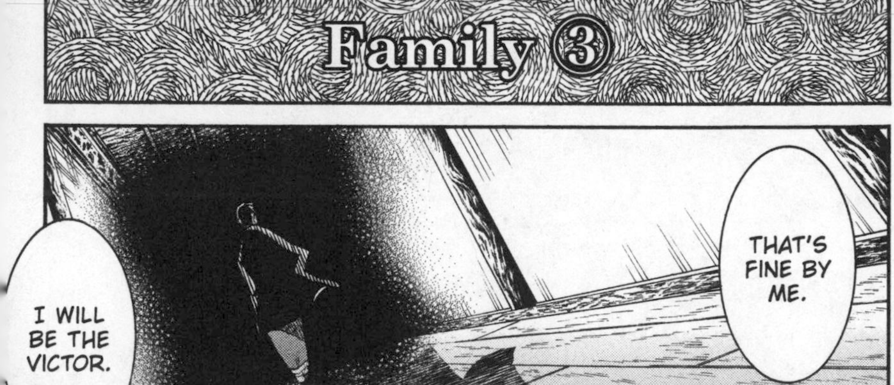
THAT'S FINE BY ME.
I WILL BE THE VICTOR.

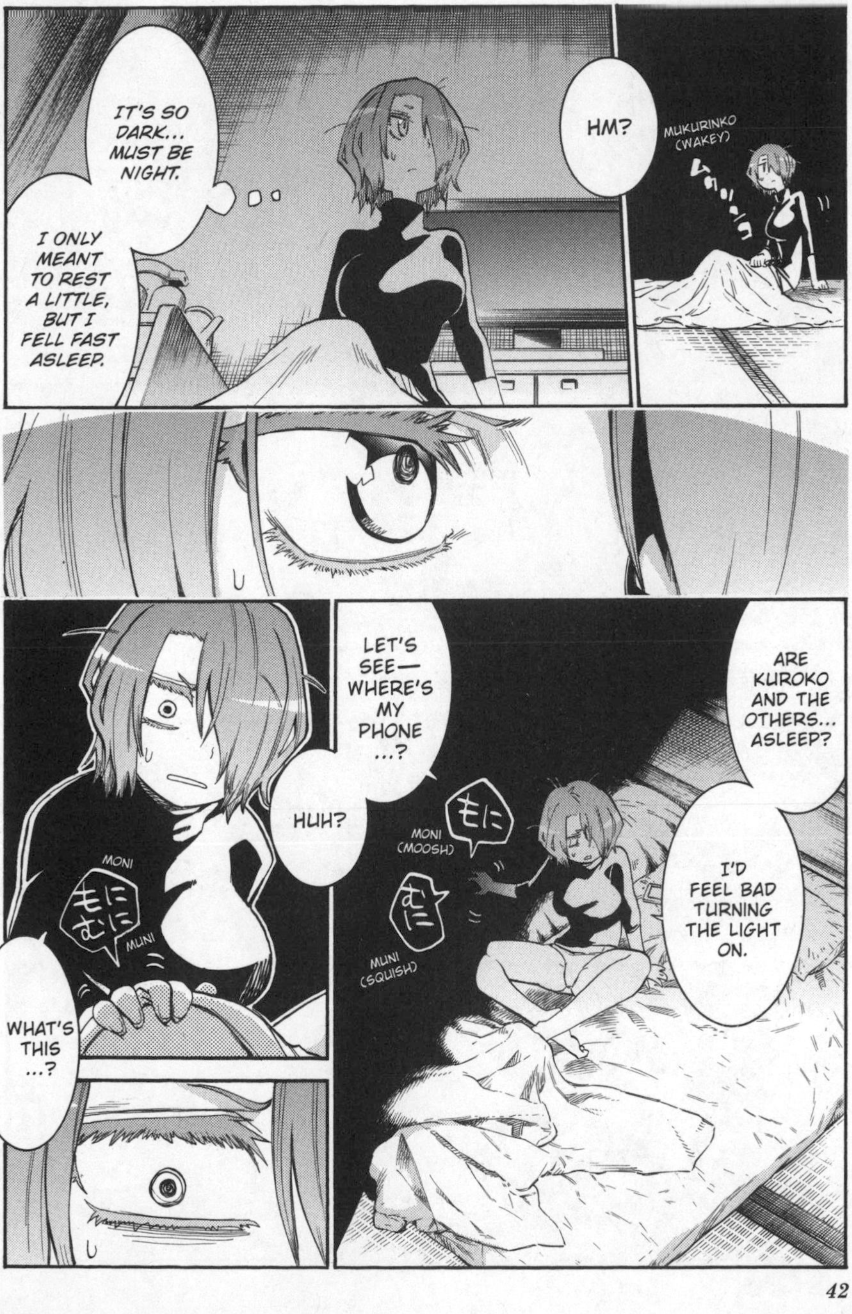
HM?
MUKURINKO (WAKEY)
IT'S SO DARK... MUST BE NIGHT.
I ONLY MEANT TO REST A LITTLE, BUT I FELL FAST ASLEEP.
ARE KUROKO AND THE OTHERS... ASLEEP?
I'D FEEL BAD TURNING THE LIGHT ON.
LET'S SEE— WHERE'S MY PHONE ...?
もに
MONI (MOOSH)
むに
MUNI (SQUISH)
HUH?
もにむに
MONI
MUNI
WHAT'S THIS ...?

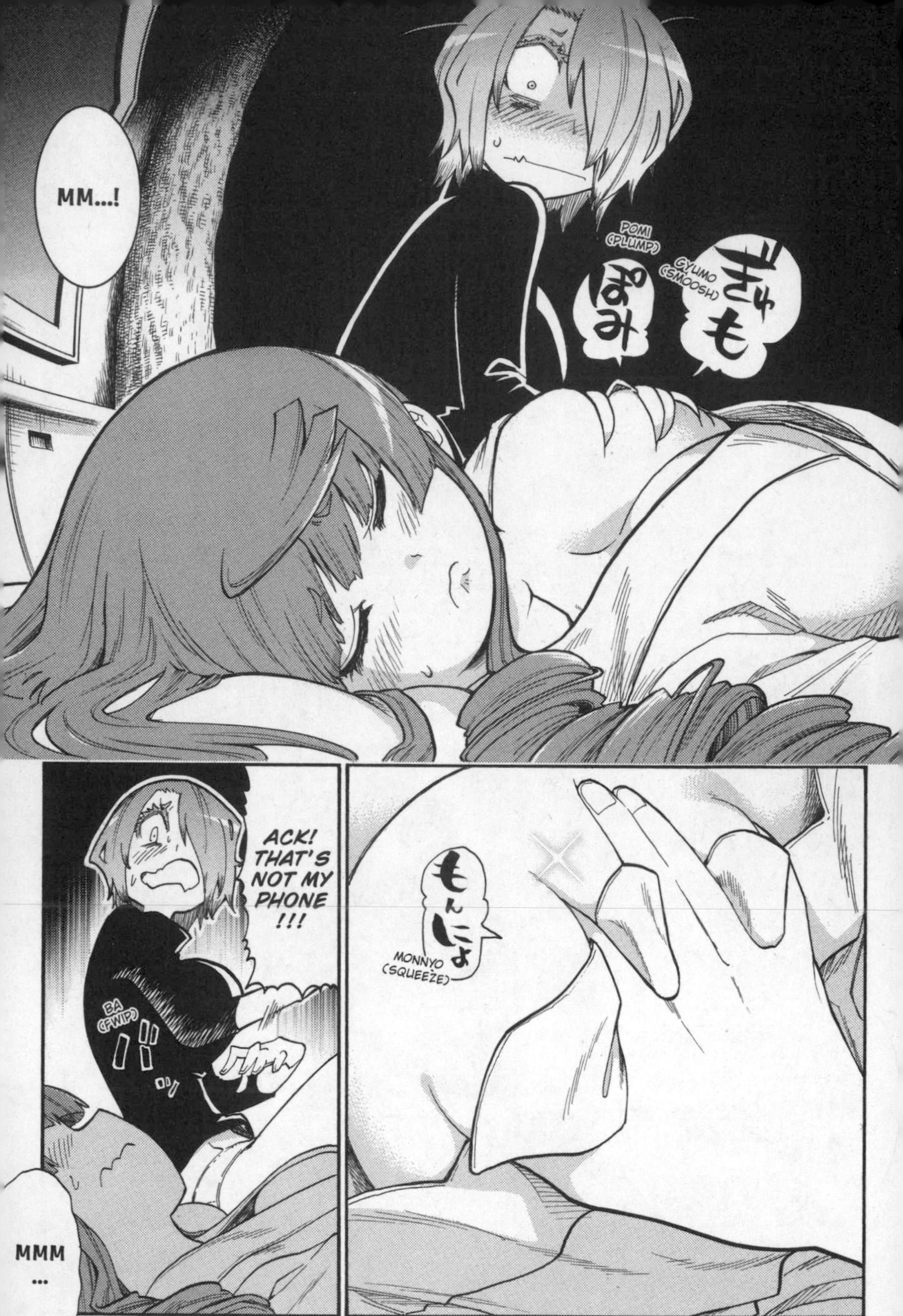
ぎゅも
GYUMO (SMOOSH)
ぽみ
POMI (PLUMP)
MM...!
もんにょ
MONNYO (SQUEEZE)
ACK! THAT'S NOT MY PHONE!!!
BA (FWIP)
MMM...

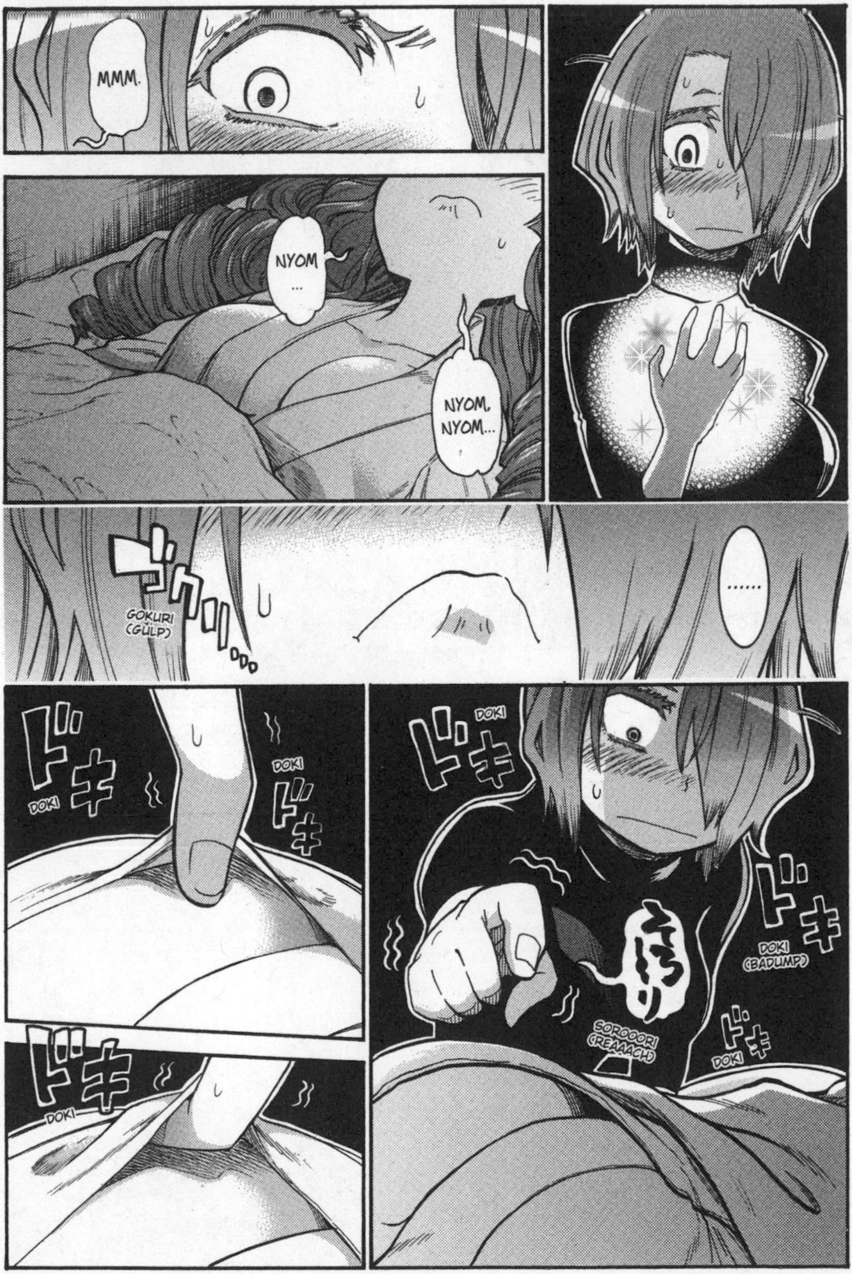
MMM.
NYOM
...
NYOM, NYOM...
......
ゴクリ
GOKURI (GULP)
ドキ
DOKI
ドキ
DOKI (BADUMP)
そろ~り
SOROOORI (REAAACH)
ドキ
DOKI
ドキ
DOKI
ドキ
DOKI
ドキ
DOKI

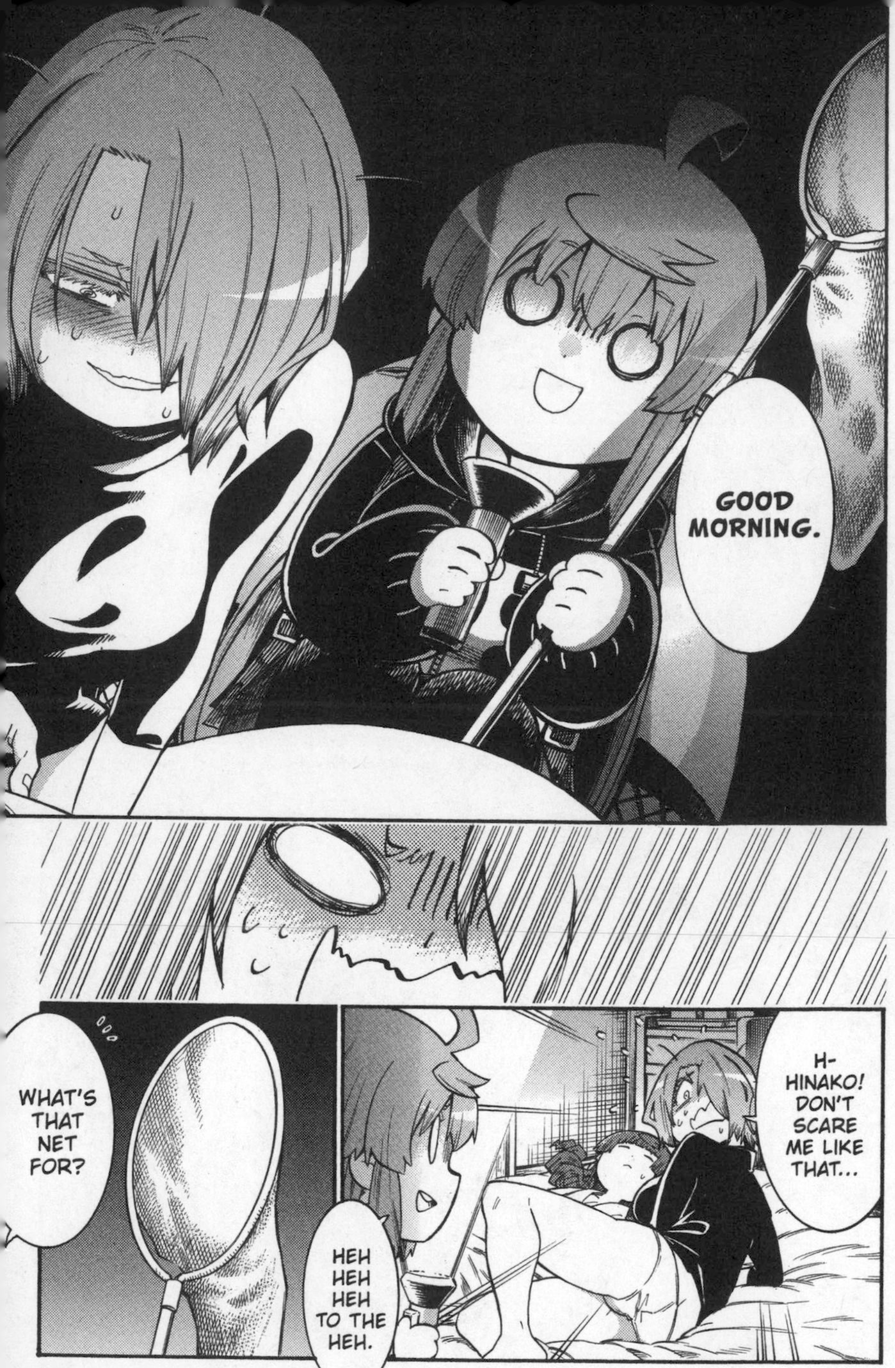
GOOD MORNING.
H-HINAKO! DON'T SCARE ME LIKE THAT...
HEH HEH HEH TO THE HEH.
WHAT'S THAT NET FOR?

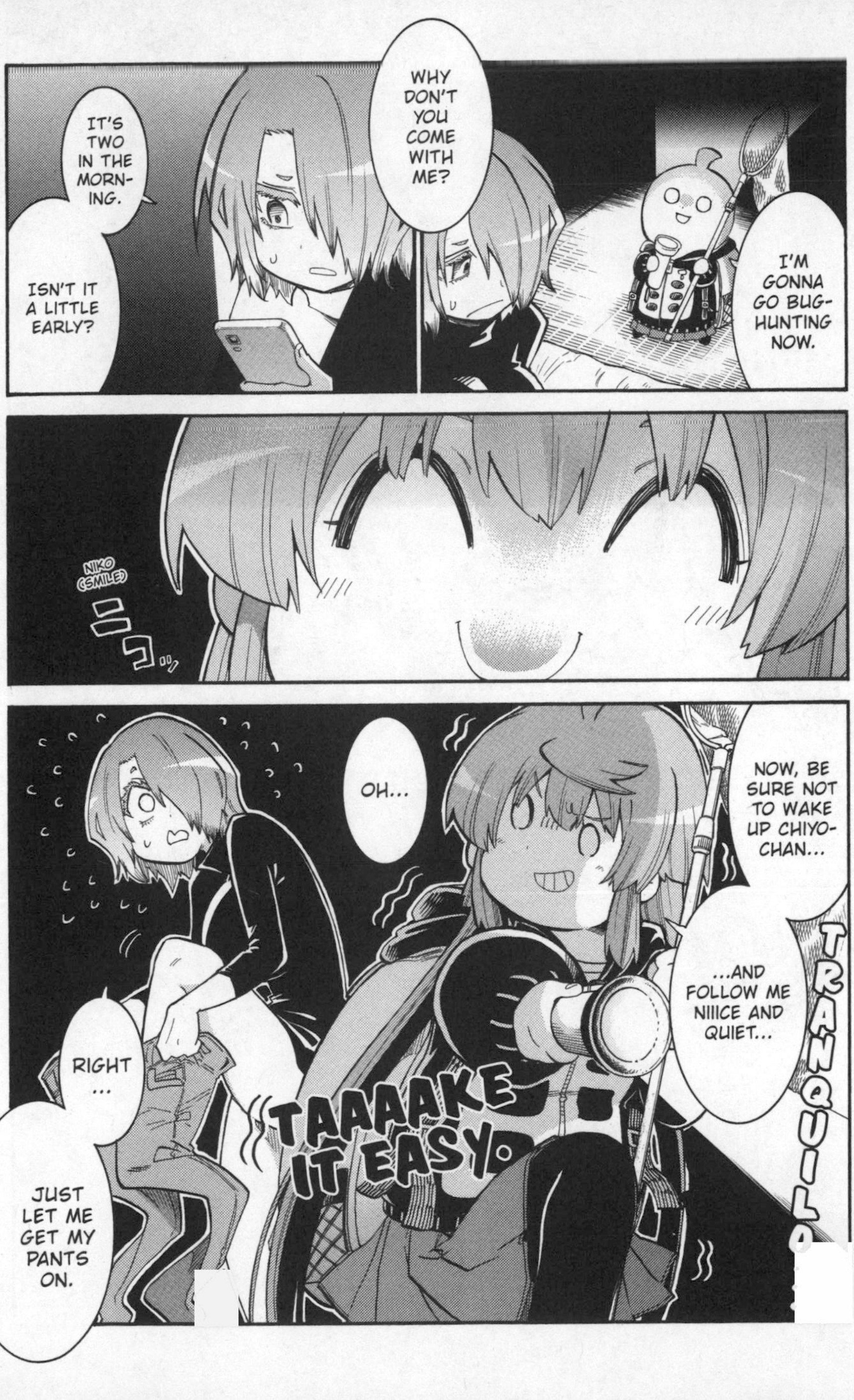
I'M GONNA GO BUG-HUNTING NOW.
WHY DON'T YOU COME WITH ME?
IT'S TWO IN THE MORNING.
ISN'T IT A LITTLE EARLY?
NIKO (SMILE)
ニコッ
NOW, BE SURE NOT TO WAKE UP CHIYO-CHAN...
...AND FOLLOW ME NIIICE AND QUIET...
TRANQUILO...
TAAAAKE IT EASY
OH...
RIGHT...
JUST LET ME GET MY PANTS ON.

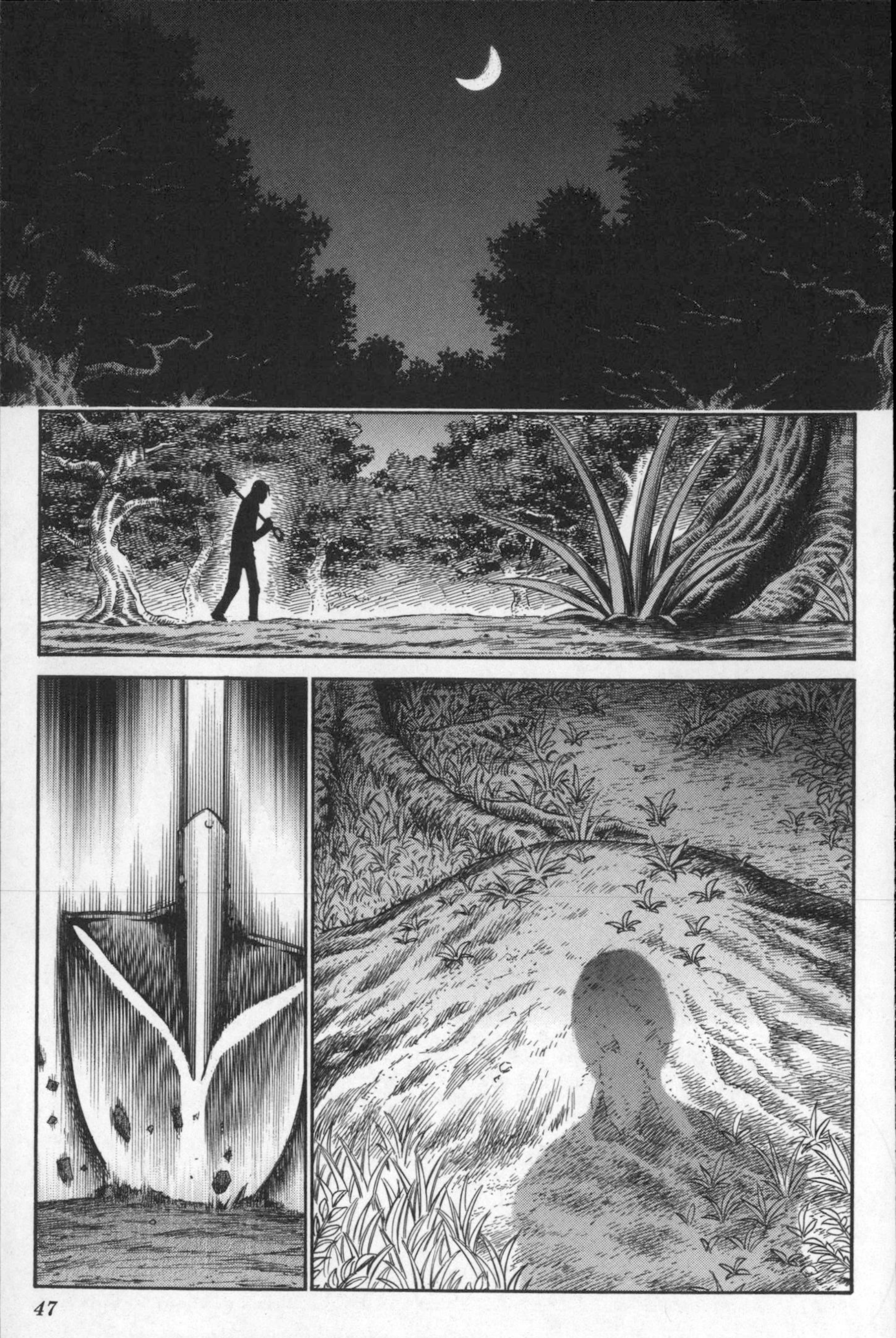

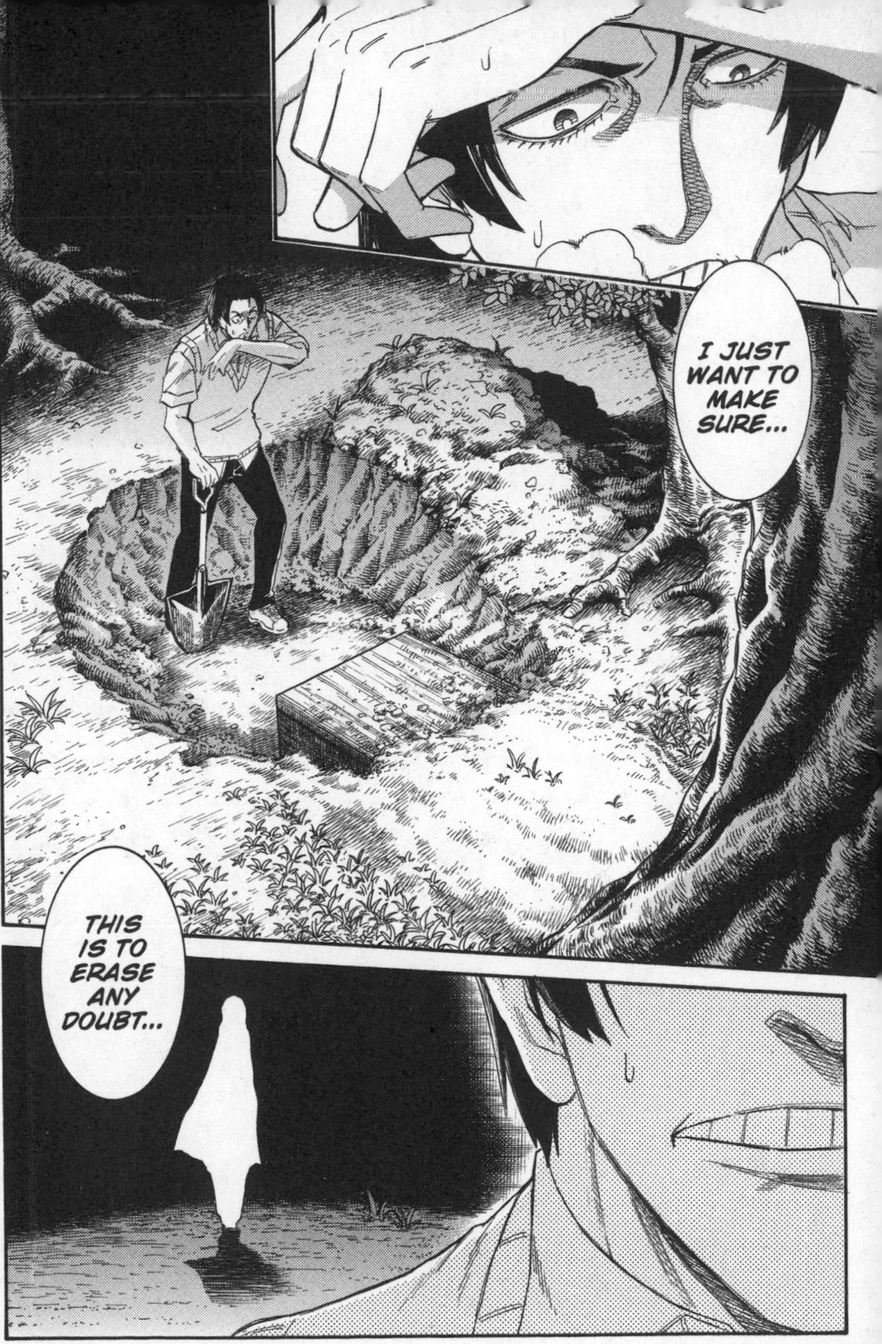
I JUST WANT TO MAKE SURE...
THIS IS TO ERASE ANY DOUBT...

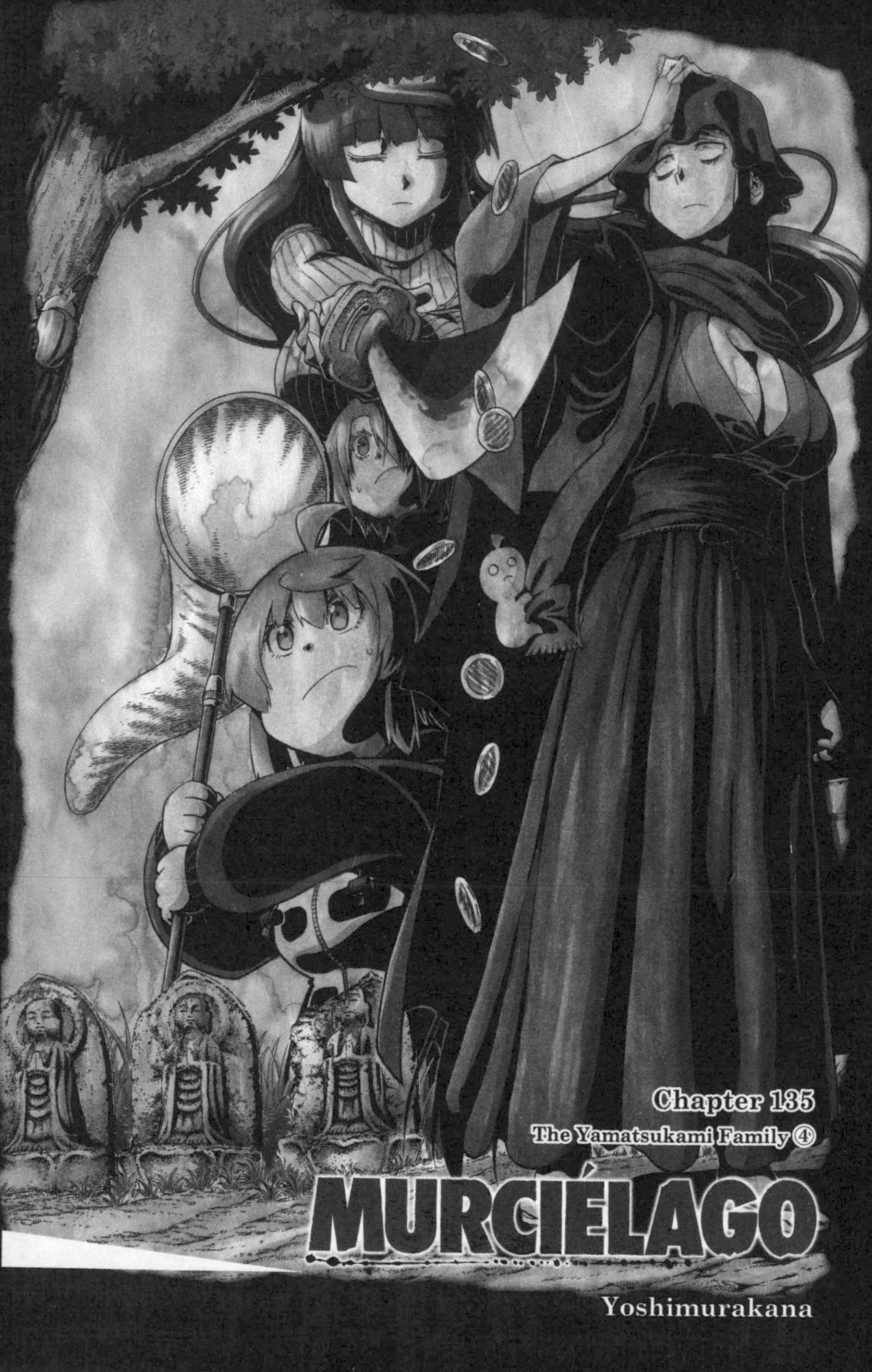
Chapter 135
The Yamatsukami Family ④
MURCIÉLAGO
Yoshimurakana

MURCIÉLAGO

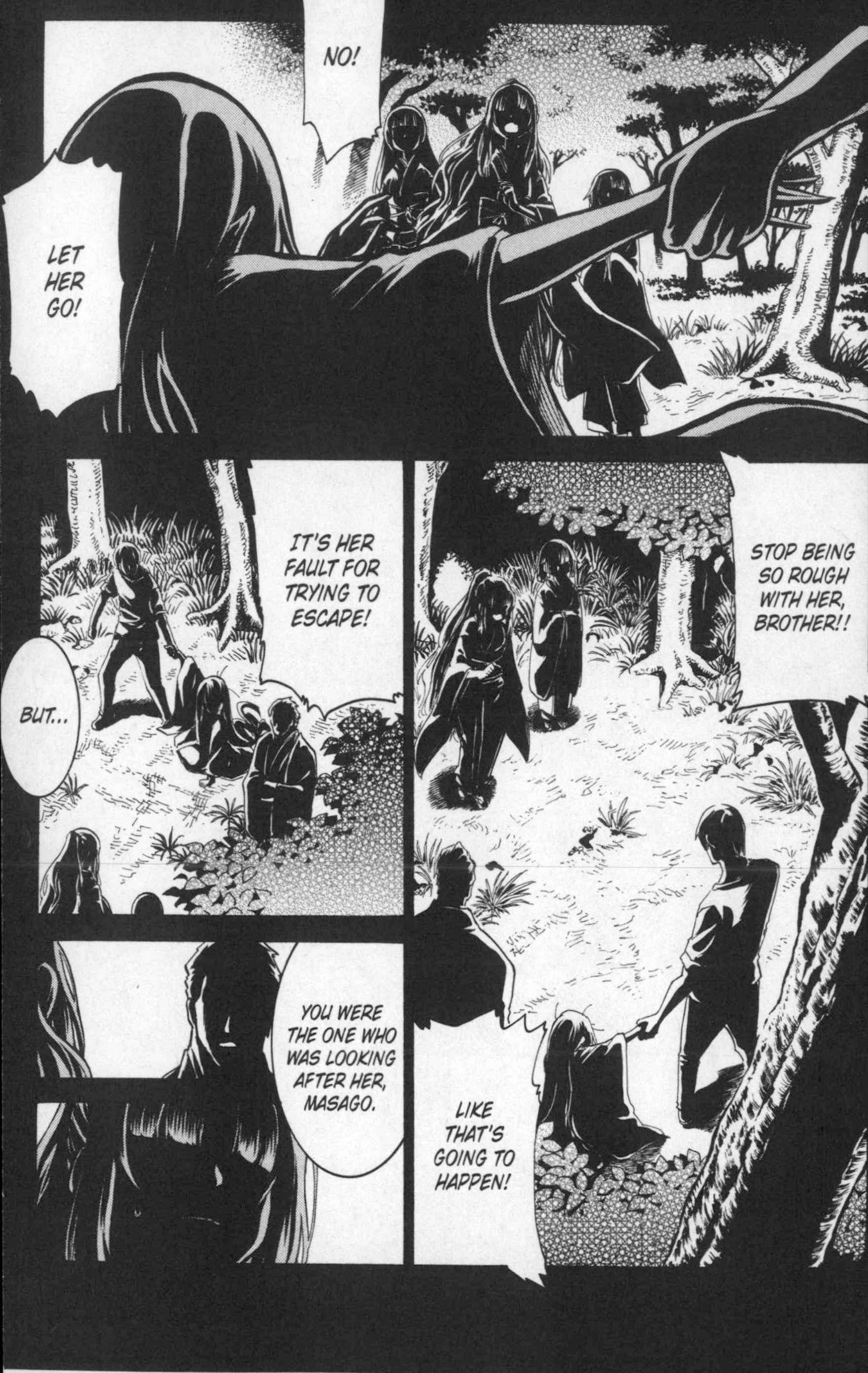
NO!
LET HER GO!
STOP BEING SO ROUGH WITH HER, BROTHER!!
LIKE THAT'S GOING TO HAPPEN!
IT'S HER FAULT FOR TRYING TO ESCAPE!
BUT...
YOU WERE THE ONE WHO WAS LOOKING AFTER HER, MASAGO.

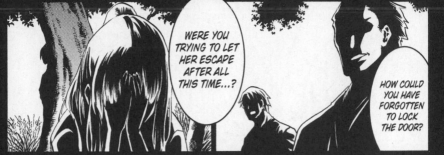

HOW COULD YOU HAVE FORGOTTEN TO LOCK THE DOOR?
WERE YOU TRYING TO LET HER ESCAPE AFTER ALL THIS TIME...?
HOW CAN YOU BE......
......
...SO CRUEL...?

MURCIÉLAGO

Yoshimurakana

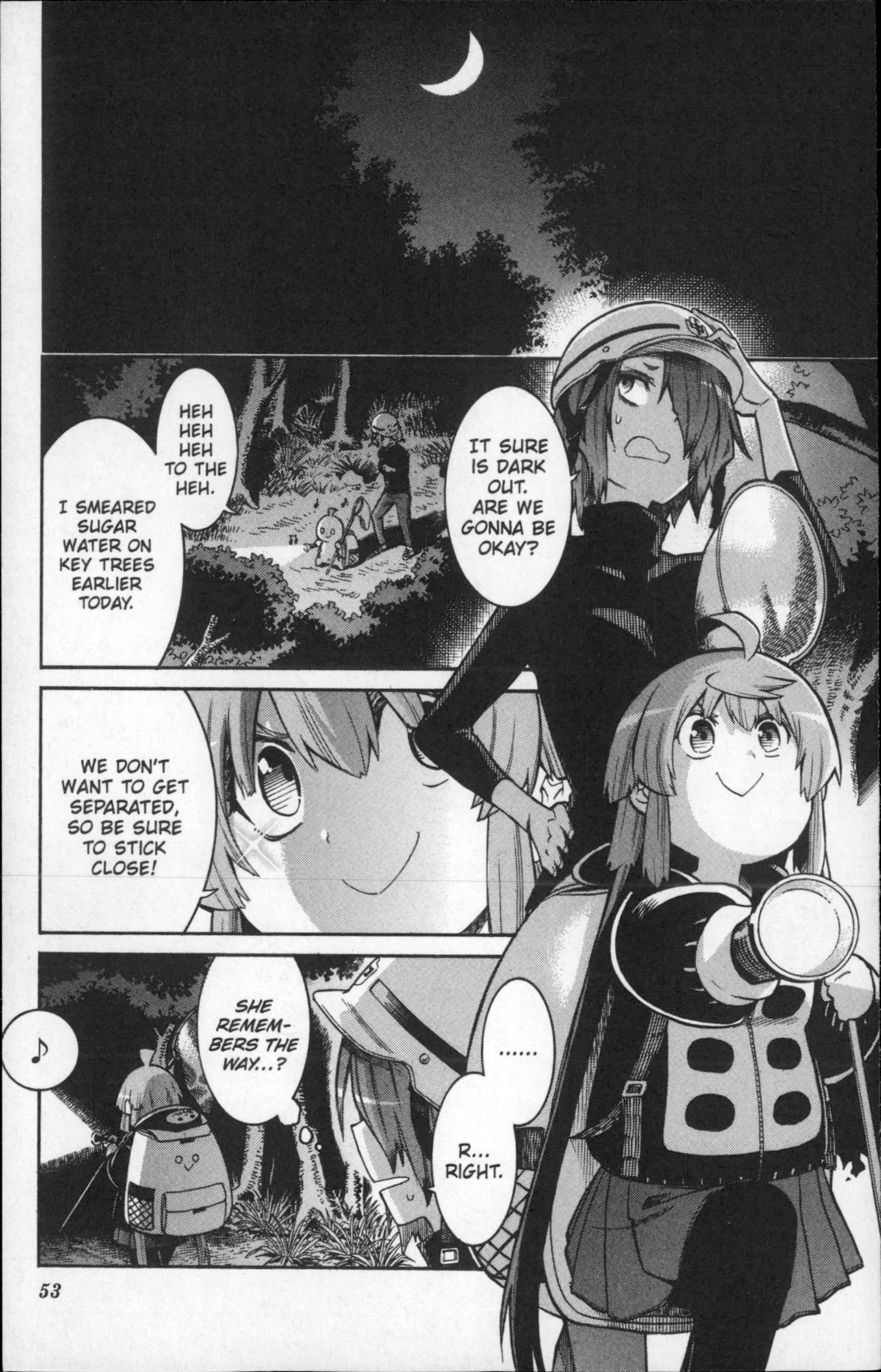

IT SURE IS DARK OUT. ARE WE GONNA BE OKAY?
HEH HEH HEH TO THE HEH.
I SMEARED SUGAR WATER ON KEY TREES EARLIER TODAY.
WE DON'T WANT TO GET SEPARATED, SO BE SURE TO STICK CLOSE!
SHE REMEM-BERS THE WAY...?
......
R... RIGHT.
♪

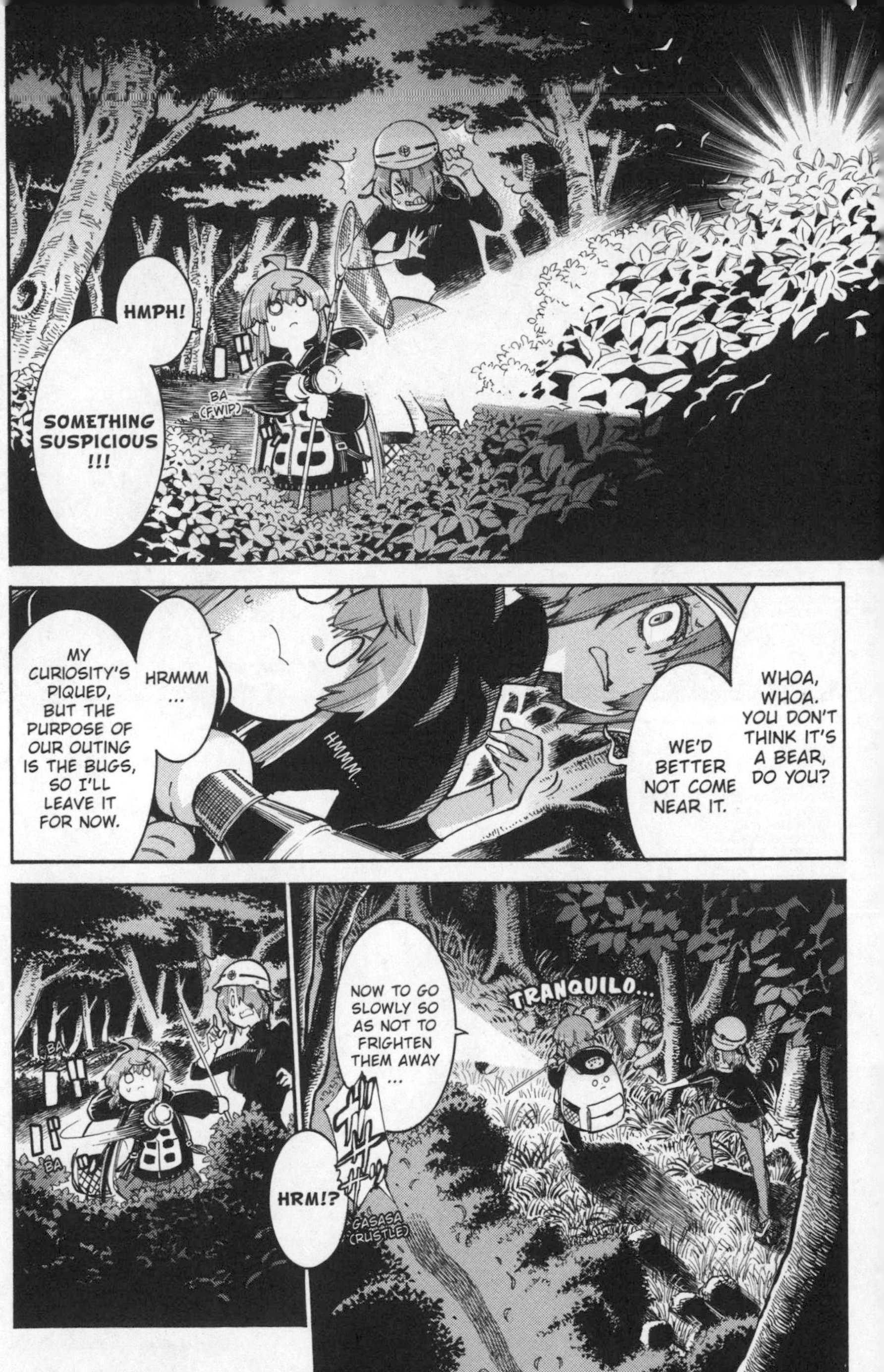
HMPH!
SOMETHING SUSPICIOUS!!!
BA (FWIP)
WHOA, WHOA. YOU DON'T THINK IT'S A BEAR, DO YOU?
WE'D BETTER NOT COME NEAR IT.
HMMM...
HRMMM...
MY CURIOSITY'S PIQUED, BUT THE PURPOSE OF OUR OUTING IS THE BUGS, SO I'LL LEAVE IT FOR NOW.
TRANQUILO...
NOW TO GO SLOWLY SO AS NOT TO FRIGHTEN THEM AWAY...
HRM!?
GASASA (RUSTLE)
BA
BA

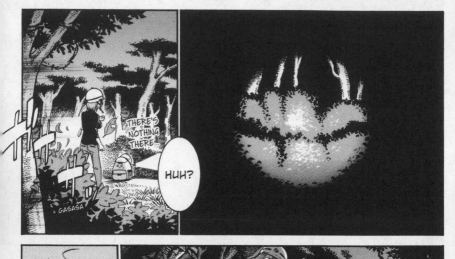

THERE'S NOTHING THERE

HUH?

GASASA

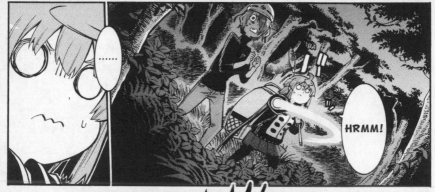

......

HRMM!

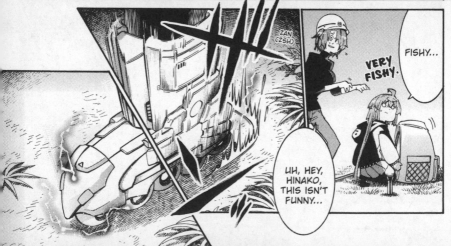

ZAN (ZSH)

FISHY...

VERY FISHY.

UH, HEY, HINAKO, THIS ISN'T FUNNY...

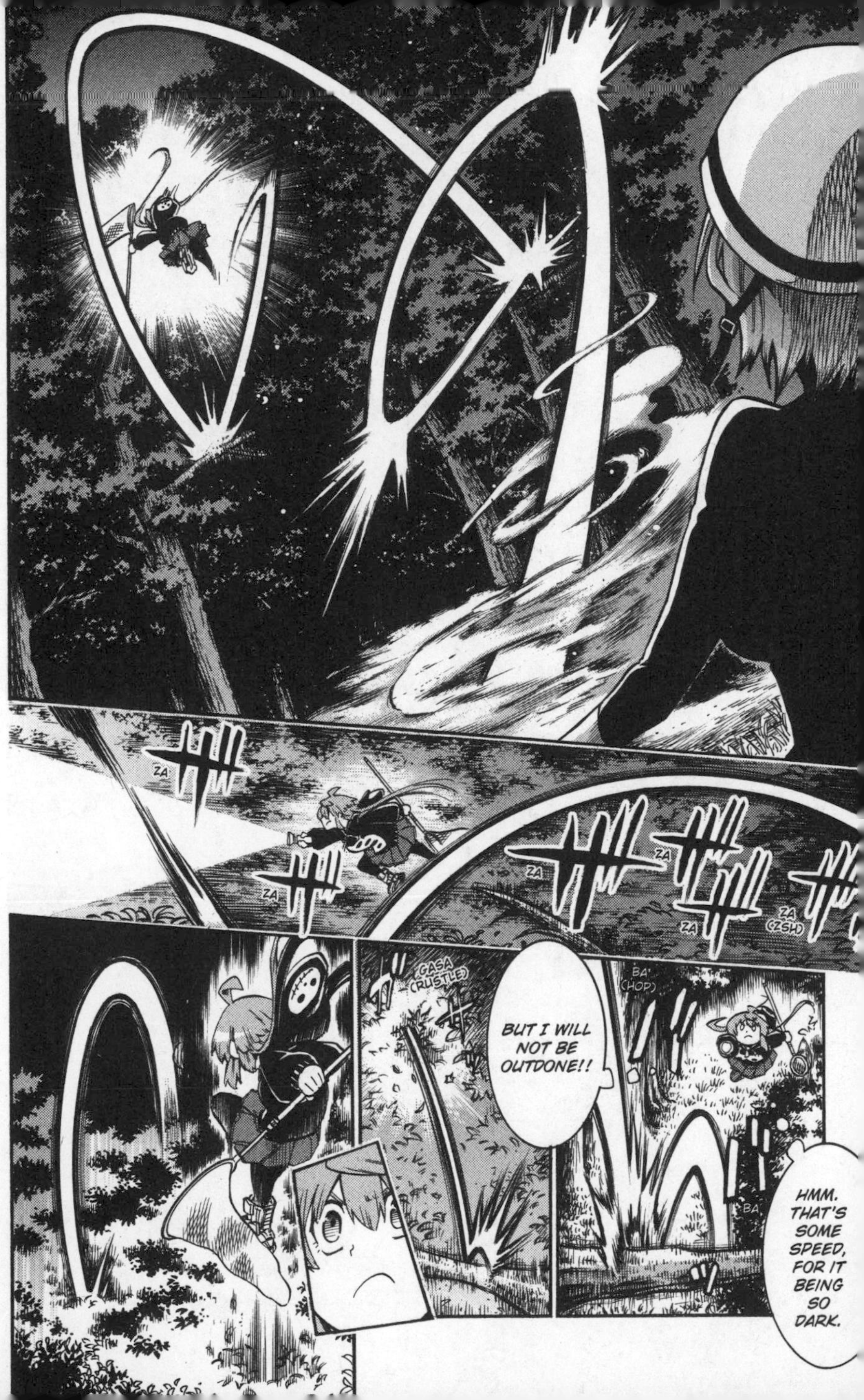
ZA (ZSH)
ZA
ZA
ZA
ZA
ZA
BA (HOP)
HMM. THAT'S SOME SPEED, FOR IT BEING SO DARK.
BA
BUT I WILL NOT BE OUTDONE!!
GASA (RUSTLE)

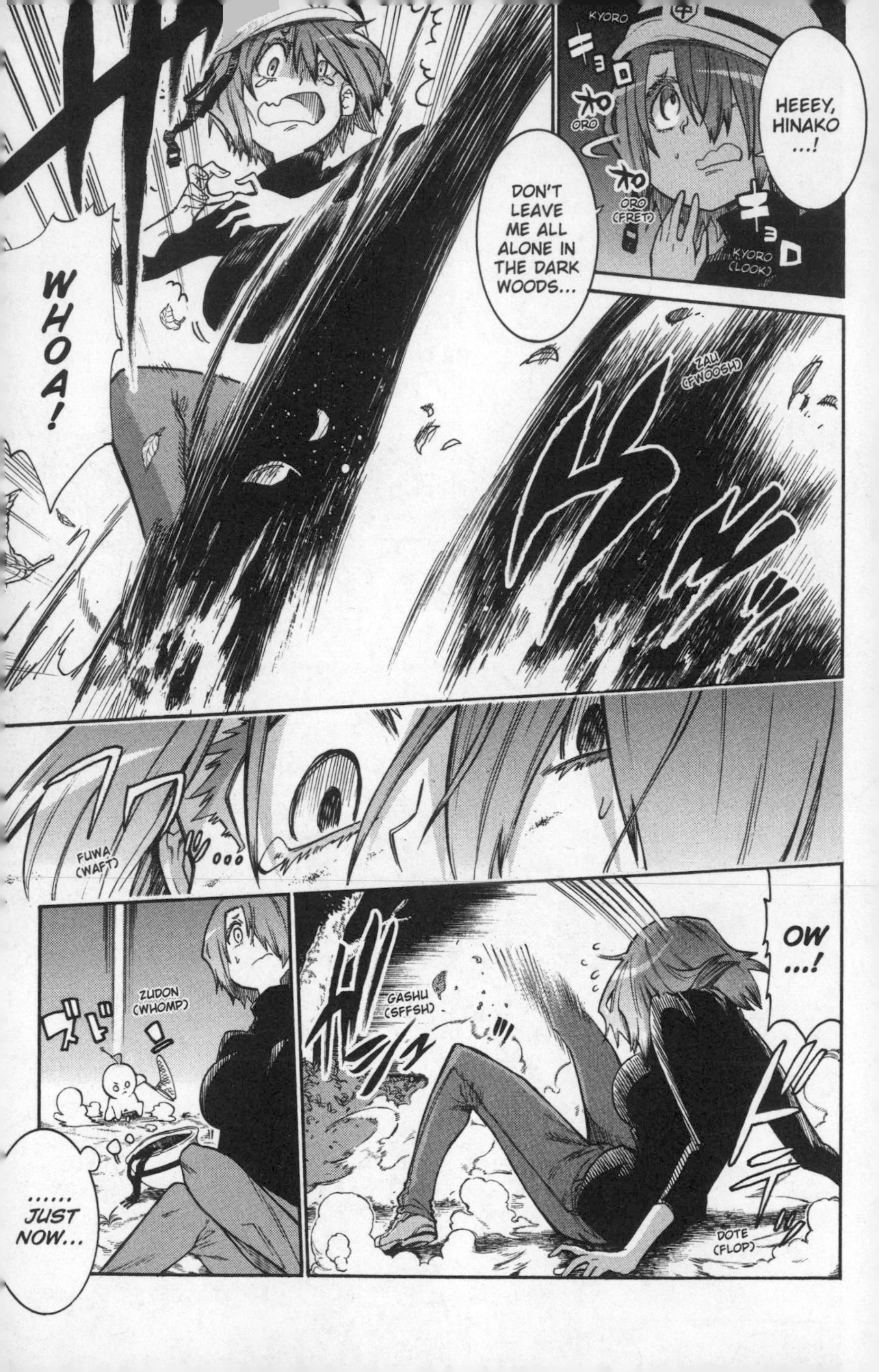
KYORO
HEEEY, HINAKO ...!
ORO
ORO (FRET)
KYORO (LOOK)
DON'T LEAVE ME ALL ALONE IN THE DARK WOODS...
WHOA!
ZAU (FWOOSH)
FUWA (WAFT)
OW ...!
GASHU (SFFSH)
DOTE (FLOP)
ZUDON (WHOMP)
...... JUST NOW...

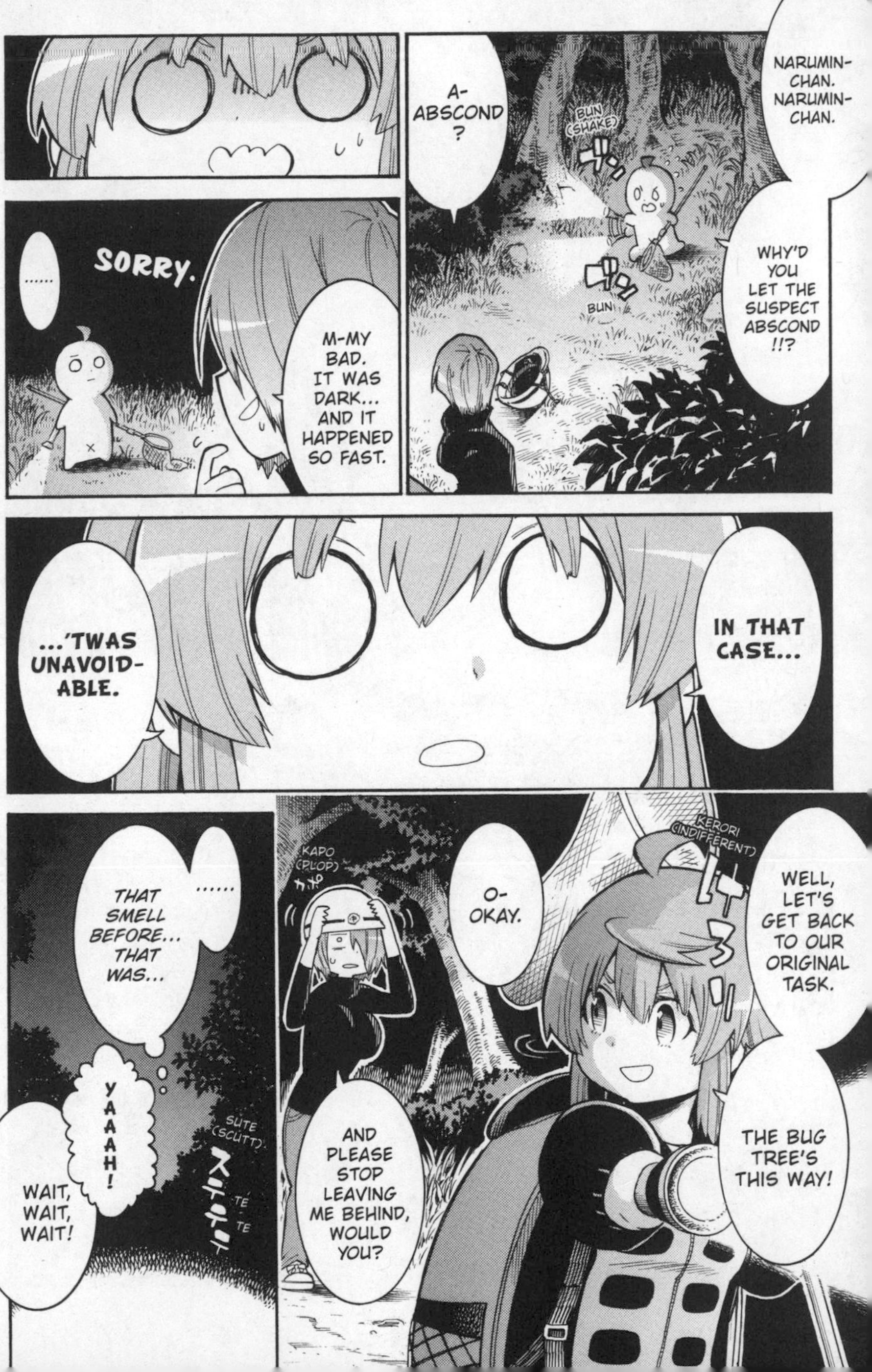
NARUMIN-CHAN. NARUMIN-CHAN.
BUN (SHAKE)
WHY'D YOU LET THE SUSPECT ABSCOND!!?
BUN
A-ABSCOND?
M-MY BAD. IT WAS DARK... AND IT HAPPENED SO FAST.
SORRY.
......
IN THAT CASE...
...'TWAS UNAVOIDABLE.
KERORI (INDIFFERENT)
WELL, LET'S GET BACK TO OUR ORIGINAL TASK.
THE BUG TREE'S THIS WAY!
O-OKAY.
KAPO (PLOP)
AND PLEASE STOP LEAVING ME BEHIND, WOULD YOU?
......
THAT SMELL BEFORE... THAT WAS...
SUTE (SCUTT)
TE TE
YAAAH!
WAIT, WAIT, WAIT!

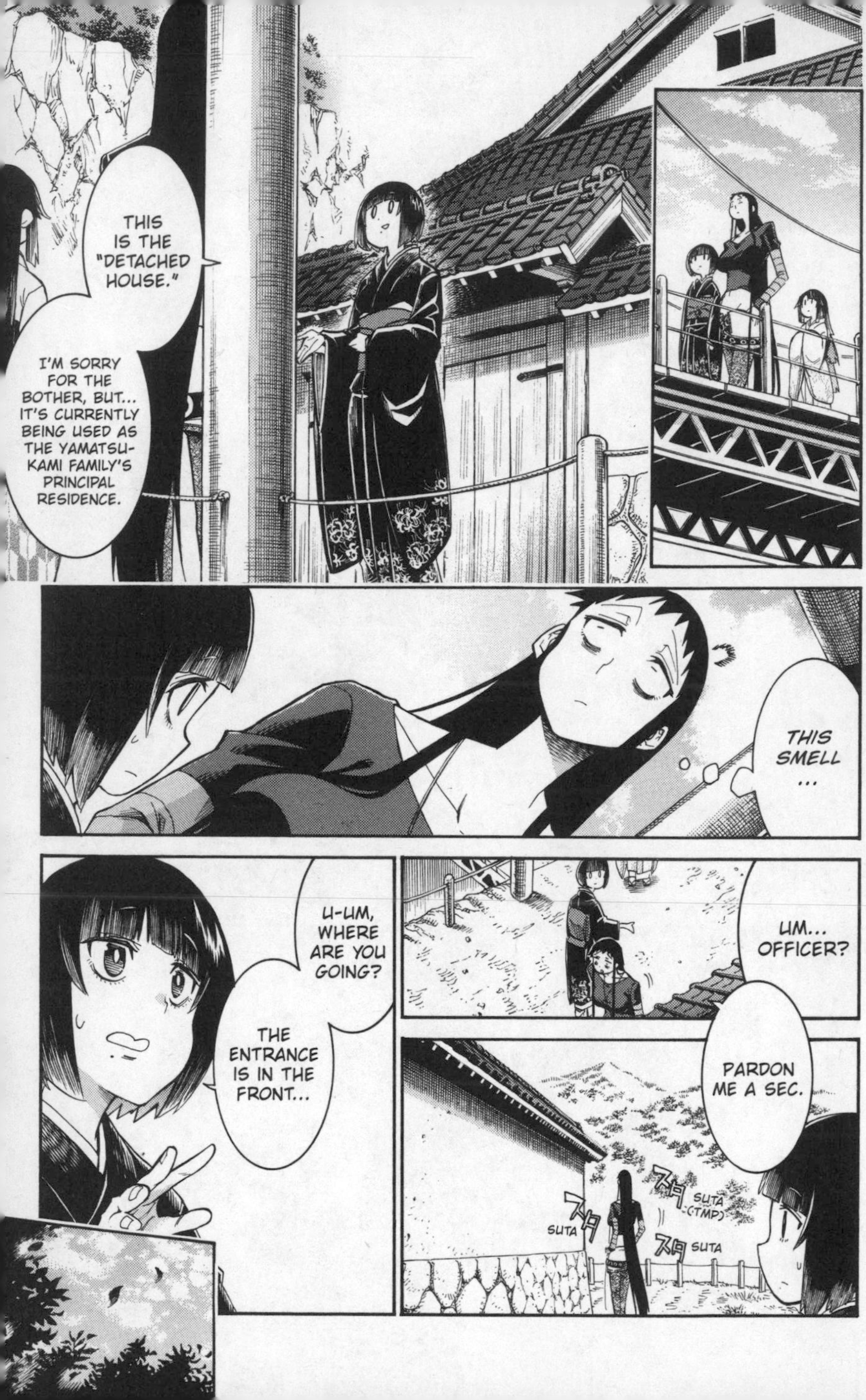
THIS IS THE "DETACHED HOUSE."
I'M SORRY FOR THE BOTHER, BUT... IT'S CURRENTLY BEING USED AS THE YAMATSU-KAMI FAMILY'S PRINCIPAL RESIDENCE.
THIS SMELL ...
UM... OFFICER?
PARDON ME A SEC.
SUTA (TMP)
SUTA
SUTA
U-UM, WHERE ARE YOU GOING?
THE ENTRANCE IS IN THE FRONT...

Chapter 135

The Yamatsukami Family ④

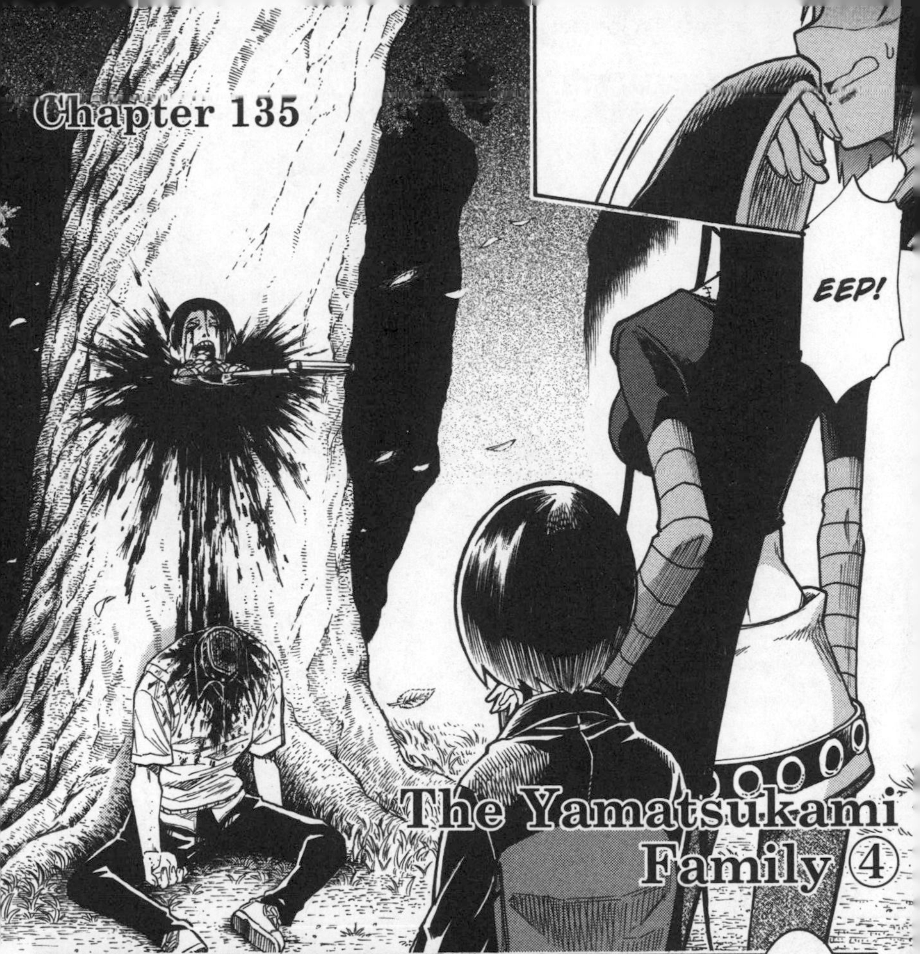
EEP!

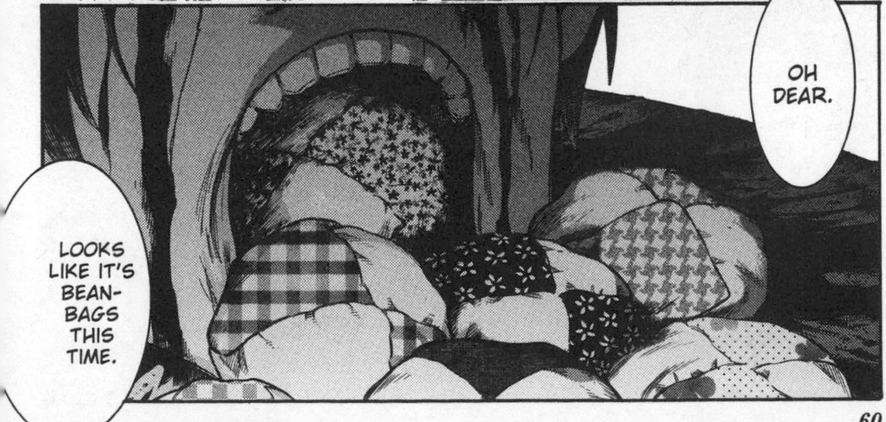
OH DEAR.
LOOKS LIKE IT'S BEAN-BAGS THIS TIME.

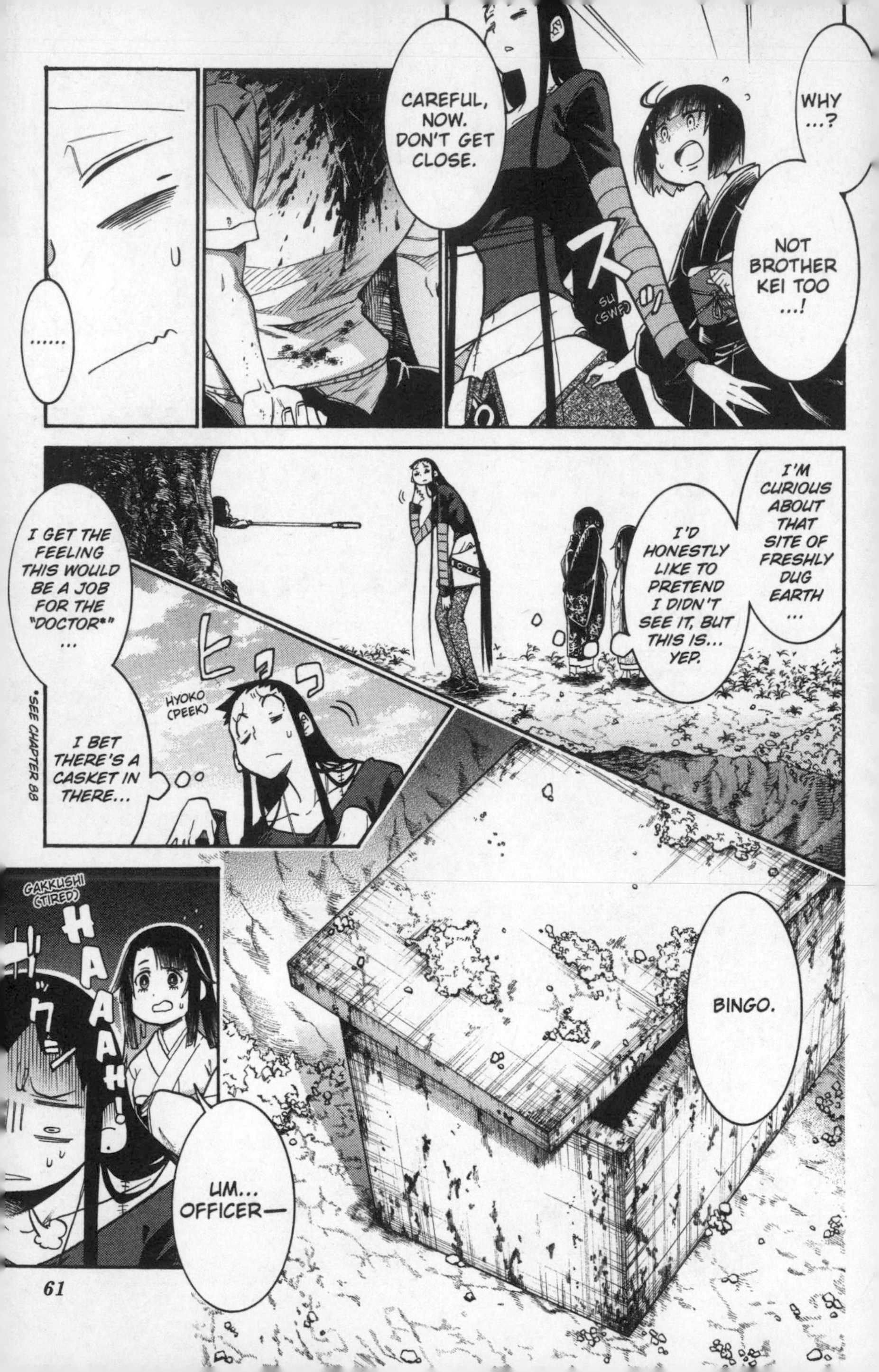
WHY ...?
NOT BROTHER KEI TOO ...!
CAREFUL, NOW. DON'T GET CLOSE.
SU (SWF)
......
I'M CURIOUS ABOUT THAT SITE OF FRESHLY DUG EARTH ...
I'D HONESTLY LIKE TO PRETEND I DIDN'T SEE IT, BUT THIS IS... YEP.
I GET THE FEELING THIS WOULD BE A JOB FOR THE "DOCTOR*" ...
HYOKO (PEEK)
I BET THERE'S A CASKET IN THERE...
*SEE CHAPTER 88
BINGO.
GAKKUSHI (TIRED)
HAAAH!
UM... OFFICER—

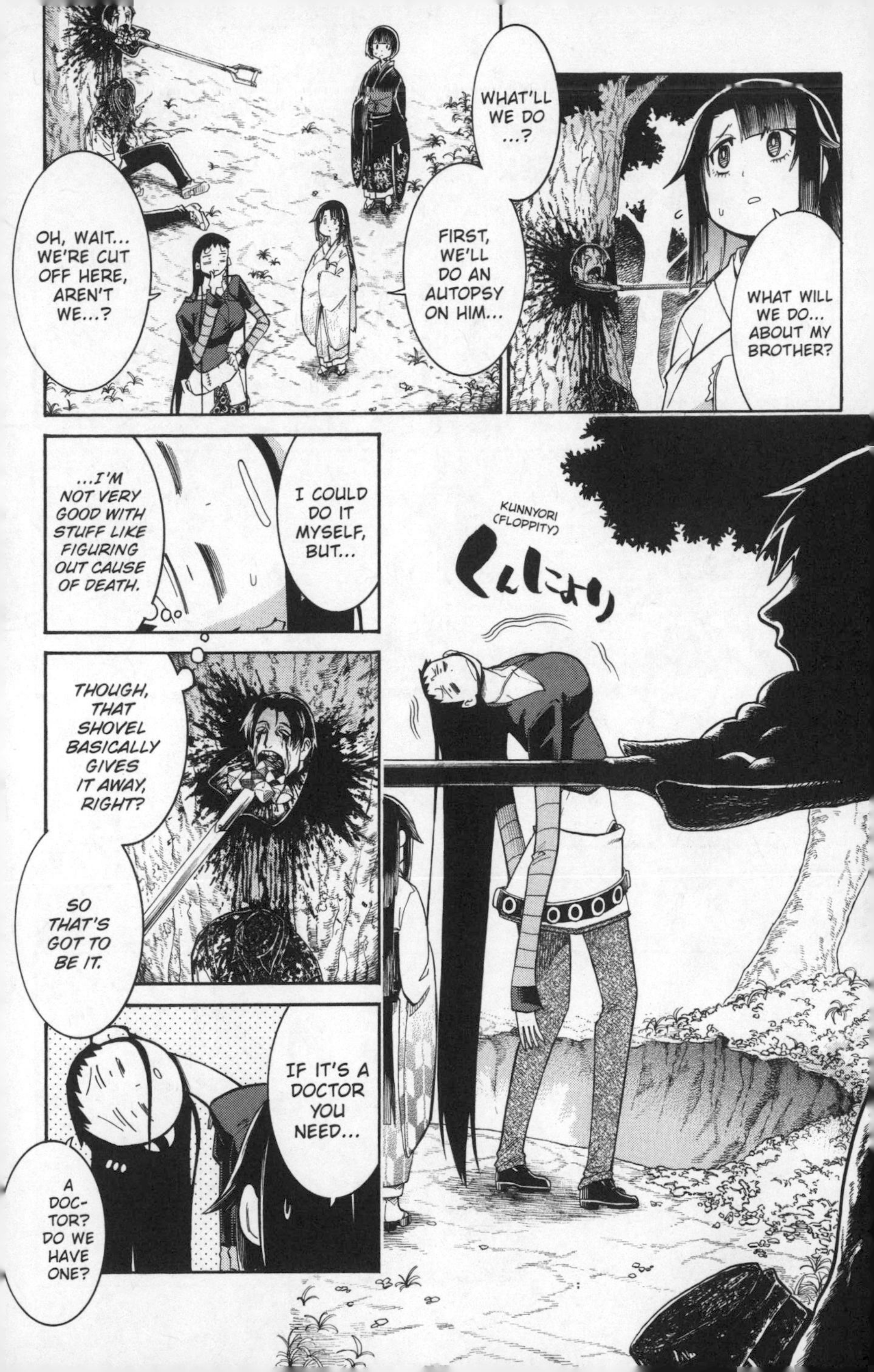
WHAT WILL WE DO... ABOUT MY BROTHER?
WHAT'LL WE DO ...?
FIRST, WE'LL DO AN AUTOPSY ON HIM...
OH, WAIT... WE'RE CUT OFF HERE, AREN'T WE...?
KUNNYORI (FLOPPITY)
くんにょり
I COULD DO IT MYSELF, BUT...
...I'M NOT VERY GOOD WITH STUFF LIKE FIGURING OUT CAUSE OF DEATH.
THOUGH, THAT SHOVEL BASICALLY GIVES IT AWAY, RIGHT?
SO THAT'S GOT TO BE IT.
IF IT'S A DOCTOR YOU NEED...
A DOC-TOR? DO WE HAVE ONE?

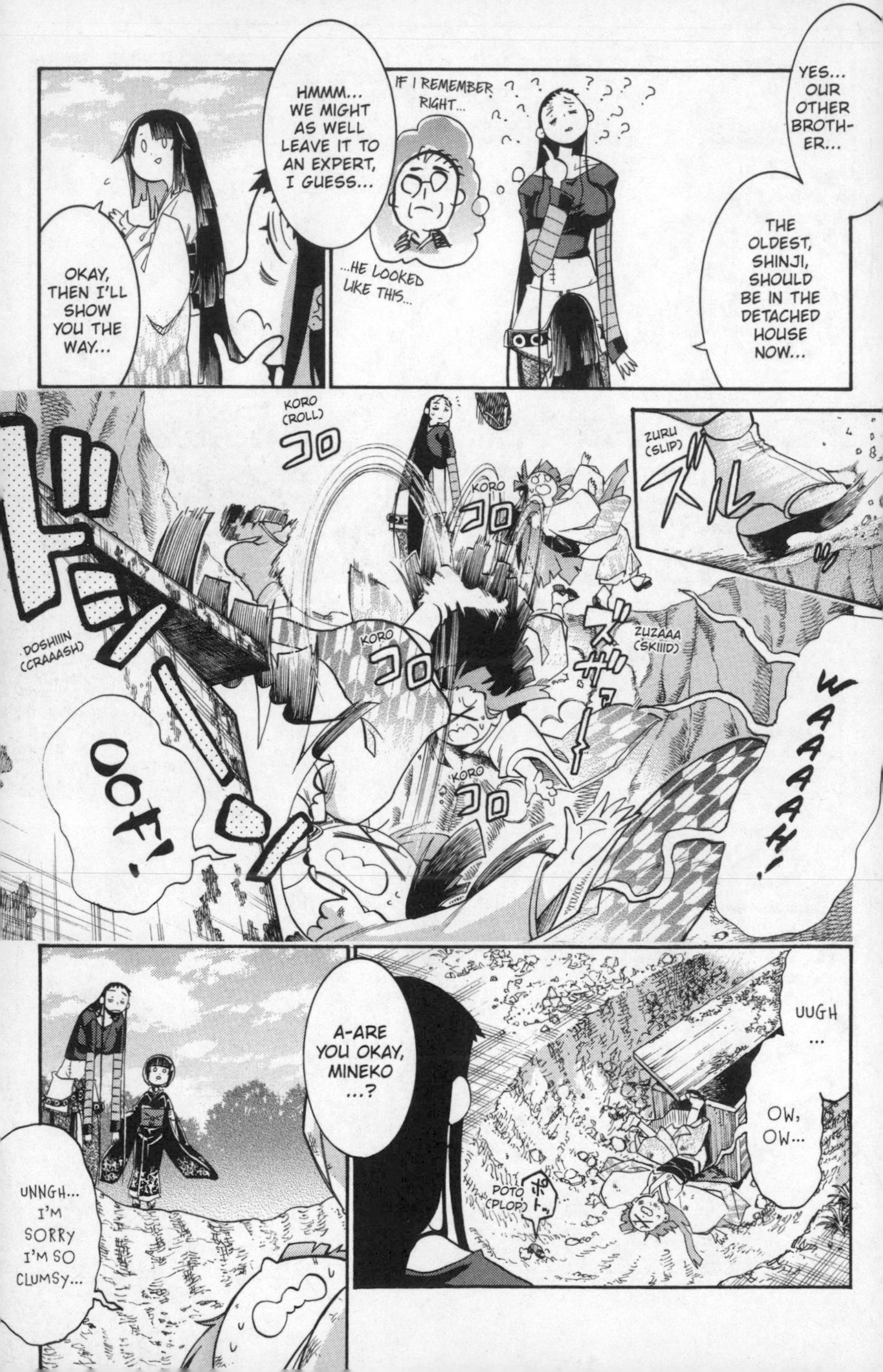
YES... OUR OTHER BROTHER...
THE OLDEST, SHINJI, SHOULD BE IN THE DETACHED HOUSE NOW...
IF I REMEMBER RIGHT...
...HE LOOKED LIKE THIS...
HMMM... WE MIGHT AS WELL LEAVE IT TO AN EXPERT, I GUESS...
OKAY, THEN I'LL SHOW YOU THE WAY...
ZURU (SLIP)
ズル
WAAAAAH!
ZUZAAA (SKIIID)
ズザァー
KORO (ROLL)
コロ
KORO
コロ
KORO
コロ
KORO
コロ
DOSHIIIN (CRAAASH)
OOF!
UUGH...
OW, OW...
A-ARE YOU OKAY, MINEKO...?
POTO (PLOP)
ポトッ
UNNGH... I'M SORRY I'M SO CLUMSY...

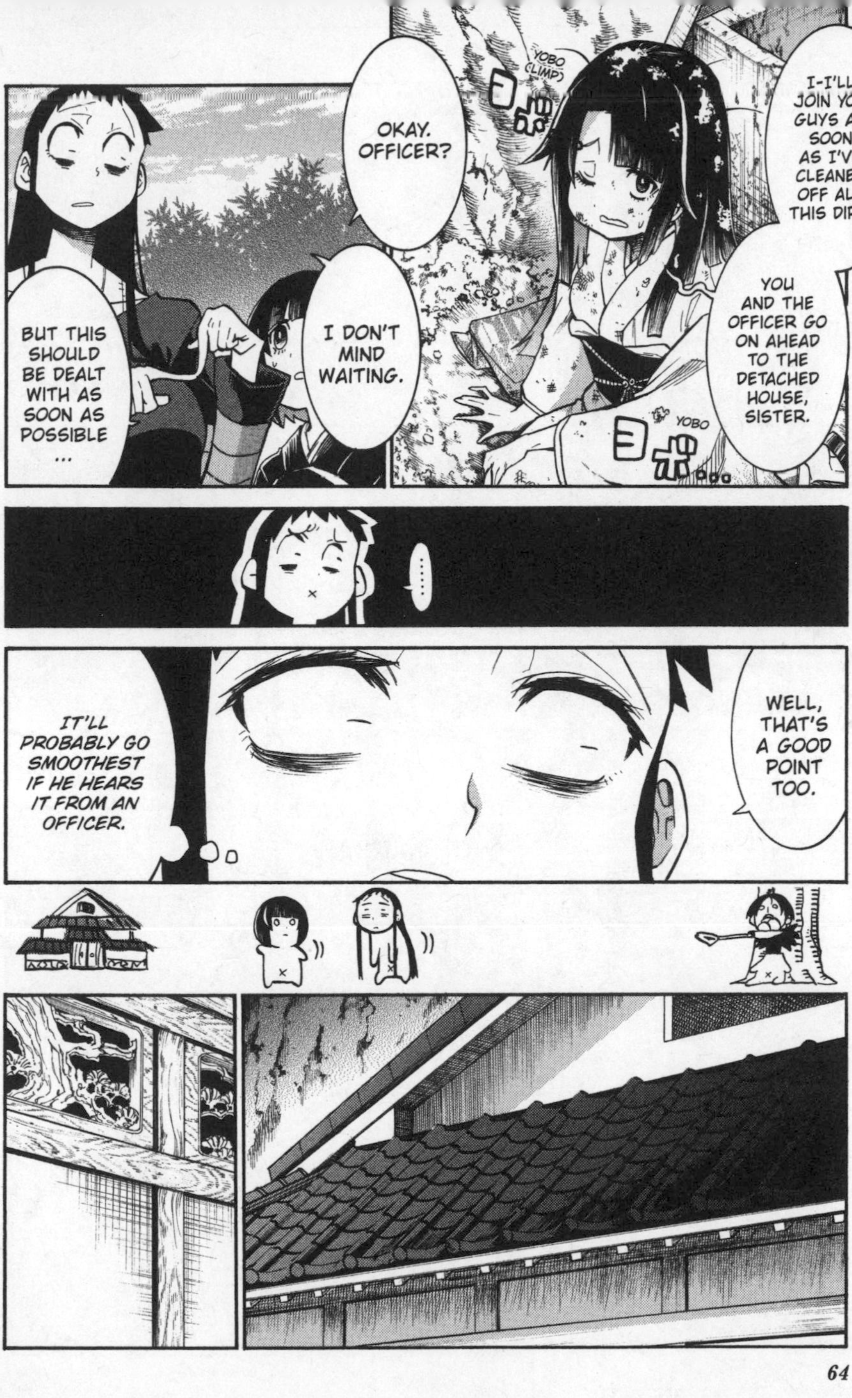
YOBO (LIMP)
I-I'LL JOIN YOU GUYS AS SOON AS I'VE CLEANED OFF ALL THIS DIRT.
YOU AND THE OFFICER GO ON AHEAD TO THE DETACHED HOUSE, SISTER.
YOBO
OKAY. OFFICER?
I DON'T MIND WAITING.
BUT THIS SHOULD BE DEALT WITH AS SOON AS POSSIBLE ...
......
WELL, THAT'S A GOOD POINT TOO.
IT'LL PROBABLY GO SMOOTHEST IF HE HEARS IT FROM AN OFFICER.

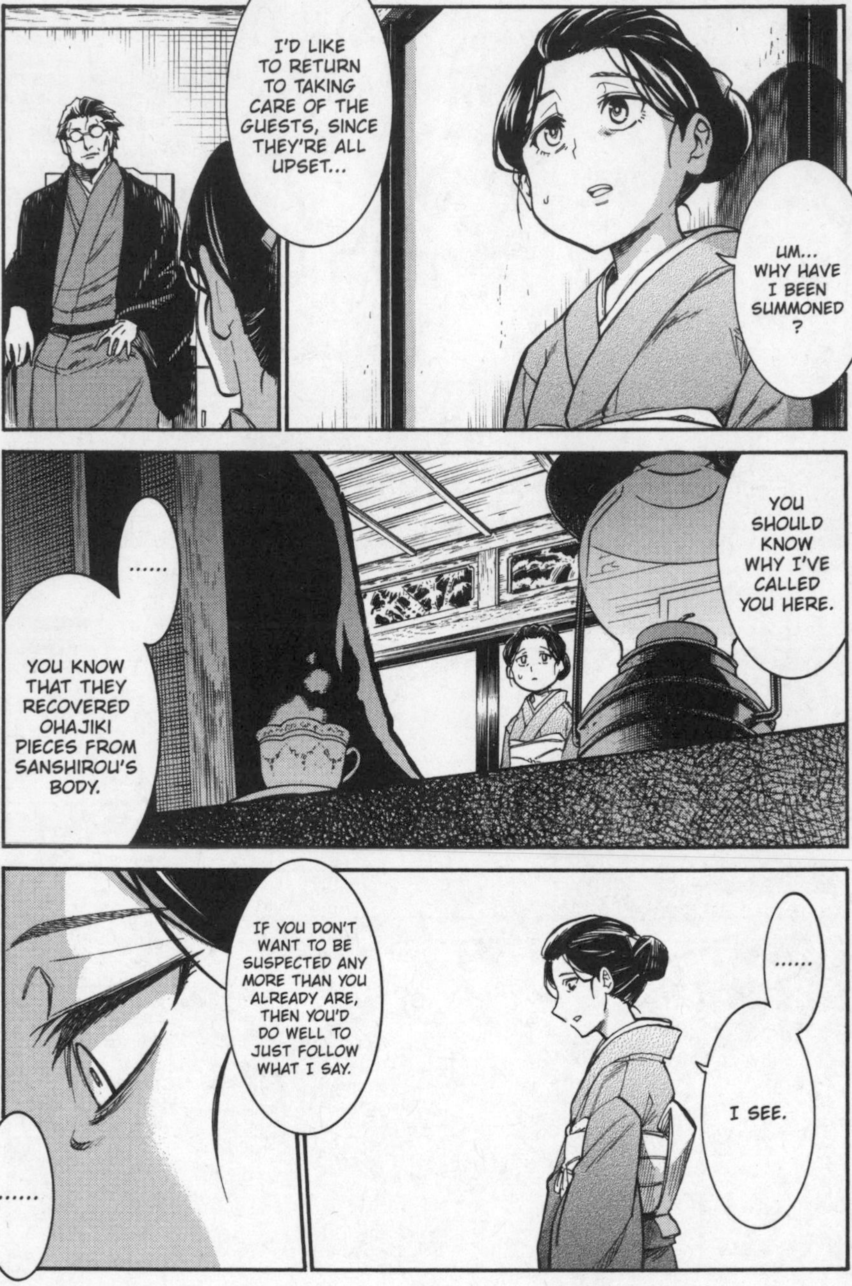
UM... WHY HAVE I BEEN SUMMONED ?
I'D LIKE TO RETURN TO TAKING CARE OF THE GUESTS, SINCE THEY'RE ALL UPSET...
YOU SHOULD KNOW WHY I'VE CALLED YOU HERE.
......
YOU KNOW THAT THEY RECOVERED OHAJIKI PIECES FROM SANSHIROU'S BODY.
IF YOU DON'T WANT TO BE SUSPECTED ANY MORE THAN YOU ALREADY ARE, THEN YOU'D DO WELL TO JUST FOLLOW WHAT I SAY.
......
I SEE.
......

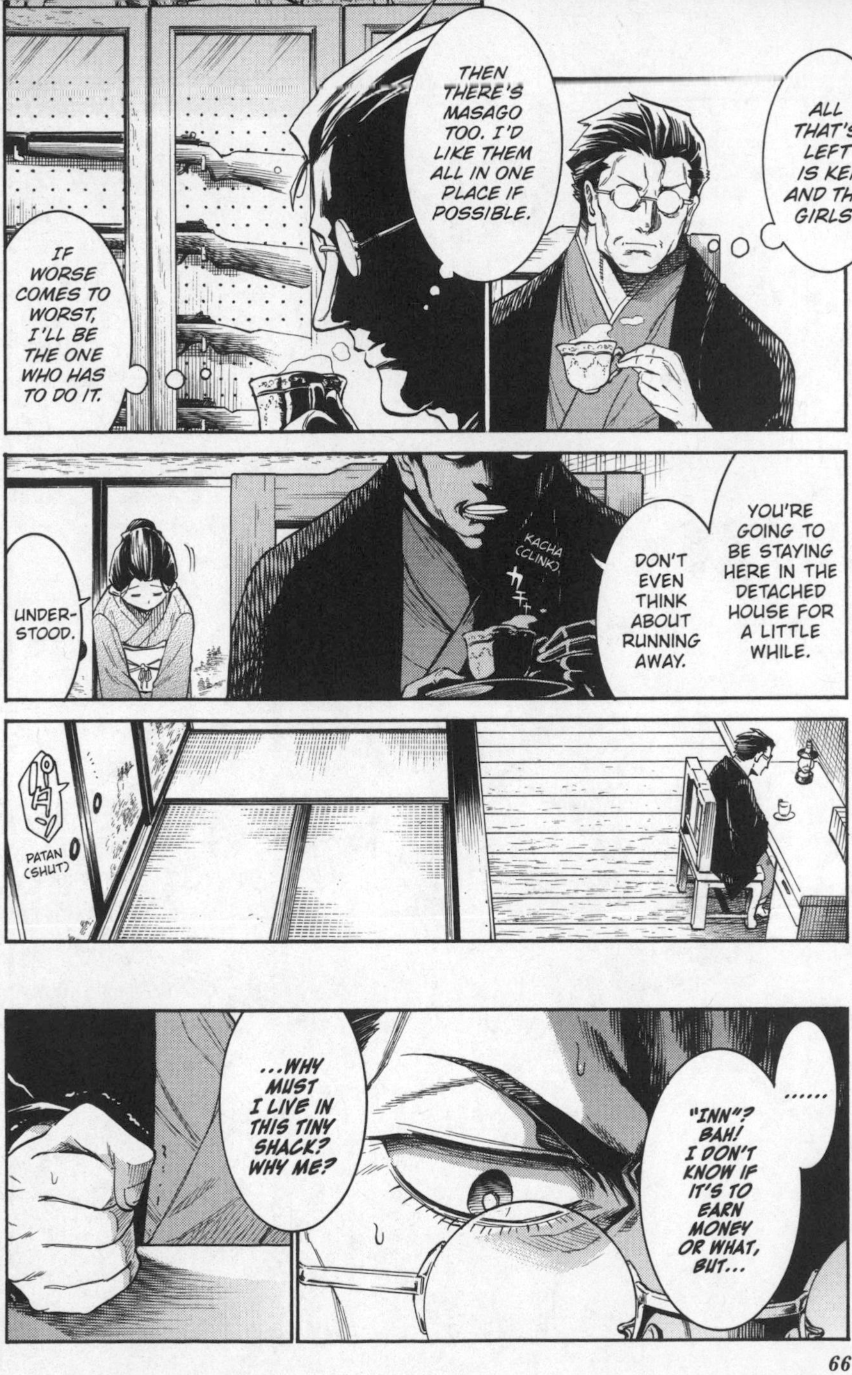
ALL THAT'S LEFT IS KEI AND THE GIRLS.
THEN THERE'S MASAGO TOO. I'D LIKE THEM ALL IN ONE PLACE IF POSSIBLE.
IF WORSE COMES TO WORST, I'LL BE THE ONE WHO HAS TO DO IT.
YOU'RE GOING TO BE STAYING HERE IN THE DETACHED HOUSE FOR A LITTLE WHILE.
DON'T EVEN THINK ABOUT RUNNING AWAY.
KACHA (CLINK)
UNDERSTOOD.
PATAN (SHUT)
......
"INN"? BAH! I DON'T KNOW IF IT'S TO EARN MONEY OR WHAT, BUT...
...WHY MUST I LIVE IN THIS TINY SHACK? WHY ME?

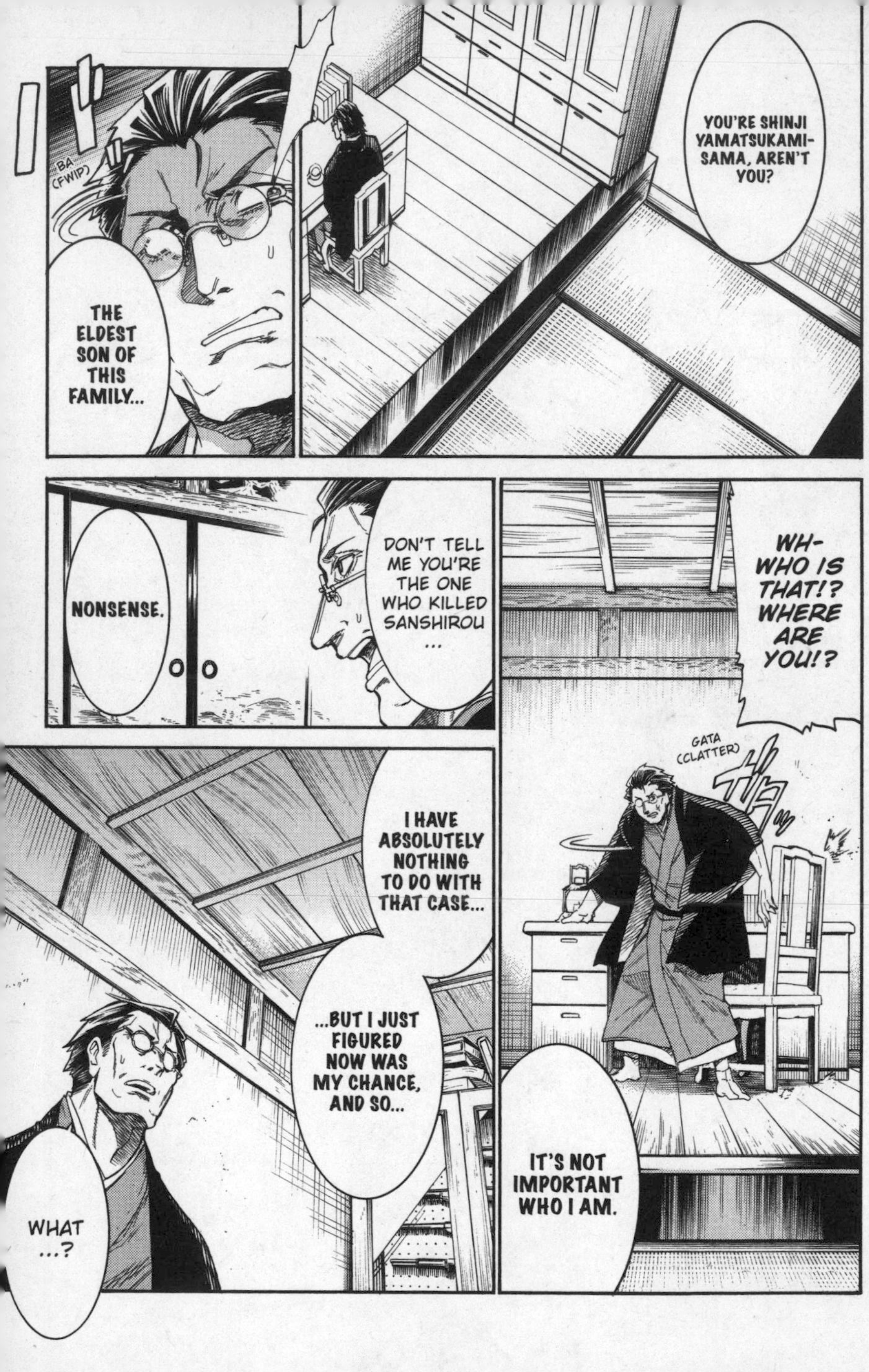
YOU'RE SHINJI YAMATSUKAMI-SAMA, AREN'T YOU?
BA (FWIP)
THE ELDEST SON OF THIS FAMILY...
WH-WHO IS THAT!? WHERE ARE YOU!?
GATA (CLATTER)
IT'S NOT IMPORTANT WHO I AM.
DON'T TELL ME YOU'RE THE ONE WHO KILLED SANSHIROU ...
NONSENSE.
I HAVE ABSOLUTELY NOTHING TO DO WITH THAT CASE...
...BUT I JUST FIGURED NOW WAS MY CHANCE, AND SO...
WHAT ...?

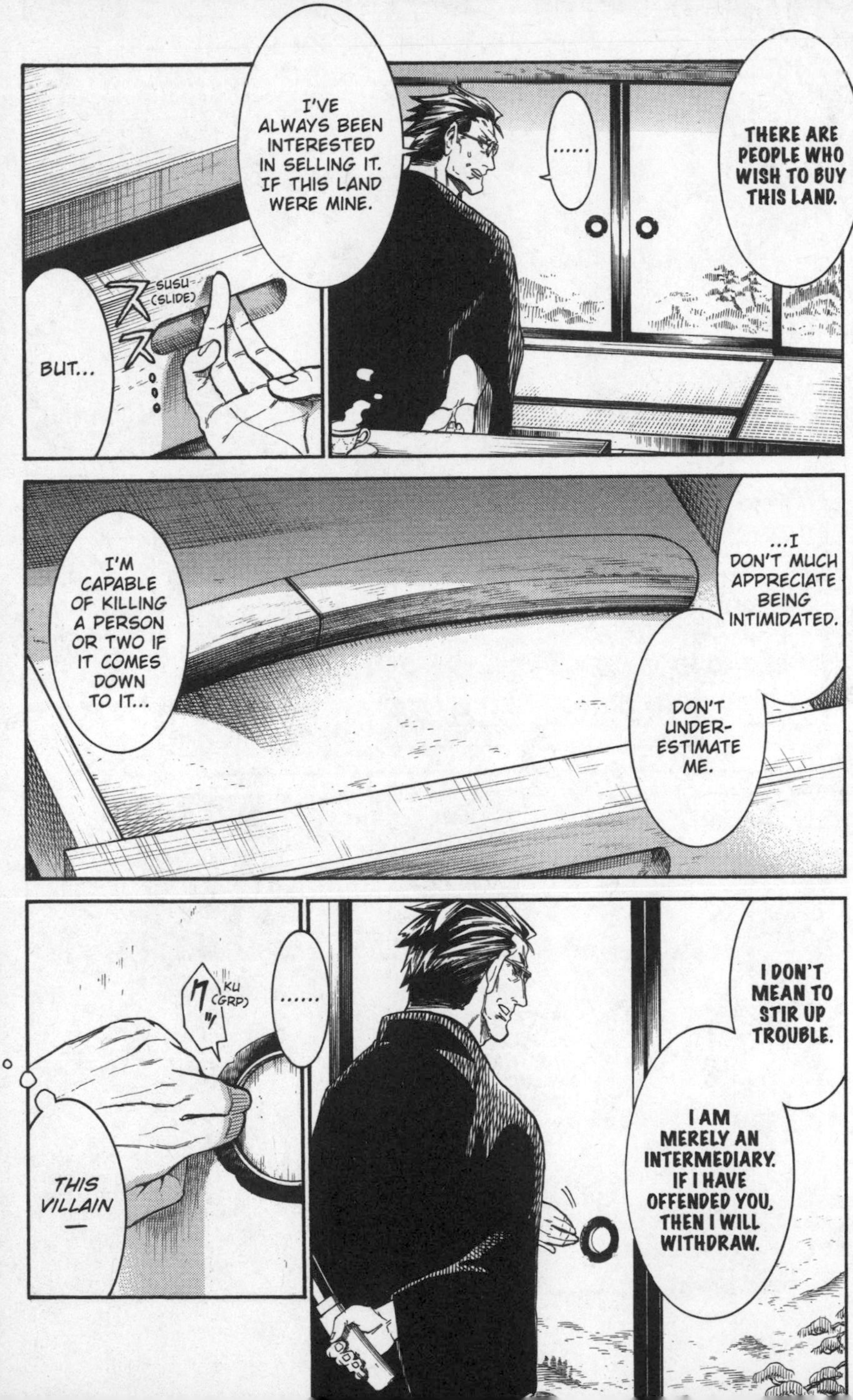
THERE ARE PEOPLE WHO WISH TO BUY THIS LAND.
......
I'VE ALWAYS BEEN INTERESTED IN SELLING IT. IF THIS LAND WERE MINE.
SUSU (SLIDE)
BUT...
...I DON'T MUCH APPRECIATE BEING INTIMIDATED.
DON'T UNDER-ESTIMATE ME.
I'M CAPABLE OF KILLING A PERSON OR TWO IF IT COMES DOWN TO IT...
I DON'T MEAN TO STIR UP TROUBLE.
I AM MERELY AN INTERMEDIARY. IF I HAVE OFFENDED YOU, THEN I WILL WITHDRAW.
......
KU (GRP)
THIS VILLAIN —

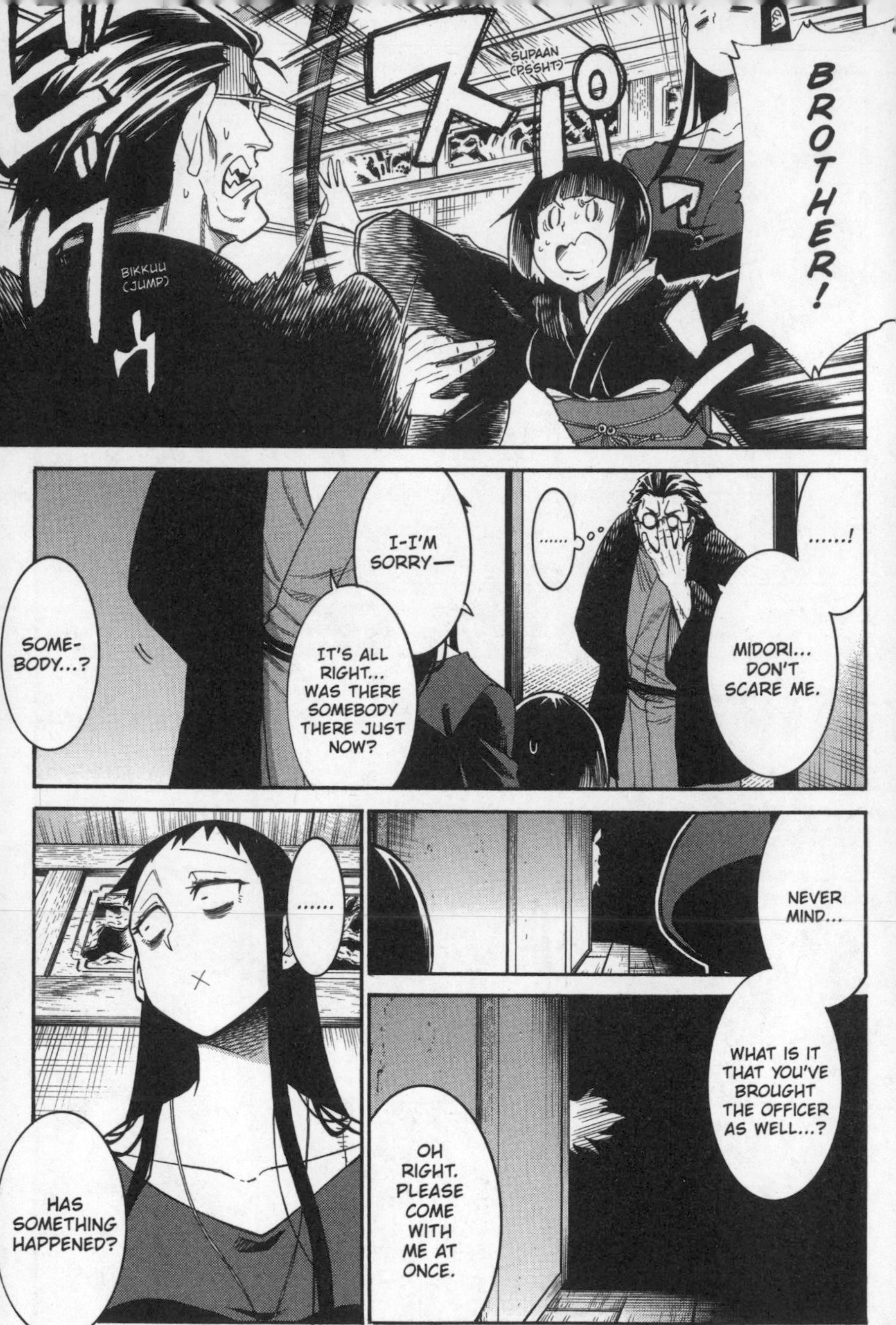
BROTHER!
SUPAAN (PSSHT)
BIKKUU (JUMP)
......!
MIDORI... DON'T SCARE ME.
......
I-I'M SORRY—
IT'S ALL RIGHT... WAS THERE SOMEBODY THERE JUST NOW?
SOME-BODY...?
NEVER MIND...
WHAT IS IT THAT YOU'VE BROUGHT THE OFFICER AS WELL...?
OH RIGHT. PLEASE COME WITH ME AT ONCE.
......
HAS SOMETHING HAPPENED?

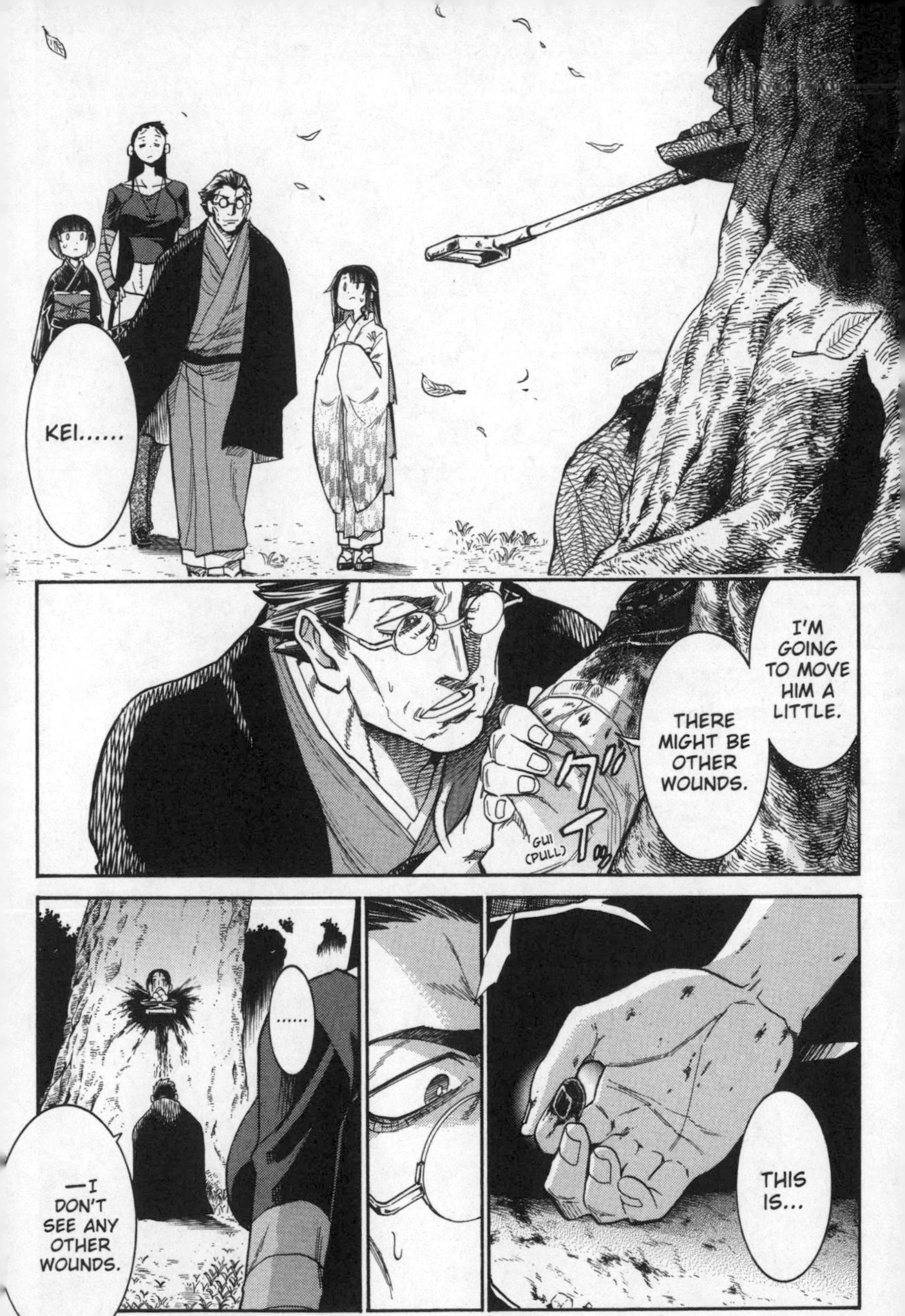
KEI......
I'M GOING TO MOVE HIM A LITTLE.
THERE MIGHT BE OTHER WOUNDS.
GUI (PULL)
THIS IS...
......
—I DON'T SEE ANY OTHER WOUNDS.

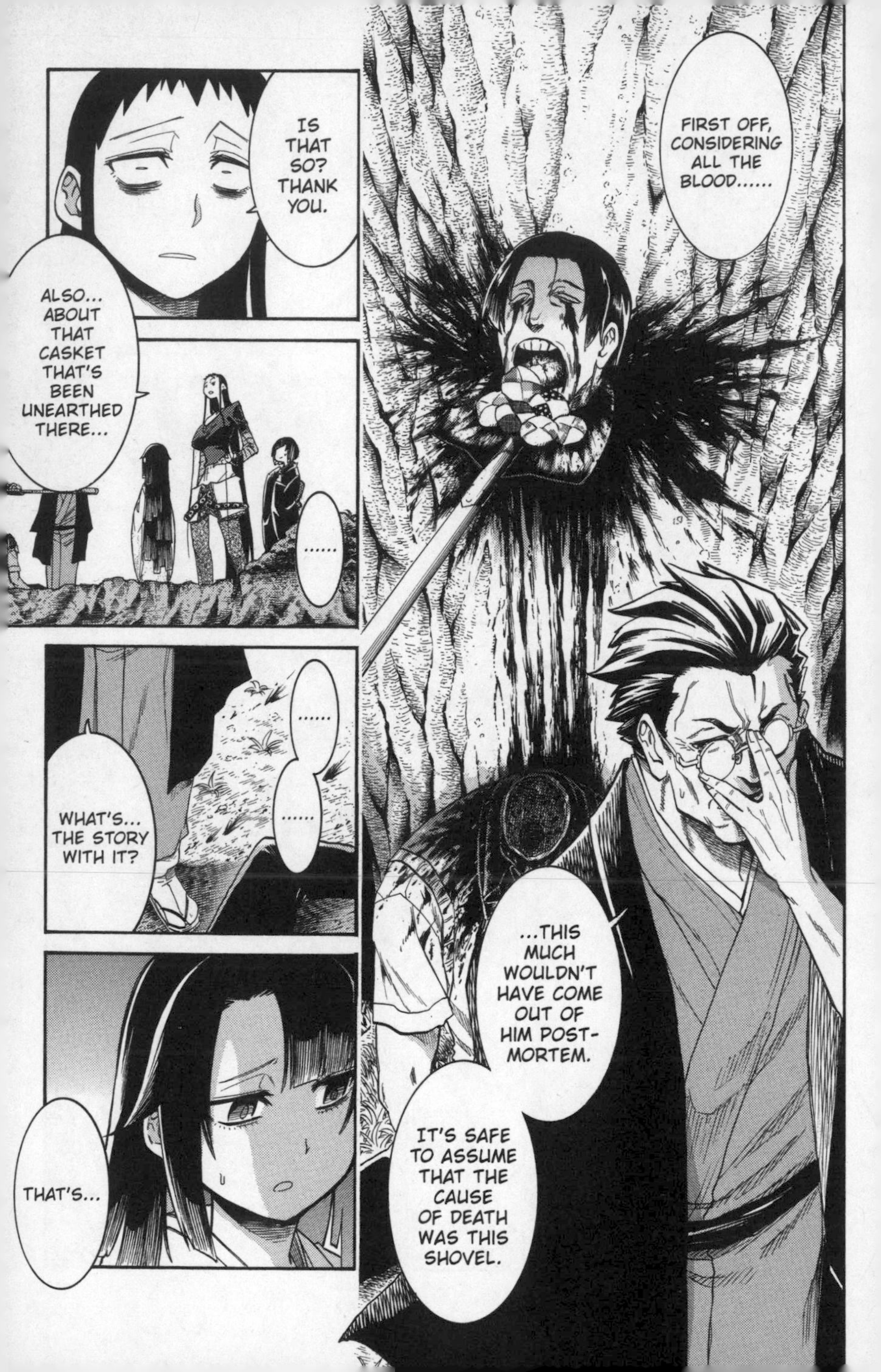
FIRST OFF, CONSIDERING ALL THE BLOOD......
...THIS MUCH WOULDN'T HAVE COME OUT OF HIM POST-MORTEM.
IT'S SAFE TO ASSUME THAT THE CAUSE OF DEATH WAS THIS SHOVEL.
IS THAT SO? THANK YOU.
ALSO... ABOUT THAT CASKET THAT'S BEEN UNEARTHED THERE...
......
......
......
WHAT'S... THE STORY WITH IT?
THAT'S...

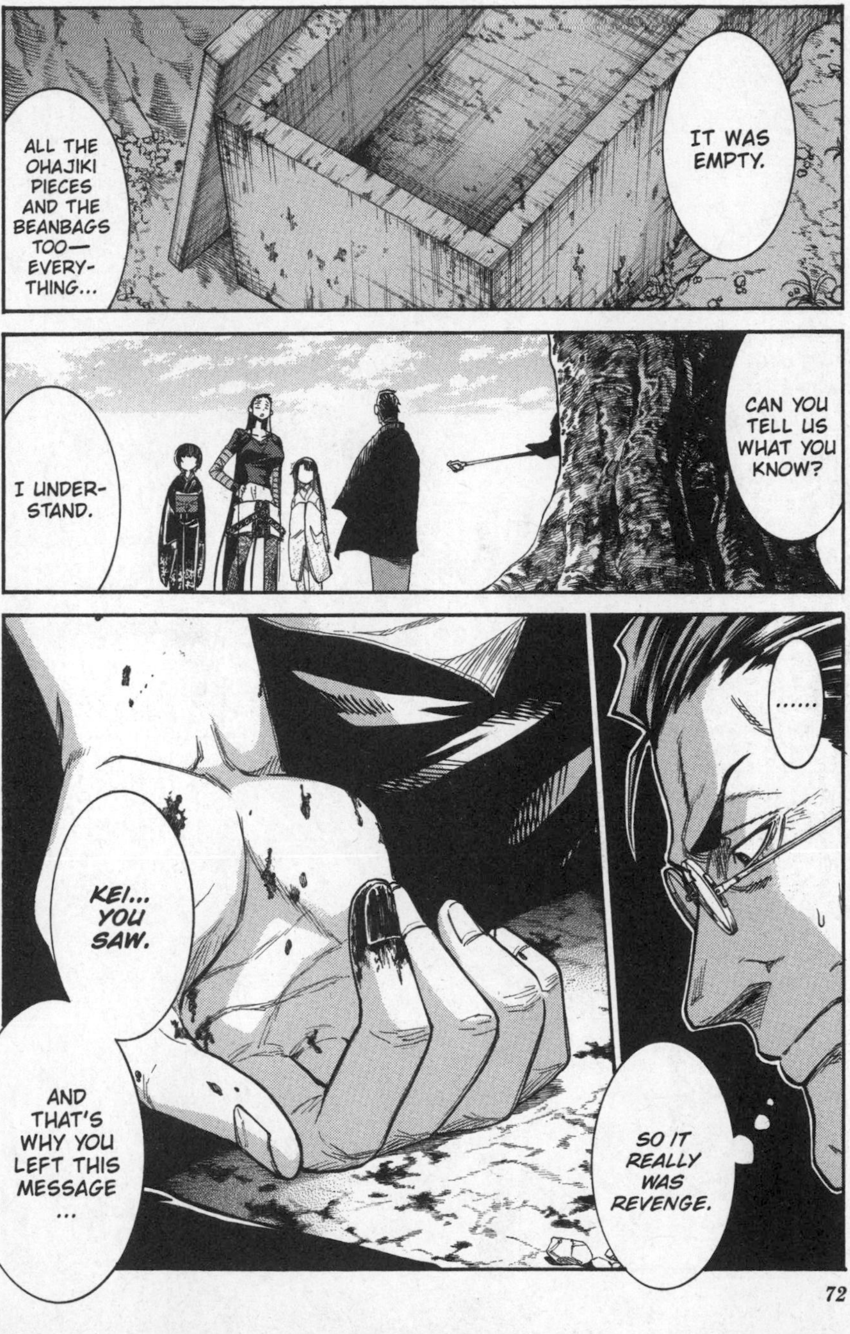
IT WAS EMPTY.
ALL THE OHAJIKI PIECES AND THE BEANBAGS TOO—EVERYTHING...
CAN YOU TELL US WHAT YOU KNOW?
I UNDERSTAND.
......
KEI... YOU SAW.
AND THAT'S WHY YOU LEFT THIS MESSAGE...
SO IT REALLY WAS REVENGE.

MURCIÉLAGO

MURCIÉLAGO

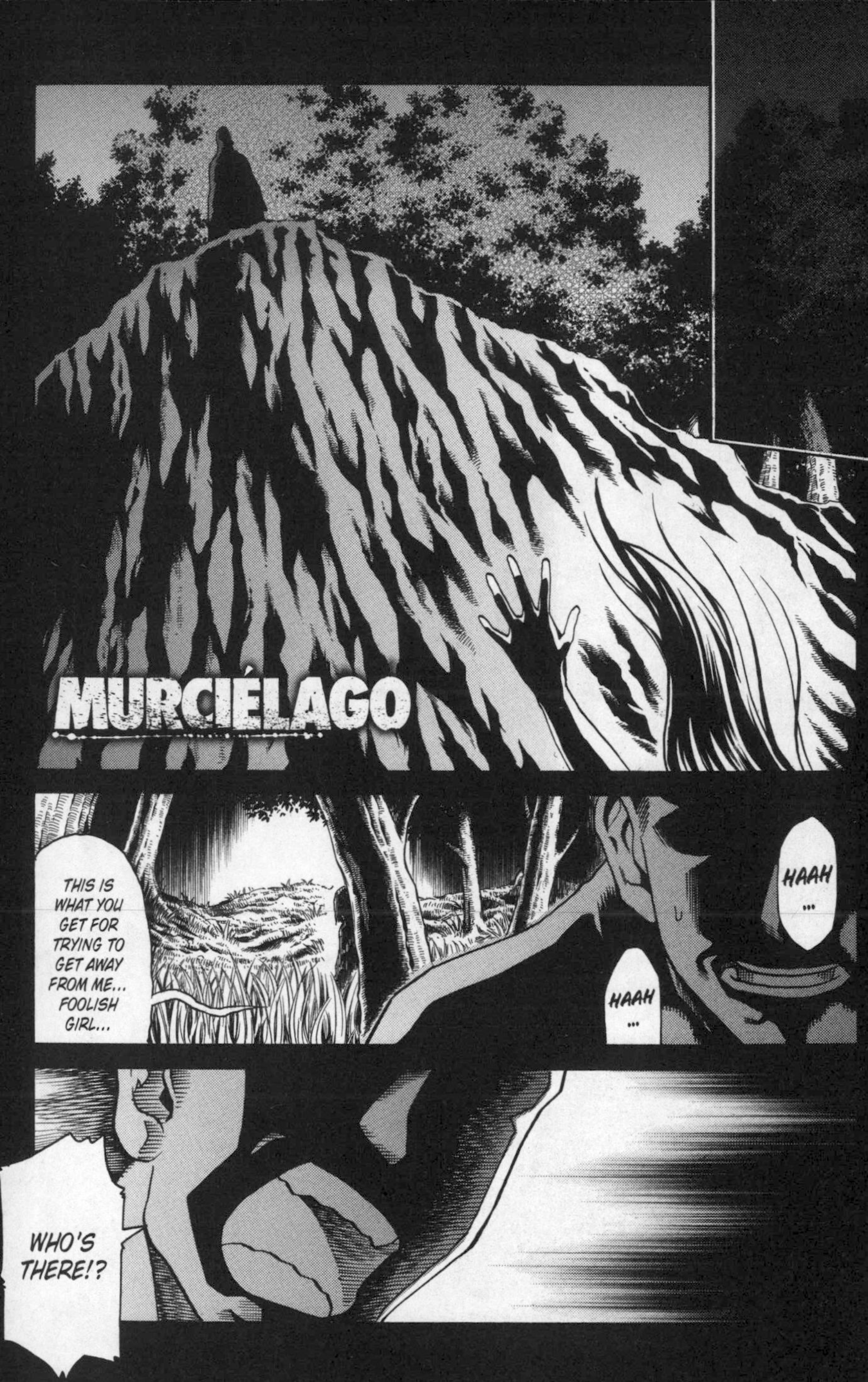
MURCIÉLAGO
HAAH...
HAAH...
THIS IS WHAT YOU GET FOR TRYING TO GET AWAY FROM ME... FOOLISH GIRL...
WHO'S THERE!?

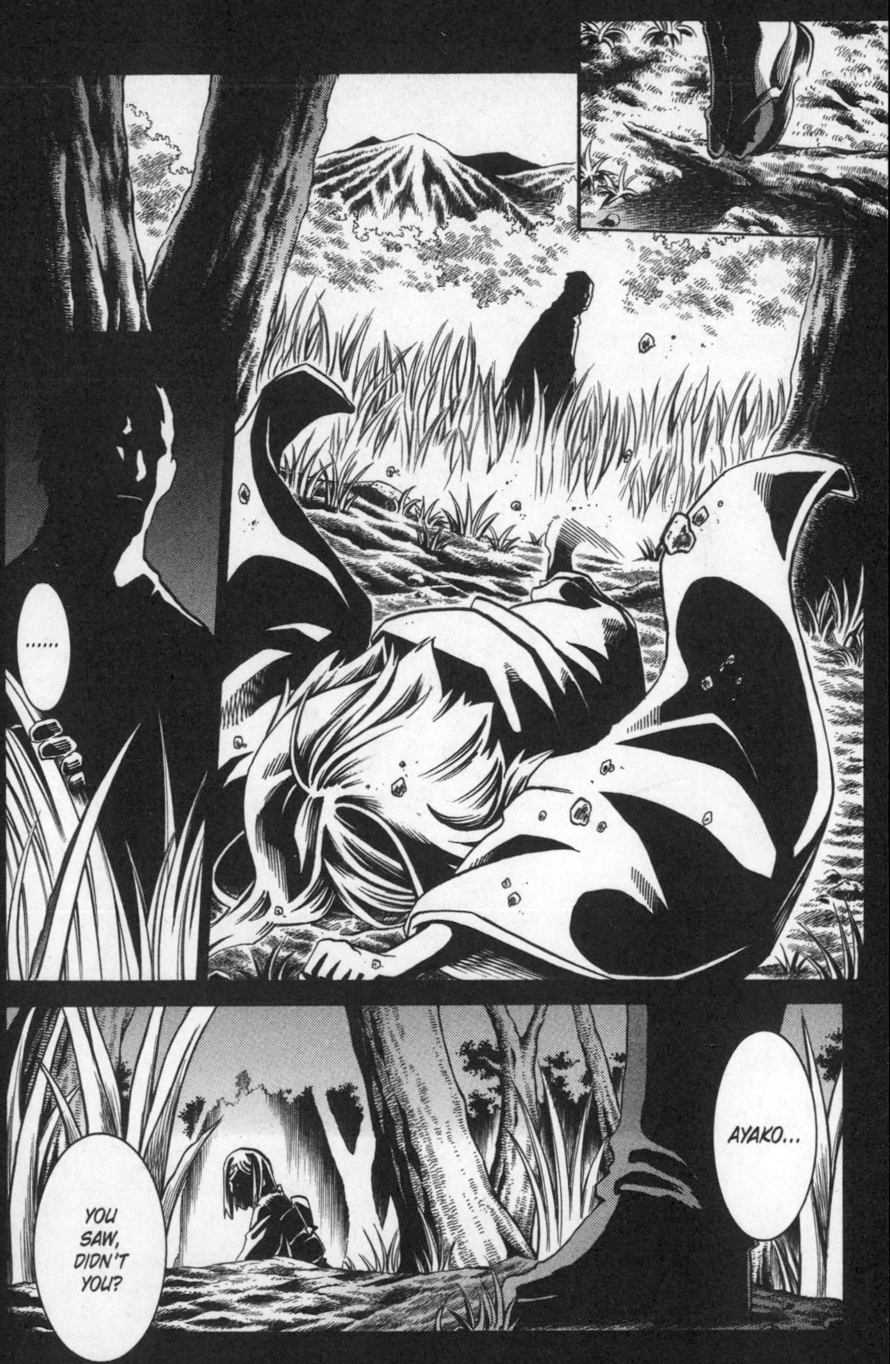
......
AYAKO...
YOU SAW,
DIDN'T
YOU?

MURCIÉLAGO

Yoshimurakana

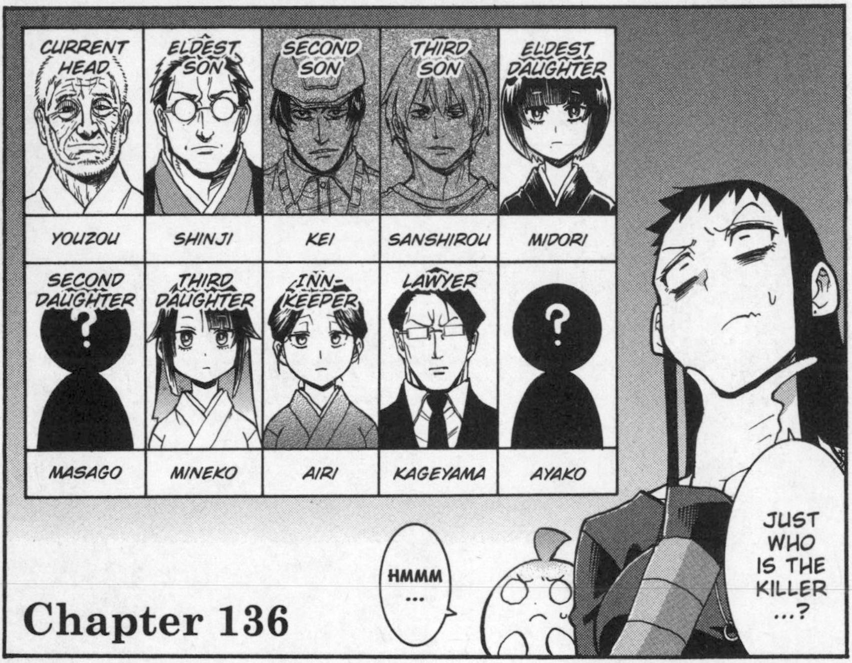
CURRENT HEAD
YOUZOU
ELDEST SON
SHINJI
SECOND SON
KEI
THIRD SON
SANSHIROU
ELDEST DAUGHTER
MIDORI
SECOND DAUGHTER
MASAGO
THIRD DAUGHTER
MINEKO
INN-KEEPER
AIRI
LAWYER
KAGEYAMA
?
AYAKO
JUST WHO IS THE KILLER ...?
HMMM ...

Chapter 136

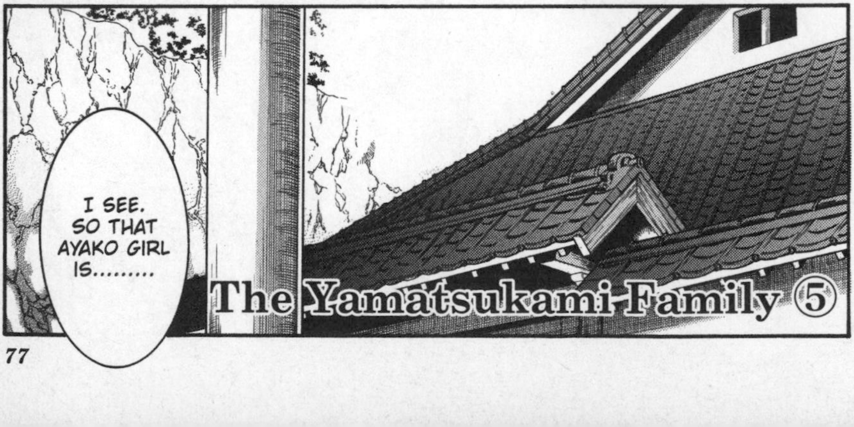
I SEE. SO THAT AYAKO GIRL IS.........

The Yamatsukami Family ⑤

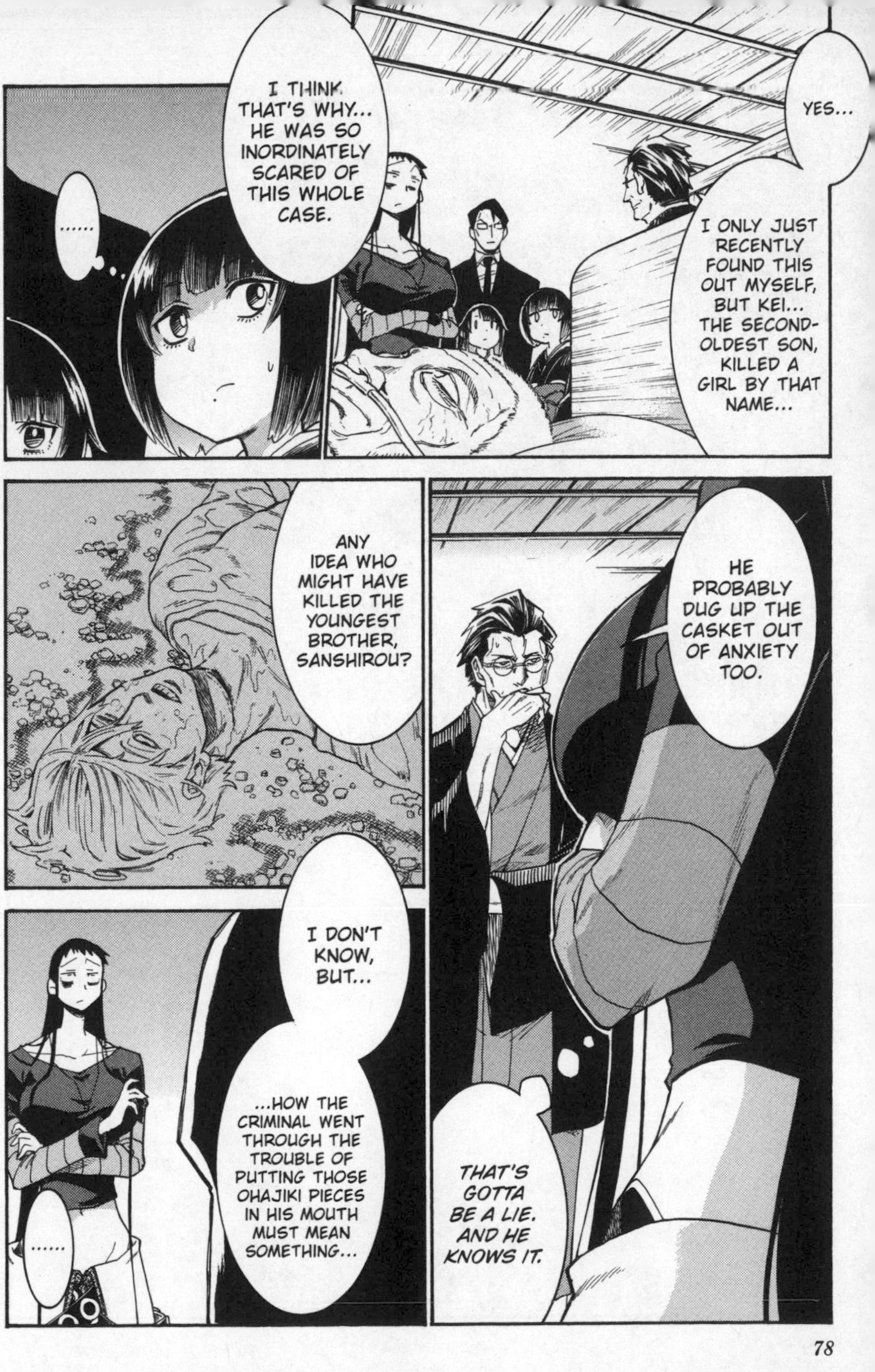
YES...
I ONLY JUST RECENTLY FOUND THIS OUT MYSELF, BUT KEI... THE SECOND-OLDEST SON, KILLED A GIRL BY THAT NAME...
I THINK THAT'S WHY... HE WAS SO INORDINATELY SCARED OF THIS WHOLE CASE.
......
HE PROBABLY DUG UP THE CASKET OUT OF ANXIETY TOO.
THAT'S GOTTA BE A LIE. AND HE KNOWS IT.
ANY IDEA WHO MIGHT HAVE KILLED THE YOUNGEST BROTHER, SANSHIROU?
I DON'T KNOW, BUT...
...HOW THE CRIMINAL WENT THROUGH THE TROUBLE OF PUTTING THOSE OHAJIKI PIECES IN HIS MOUTH MUST MEAN SOMETHING...
......

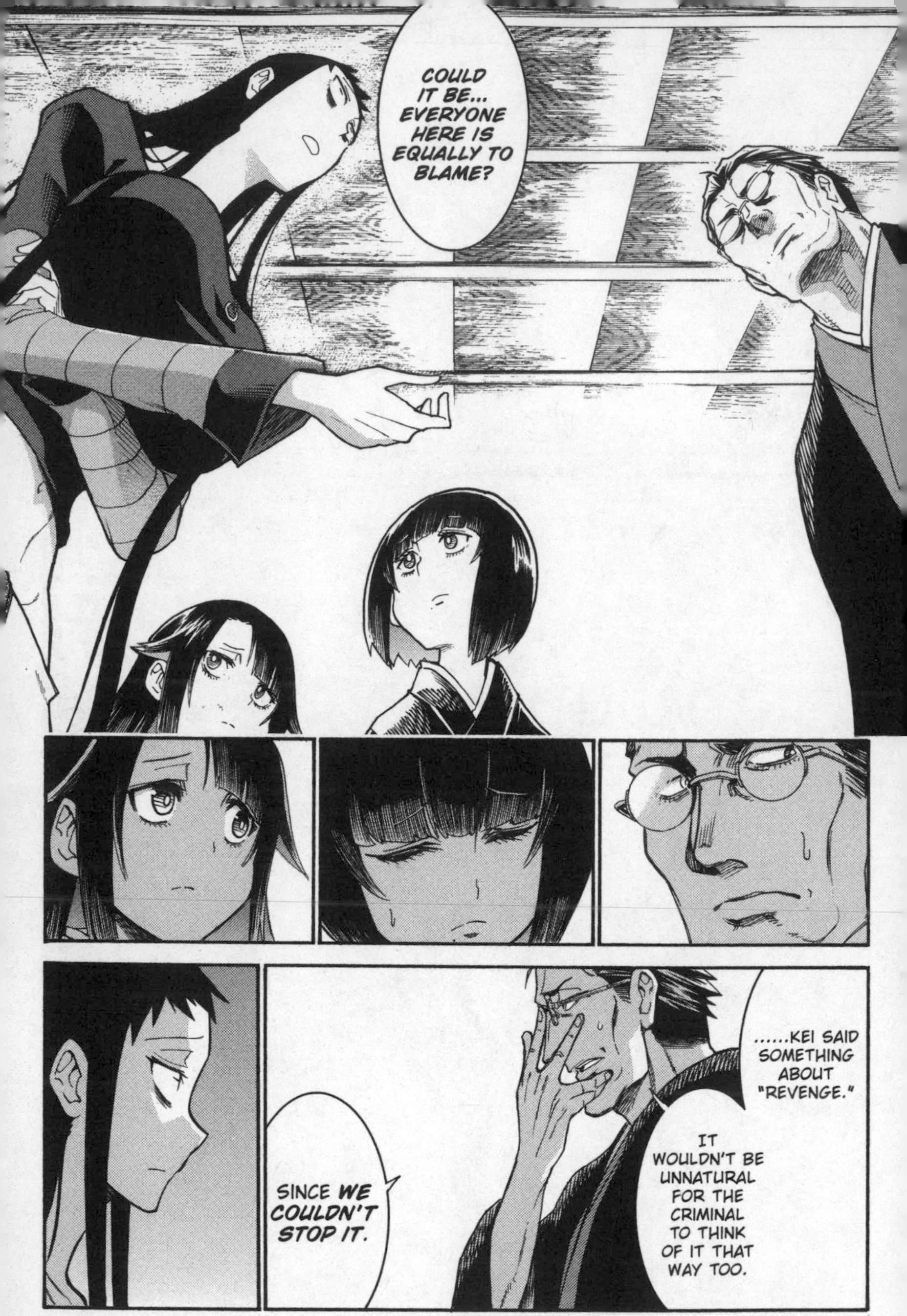
COULD IT BE... EVERYONE HERE IS EQUALLY TO BLAME?
......KEI SAID SOMETHING ABOUT "REVENGE."
IT WOULDN'T BE UNNATURAL FOR THE CRIMINAL TO THINK OF IT THAT WAY TOO.
SINCE *WE* COULDN'T STOP IT.

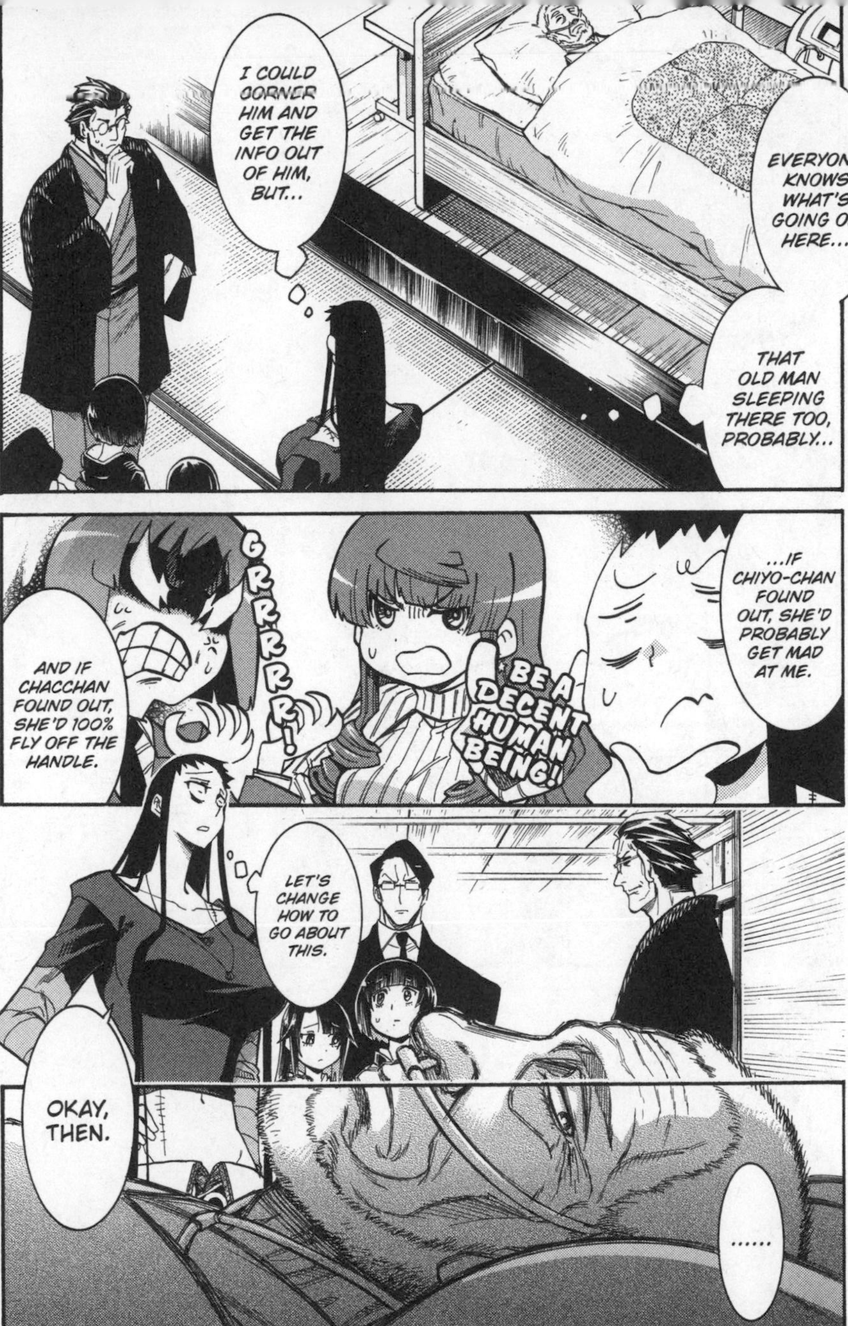
EVERYONE KNOWS WHAT'S GOING ON HERE...
THAT OLD MAN SLEEPING THERE TOO, PROBABLY...
I COULD CORNER HIM AND GET THE INFO OUT OF HIM, BUT...
...IF CHIYO-CHAN FOUND OUT, SHE'D PROBABLY GET MAD AT ME.
BE A DECENT HUMAN BEING!!
GRRRRR!
AND IF CHACCHAN FOUND OUT, SHE'D 100% FLY OFF THE HANDLE.
LET'S CHANGE HOW TO GO ABOUT THIS.
......
OKAY, THEN.

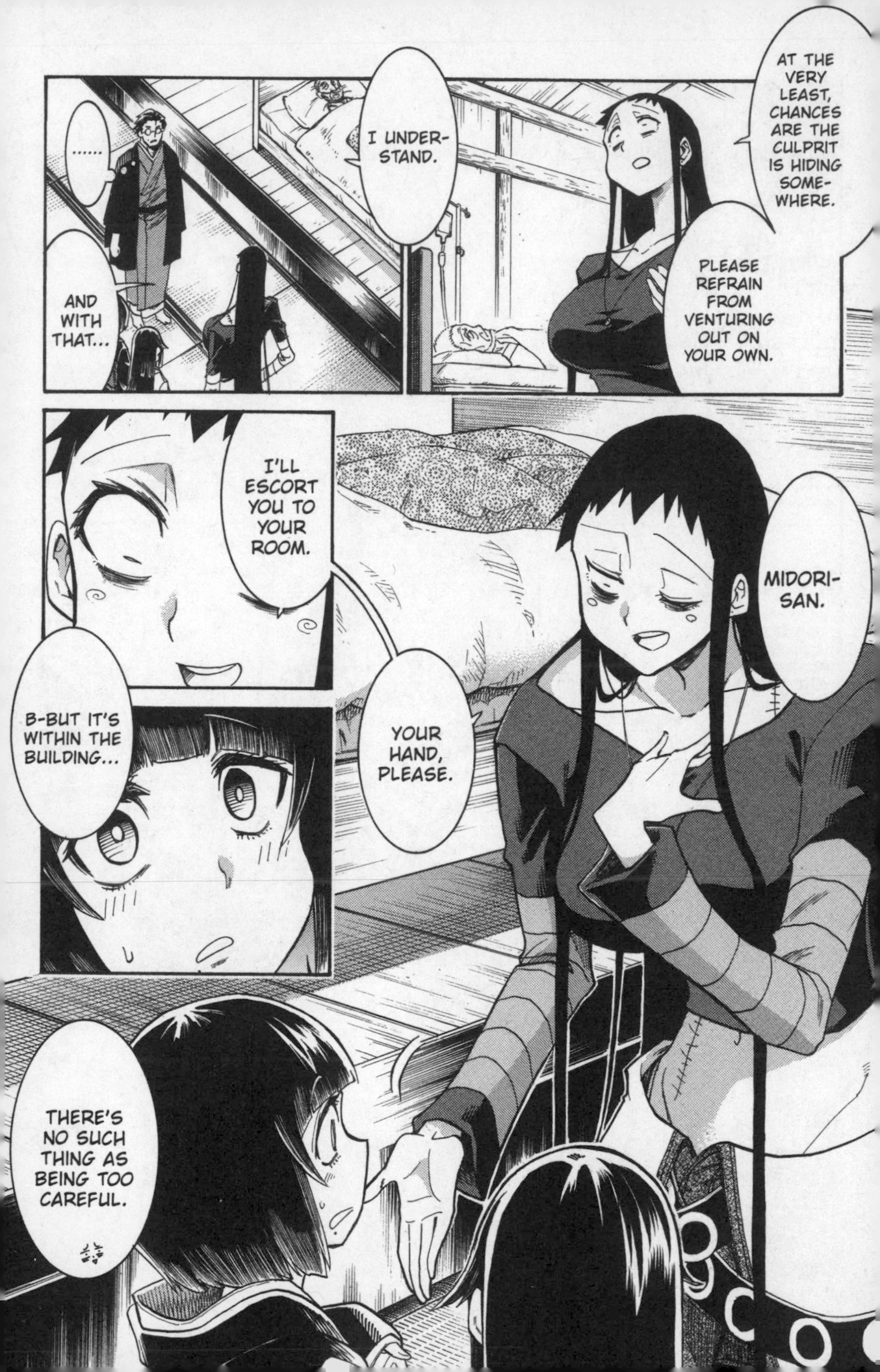
AT THE VERY LEAST, CHANCES ARE THE CULPRIT IS HIDING SOMEWHERE.
PLEASE REFRAIN FROM VENTURING OUT ON YOUR OWN.
I UNDERSTAND.
......
AND WITH THAT...
MIDORI-SAN.
YOUR HAND, PLEASE.
I'LL ESCORT YOU TO YOUR ROOM.
B-BUT IT'S WITHIN THE BUILDING...
THERE'S NO SUCH THING AS BEING TOO CAREFUL.

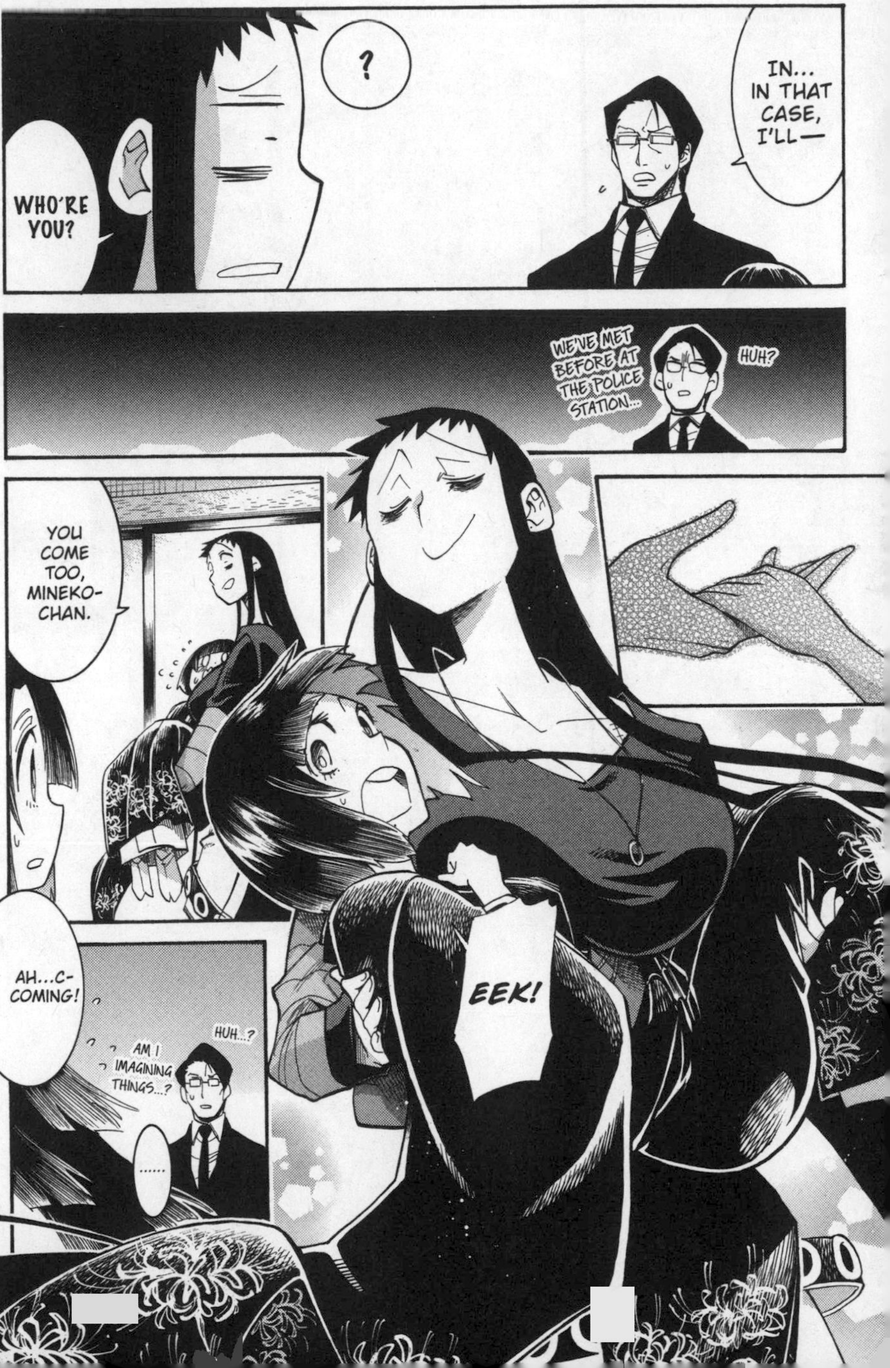
IN... IN THAT CASE, I'LL—
?
WHO'RE YOU?
WE'VE MET BEFORE AT THE POLICE STATION...
HUH?
EEK!
YOU COME TOO, MINEKO-CHAN.
AH...C-COMING!
HUH...?
AM I IMAGINING THINGS...?
......

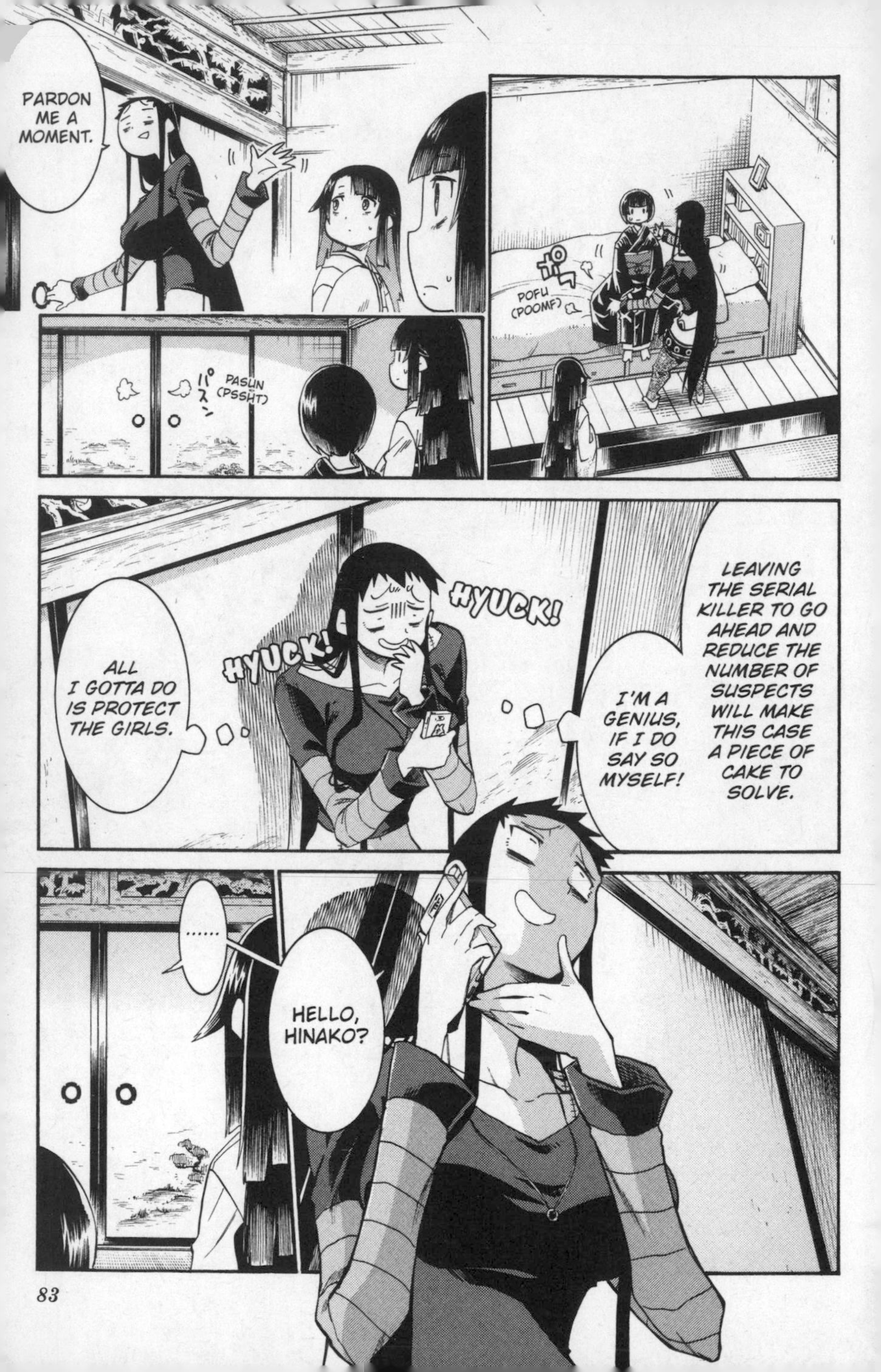
ポフ
POFU (POOMF)
PARDON ME A MOMENT.
パスン
PASUN (PSSHT)
LEAVING THE SERIAL KILLER TO GO AHEAD AND REDUCE THE NUMBER OF SUSPECTS WILL MAKE THIS CASE A PIECE OF CAKE TO SOLVE.
I'M A GENIUS, IF I DO SAY SO MYSELF!
HYUCK!
HYUCK!
ALL I GOTTA DO IS PROTECT THE GIRLS.
HELLO, HINAKO?
......

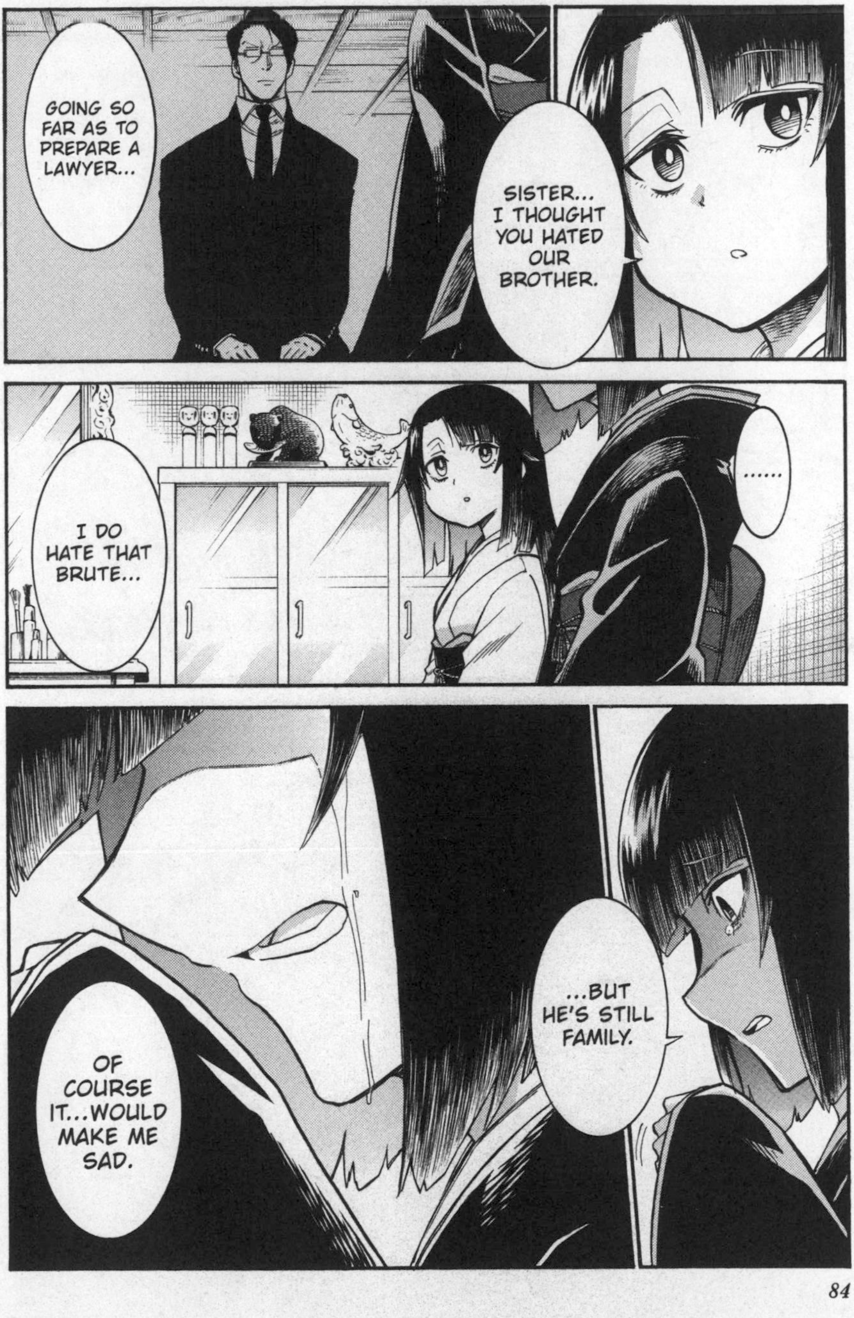
SISTER... I THOUGHT YOU HATED OUR BROTHER.
GOING SO FAR AS TO PREPARE A LAWYER...
......
I DO HATE THAT BRUTE...
...BUT HE'S STILL FAMILY.
OF COURSE IT...WOULD MAKE ME SAD.

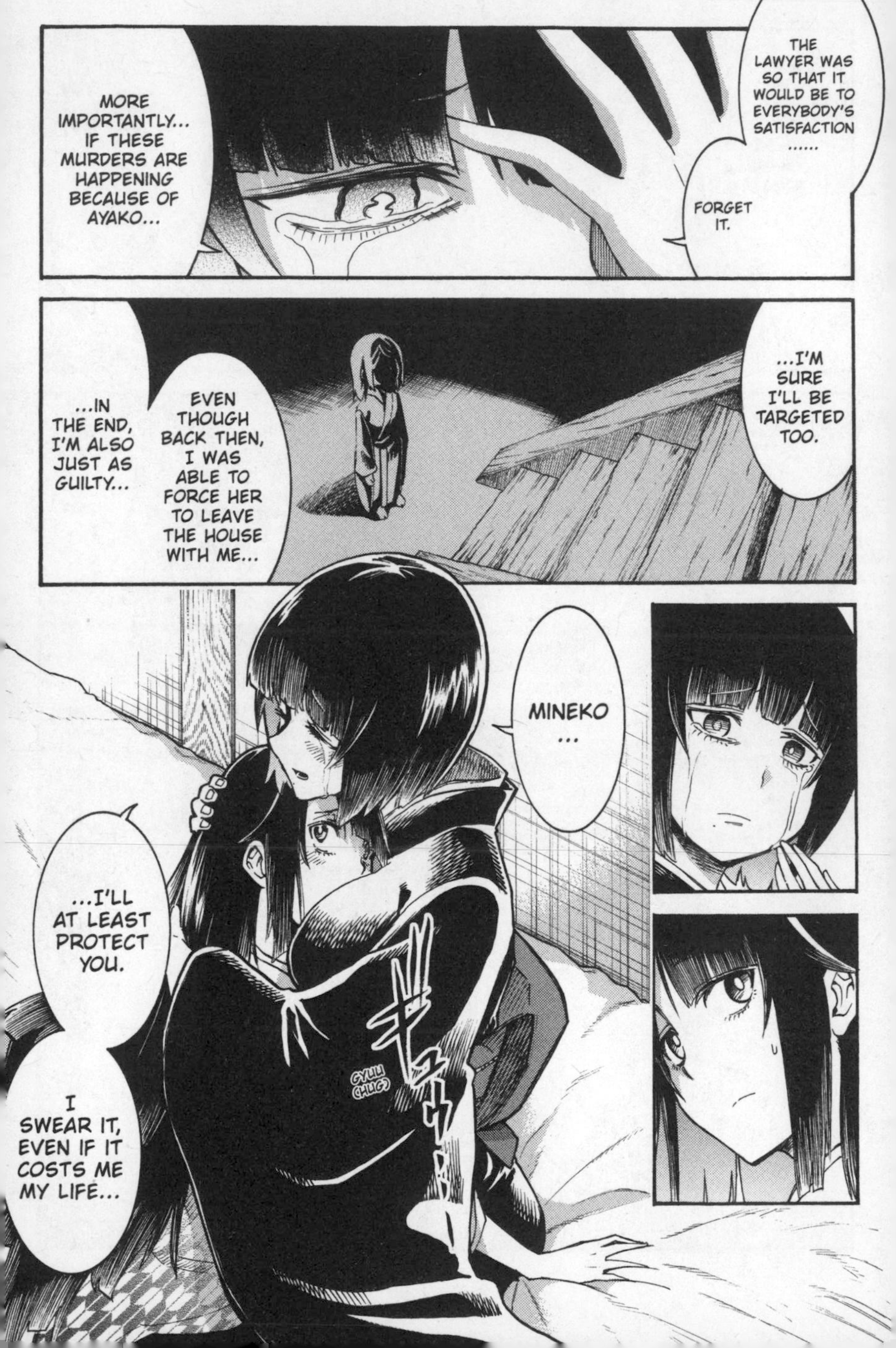
THE LAWYER WAS SO THAT IT WOULD BE TO EVERYBODY'S SATISFACTION ......
FORGET IT.
MORE IMPORTANTLY... IF THESE MURDERS ARE HAPPENING BECAUSE OF AYAKO...
...I'M SURE I'LL BE TARGETED TOO.
EVEN THOUGH BACK THEN, I WAS ABLE TO FORCE HER TO LEAVE THE HOUSE WITH ME...
...IN THE END, I'M ALSO JUST AS GUILTY...
MINEKO ...
...I'LL AT LEAST PROTECT YOU.
GYUU (HUG)
I SWEAR IT, EVEN IF IT COSTS ME MY LIFE...

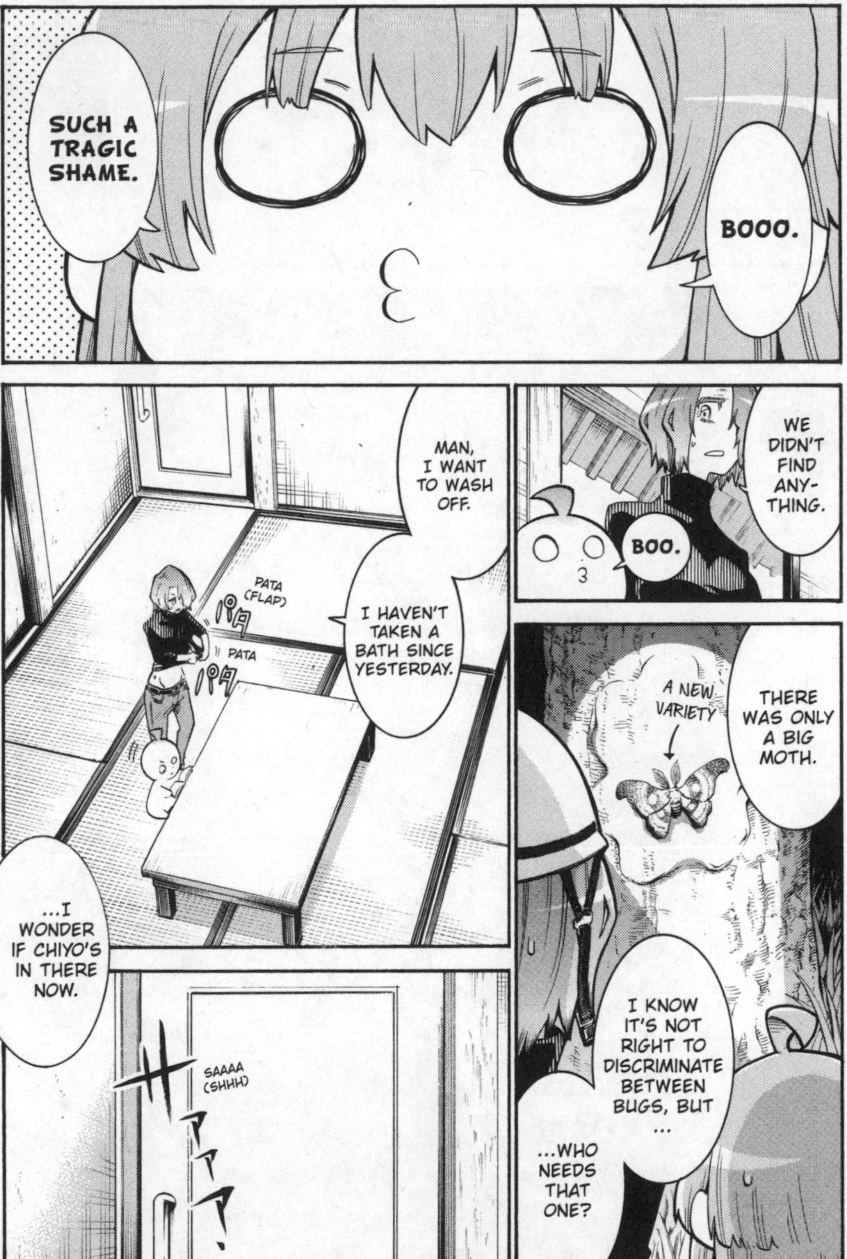

SUCH A TRAGIC SHAME.
BOOO.
WE DIDN'T FIND ANYTHING.
BOO.
THERE WAS ONLY A BIG MOTH.
A NEW VARIETY
I KNOW IT'S NOT RIGHT TO DISCRIMINATE BETWEEN BUGS, BUT ...
...WHO NEEDS THAT ONE?
MAN, I WANT TO WASH OFF.
I HAVEN'T TAKEN A BATH SINCE YESTERDAY.
PATA (FLAP)
PATA
...I WONDER IF CHIYO'S IN THERE NOW.
SAAAA (SHHH)

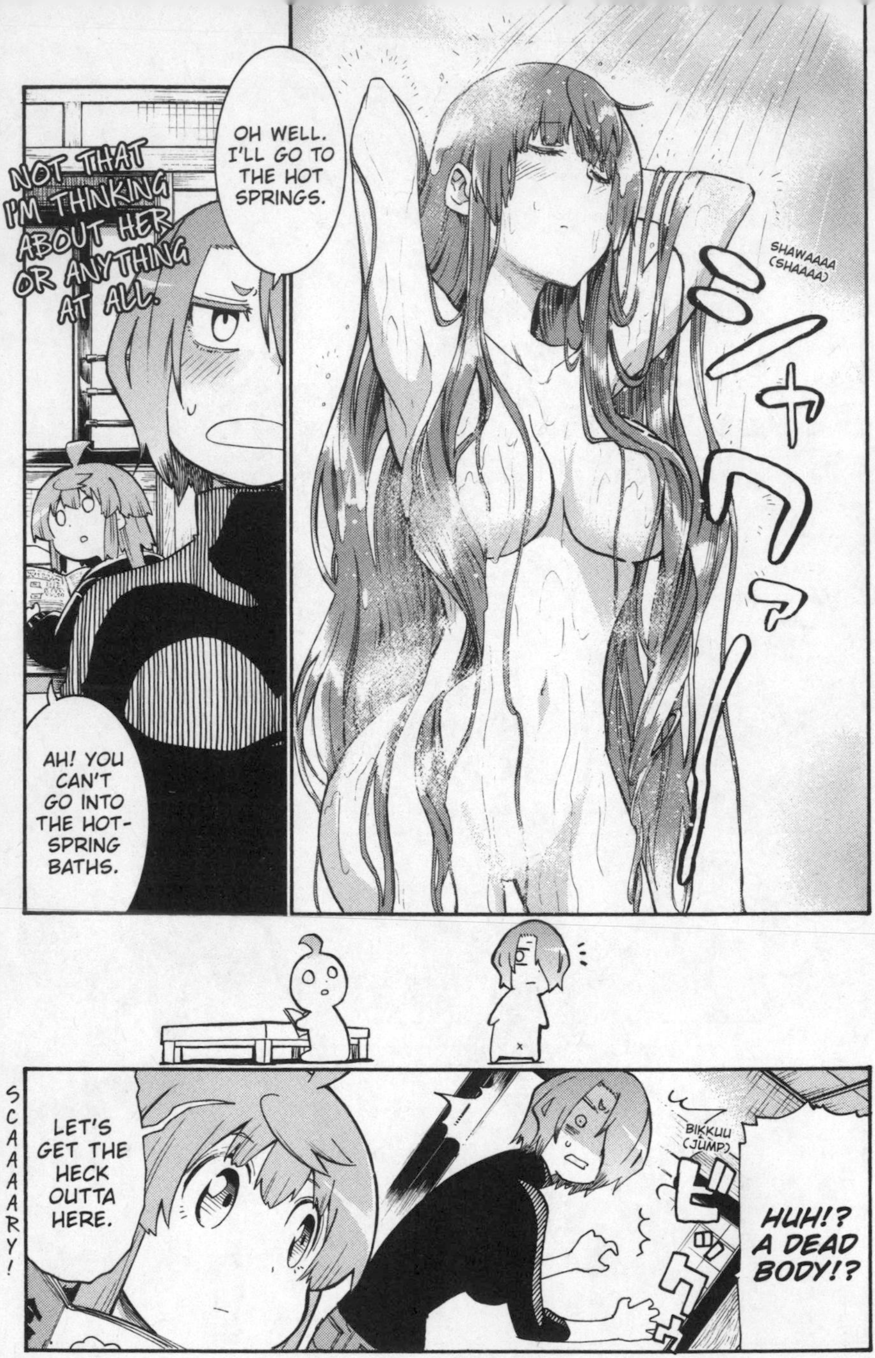
SHAWAAAA (SHAAAAA)
OH WELL. I'LL GO TO THE HOT SPRINGS.
NOT THAT I'M THINKING ABOUT HER OR ANYTHING AT ALL.
AH! YOU CAN'T GO INTO THE HOT-SPRING BATHS.
HUH!? A DEAD BODY!?
BIKKUU (JUMP)
LET'S GET THE HECK OUTTA HERE.
SCAAAAARY!

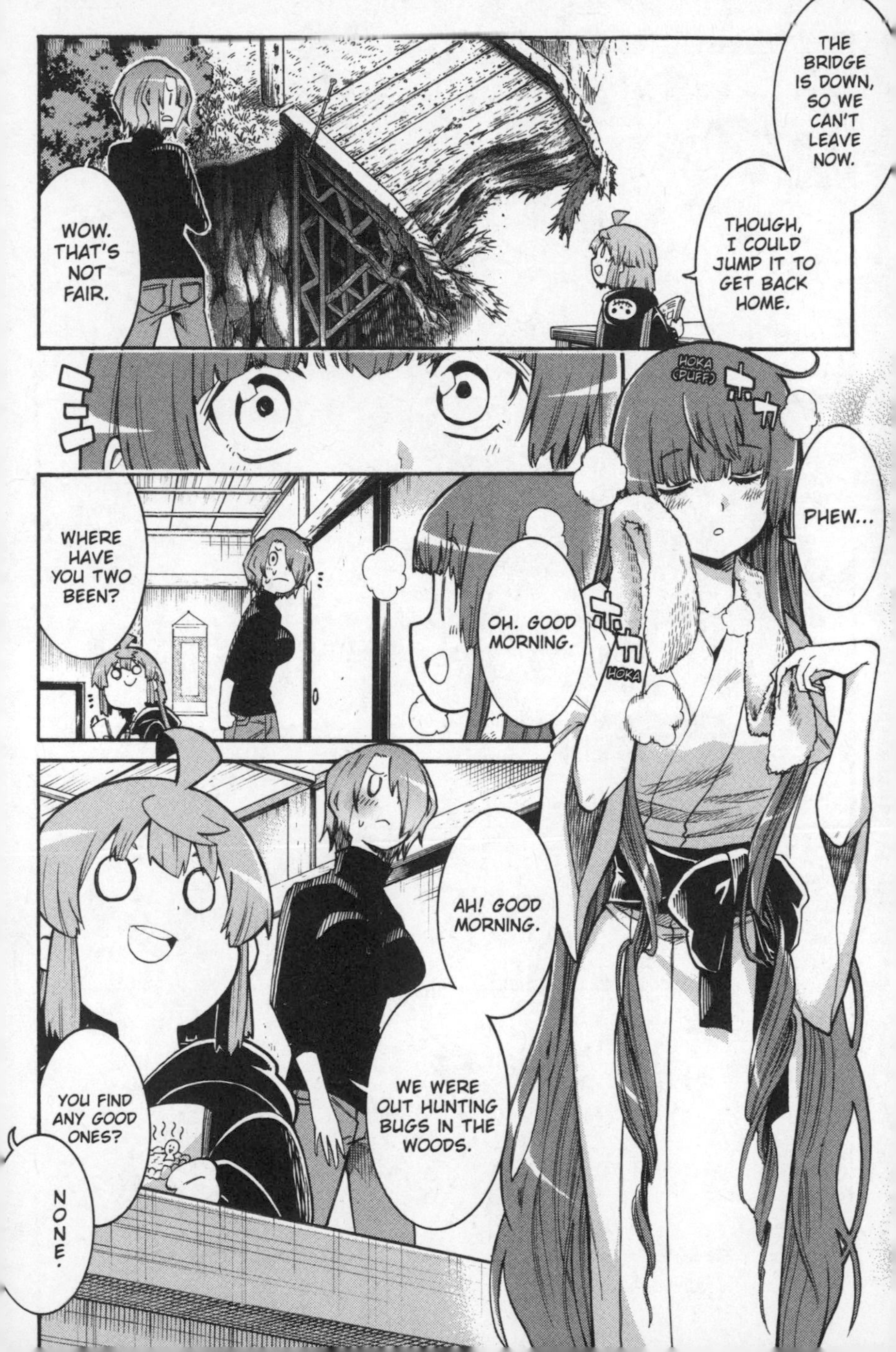
THE BRIDGE IS DOWN, SO WE CAN'T LEAVE NOW.
THOUGH, I COULD JUMP IT TO GET BACK HOME.
WOW. THAT'S NOT FAIR.
HOKA (PUFF)
PHEW...
HOKA
WHERE HAVE YOU TWO BEEN?
OH. GOOD MORNING.
AH! GOOD MORNING.
WE WERE OUT HUNTING BUGS IN THE WOODS.
YOU FIND ANY GOOD ONES?
NONE.

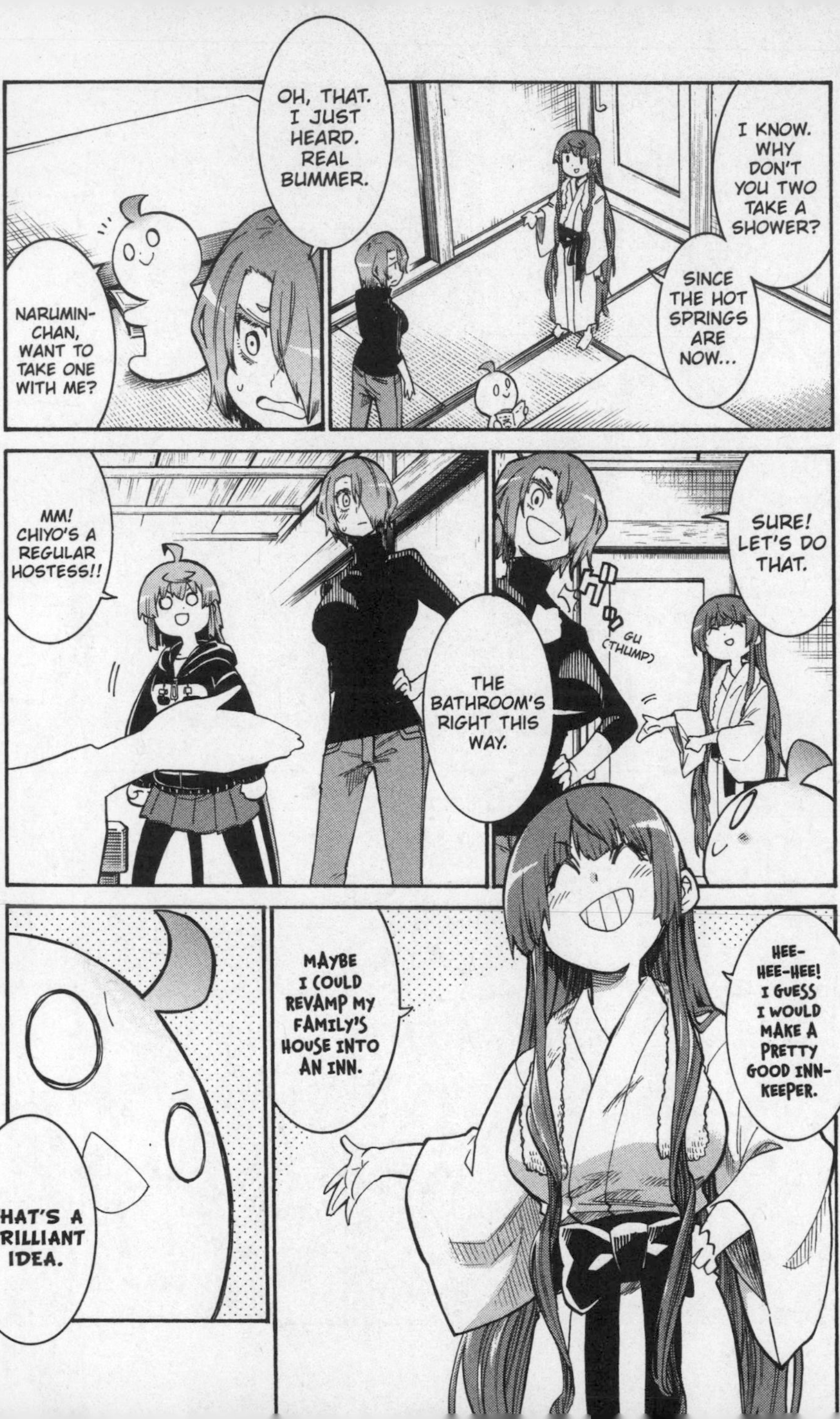
I KNOW. WHY DON'T YOU TWO TAKE A SHOWER?
SINCE THE HOT SPRINGS ARE NOW...
OH, THAT. I JUST HEARD. REAL BUMMER.
NARUMIN-CHAN, WANT TO TAKE ONE WITH ME?
SURE! LET'S DO THAT.
GU (THUMP)
THE BATHROOM'S RIGHT THIS WAY.
MM! CHIYO'S A REGULAR HOSTESS!!
HEE-HEE-HEE! I GUESS I WOULD MAKE A PRETTY GOOD INN-KEEPER.
MAYBE I COULD REVAMP MY FAMILY'S HOUSE INTO AN INN.
THAT'S A BRILLIANT IDEA.

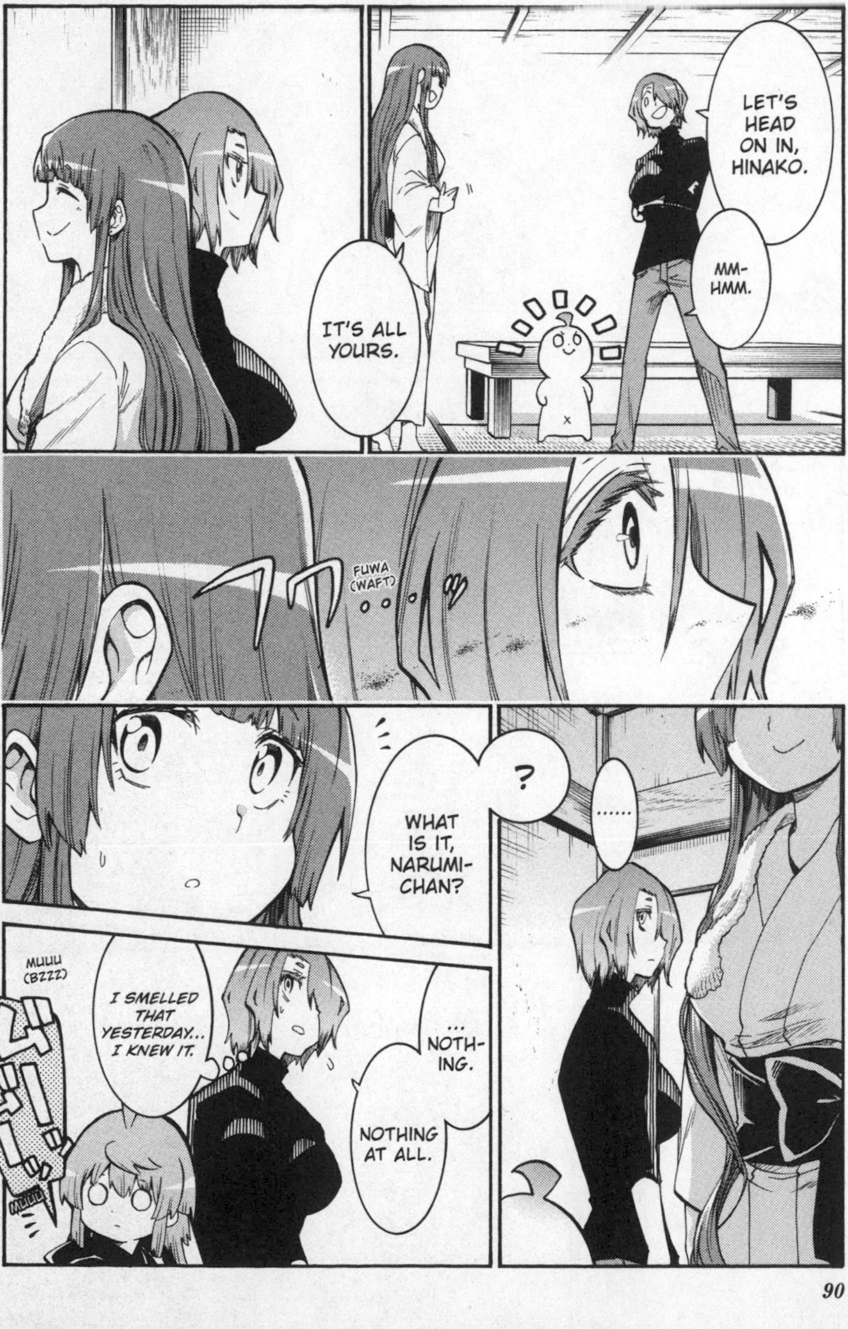
LET'S HEAD ON IN, HINAKO.
MM-HMM.
IT'S ALL YOURS.
FUWA (WAFT)
......
?
WHAT IS IT, NARUMI-CHAN?
... NOTHING.
NOTHING AT ALL.
I SMELLED THAT YESTERDAY... I KNEW IT.
MUUU (BZZZ)

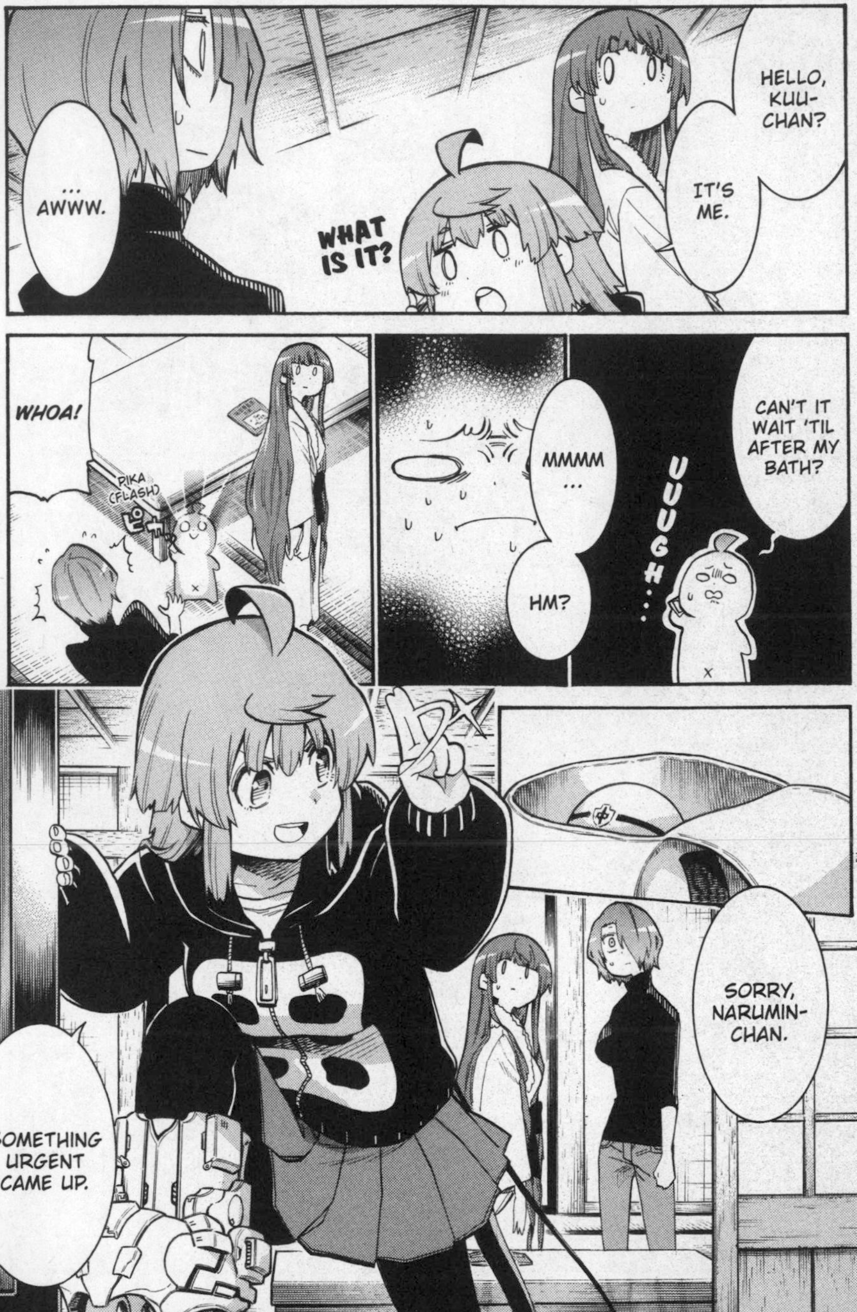
HELLO, KUU-CHAN?
IT'S ME.
WHAT IS IT?
... AWWW.
CAN'T IT WAIT 'TIL AFTER MY BATH?
UUUGH...
MMMM...
HM?
WHOA!
PIKA (FLASH)
SORRY, NARUMIN-CHAN.
SOMETHING URGENT CAME UP.

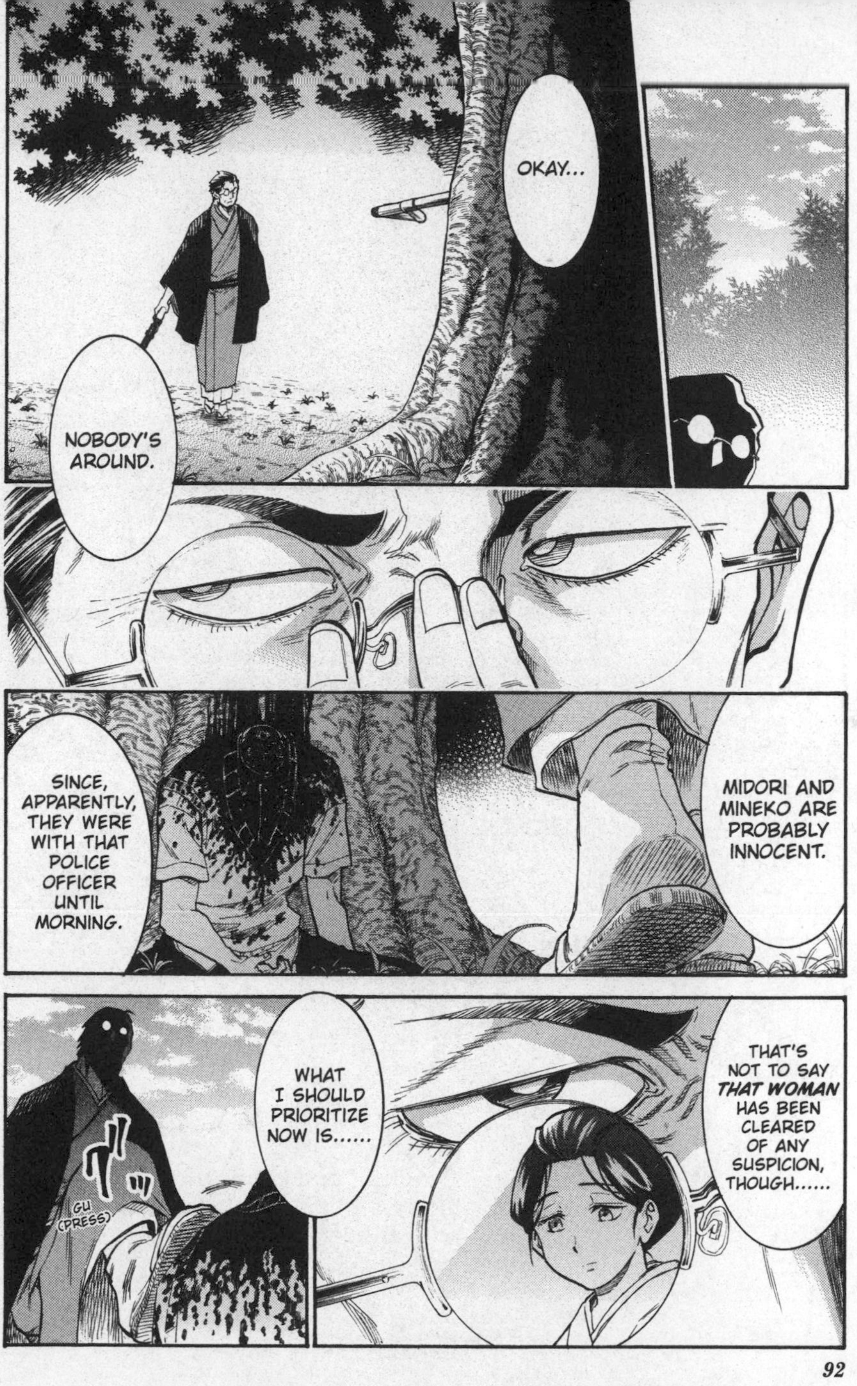
OKAY...
NOBODY'S AROUND.
MIDORI AND MINEKO ARE PROBABLY INNOCENT.
SINCE, APPARENTLY, THEY WERE WITH THAT POLICE OFFICER UNTIL MORNING.
THAT'S NOT TO SAY *THAT WOMAN* HAS BEEN CLEARED OF ANY SUSPICION, THOUGH......
WHAT I SHOULD PRIORITIZE NOW IS......
GU (PRESS)

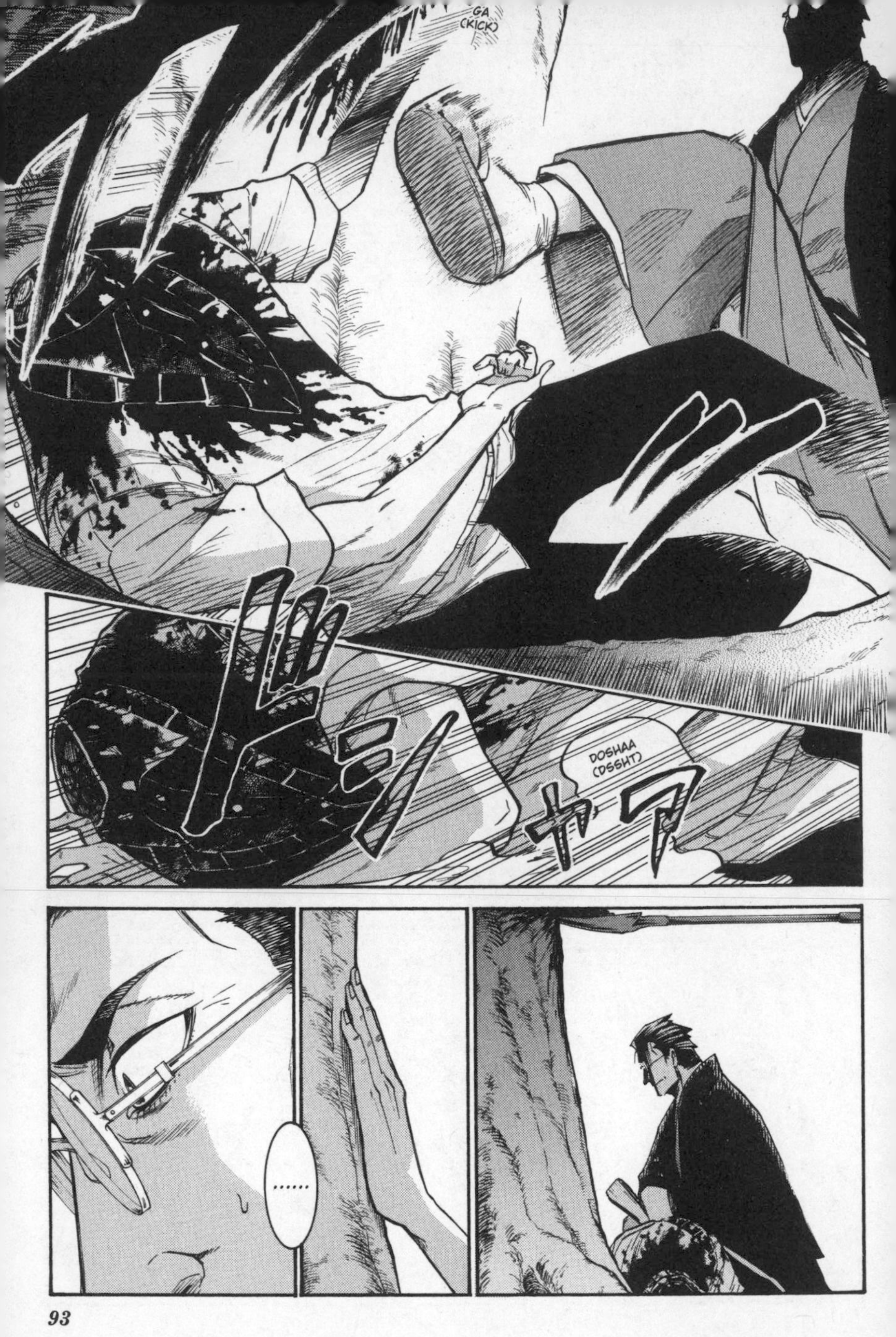
GA
(KICK)
ドシャア
DOSHAA
(DSSHT)
......

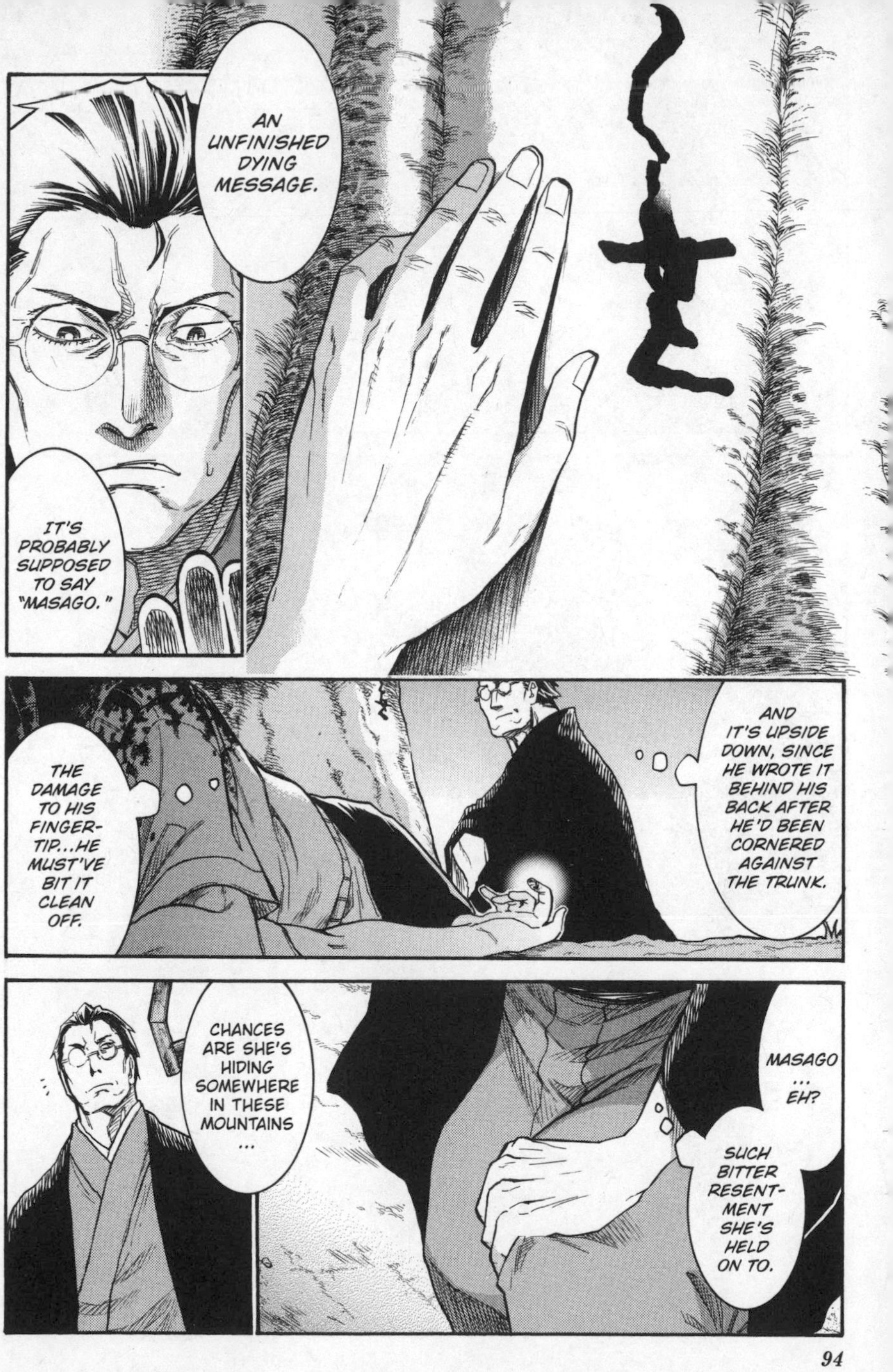
AN UNFINISHED DYING MESSAGE.
IT'S PROBABLY SUPPOSED TO SAY "MASAGO."
AND IT'S UPSIDE DOWN, SINCE HE WROTE IT BEHIND HIS BACK AFTER HE'D BEEN CORNERED AGAINST THE TRUNK.
THE DAMAGE TO HIS FINGER-TIP...HE MUST'VE BIT IT CLEAN OFF.
MASAGO ... EH?
SUCH BITTER RESENT-MENT SHE'S HELD ON TO.
CHANCES ARE SHE'S HIDING SOMEWHERE IN THESE MOUNTAINS ...

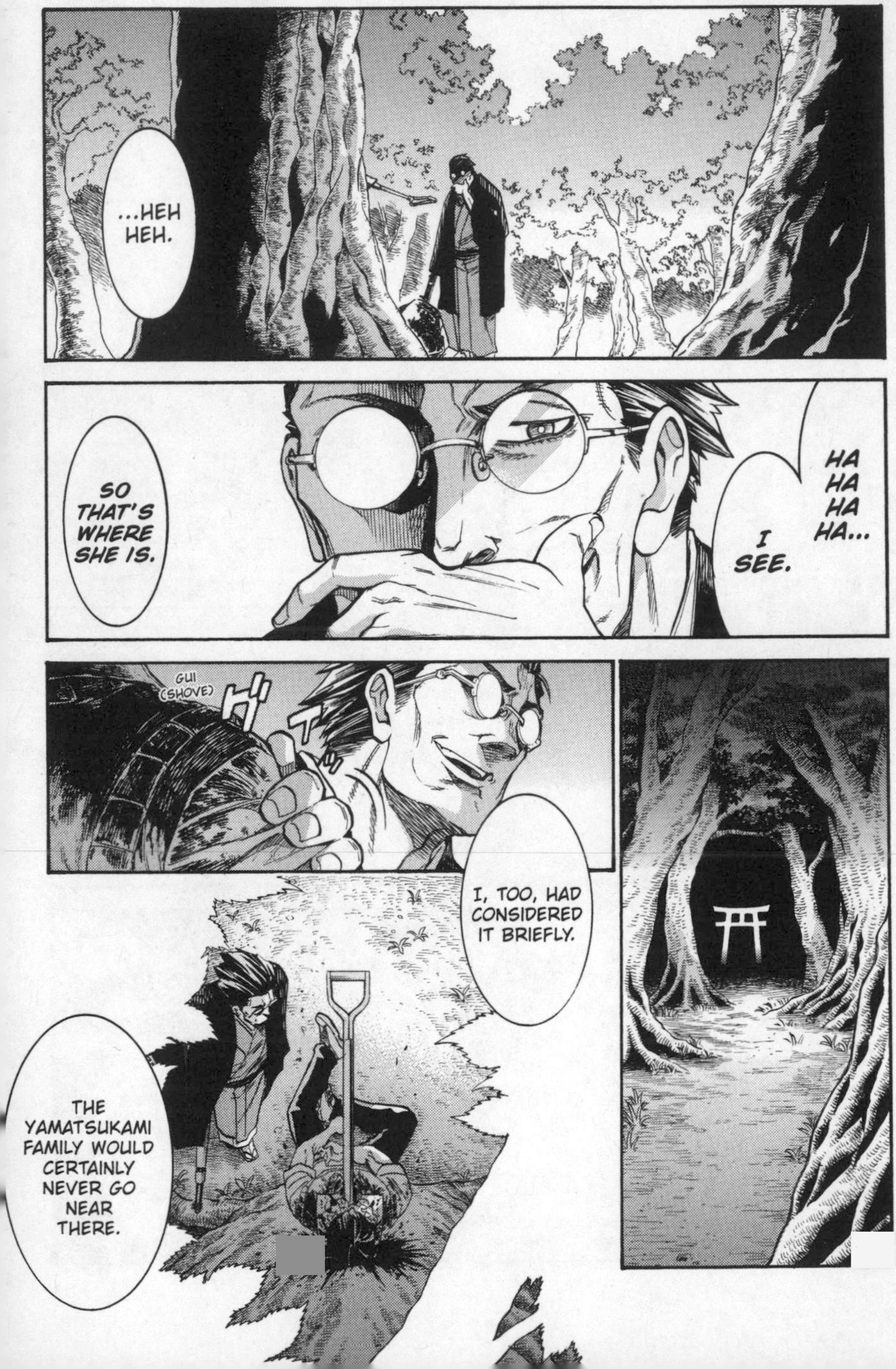
...HEH HEH.
HA HA HA HA... I SEE.
SO THAT'S WHERE SHE IS.
GUI (SHOVE)
I, TOO, HAD CONSIDERED IT BRIEFLY.
THE YAMATSUKAMI FAMILY WOULD CERTAINLY NEVER GO NEAR THERE.

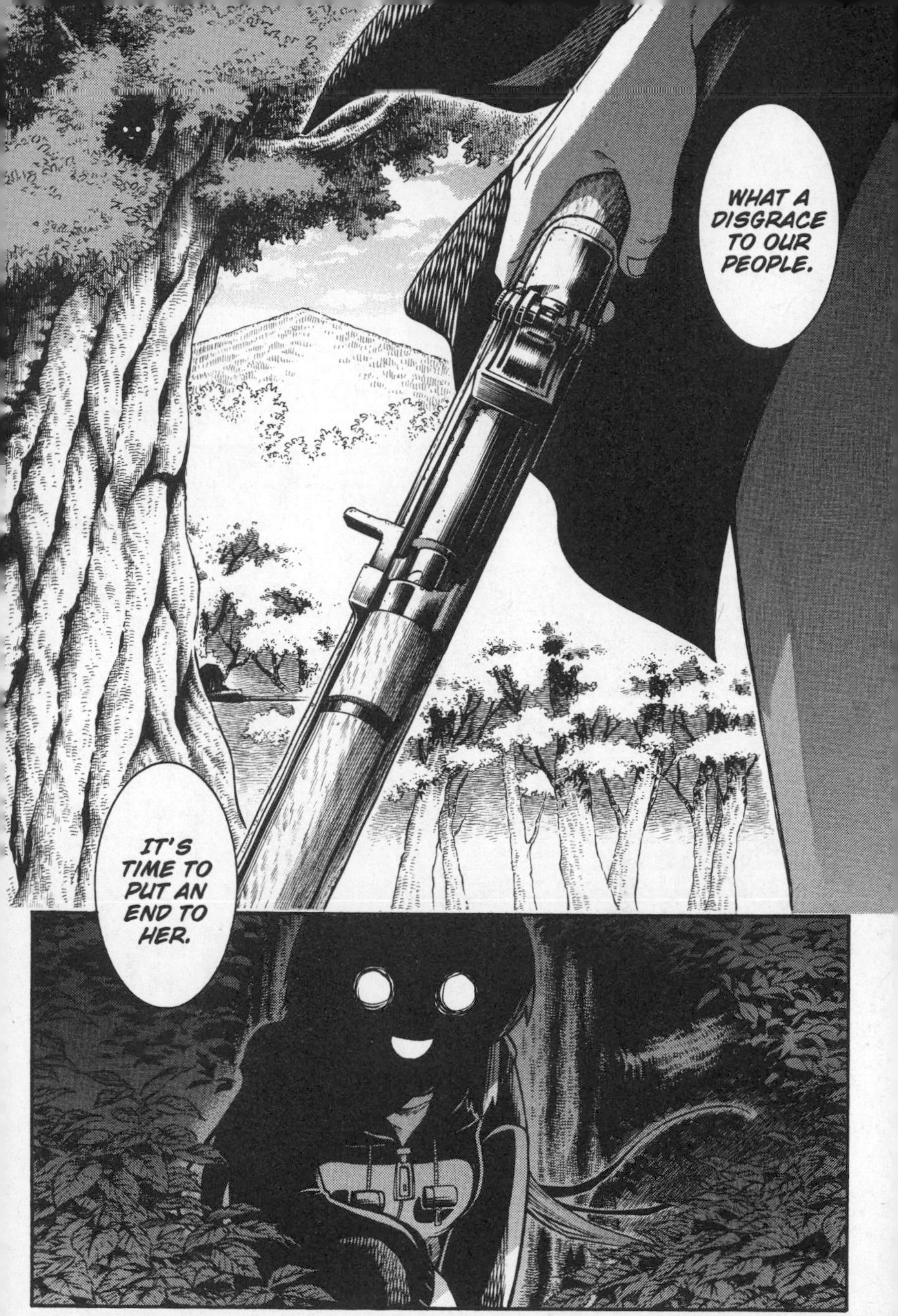
WHAT A DISGRACE TO OUR PEOPLE.
IT'S TIME TO PUT AN END TO HER.

MURCIÉLAGO

MURCIÉLAGO

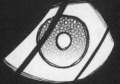 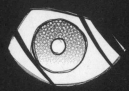

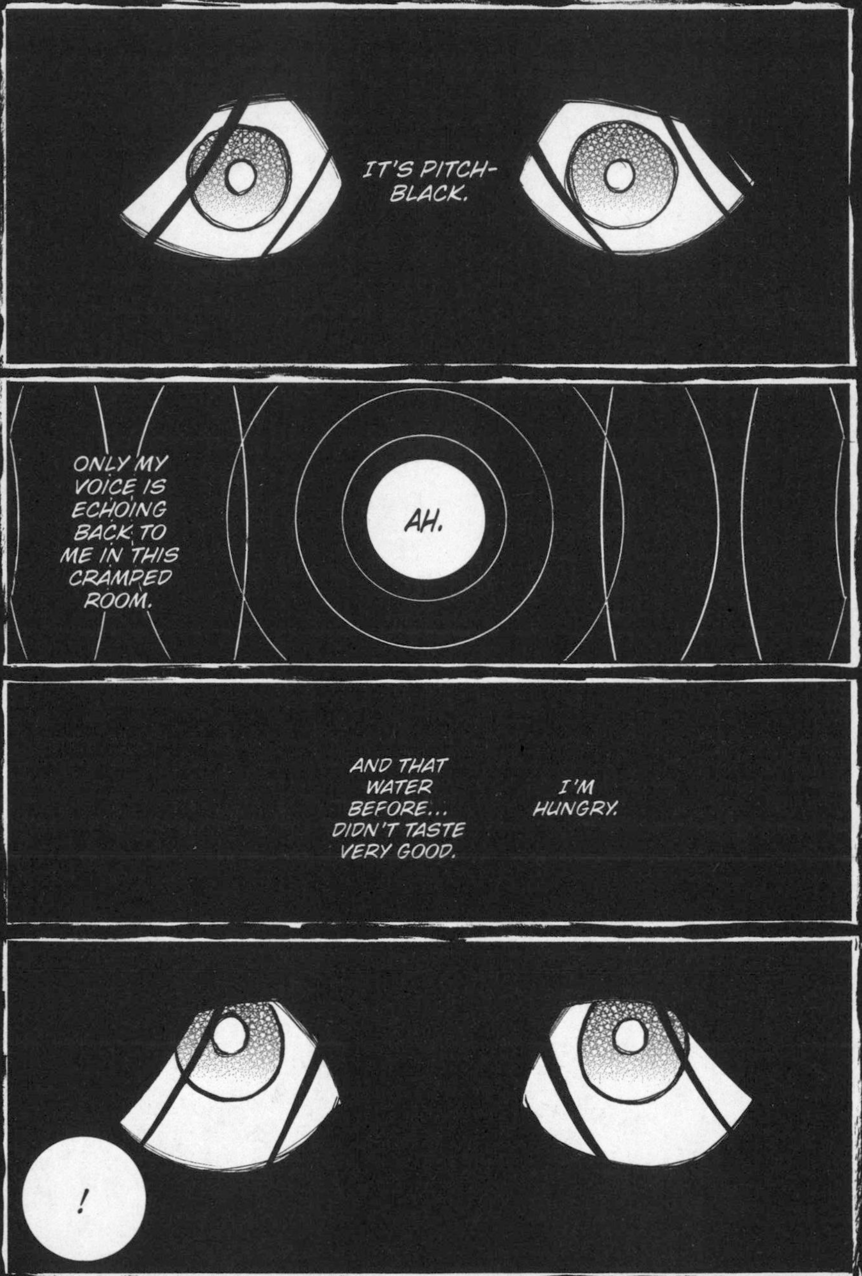

IT'S PITCH-
BLACK.

ONLY MY
VOICE IS
ECHOING
BACK TO
ME IN THIS
CRAMPED
ROOM.

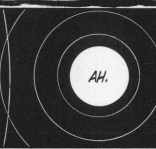

AH.

AND THAT
WATER
BEFORE...
DIDN'T TASTE
VERY GOOD.

I'M
HUNGRY.

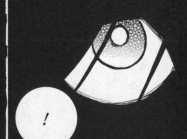 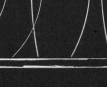 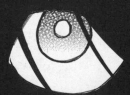

!

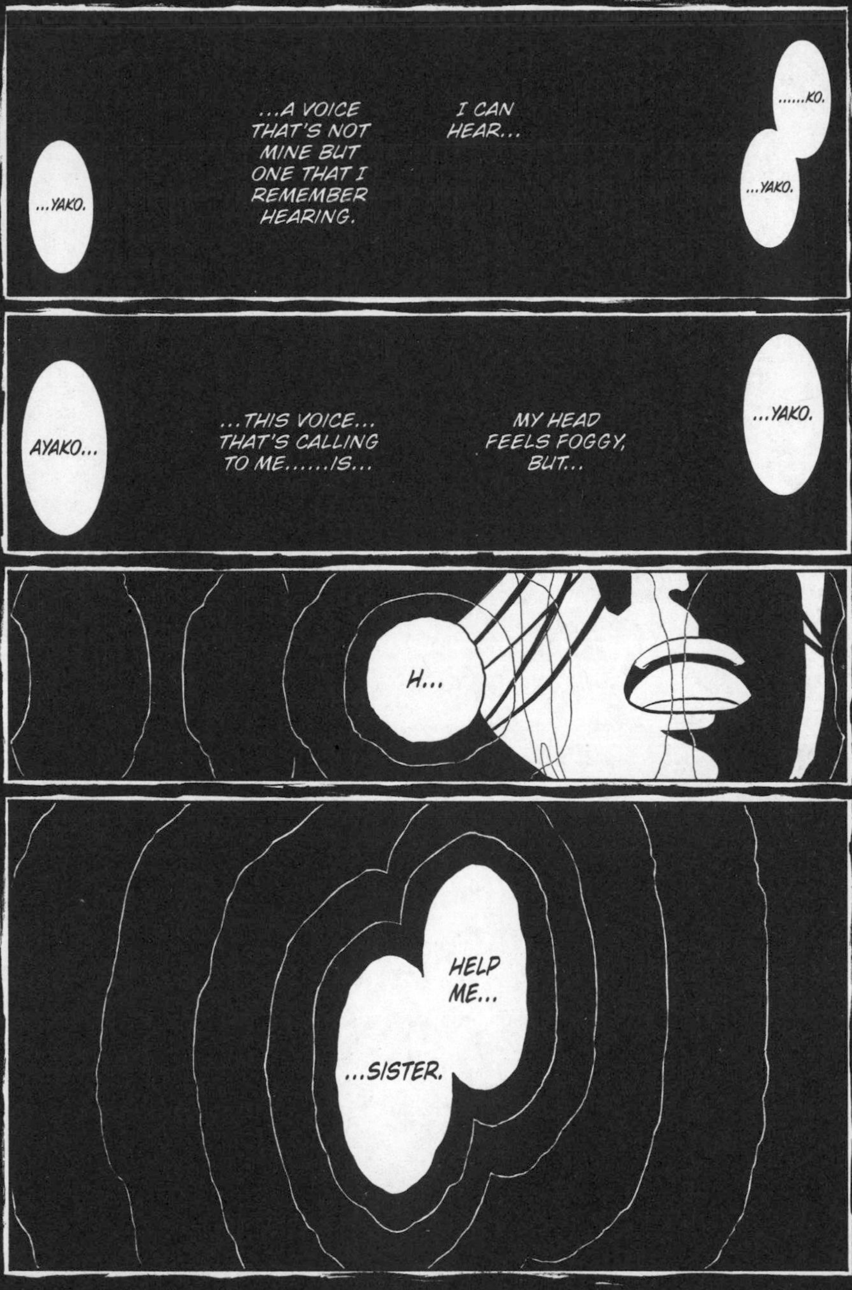
......KO.
...YAKO.
I CAN HEAR...
...A VOICE THAT'S NOT MINE BUT ONE THAT I REMEMBER HEARING.
...YAKO.
...YAKO.
MY HEAD FEELS FOGGY, BUT...
...THIS VOICE... THAT'S CALLING TO ME......IS...
AYAKO...
H...
HELP ME...
...SISTER.

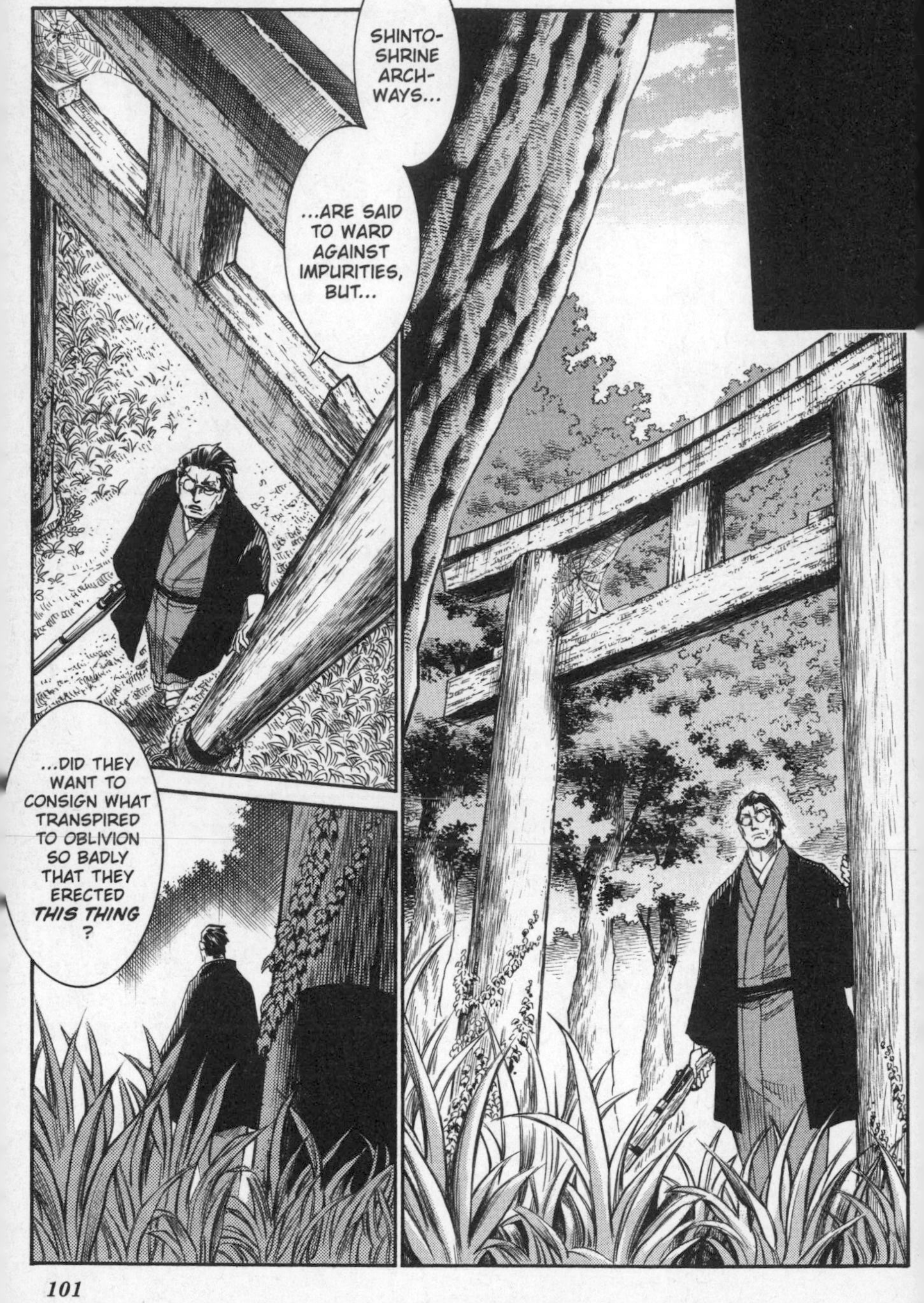
SHINTO-SHRINE ARCHWAYS...
...ARE SAID TO WARD AGAINST IMPURITIES, BUT...
...DID THEY WANT TO CONSIGN WHAT TRANSPIRED TO OBLIVION SO BADLY THAT THEY ERECTED ***THIS THING*** ?

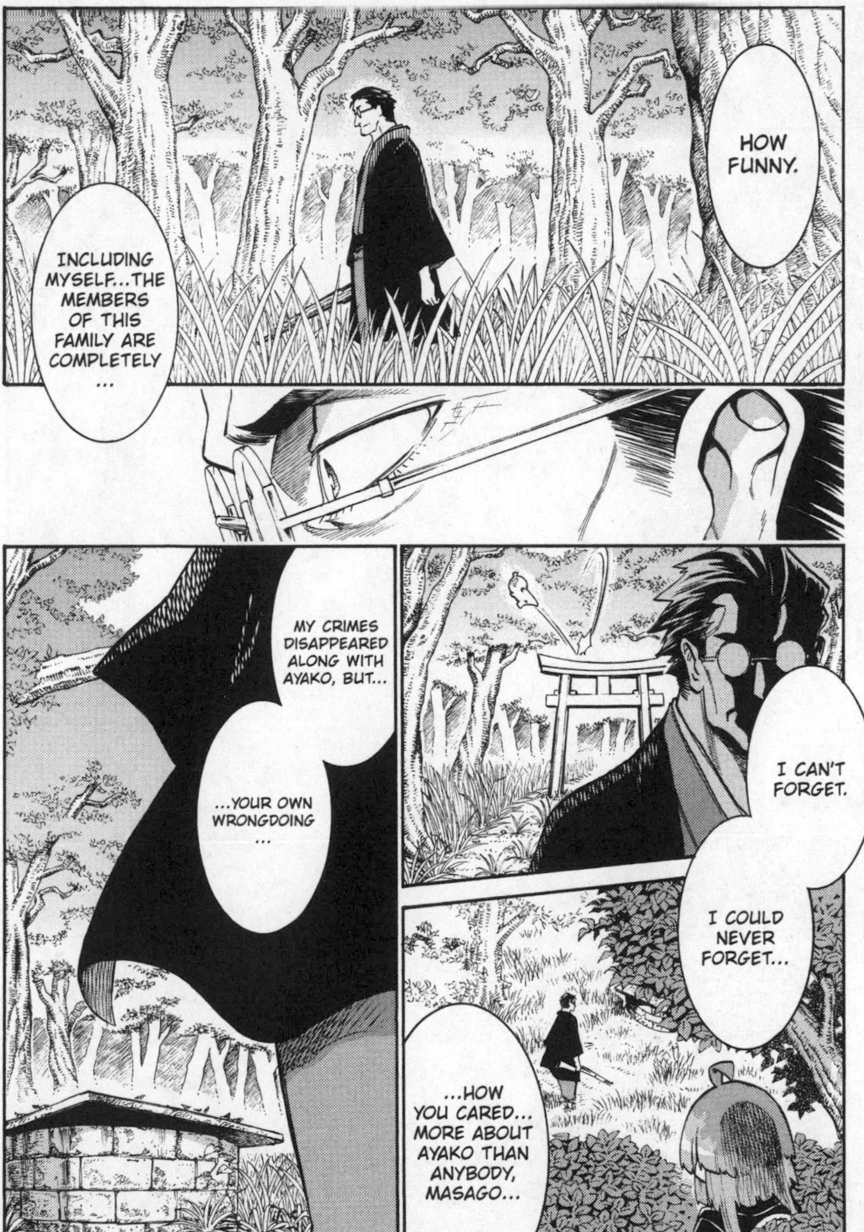
HOW FUNNY.
INCLUDING MYSELF...THE MEMBERS OF THIS FAMILY ARE COMPLETELY ...
I CAN'T FORGET.
I COULD NEVER FORGET...
...HOW YOU CARED... MORE ABOUT AYAKO THAN ANYBODY, MASAGO...
MY CRIMES DISAPPEARED ALONG WITH AYAKO, BUT...
...YOUR OWN WRONGDOING ...

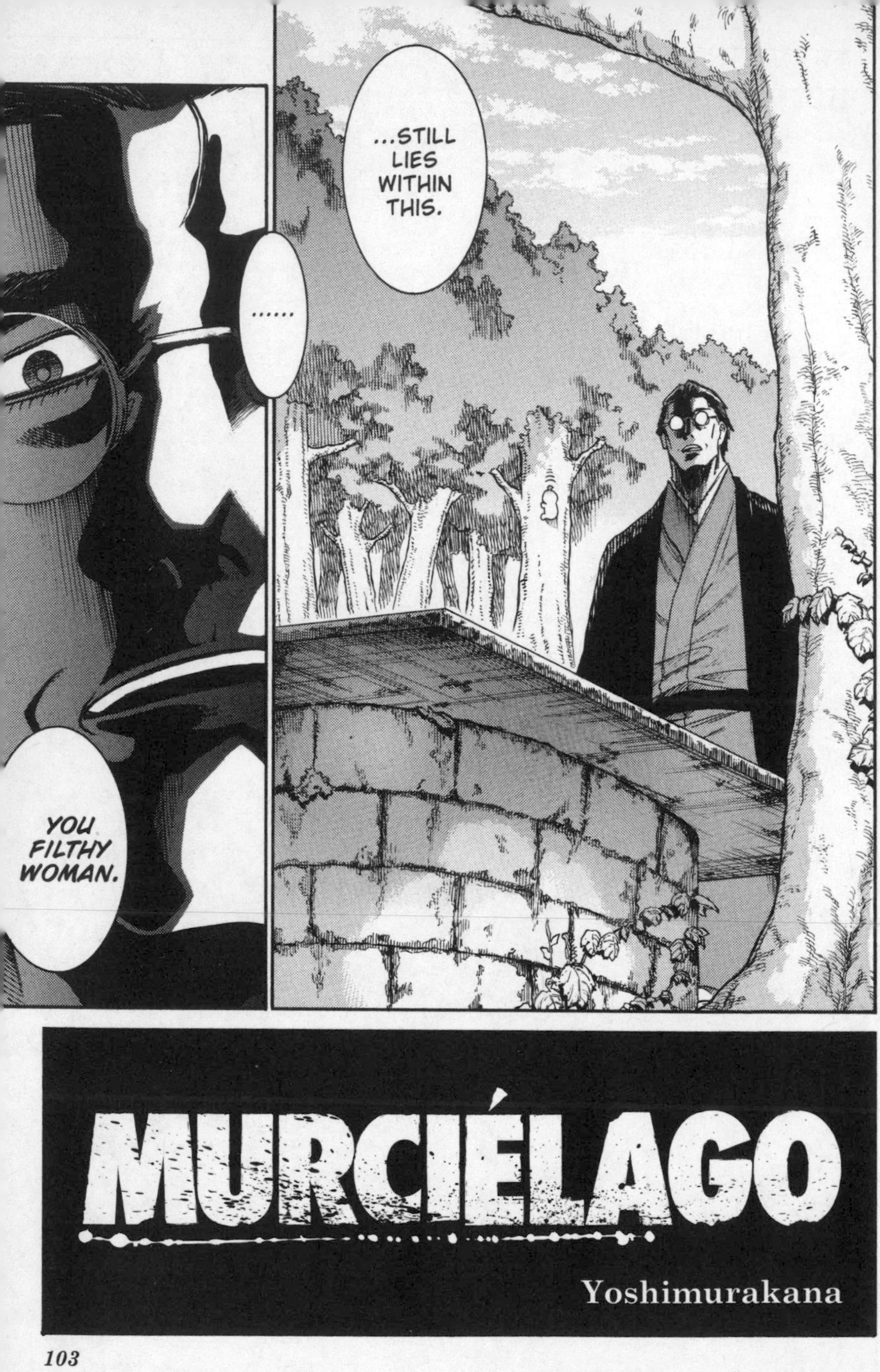
...STILL LIES WITHIN THIS.
......
YOU FILTHY WOMAN.

MURCIÉLAGO

Yoshimurakana

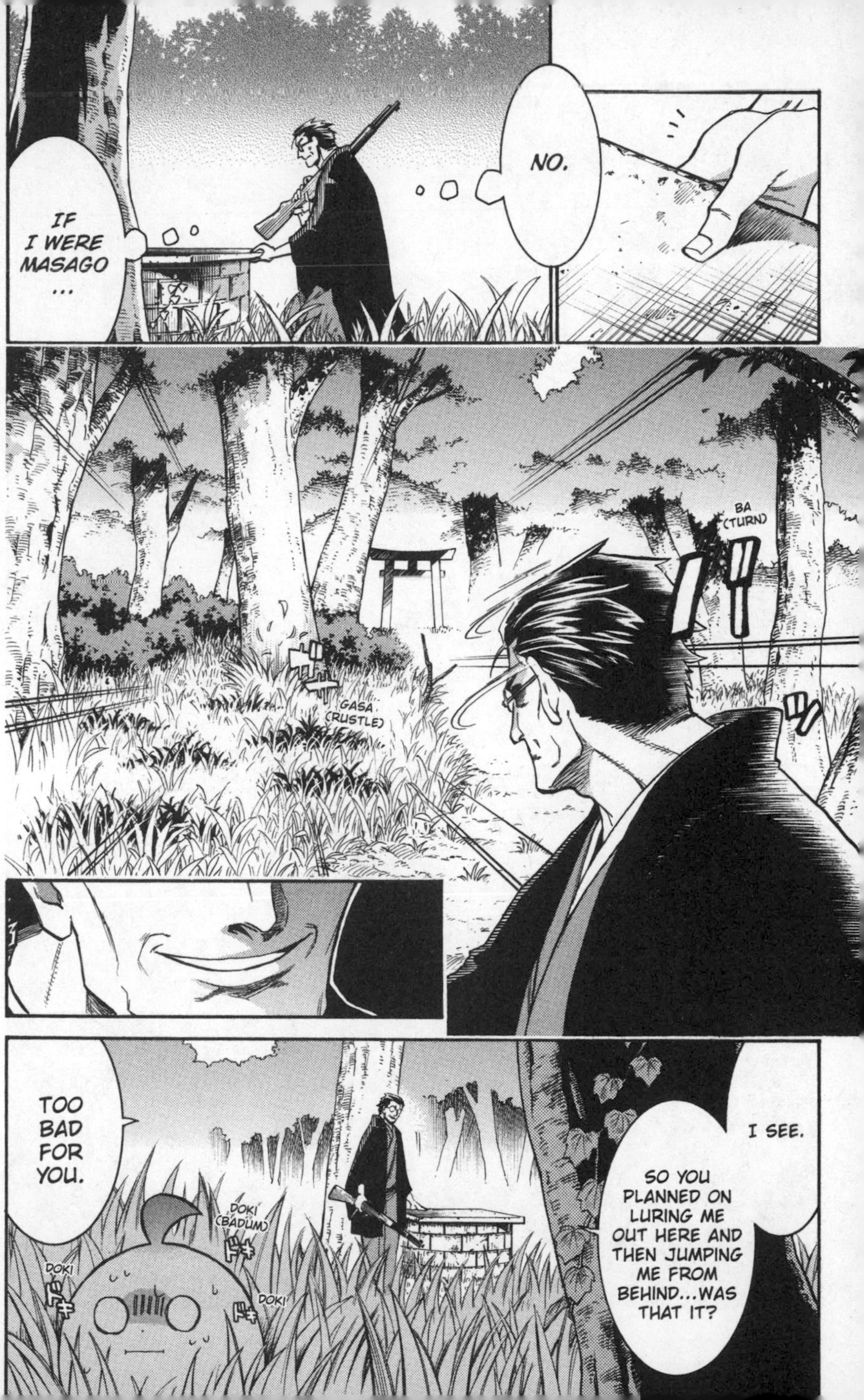
NO.
IF I WERE MASAGO ...
BA (TURN)
GASA (RUSTLE)
I SEE.
SO YOU PLANNED ON LURING ME OUT HERE AND THEN JUMPING ME FROM BEHIND...WAS THAT IT?
TOO BAD FOR YOU.
DOKI (BADUM)
DOKI
DOKI

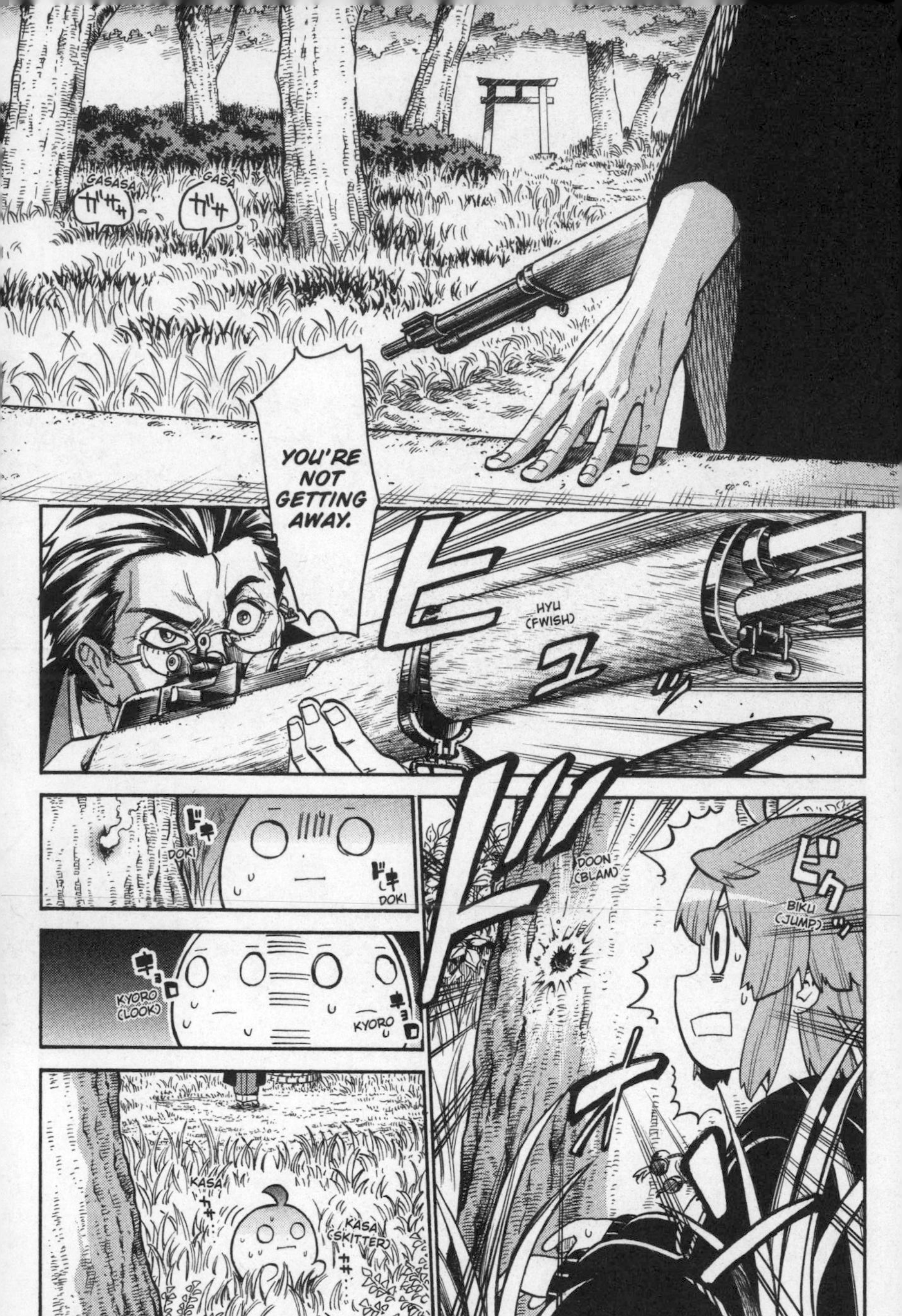
GASA
GASASA
YOU'RE NOT GETTING AWAY.
HYU (FWISH)
DOON (BLAM)
BIKU (JUMP)
DOKI
DOKI
KYORO
KYORO (LOOK)
KASA (SKITTER)
KASA

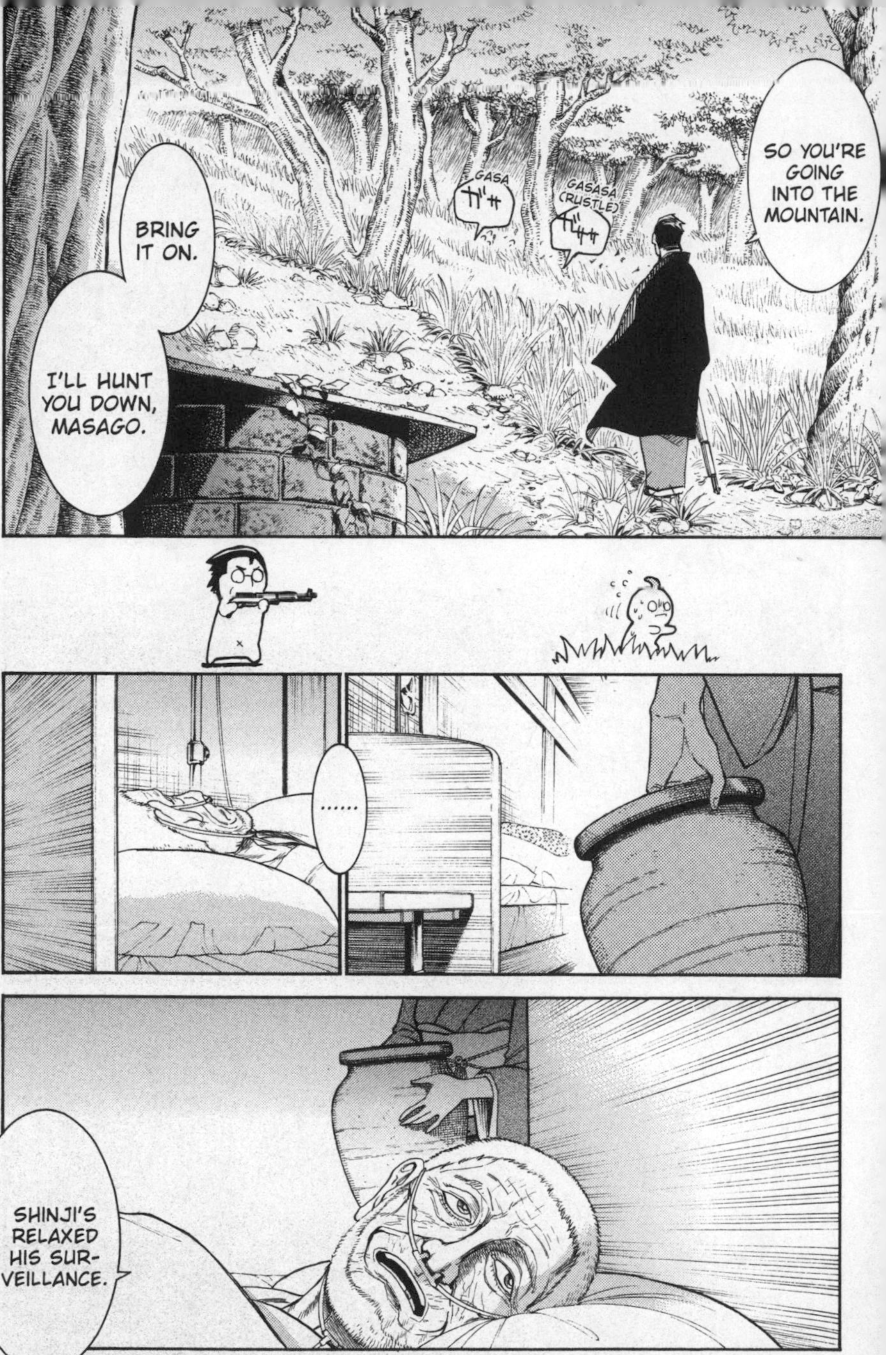
SO YOU'RE GOING INTO THE MOUNTAIN.
GASASA (RUSTLE)
GASA
BRING IT ON.
I'LL HUNT YOU DOWN, MASAGO.
......
SHINJI'S RELAXED HIS SUR-VEILLANCE.

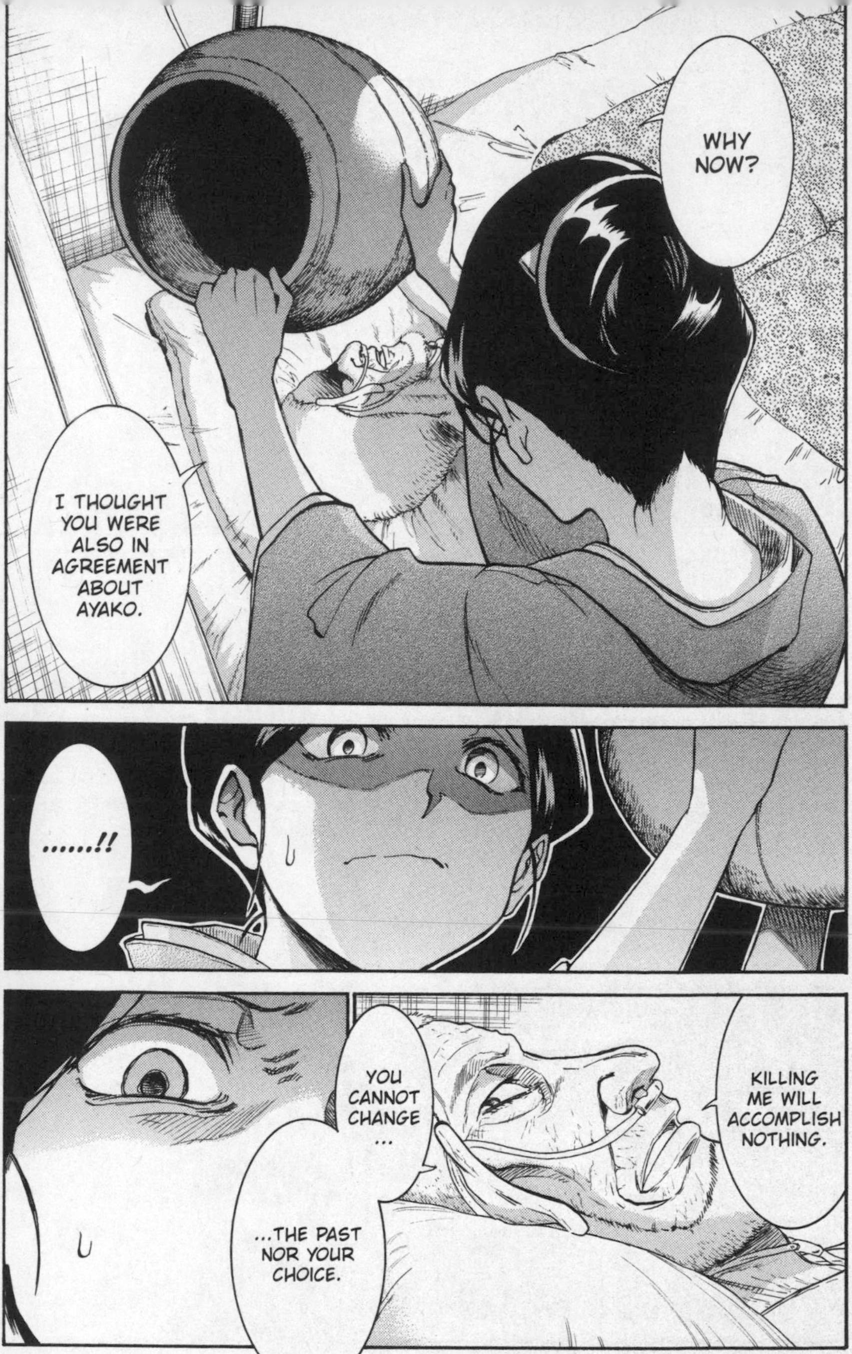
WHY NOW?
I THOUGHT YOU WERE ALSO IN AGREEMENT ABOUT AYAKO.
......!!
KILLING ME WILL ACCOMPLISH NOTHING.
YOU CANNOT CHANGE ...
...THE PAST NOR YOUR CHOICE.

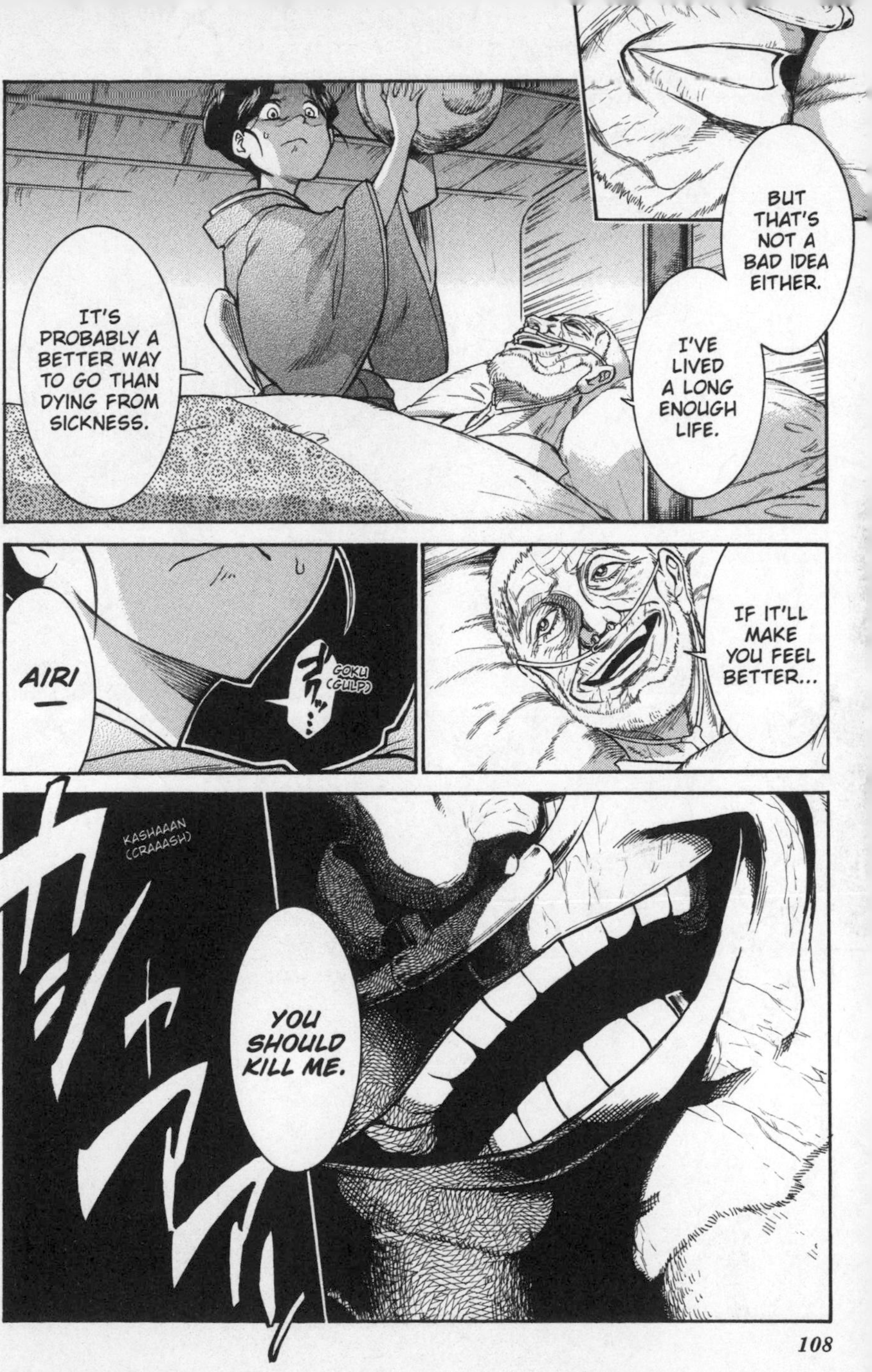
BUT THAT'S NOT A BAD IDEA EITHER.
I'VE LIVED A LONG ENOUGH LIFE.
IT'S PROBABLY A BETTER WAY TO GO THAN DYING FROM SICKNESS.
IF IT'LL MAKE YOU FEEL BETTER...
GOKU (GULP)
AIRI —
YOU SHOULD KILL ME.
KASHAAAN (CRAAASH)

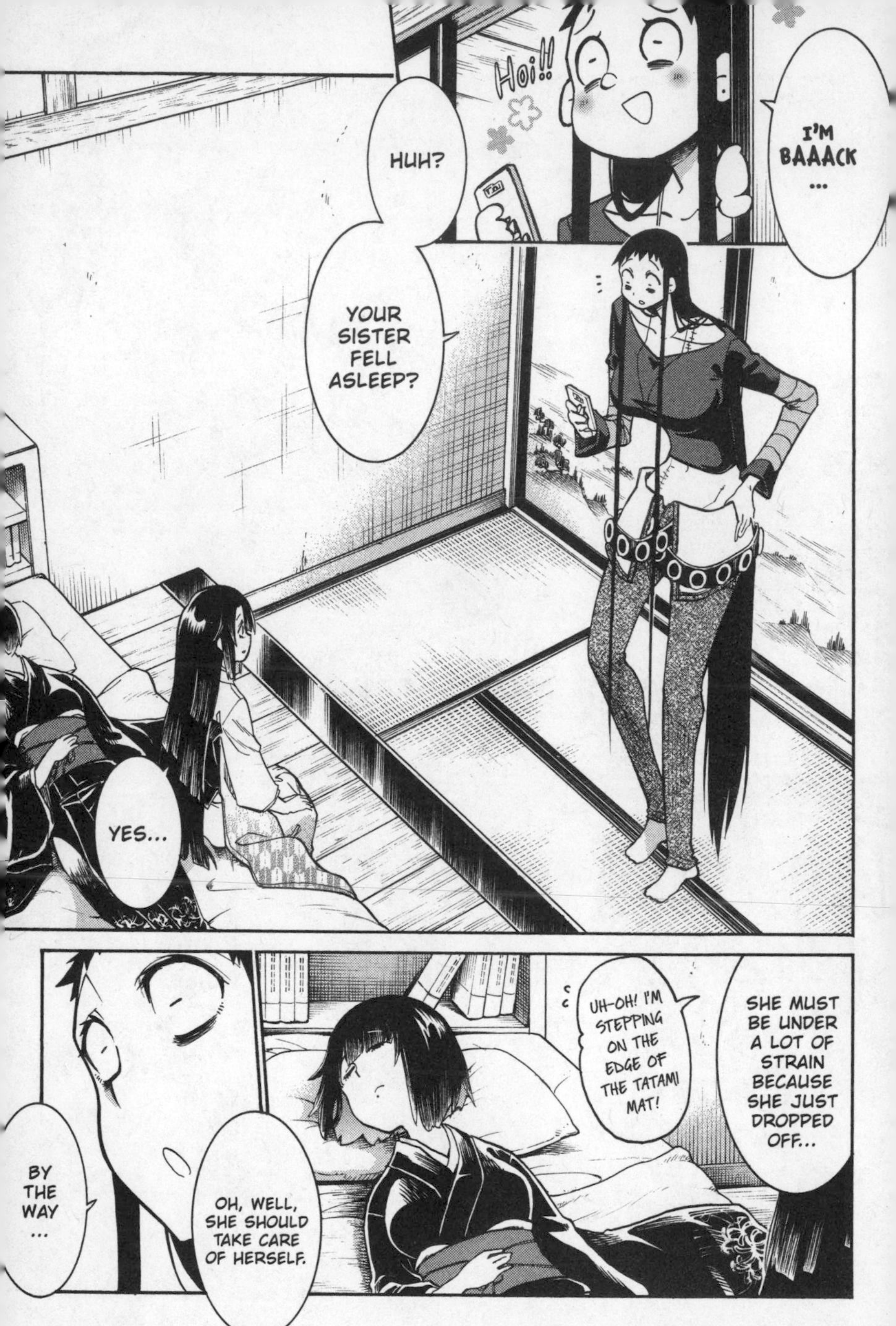
I'M BAAACK...
Hoi!!
HUH?
YOUR SISTER FELL ASLEEP?
YES...
SHE MUST BE UNDER A LOT OF STRAIN BECAUSE SHE JUST DROPPED OFF...
UH-OH! I'M STEPPING ON THE EDGE OF THE TATAMI MAT!
OH, WELL, SHE SHOULD TAKE CARE OF HERSELF.
BY THE WAY...

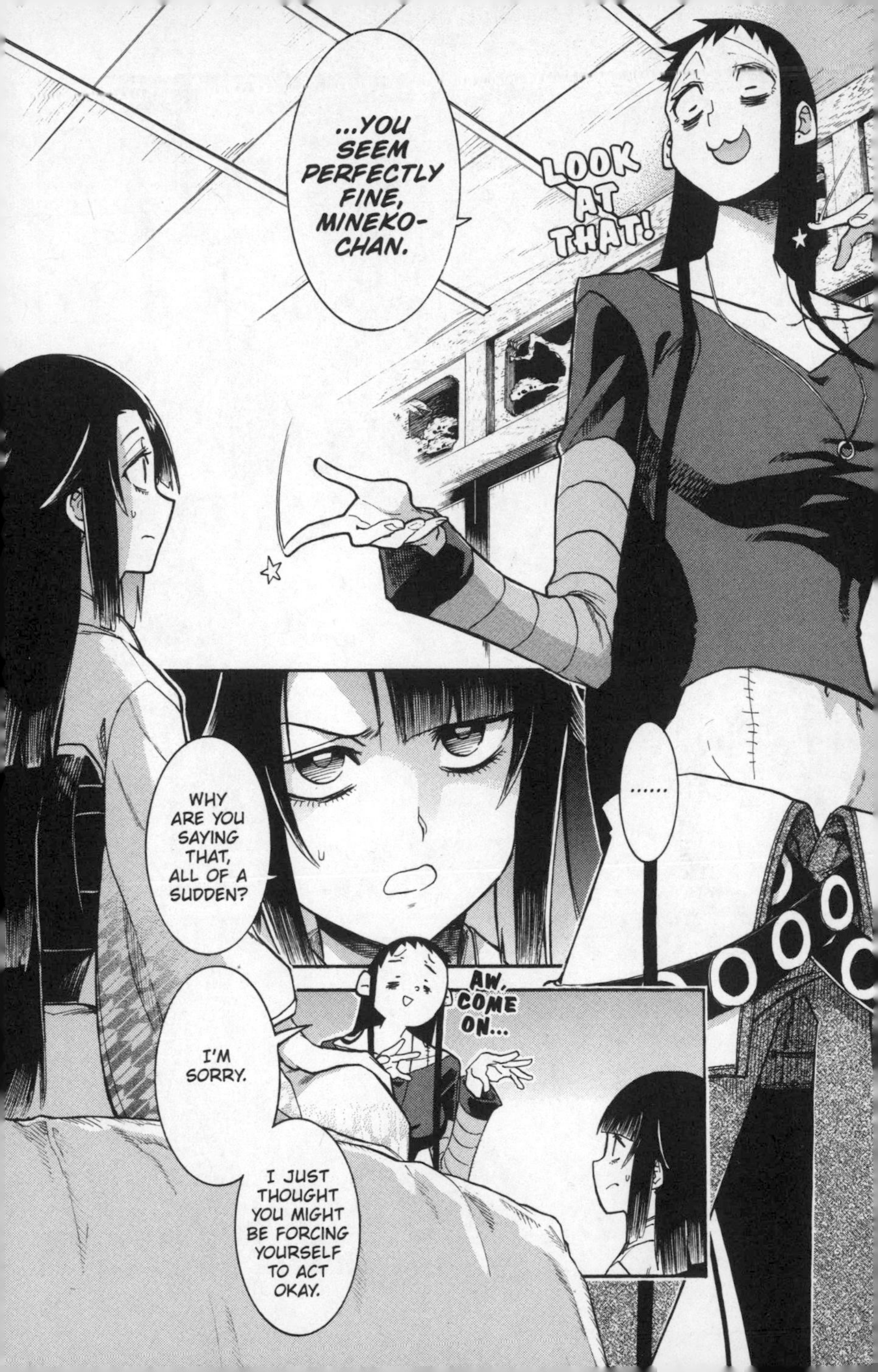
LOOK AT THAT!
...YOU SEEM PERFECTLY FINE, MINEKO-CHAN.
......
WHY ARE YOU SAYING THAT, ALL OF A SUDDEN?
AW, COME ON...
I'M SORRY.
I JUST THOUGHT YOU MIGHT BE FORCING YOURSELF TO ACT OKAY.

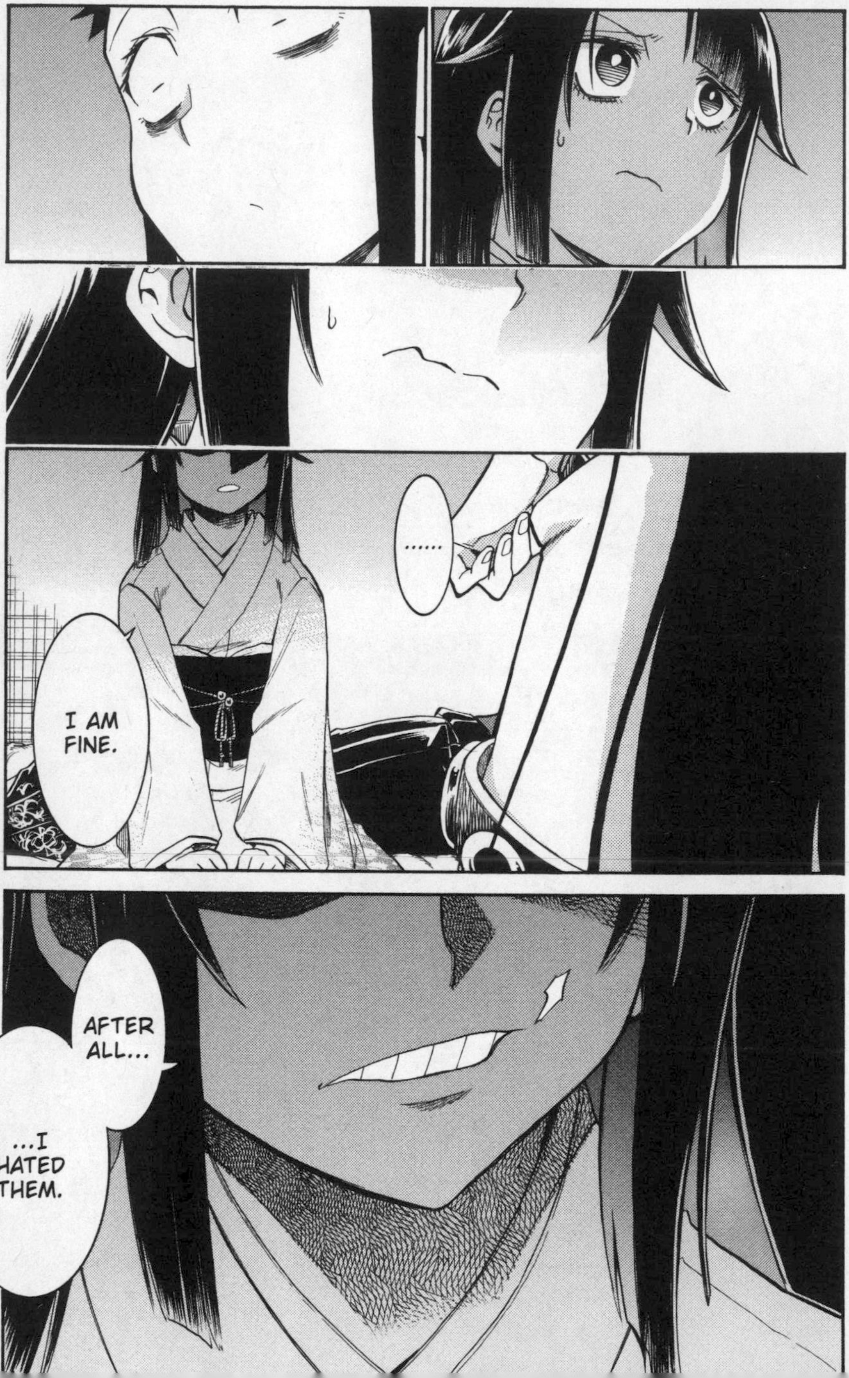
......
I AM FINE.
AFTER ALL...
...I HATED THEM.

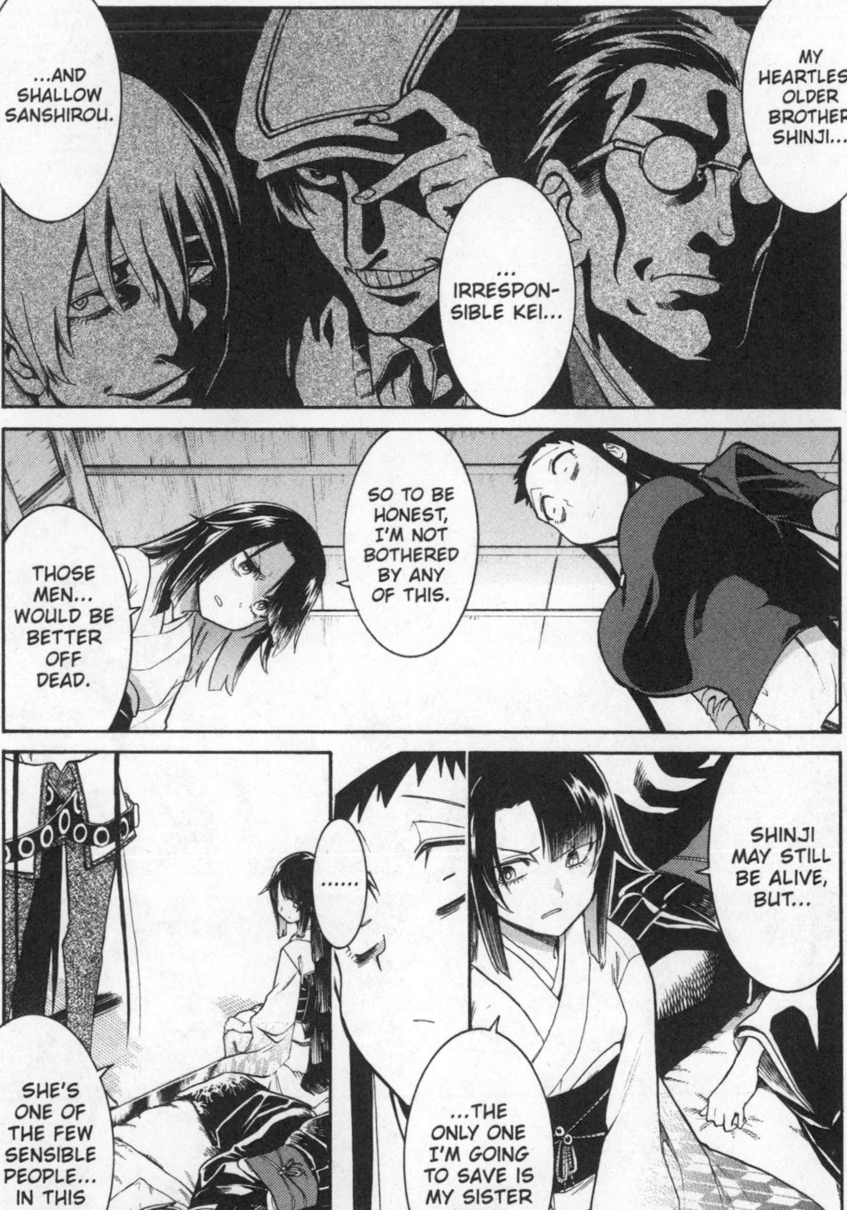
MY HEARTLESS OLDER BROTHER SHINJI...
... IRRESPONSIBLE KEI...
...AND SHALLOW SANSHIROU.
SO TO BE HONEST, I'M NOT BOTHERED BY ANY OF THIS.
THOSE MEN... WOULD BE BETTER OFF DEAD.
SHINJI MAY STILL BE ALIVE, BUT...
...THE ONLY ONE I'M GOING TO SAVE IS MY SISTER MIDORI.
......
SHE'S ONE OF THE FEW SENSIBLE PEOPLE... IN THIS HOUSE.

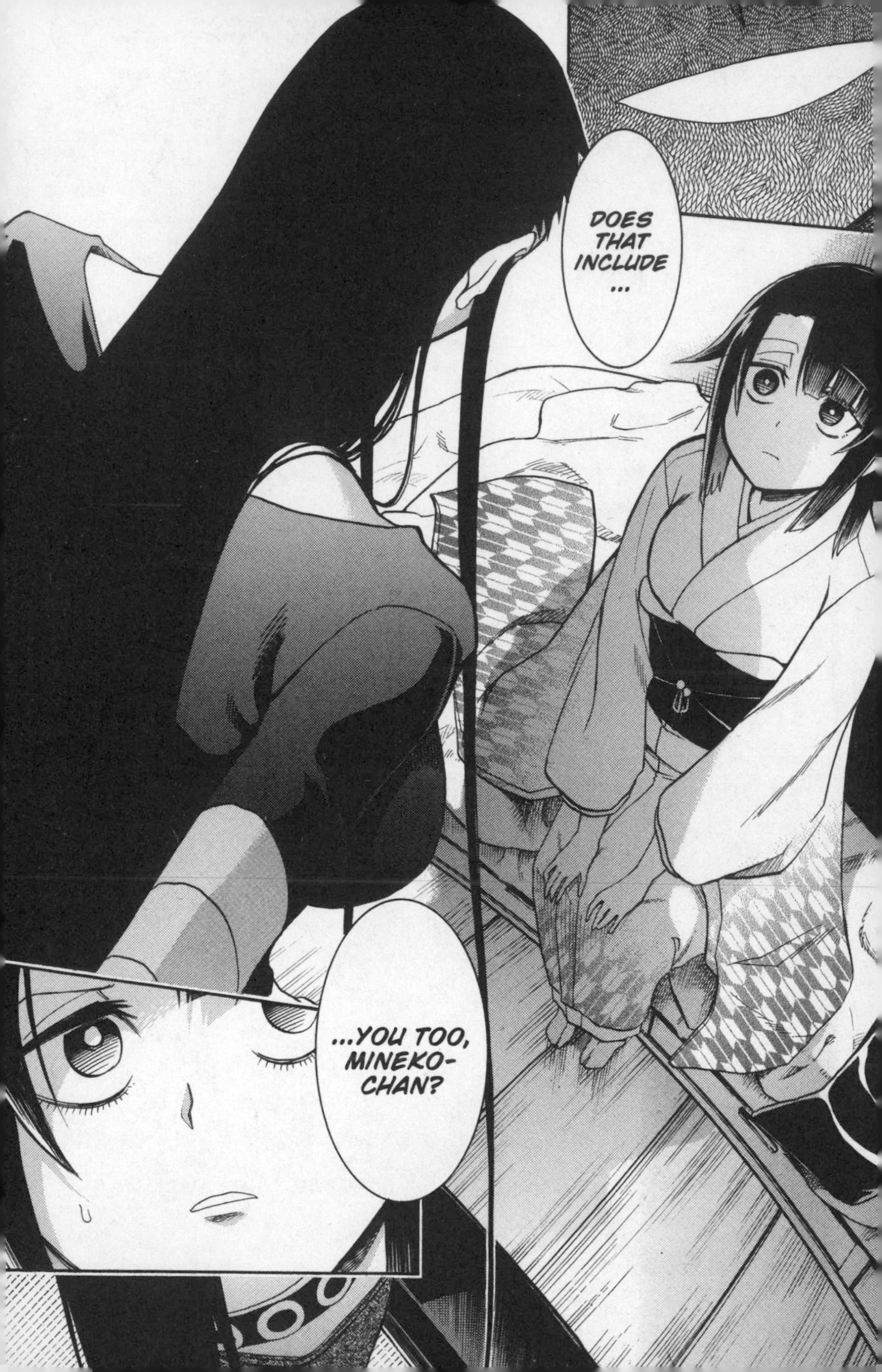
DOES THAT INCLUDE ...
...YOU TOO, MINEKO-CHAN?

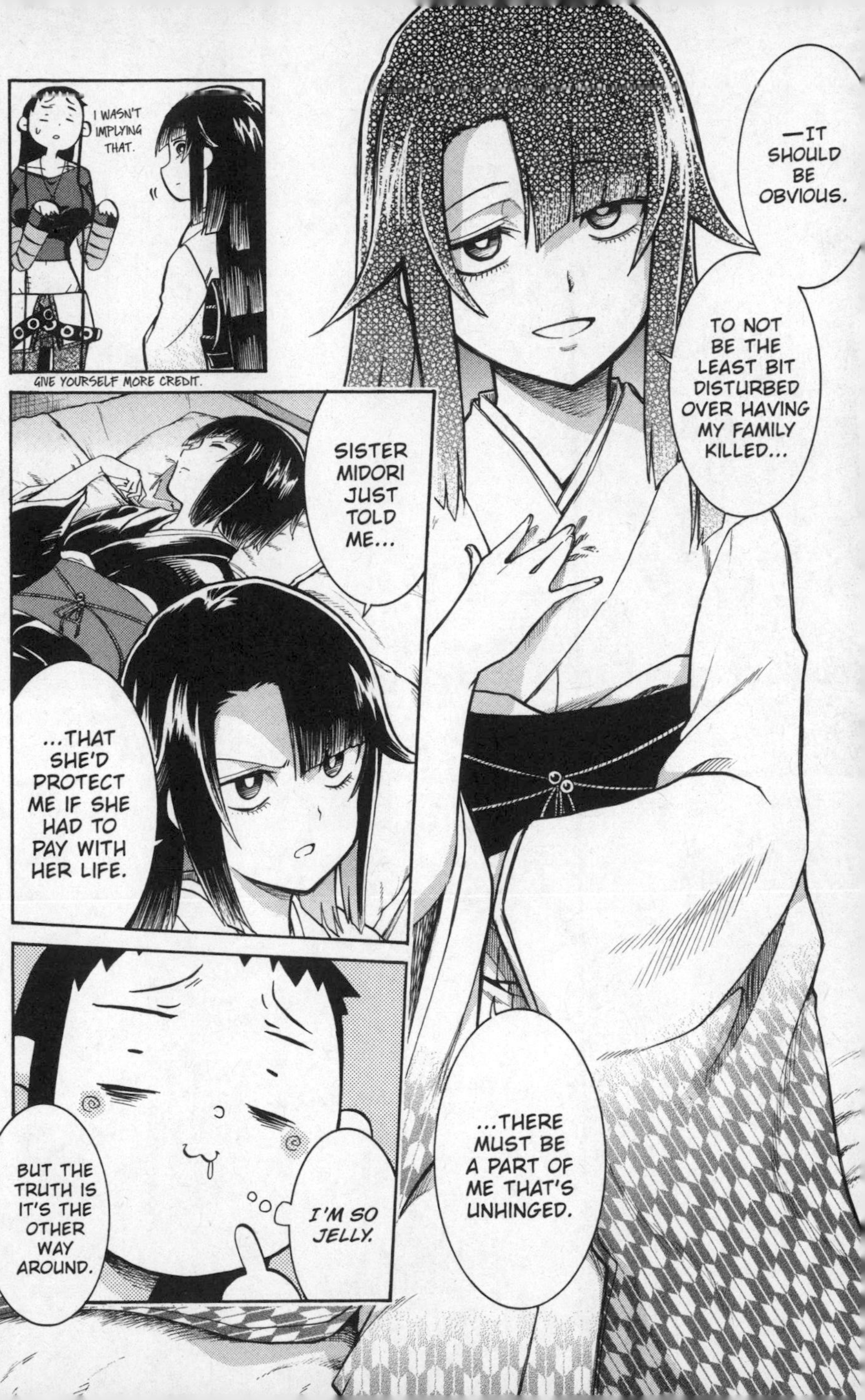
—IT SHOULD BE OBVIOUS.
TO NOT BE THE LEAST BIT DISTURBED OVER HAVING MY FAMILY KILLED...
...THERE MUST BE A PART OF ME THAT'S UNHINGED.
I WASN'T IMPLYING THAT.
GIVE YOURSELF MORE CREDIT.
SISTER MIDORI JUST TOLD ME...
...THAT SHE'D PROTECT ME IF SHE HAD TO PAY WITH HER LIFE.
I'M SO JELLY.
BUT THE TRUTH IS IT'S THE OTHER WAY AROUND.

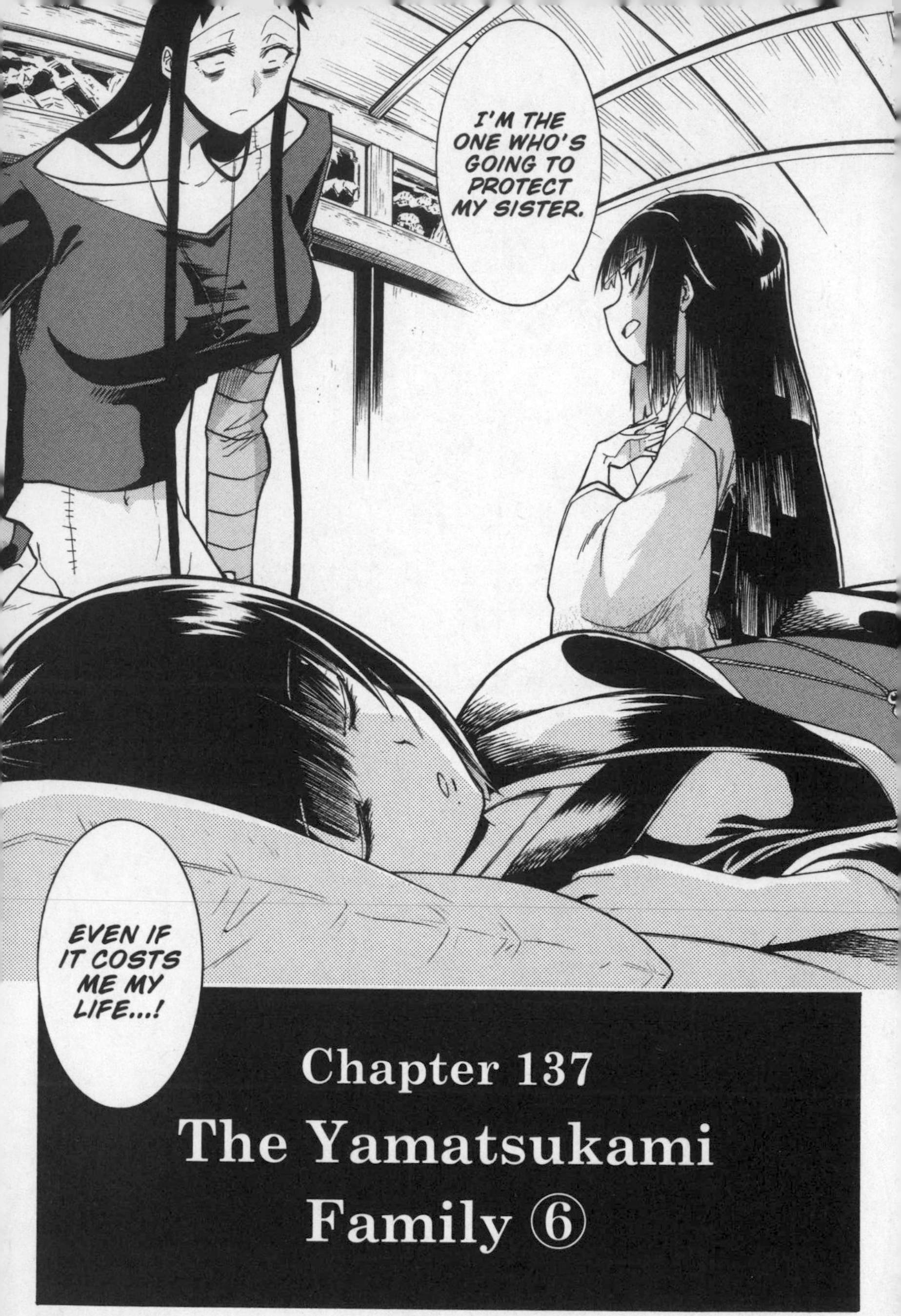
I'M THE ONE WHO'S GOING TO PROTECT MY SISTER.
EVEN IF IT COSTS ME MY LIFE...!

Chapter 137
The Yamatsukami Family ⑥

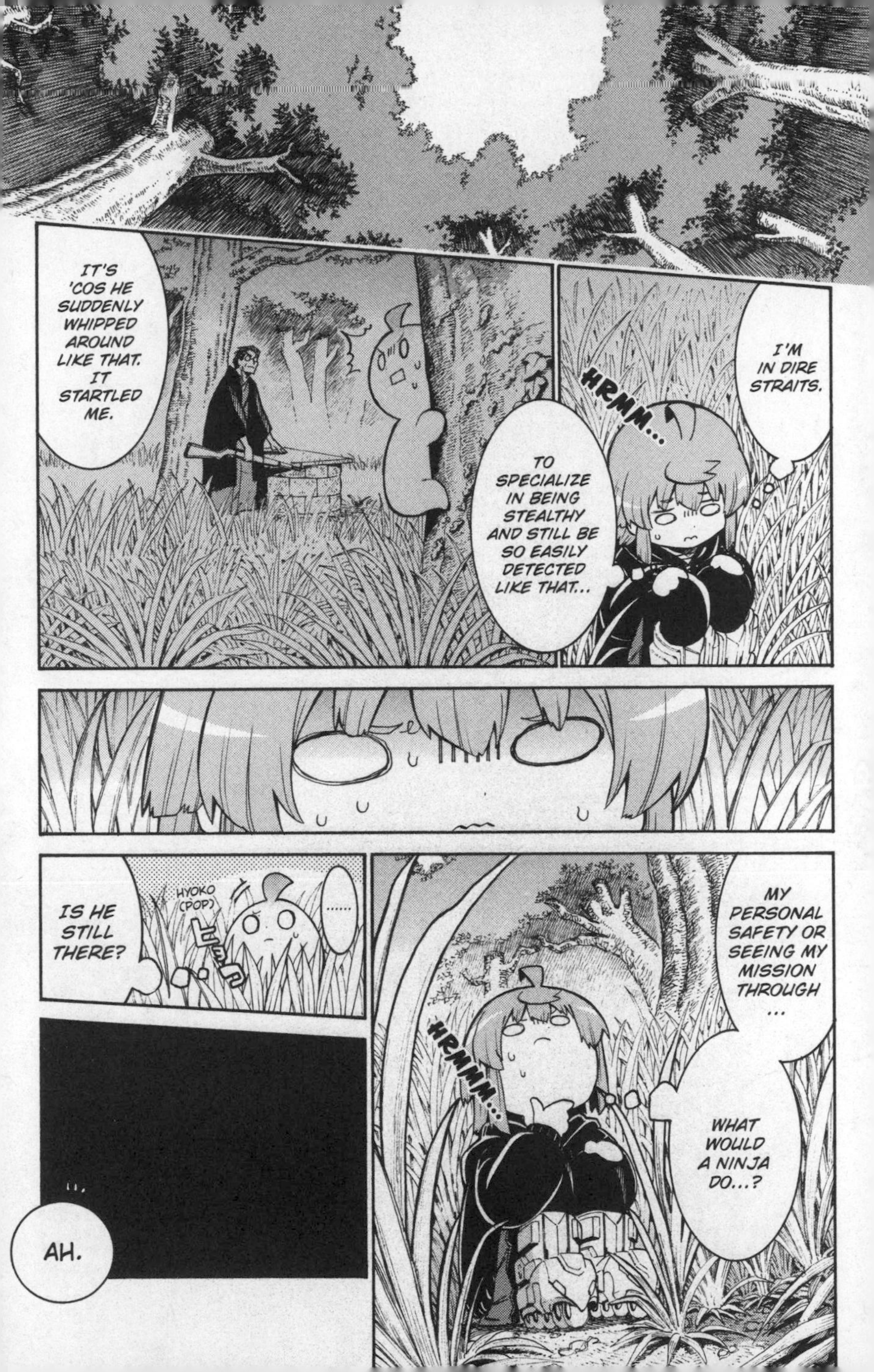
I'M IN DIRE STRAITS.
HRMMM...
TO SPECIALIZE IN BEING STEALTHY AND STILL BE SO EASILY DETECTED LIKE THAT...
IT'S 'COS HE SUDDENLY WHIPPED AROUND LIKE THAT. IT STARTLED ME.
MY PERSONAL SAFETY OR SEEING MY MISSION THROUGH...
HRMMM...
WHAT WOULD A NINJA DO...?
......
HYOKO (POP)
IS HE STILL THERE?
AH.

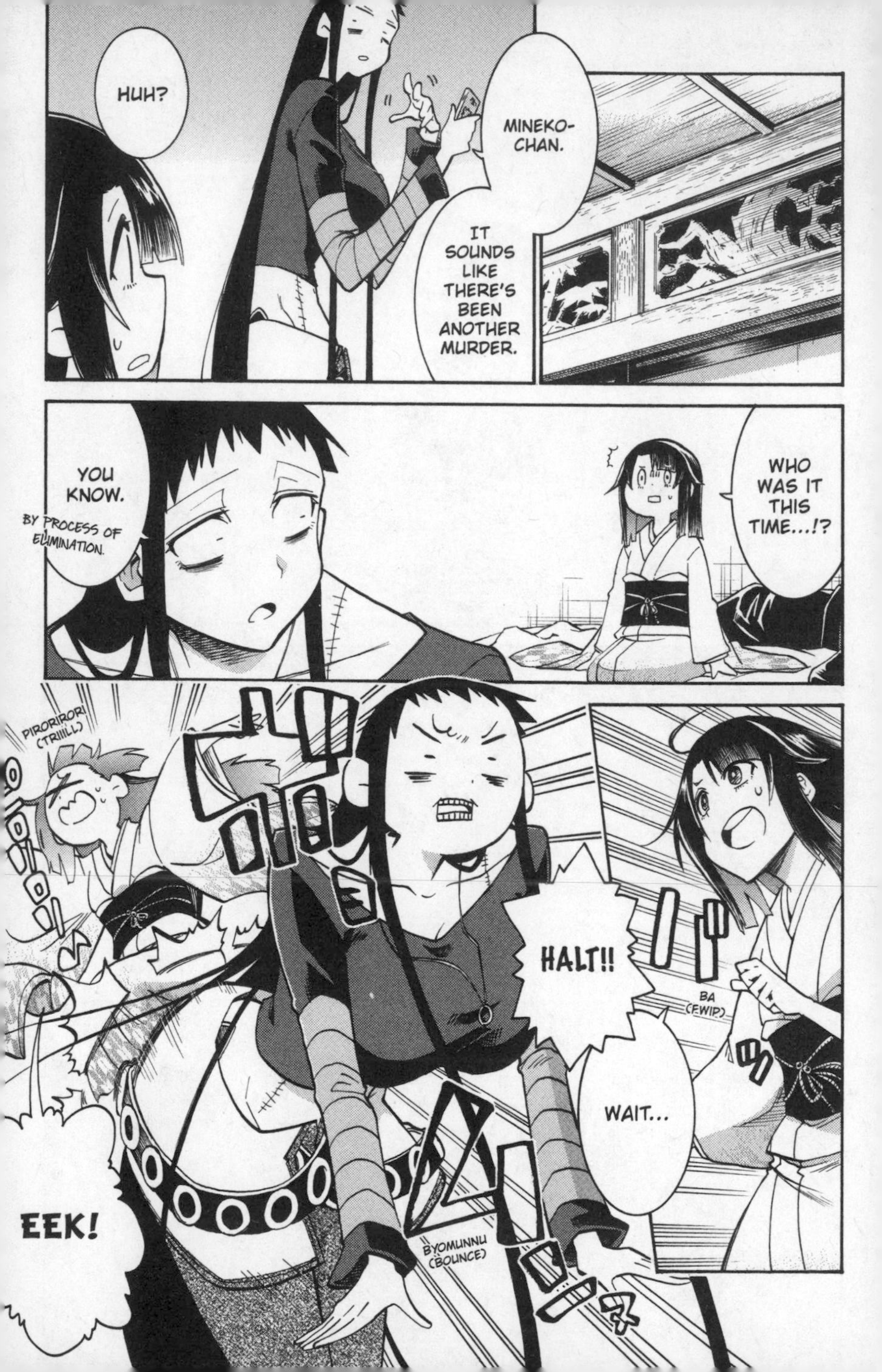
MINEKO-CHAN.
HUH?
IT SOUNDS LIKE THERE'S BEEN ANOTHER MURDER.
WHO WAS IT THIS TIME...!?
YOU KNOW.
BY PROCESS OF ELIMINATION.
HALT!!
BA (FWIP)
WAIT...
PIRORIRORI (TRIIILL)
BYOMUNNU (BOUNCE)
EEK!

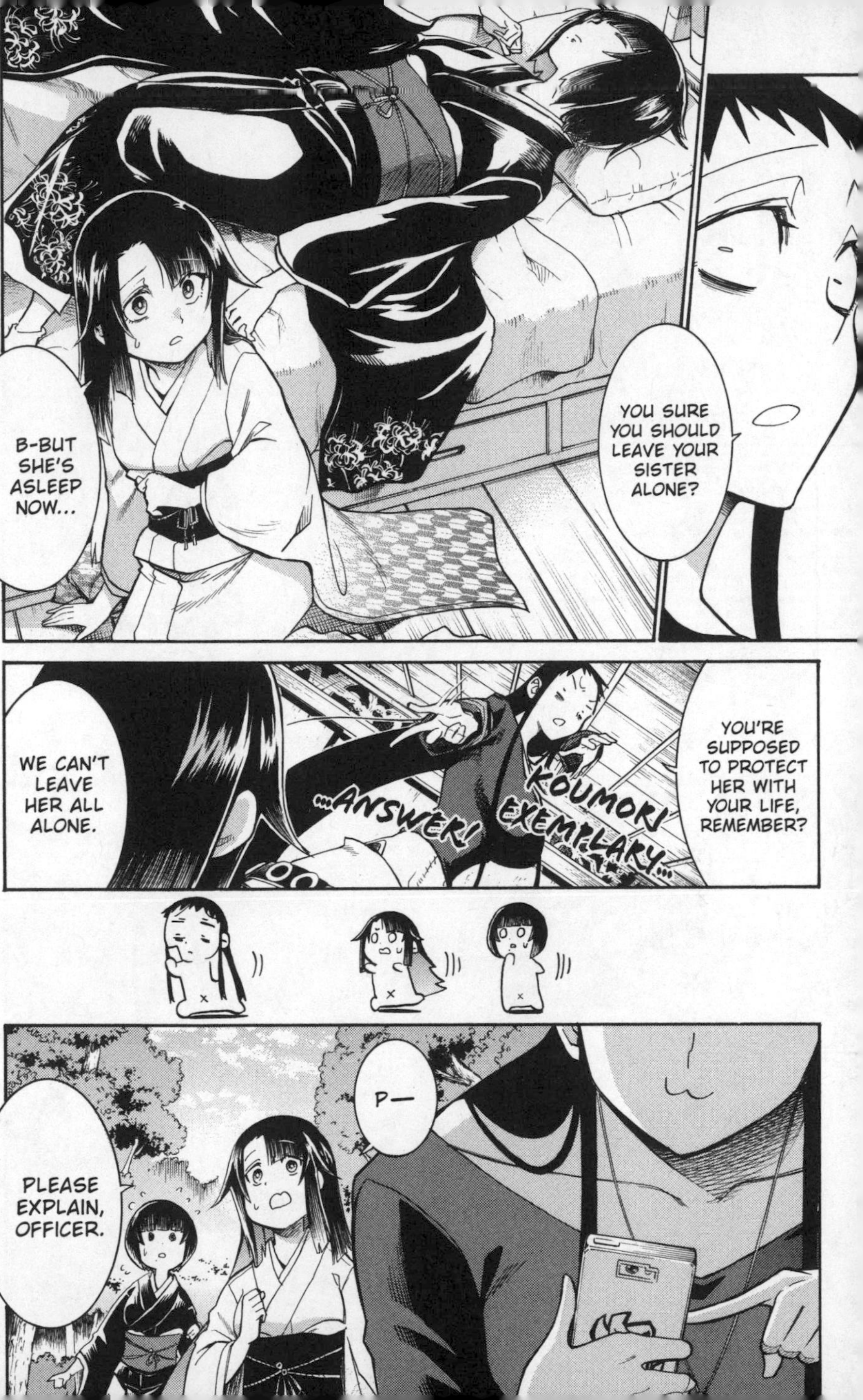
YOU SURE YOU SHOULD LEAVE YOUR SISTER ALONE?
B-BUT SHE'S ASLEEP NOW...
YOU'RE SUPPOSED TO PROTECT HER WITH YOUR LIFE, REMEMBER?
KOUMORI EXEMPLARY...
...ANSWER!
WE CAN'T LEAVE HER ALL ALONE.
P—
PLEASE EXPLAIN, OFFICER.

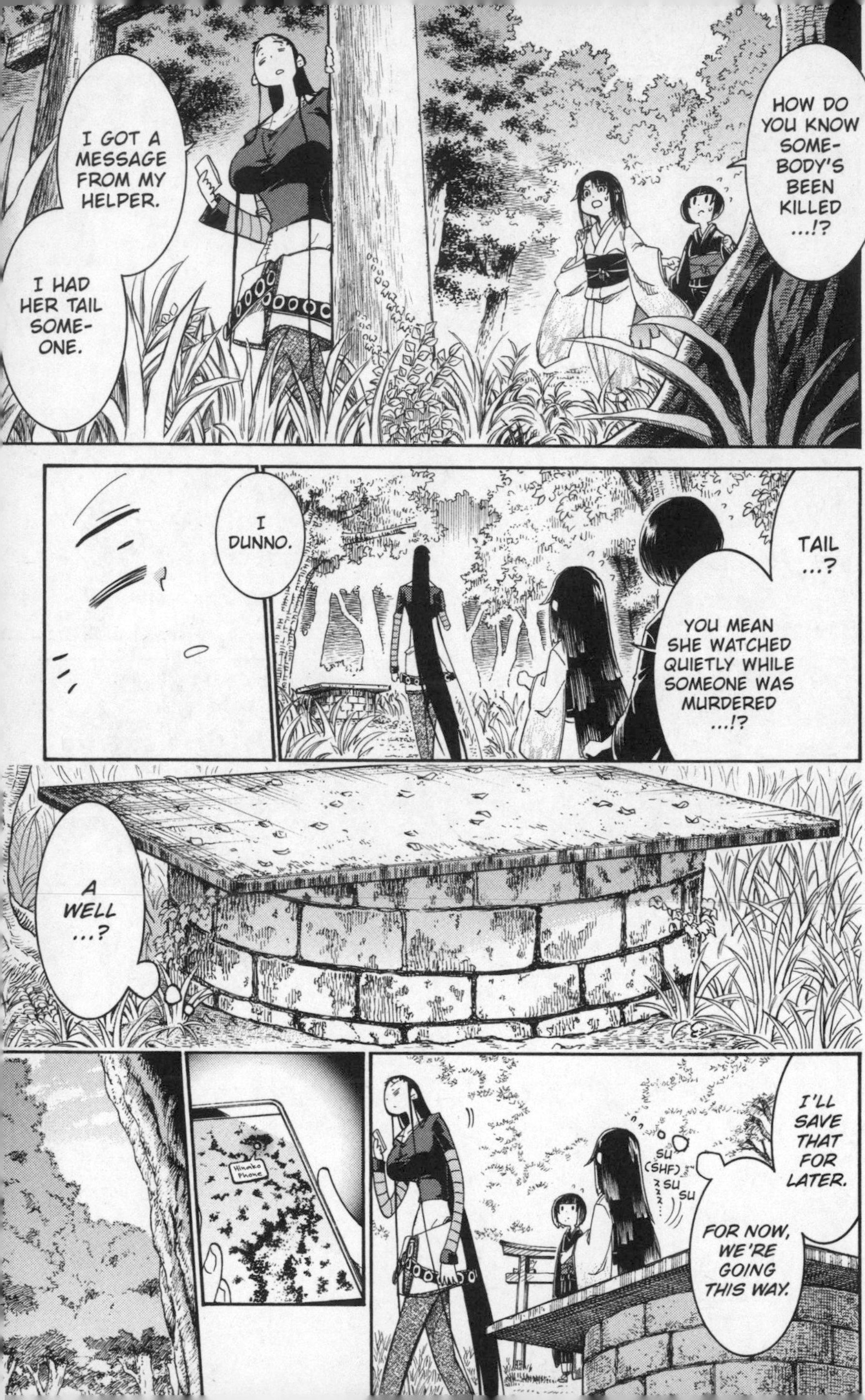
HOW DO YOU KNOW SOMEBODY'S BEEN KILLED ...!?
I GOT A MESSAGE FROM MY HELPER.
I HAD HER TAIL SOMEONE.
TAIL ...?
YOU MEAN SHE WATCHED QUIETLY WHILE SOMEONE WAS MURDERED ...!?
I DUNNO.
A WELL ...?
I'LL SAVE THAT FOR LATER.
FOR NOW, WE'RE GOING THIS WAY.
SU (SHF) SU SU
Hinako Phone

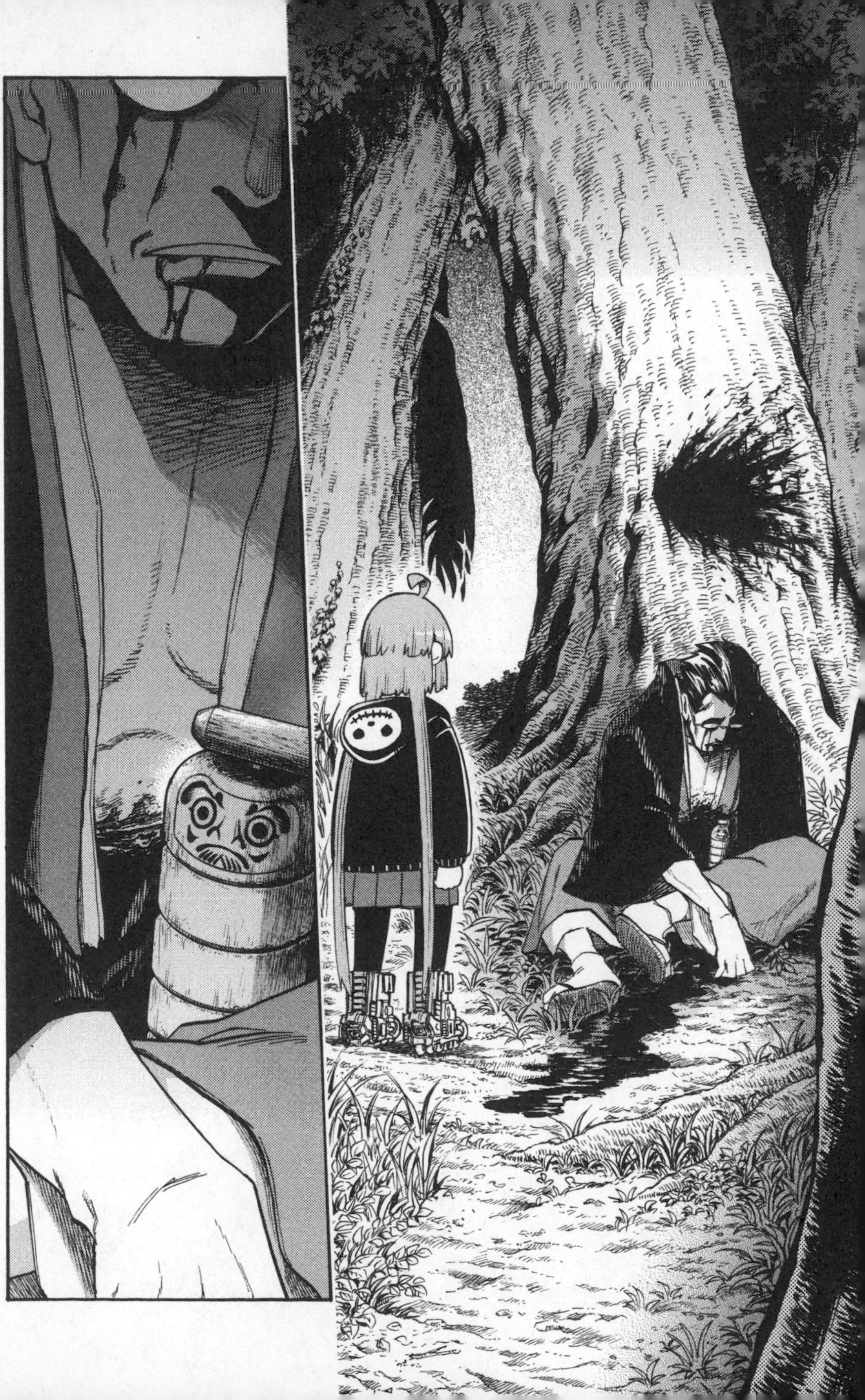

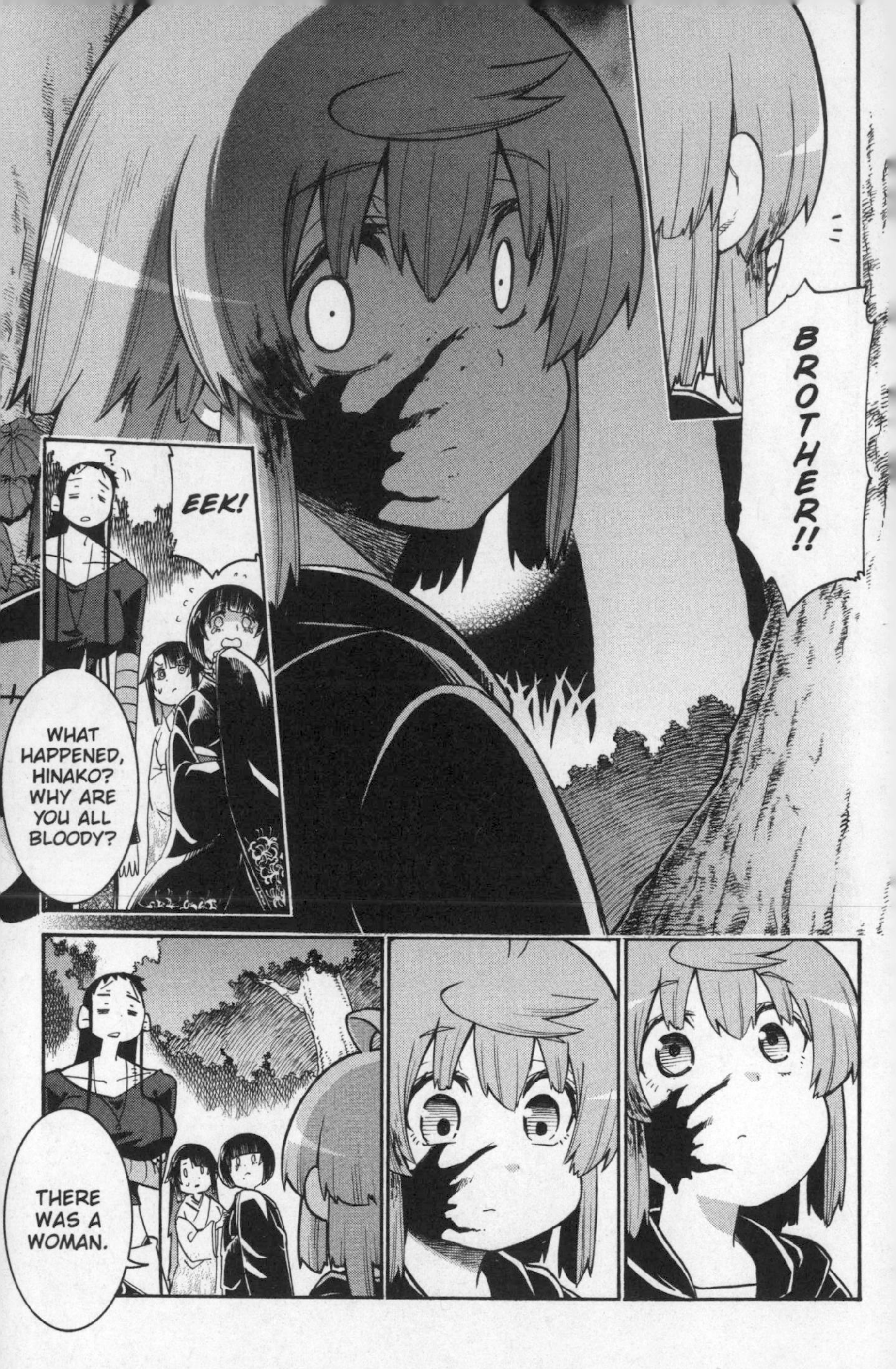
BROTHER!!
EEK!
WHAT HAPPENED, HINAKO? WHY ARE YOU ALL BLOODY?
THERE WAS A WOMAN.

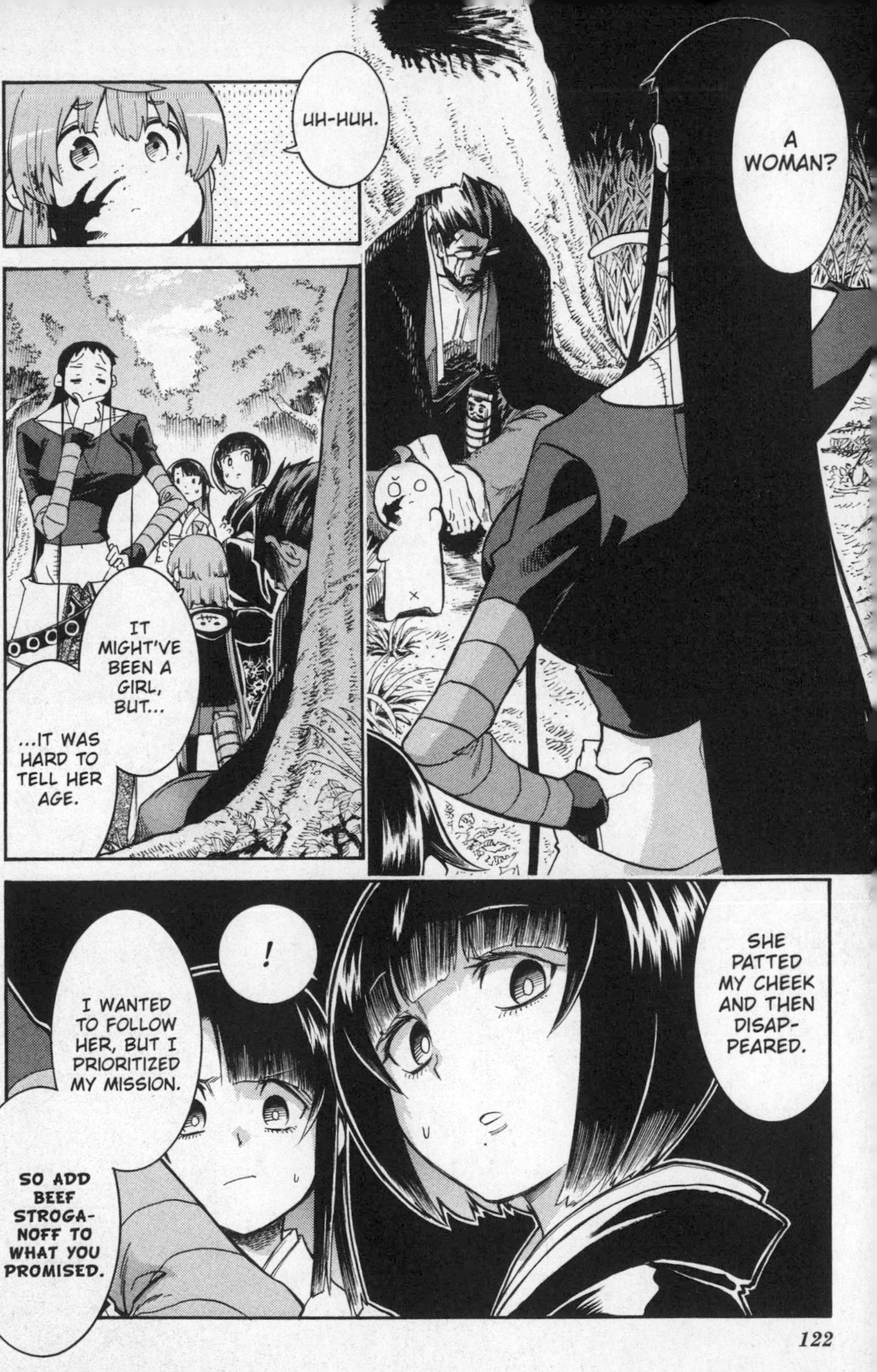
A WOMAN?
UH-HUH.
IT MIGHT'VE BEEN A GIRL, BUT...
...IT WAS HARD TO TELL HER AGE.
SHE PATTED MY CHEEK AND THEN DISAP-PEARED.
!
I WANTED TO FOLLOW HER, BUT I PRIORITIZED MY MISSION.
SO ADD BEEF STROGA-NOFF TO WHAT YOU PROMISED.

MURCIÉLAGO

MURCIÉLAGO

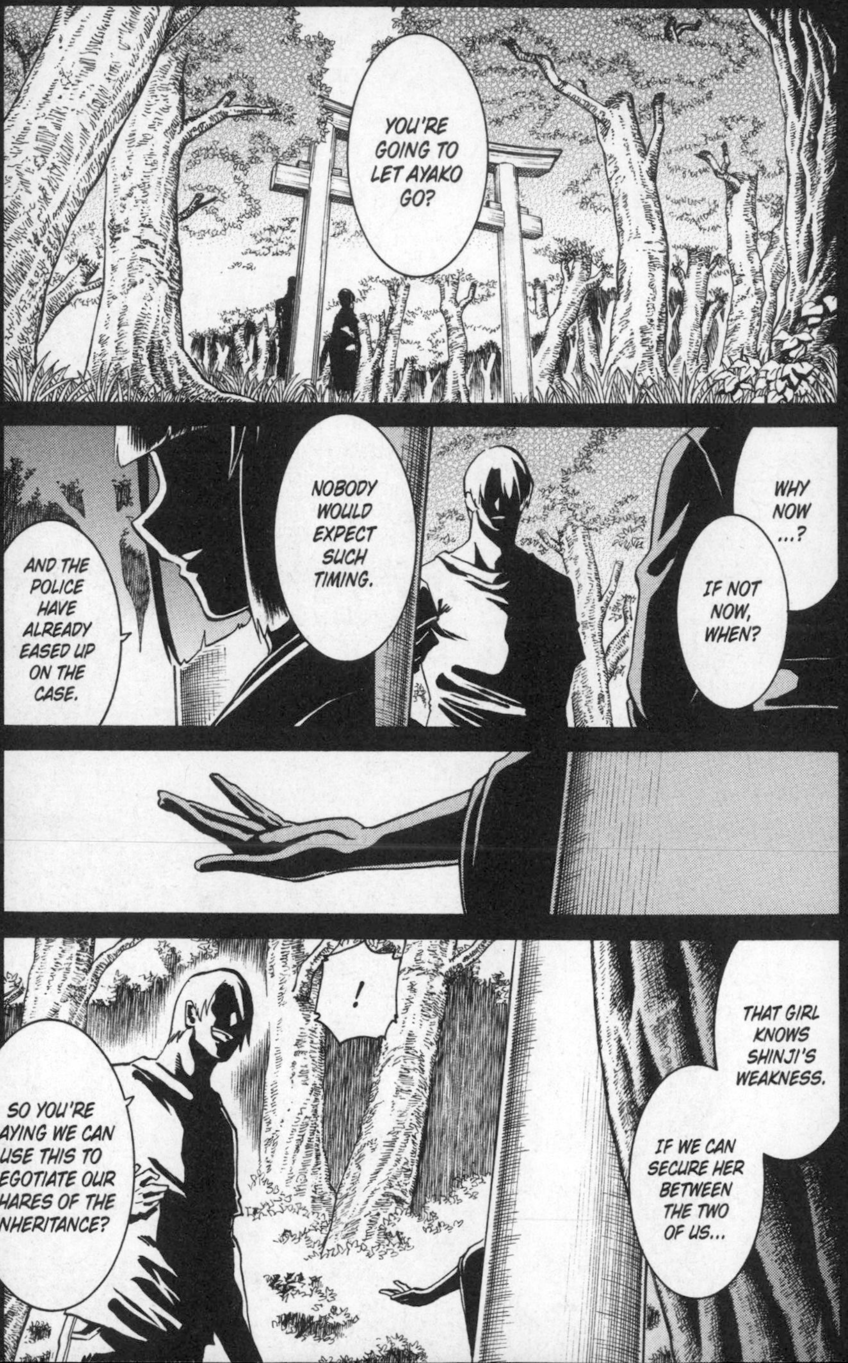
YOU'RE GOING TO LET AYAKO GO?
WHY NOW ...?
IF NOT NOW, WHEN?
NOBODY WOULD EXPECT SUCH TIMING.
AND THE POLICE HAVE ALREADY EASED UP ON THE CASE.
THAT GIRL KNOWS SHINJI'S WEAKNESS.
IF WE CAN SECURE HER BETWEEN THE TWO OF US...
!
SO YOU'RE SAYING WE CAN USE THIS TO NEGOTIATE OUR SHARES OF THE INHERITANCE?

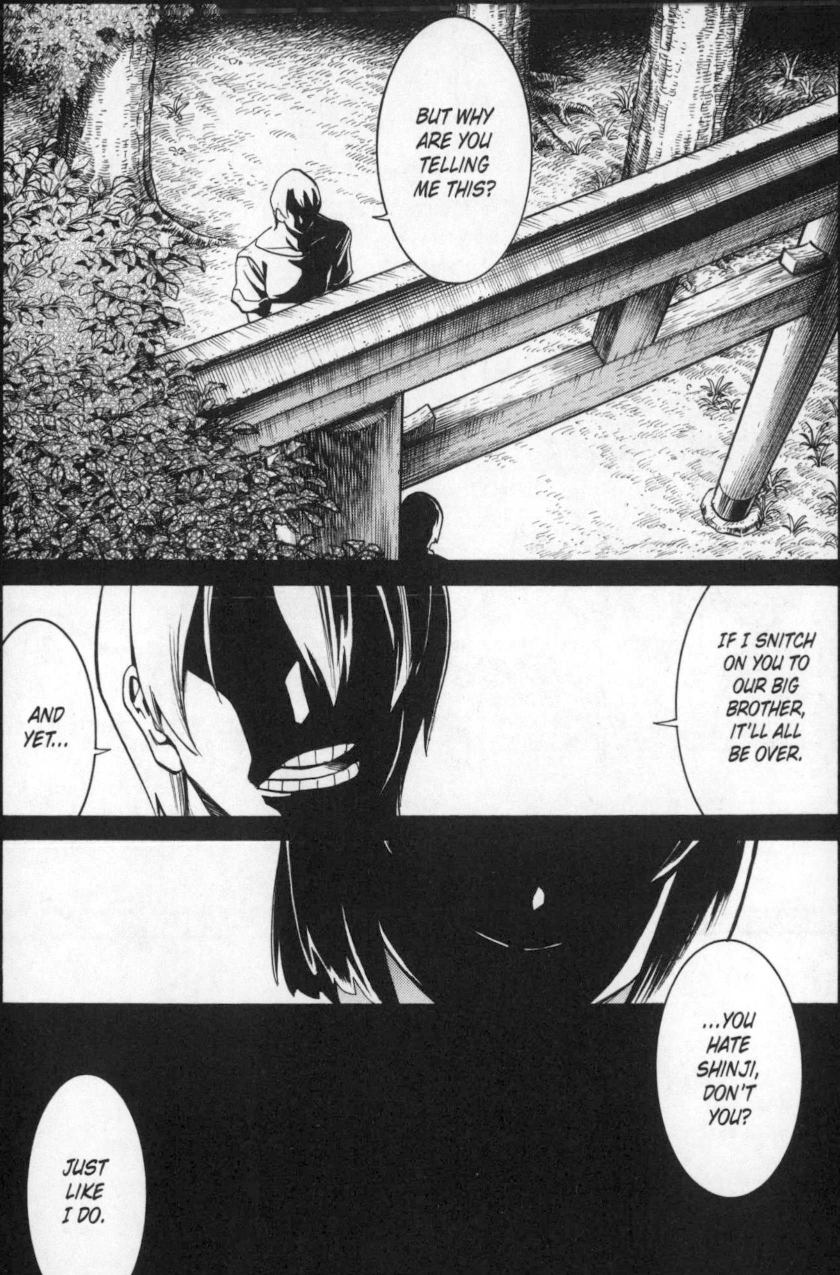
BUT WHY ARE YOU TELLING ME THIS?
IF I SNITCH ON YOU TO OUR BIG BROTHER, IT'LL ALL BE OVER.
AND YET...
...YOU HATE SHINJI, DON'T YOU?
JUST LIKE I DO.

MURCIÉLAGO

Yoshimurakana

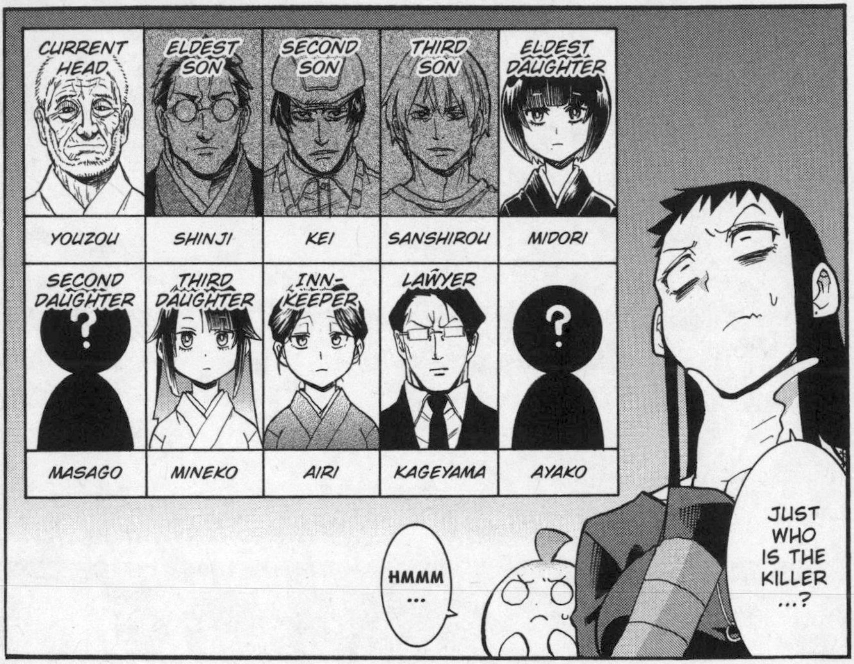
CURRENT HEAD
YOUZOU
ELDEST SON
SHINJI
SECOND SON
KEI
THIRD SON
SANSHIROU
ELDEST DAUGHTER
MIDORI
SECOND DAUGHTER
MASAGO
THIRD DAUGHTER
MINEKO
INN-KEEPER
AIRI
LAWYER
KAGEYAMA
AYAKO
JUST WHO IS THE KILLER ...?
HMMM ...

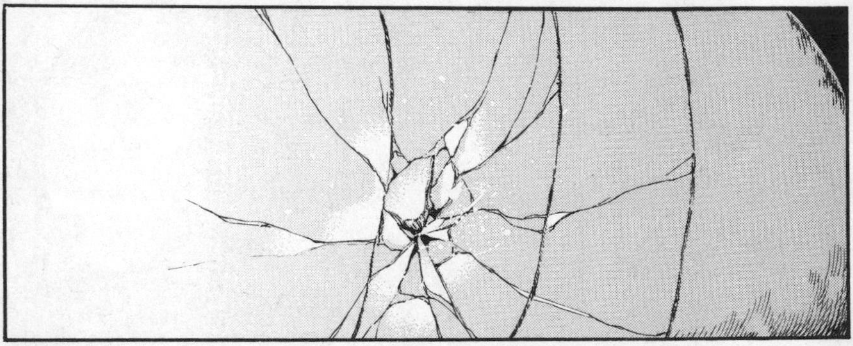

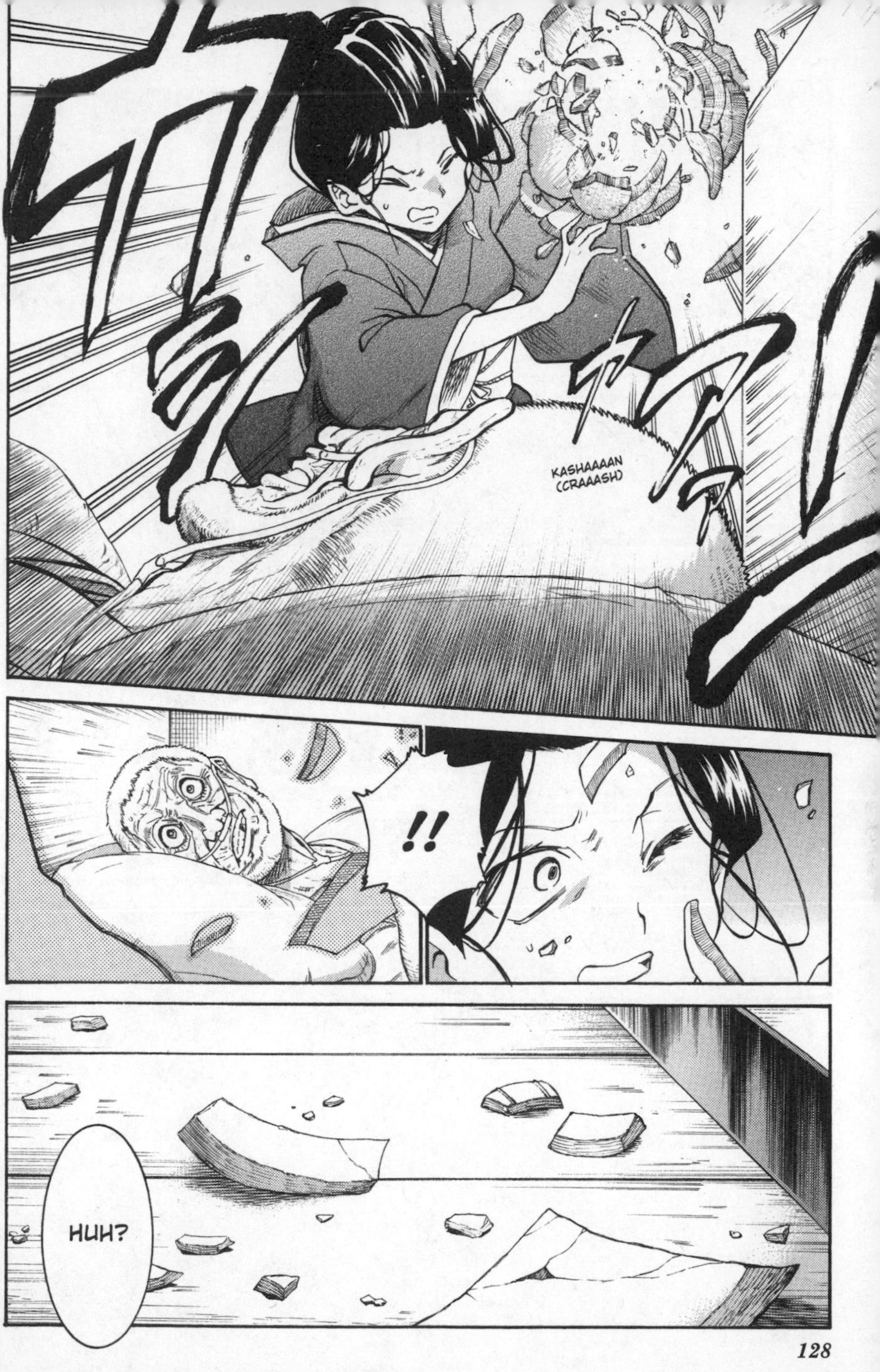
KASHAAAAN
(CRAAASH)
!!
HUH?

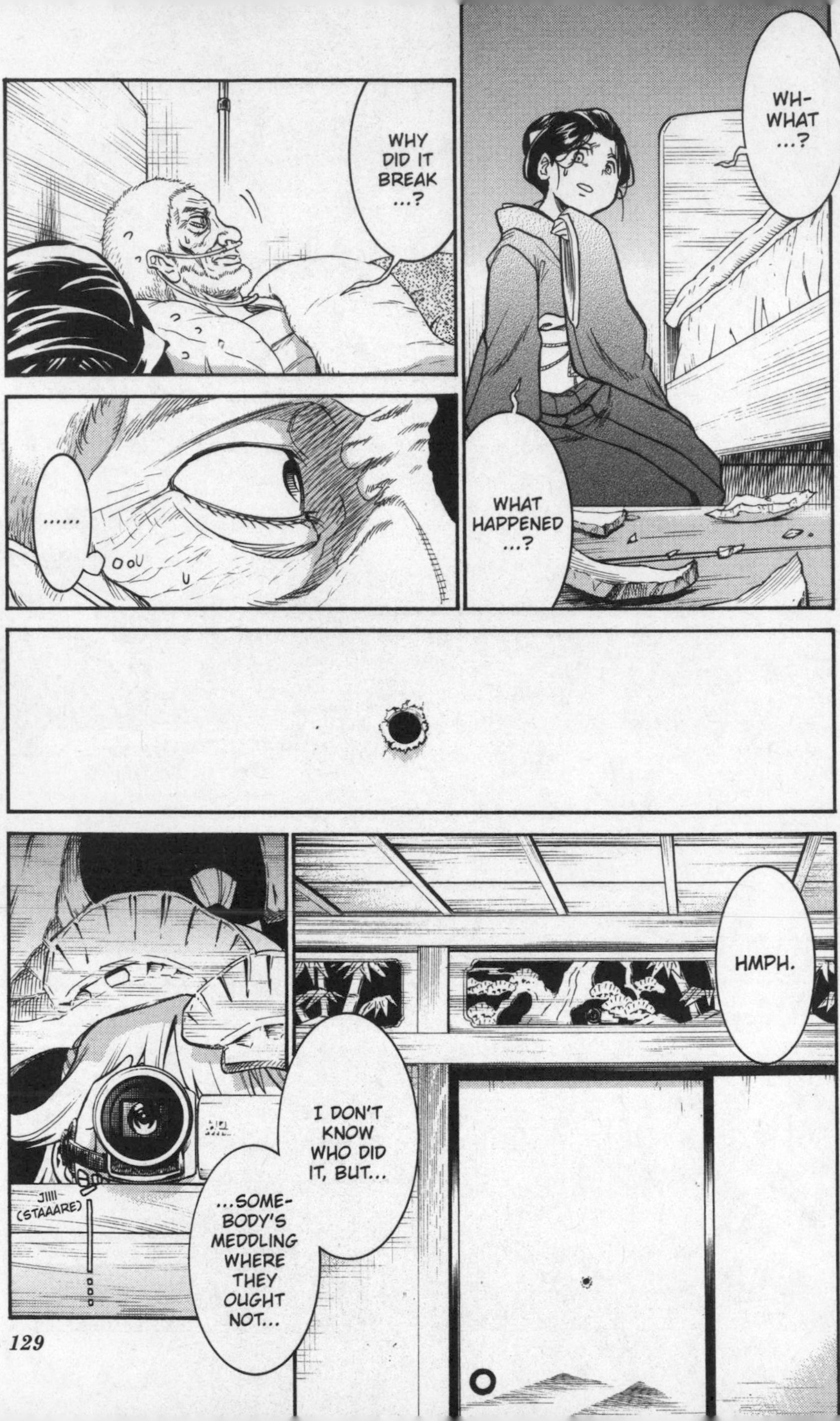
WH- WHAT ...?
WHAT HAPPENED ...?
WHY DID IT BREAK ...?
......
HMPH.
I DON'T KNOW WHO DID IT, BUT...
...SOME-BODY'S MEDDLING WHERE THEY OUGHT NOT...
JIIII (STAAARE)

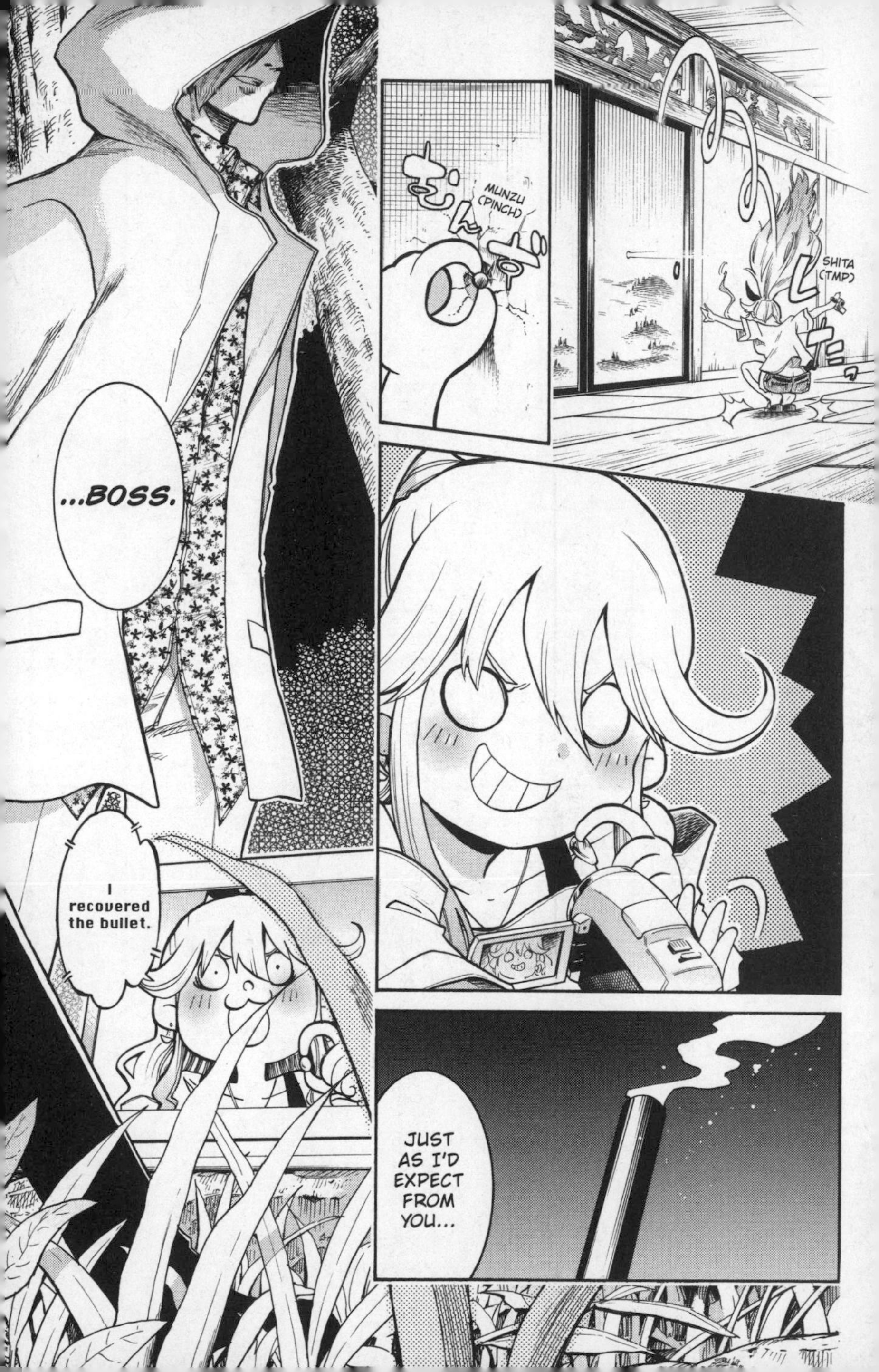
SHITA (TMP)
MUNZU (PINCH)
JUST AS I'D EXPECT FROM YOU...
...BOSS.
I recovered the bullet.

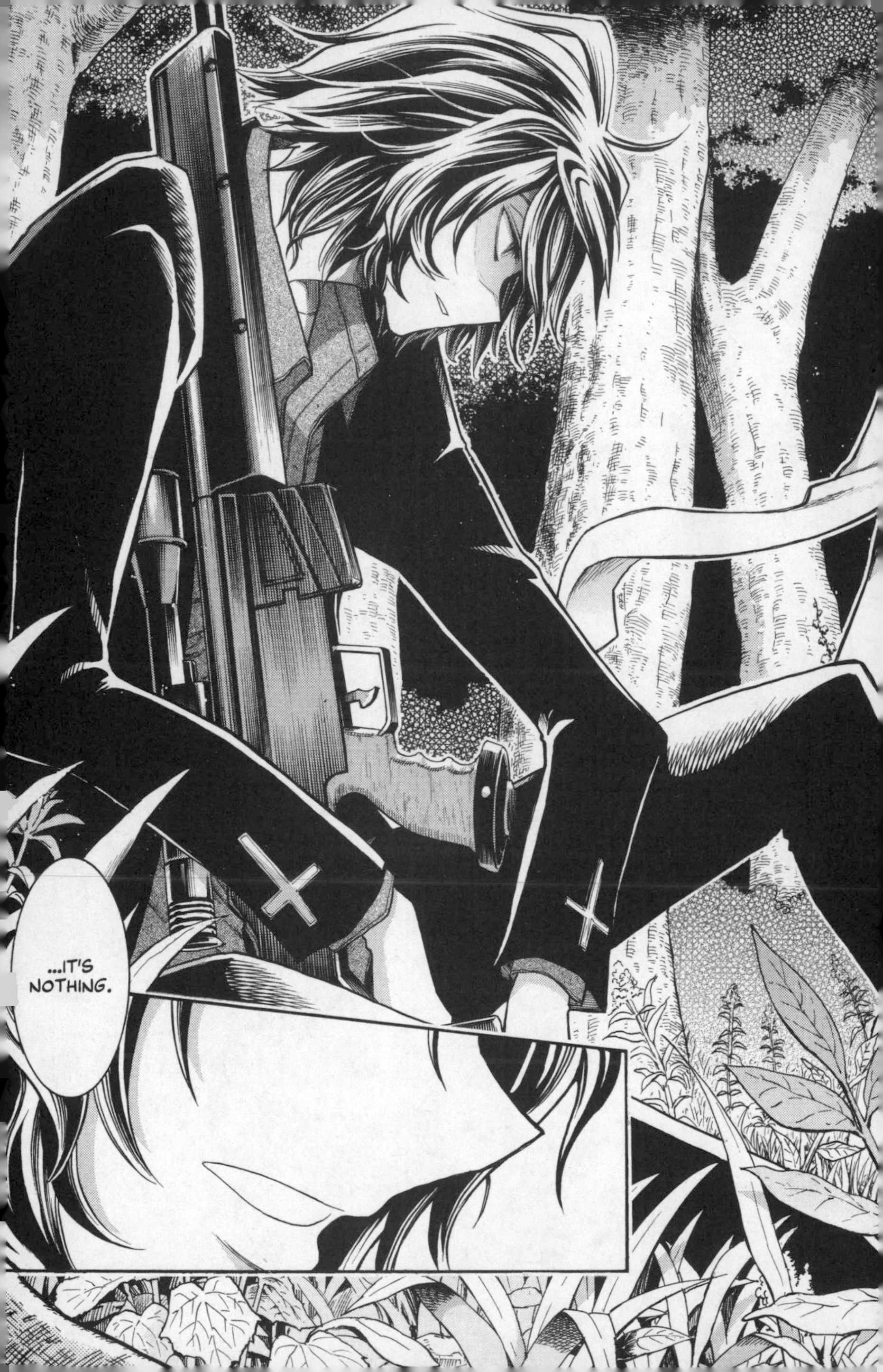
...IT'S NOTHING.

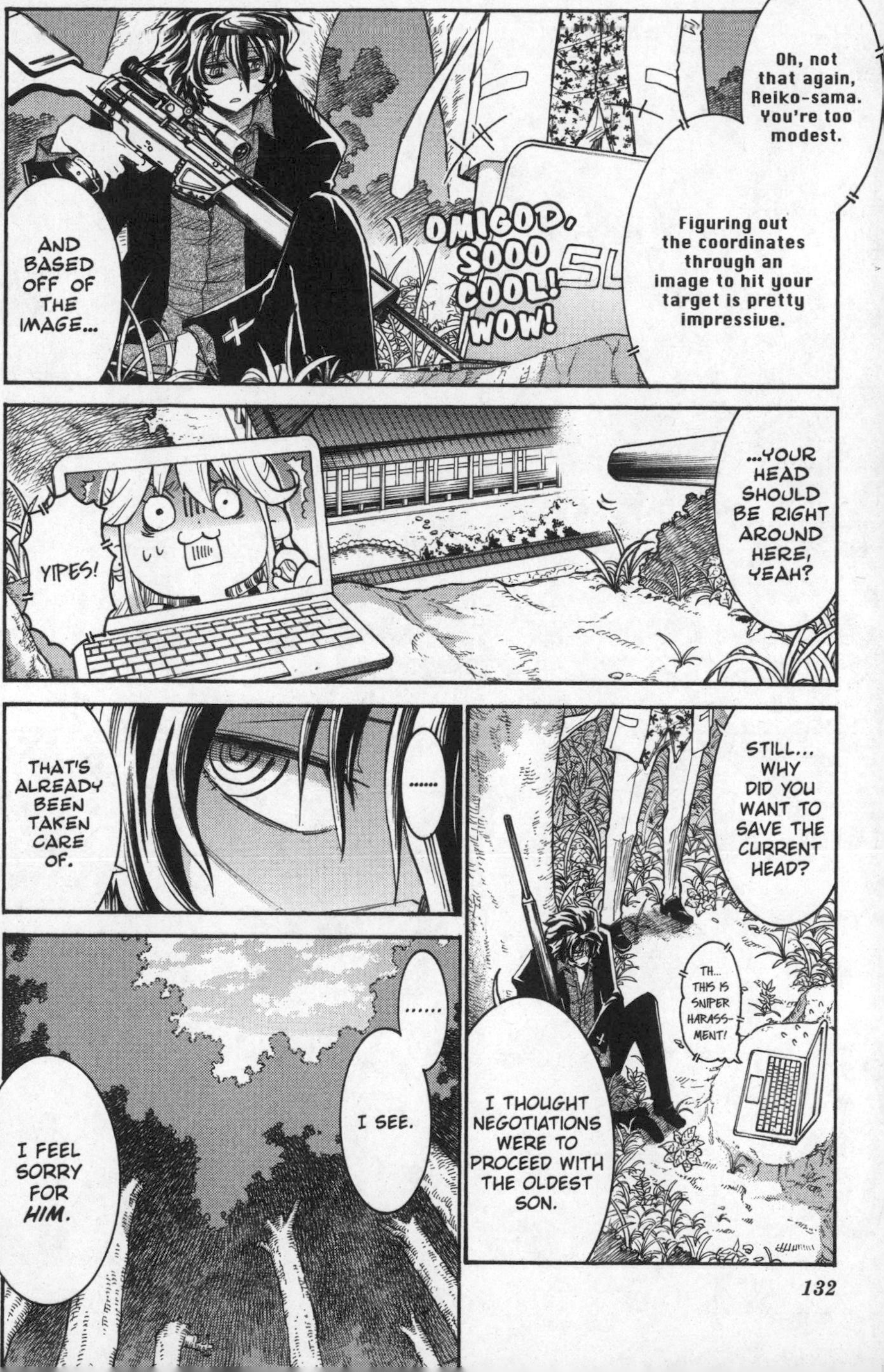

Oh, not that again, Reiko-sama. You're too modest.
Figuring out the coordinates through an image to hit your target is pretty impressive.
OMIGOD, SOOO COOL! WOW!
AND BASED OFF OF THE IMAGE...
...YOUR HEAD SHOULD BE RIGHT AROUND HERE, YEAH?
YIPES!
STILL... WHY DID YOU WANT TO SAVE THE CURRENT HEAD?
TH... THIS IS SNIPER HARASSMENT!
I THOUGHT NEGOTIATIONS WERE TO PROCEED WITH THE OLDEST SON.
......
THAT'S ALREADY BEEN TAKEN CARE OF.
......
I SEE.
I FEEL SORRY FOR *HIM*.

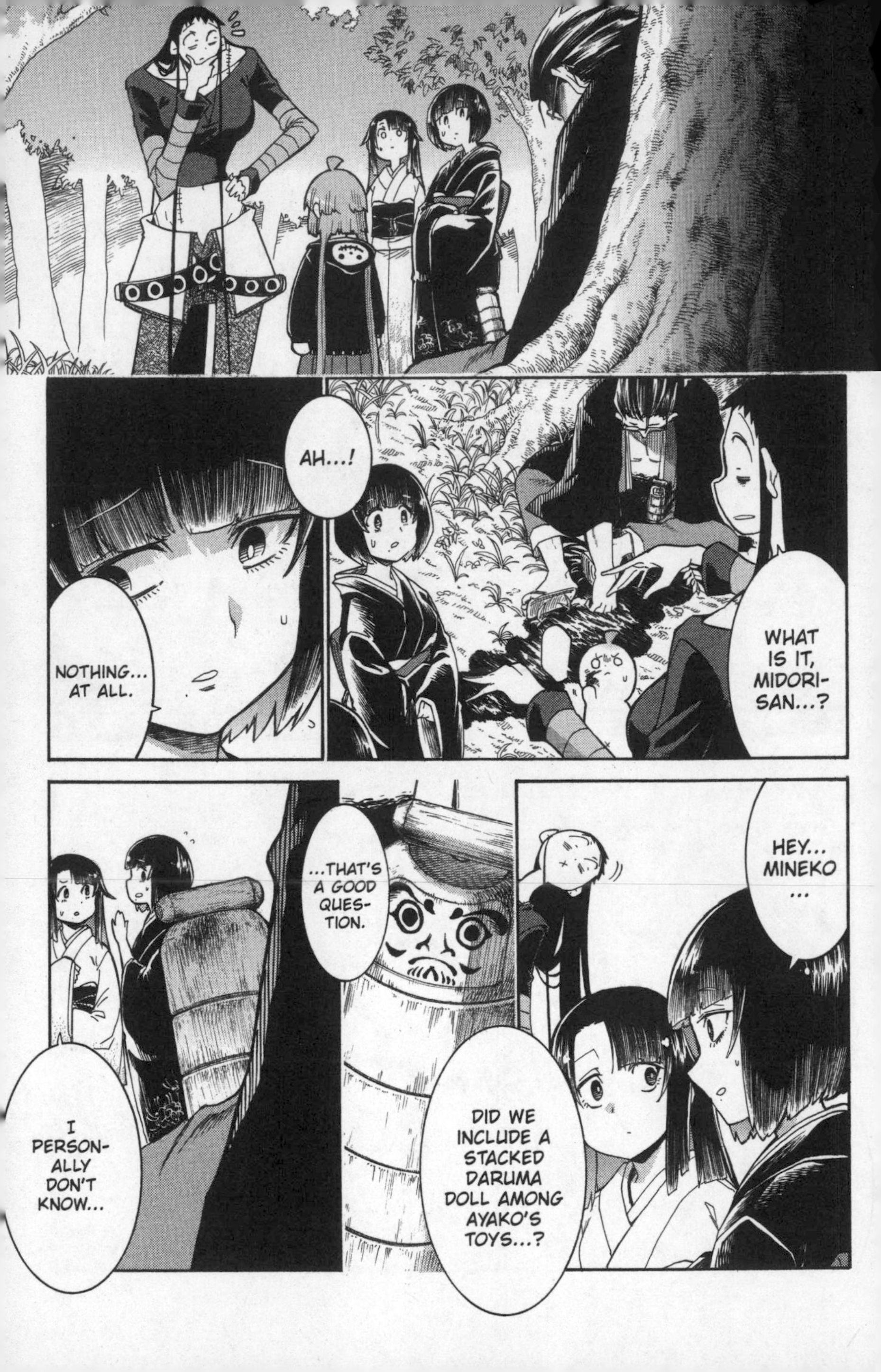
AH...!
WHAT IS IT, MIDORI-SAN...?
NOTHING... AT ALL.
HEY... MINEKO ...
DID WE INCLUDE A STACKED DARUMA DOLL AMONG AYAKO'S TOYS...?
...THAT'S A GOOD QUES-TION.
I PERSON-ALLY DON'T KNOW...

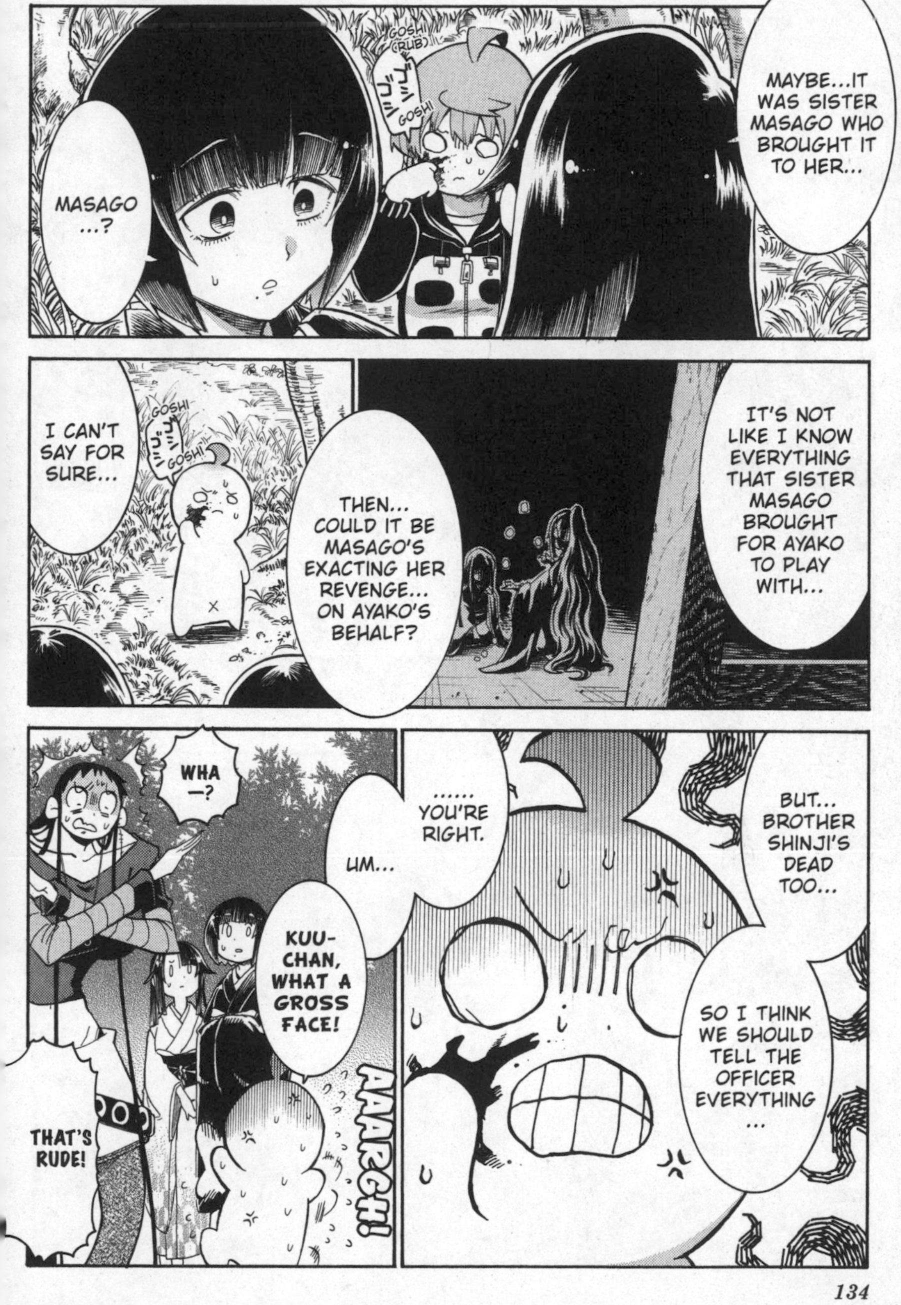
MAYBE...IT WAS SISTER MASAGO WHO BROUGHT IT TO HER...
GOSHI (RUB)
GOSHI
MASAGO ...?
IT'S NOT LIKE I KNOW EVERYTHING THAT SISTER MASAGO BROUGHT FOR AYAKO TO PLAY WITH...
THEN... COULD IT BE MASAGO'S EXACTING HER REVENGE... ON AYAKO'S BEHALF?
GOSHI
GOSHI
I CAN'T SAY FOR SURE...
BUT... BROTHER SHINJI'S DEAD TOO...
SO I THINK WE SHOULD TELL THE OFFICER EVERYTHING ...
...... YOU'RE RIGHT.
UM...
WHA —?
KUU-CHAN, WHAT A GROSS FACE!
AAARGH!
THAT'S RUDE!

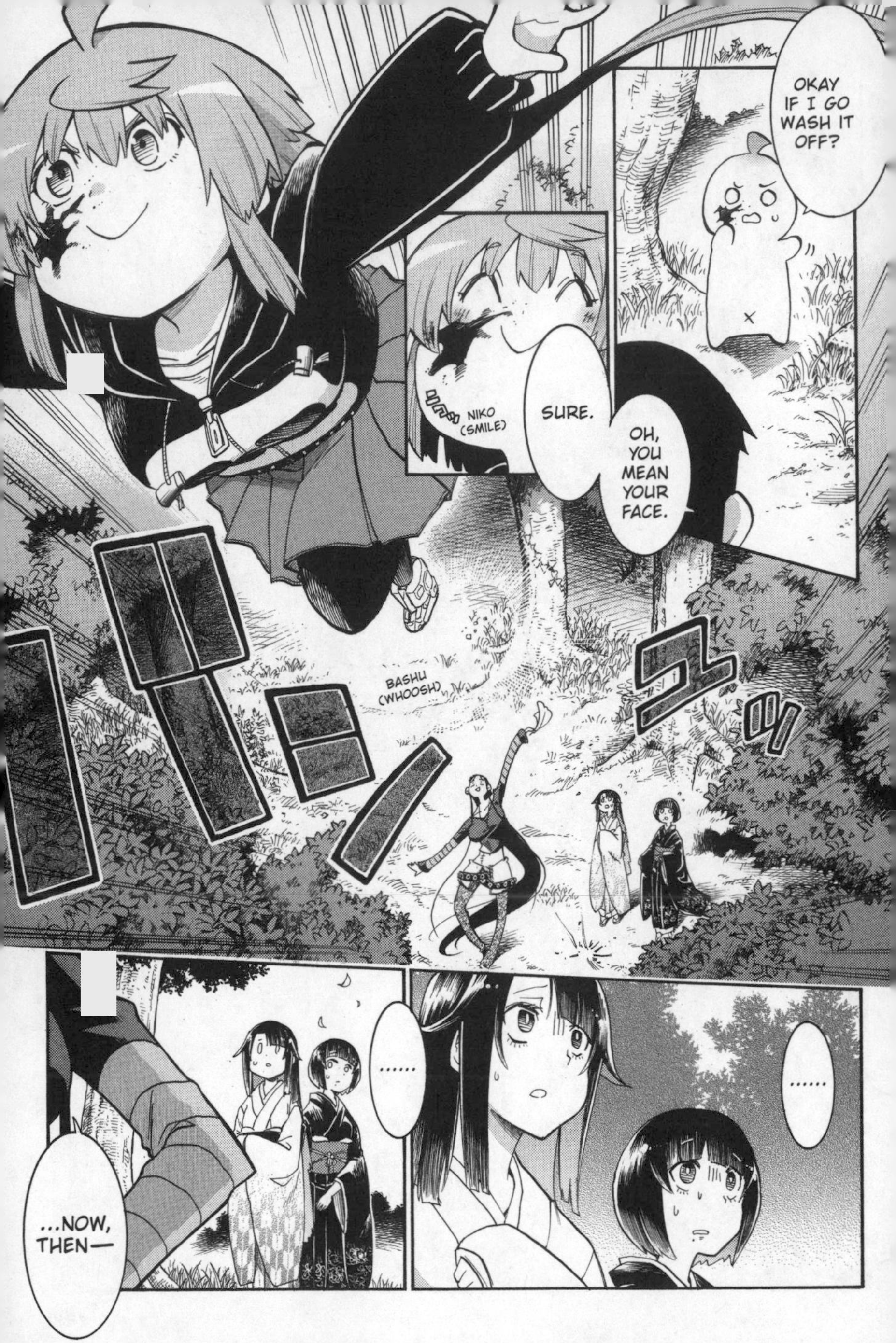
OKAY IF I GO WASH IT OFF?
OH, YOU MEAN YOUR FACE.
SURE.
NIKO (SMILE)
BASHU (WHOOSH)
......
......
...NOW, THEN—

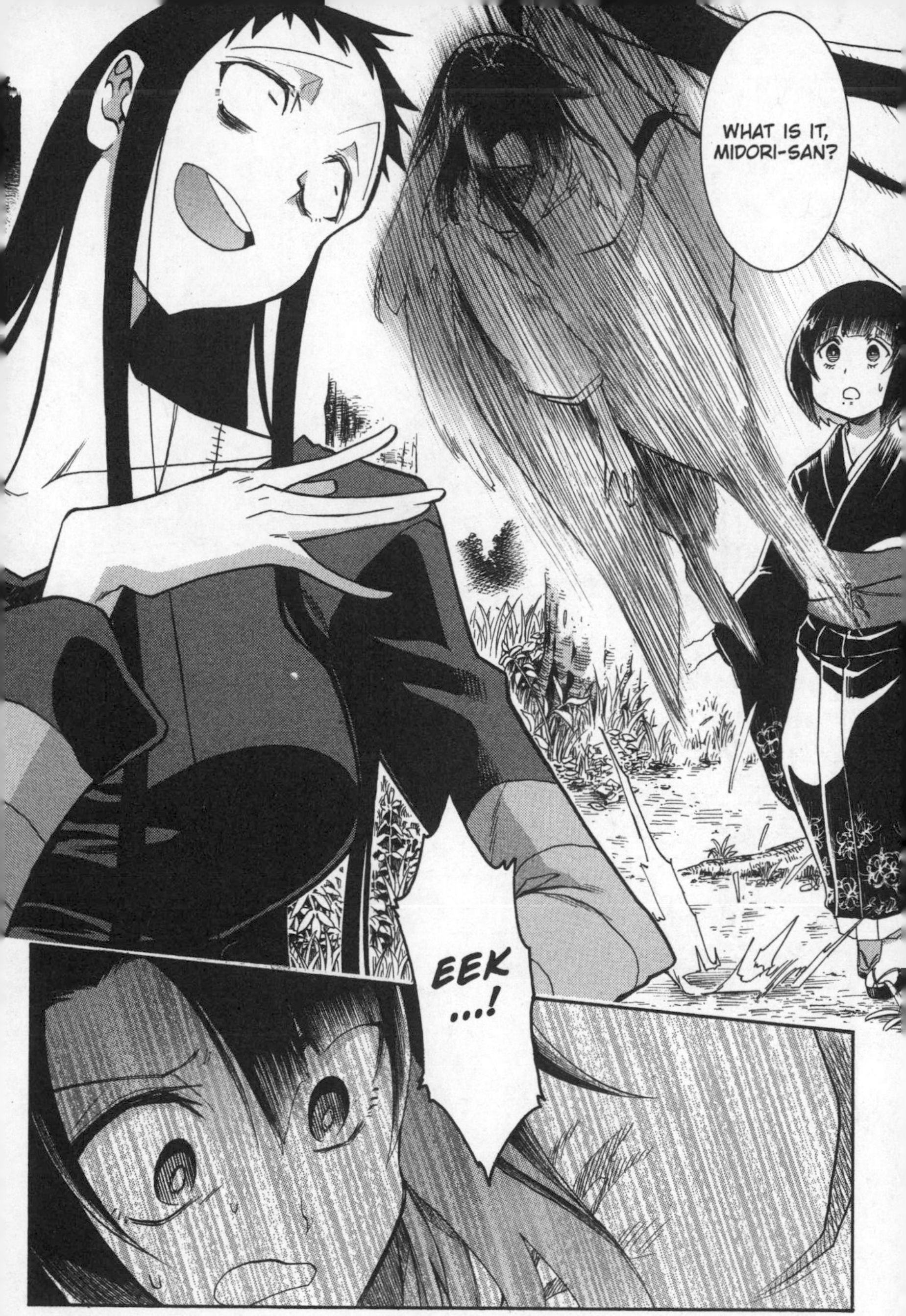
WHAT IS IT, MIDORI-SAN?
EEK ...!

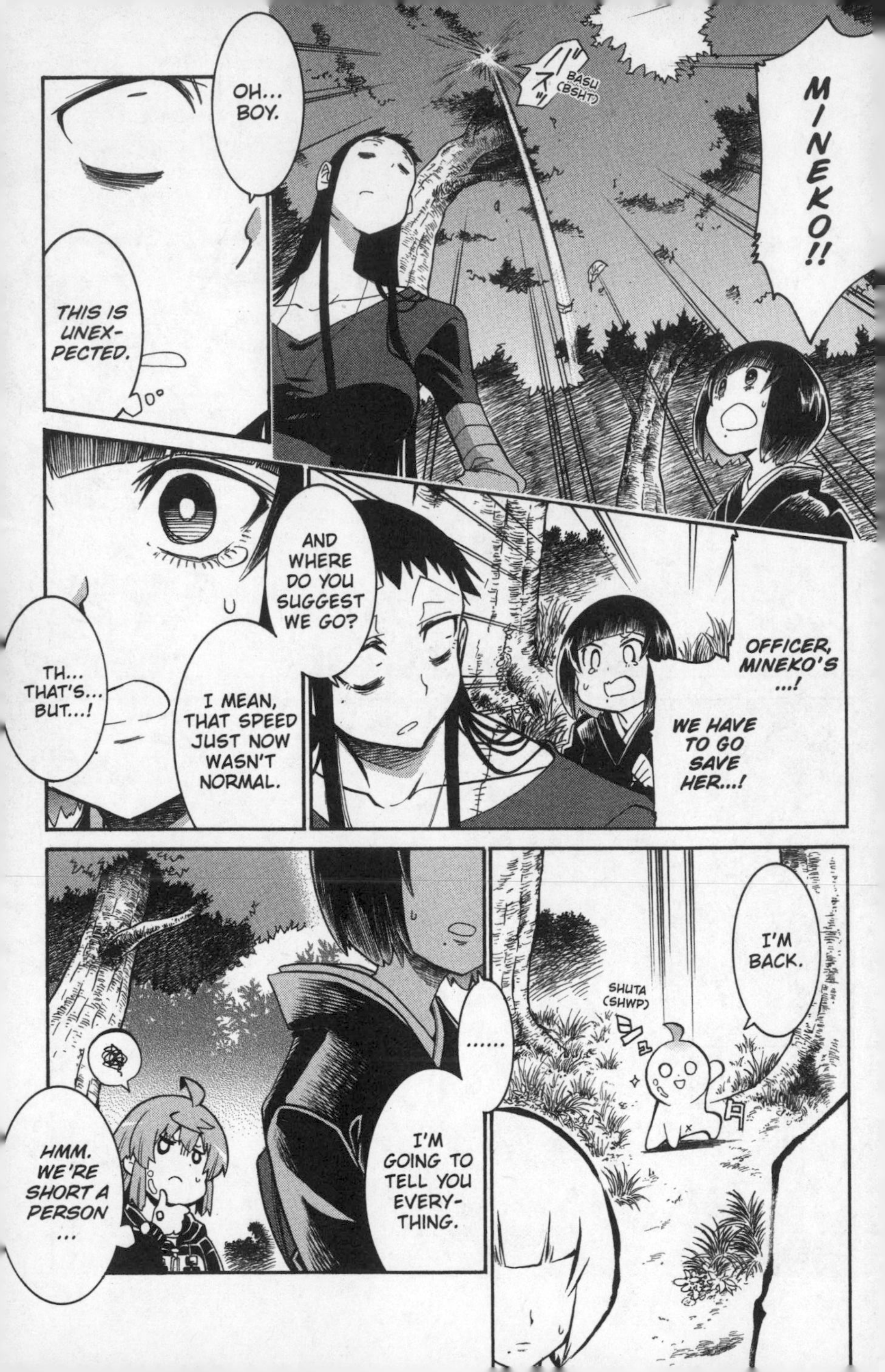
MINEKO!!
BASU (BSHT)
OH... BOY.
THIS IS UNEXPECTED.
OFFICER, MINEKO'S ...!
WE HAVE TO GO SAVE HER...!
AND WHERE DO YOU SUGGEST WE GO?
I MEAN, THAT SPEED JUST NOW WASN'T NORMAL.
TH... THAT'S... BUT...!
I'M BACK.
SHUTA (SHWP)
......
I'M GOING TO TELL YOU EVERYTHING.
HMM. WE'RE SHORT A PERSON ...

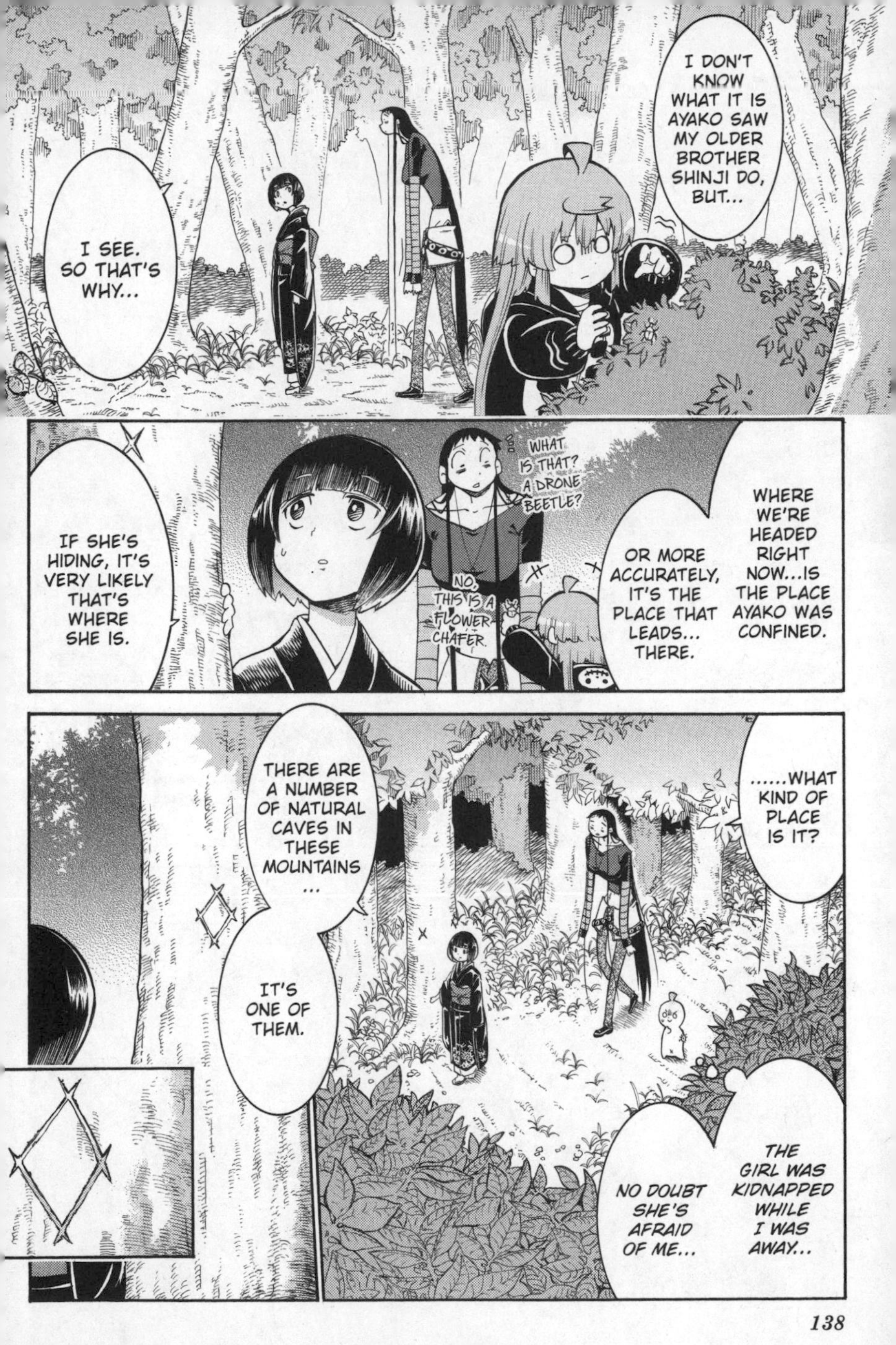

I DON'T KNOW WHAT IT IS AYAKO SAW MY OLDER BROTHER SHINJI DO, BUT...
I SEE. SO THAT'S WHY...
WHERE WE'RE HEADED RIGHT NOW...IS THE PLACE AYAKO WAS CONFINED.
OR MORE ACCURATELY, IT'S THE PLACE THAT LEADS... THERE.
WHAT IS THAT? A DRONE BEETLE?
NO, THIS IS A FLOWER CHAFER.
IF SHE'S HIDING, IT'S VERY LIKELY THAT'S WHERE SHE IS.
......WHAT KIND OF PLACE IS IT?
THERE ARE A NUMBER OF NATURAL CAVES IN THESE MOUNTAINS...
IT'S ONE OF THEM.
THE GIRL WAS KIDNAPPED WHILE I WAS AWAY...
NO DOUBT SHE'S AFRAID OF ME...

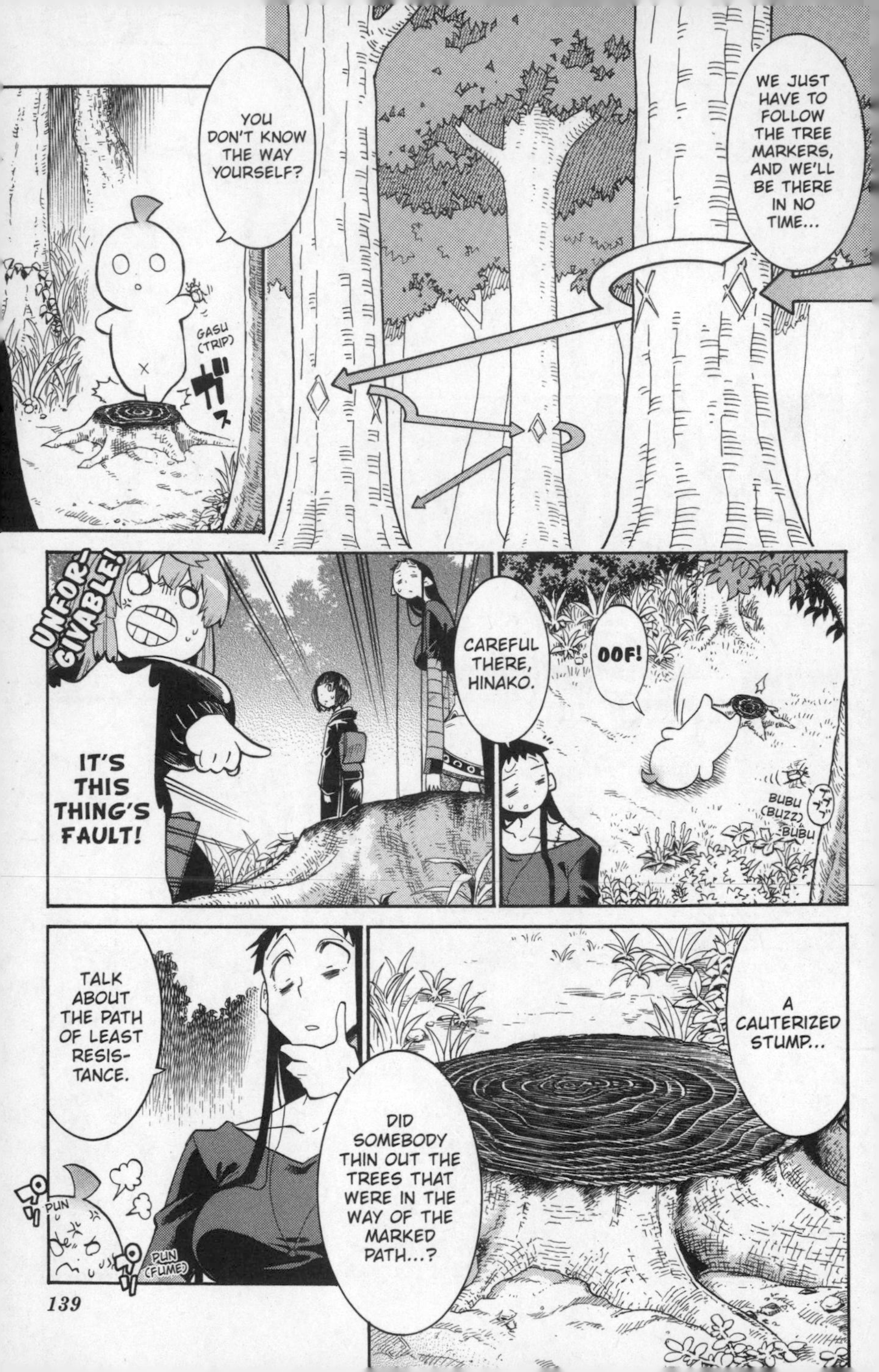
WE JUST HAVE TO FOLLOW THE TREE MARKERS, AND WE'LL BE THERE IN NO TIME...
YOU DON'T KNOW THE WAY YOURSELF?
GASU (TRIP)
OOF!
CAREFUL THERE, HINAKO.
BUBU (BUZZ) BUBU
UNFOR-GIVABLE!
IT'S THIS THING'S FAULT!
A CAUTERIZED STUMP...
DID SOMEBODY THIN OUT THE TREES THAT WERE IN THE WAY OF THE MARKED PATH...?
TALK ABOUT THE PATH OF LEAST RESIS-TANCE.
PUN
PUN (FUME)

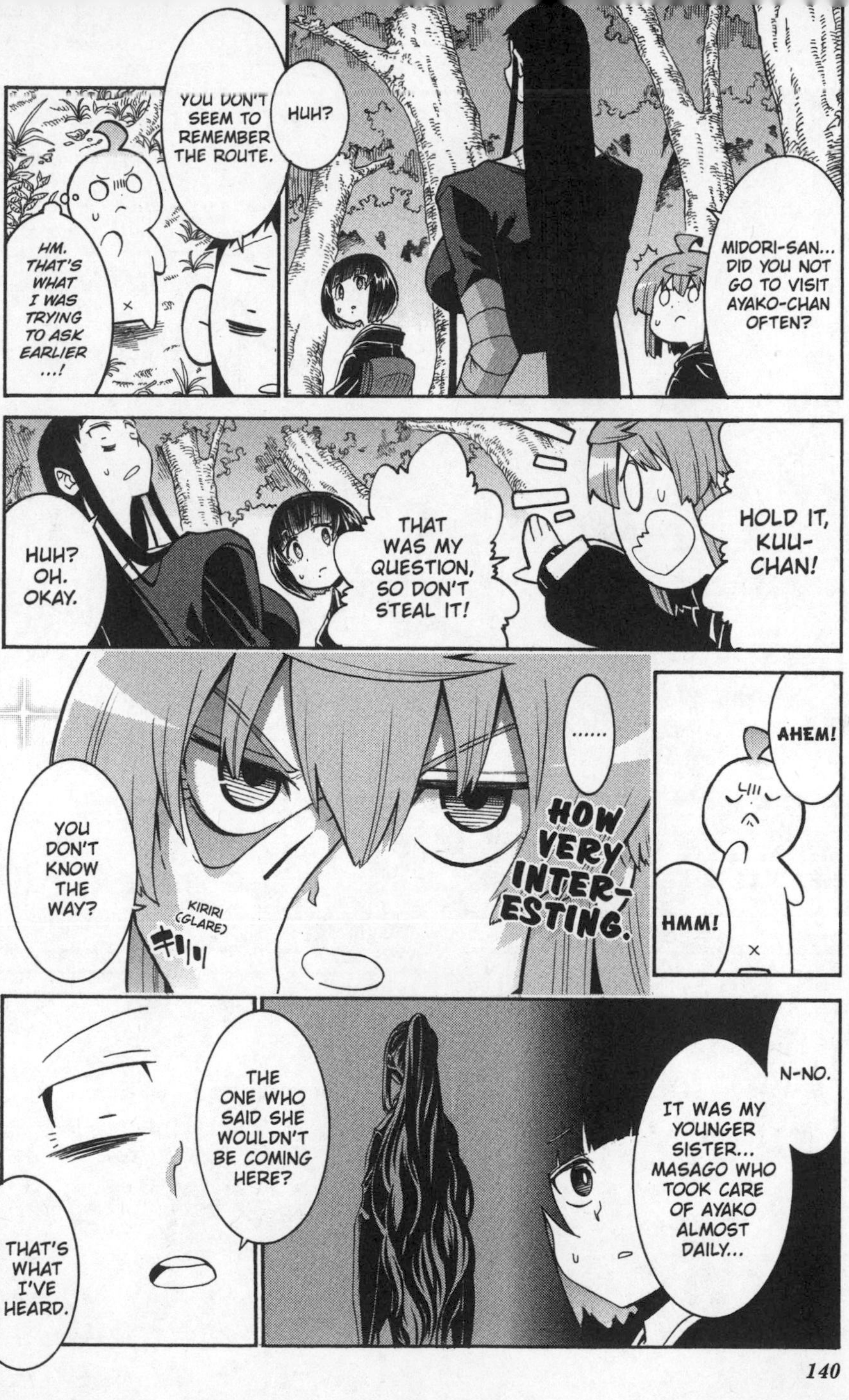
MIDORI-SAN... DID YOU NOT GO TO VISIT AYAKO-CHAN OFTEN?
HUH?
YOU DON'T SEEM TO REMEMBER THE ROUTE.
HM. THAT'S WHAT I WAS TRYING TO ASK EARLIER...!
HOLD IT, KUU-CHAN!
THAT WAS MY QUESTION, SO DON'T STEAL IT!
HUH? OH. OKAY.
AHEM!
HMM!
......
HOW VERY INTER-ESTING.
YOU DON'T KNOW THE WAY?
KIRIRI (GLARE)
N-NO.
IT WAS MY YOUNGER SISTER... MASAGO WHO TOOK CARE OF AYAKO ALMOST DAILY...
THE ONE WHO SAID SHE WOULDN'T BE COMING HERE?
THAT'S WHAT I'VE HEARD.

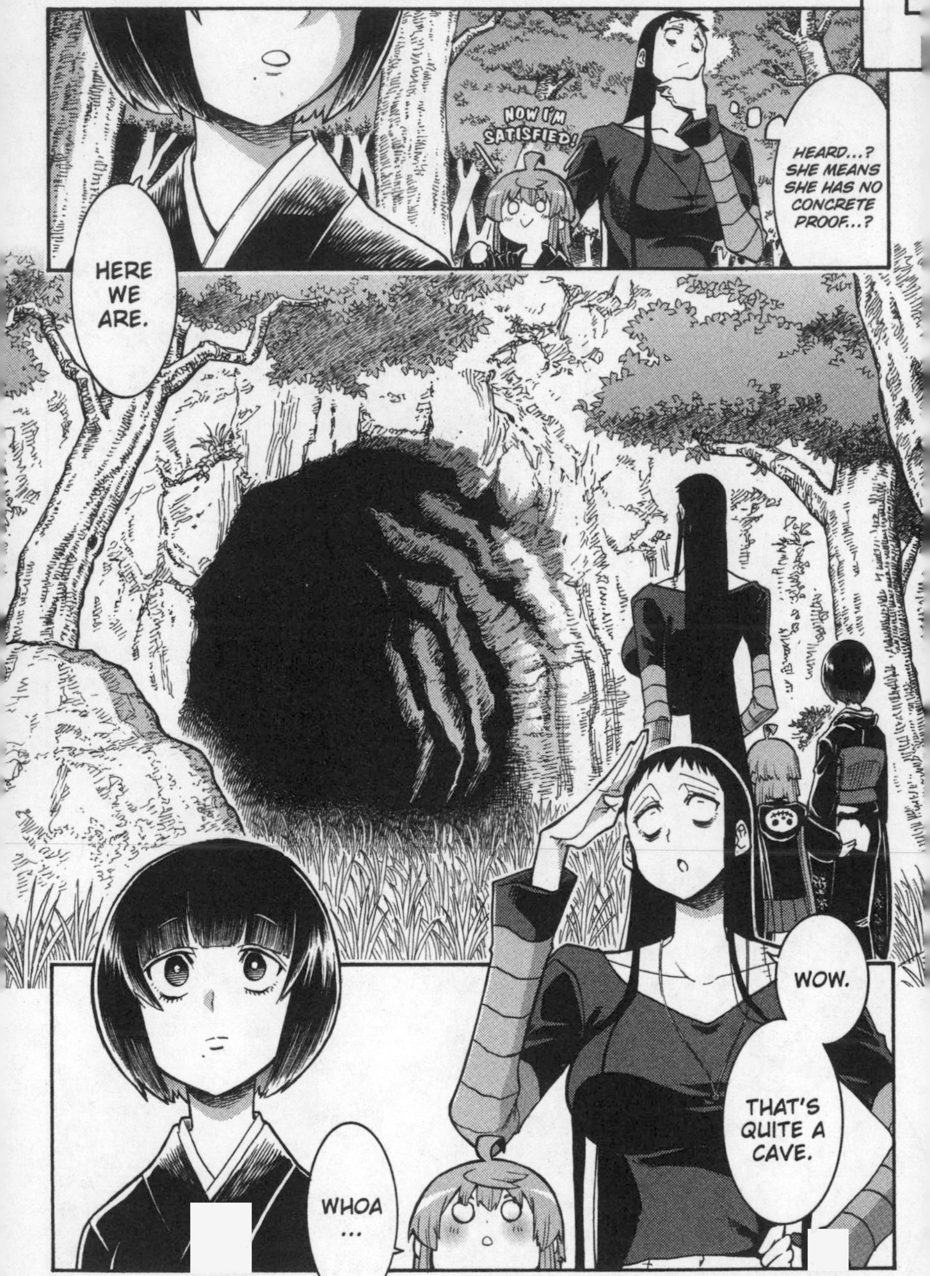
HEARD...? SHE MEANS SHE HAS NO CONCRETE PROOF...?
NOW I'M SATISFIED!
HERE WE ARE.
WOW.
THAT'S QUITE A CAVE.
WHOA ...

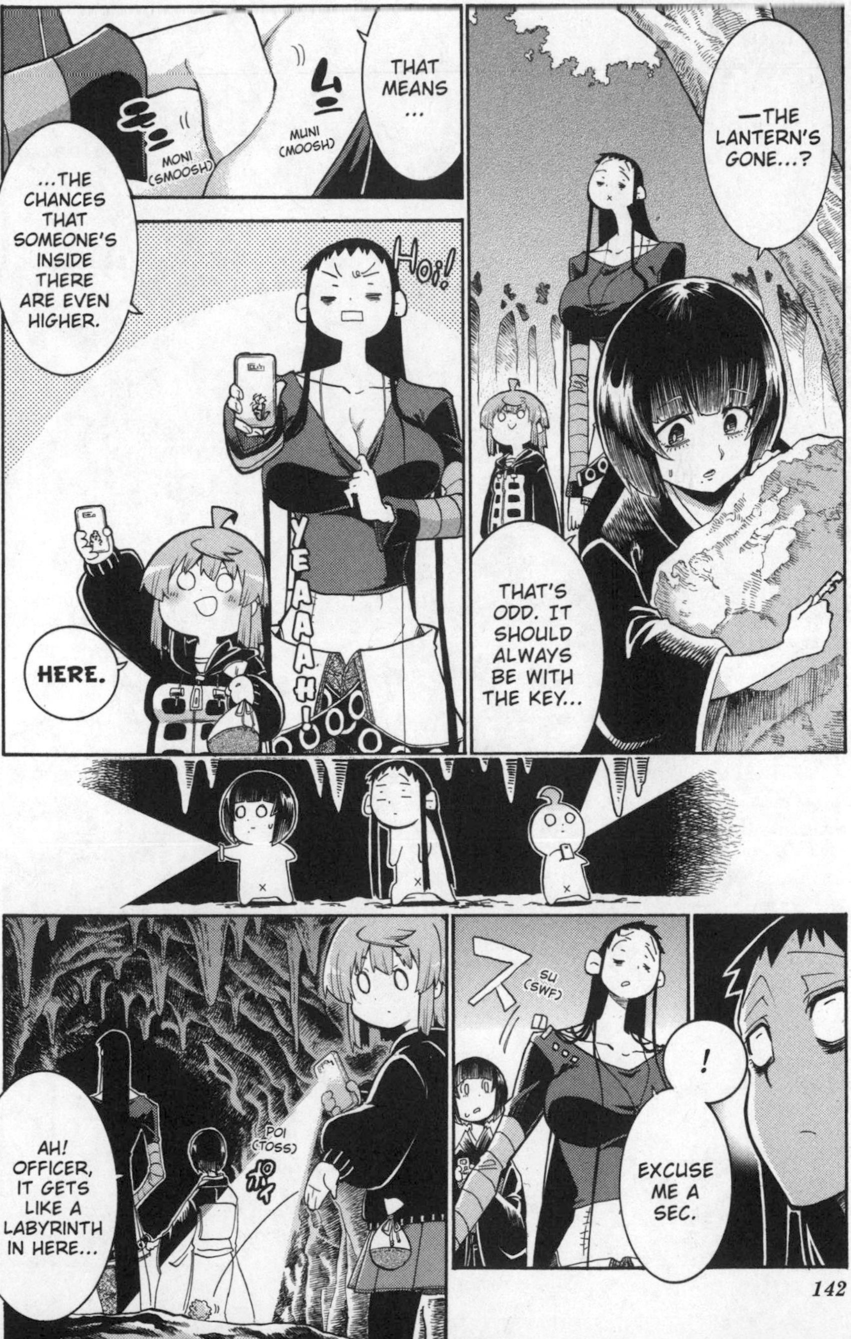
—THE LANTERN'S GONE...?
THAT'S ODD. IT SHOULD ALWAYS BE WITH THE KEY...
THAT MEANS ...
MUNI (MOOSH)
MONI (SMOOSH)
...THE CHANCES THAT SOMEONE'S INSIDE THERE ARE EVEN HIGHER.
Hoi!
YEAAAAH!
HERE.
!
EXCUSE ME A SEC.
SU (SWF)
POI (TOSS)
AH! OFFICER, IT GETS LIKE A LABYRINTH IN HERE...

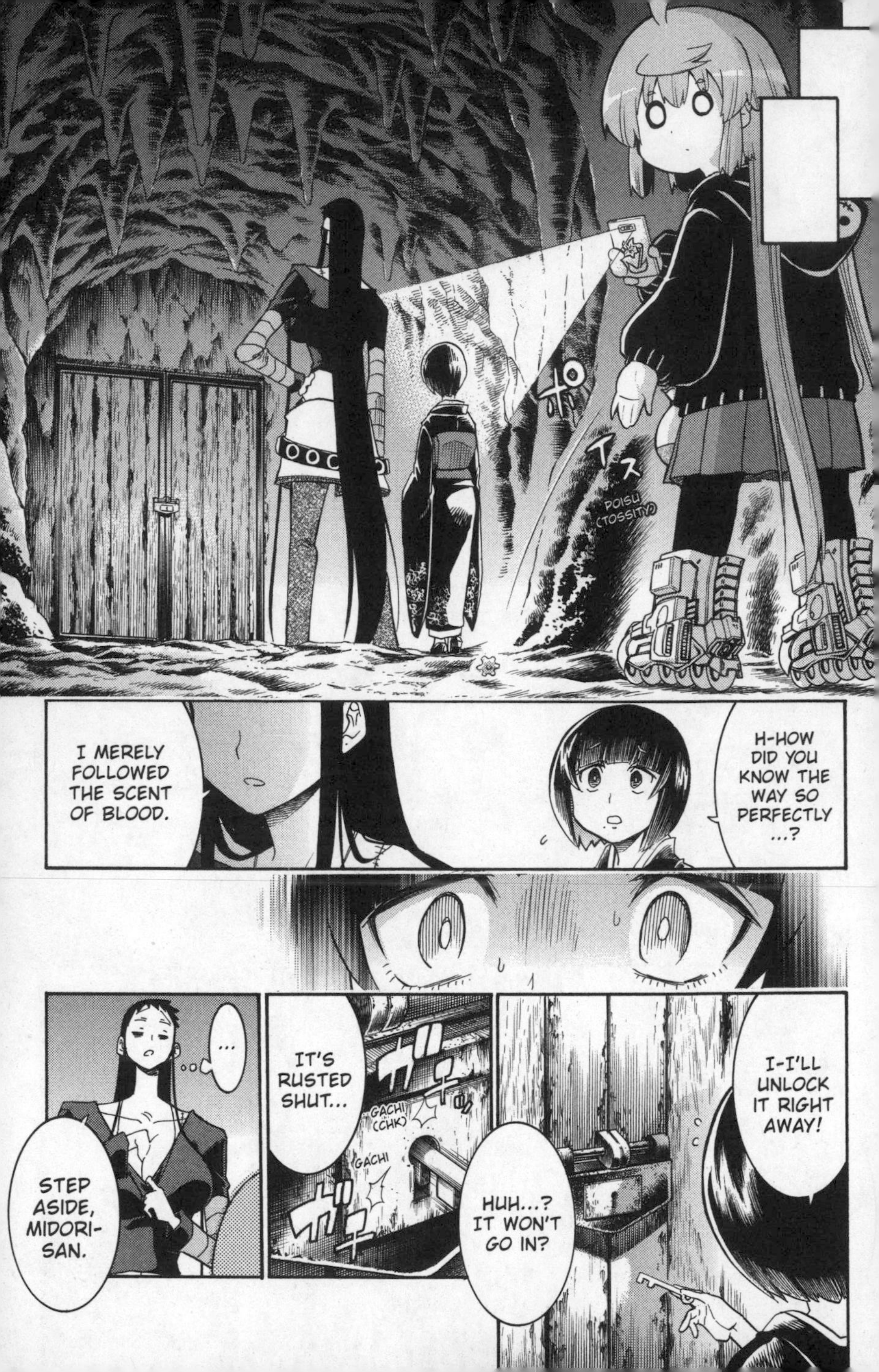
POISU (TOSSITY)
H-HOW DID YOU KNOW THE WAY SO PERFECTLY ...?
I MERELY FOLLOWED THE SCENT OF BLOOD.
I-I'LL UNLOCK IT RIGHT AWAY!
HUH...? IT WON'T GO IN?
IT'S RUSTED SHUT...
GACHI (CHK)
GACHI
...
STEP ASIDE, MIDORI-SAN.

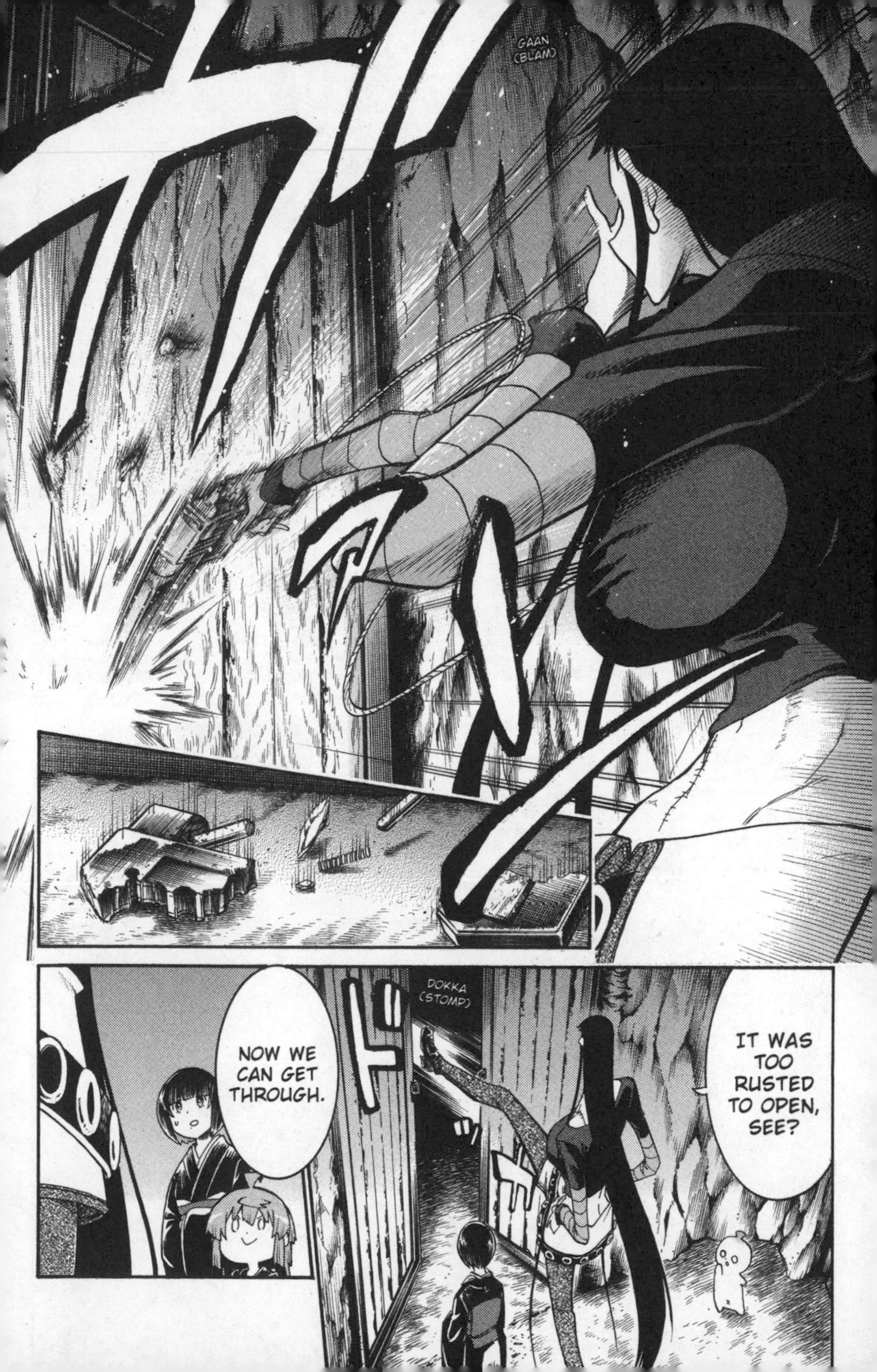
GAAN (BLAM)
DOKKA (STOMP)
IT WAS TOO RUSTED TO OPEN, SEE?
NOW WE CAN GET THROUGH.

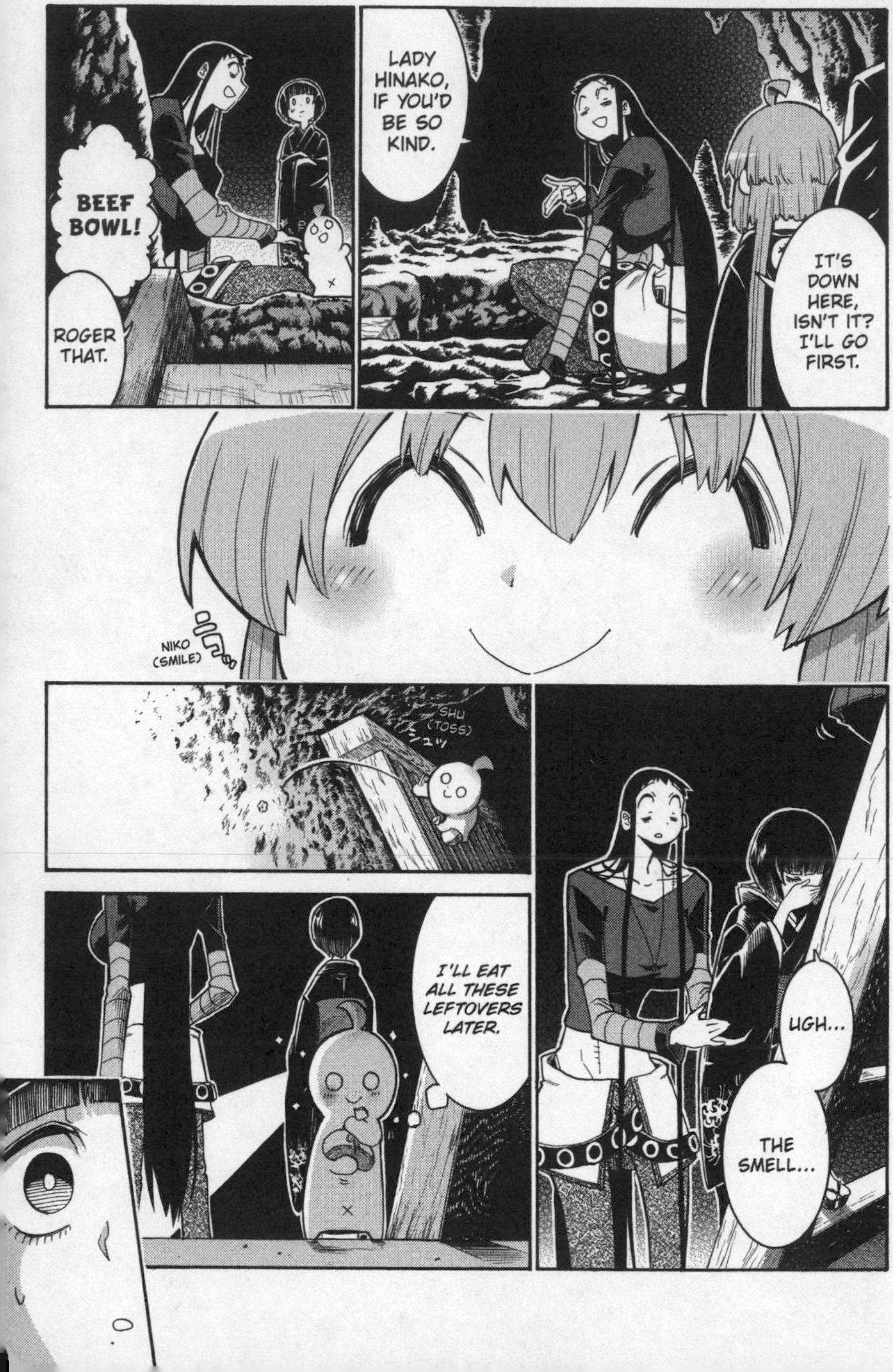

LADY HINAKO, IF YOU'D BE SO KIND.
IT'S DOWN HERE, ISN'T IT? I'LL GO FIRST.
BEEF BOWL!
ROGER THAT.
NIKO (SMILE)
UGH...
THE SMELL...
SHU (TOSS)
I'LL EAT ALL THESE LEFTOVERS LATER.

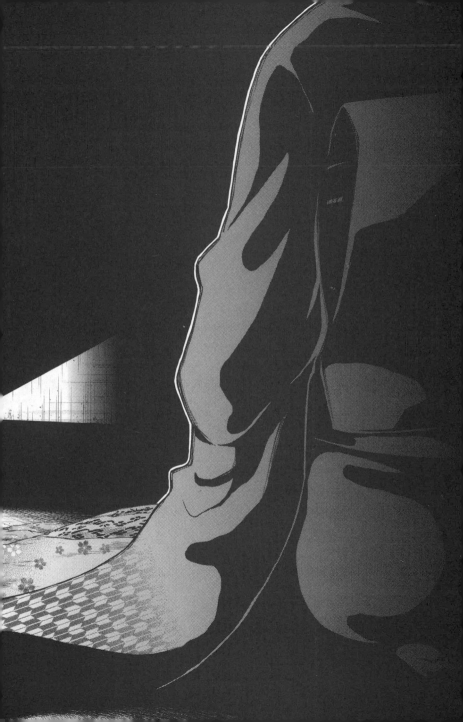

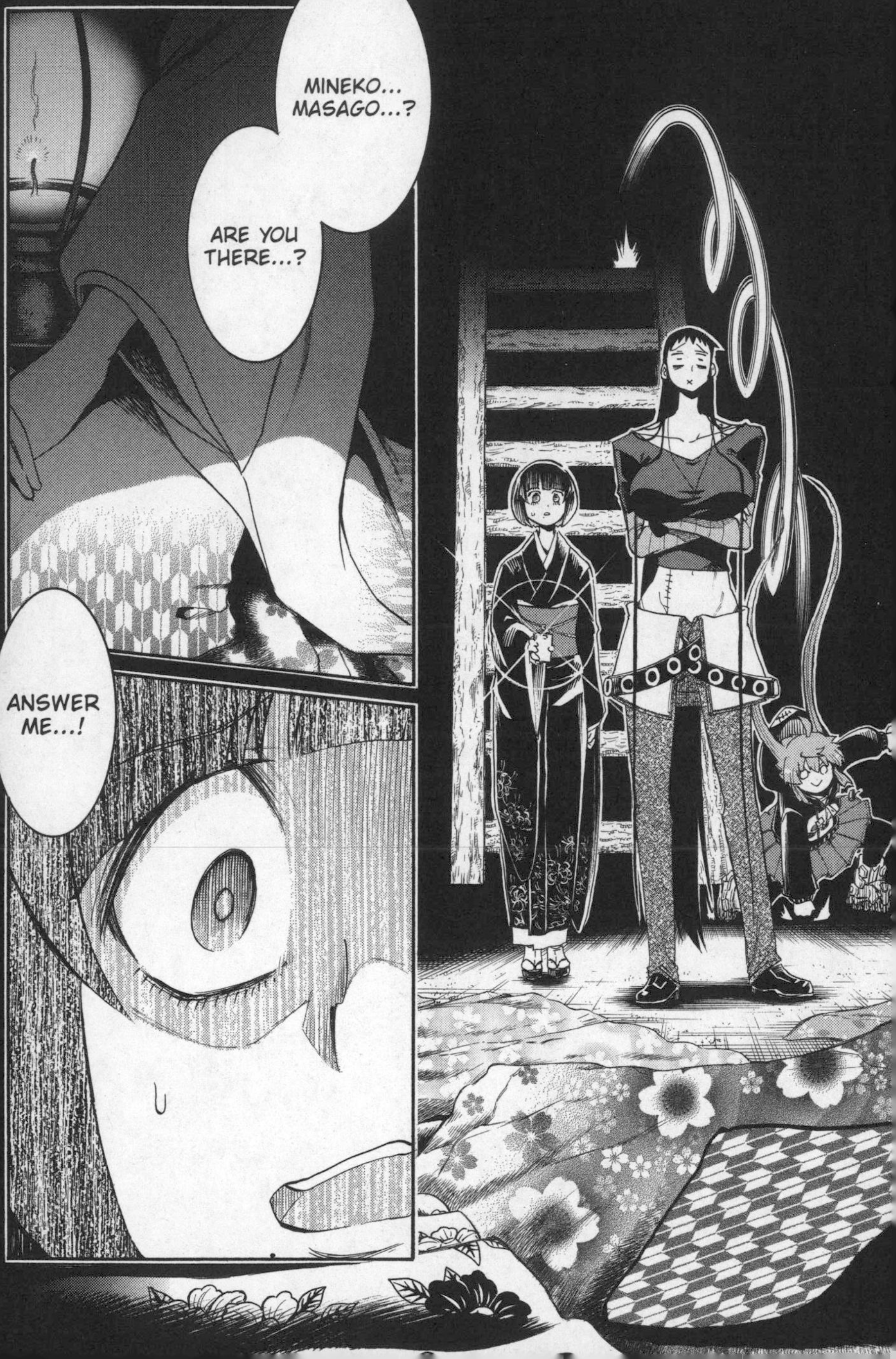
MINEKO... MASAGO...?
ARE YOU THERE...?
ANSWER ME...!

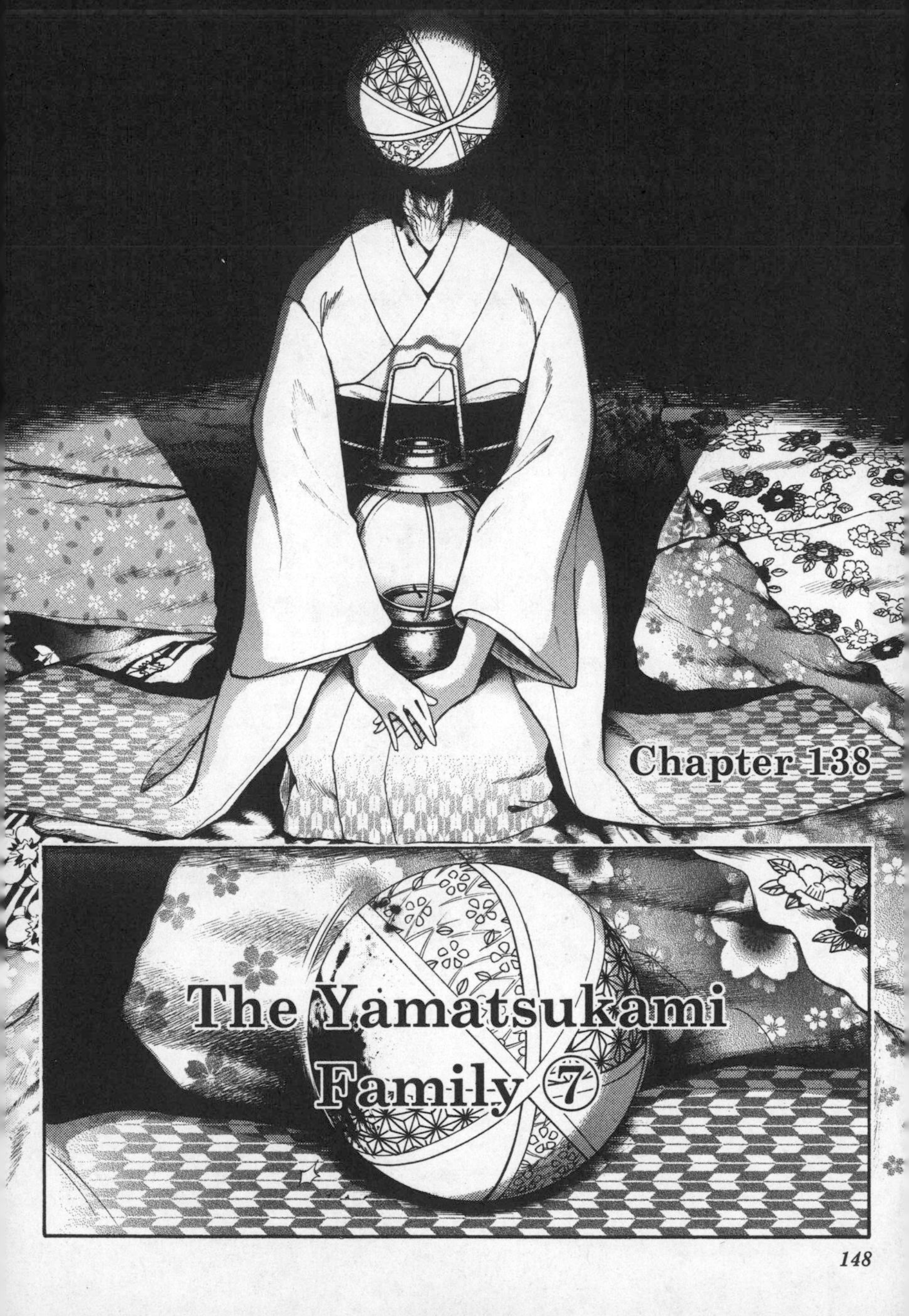
Chapter 138
The Yamatsukami Family 7

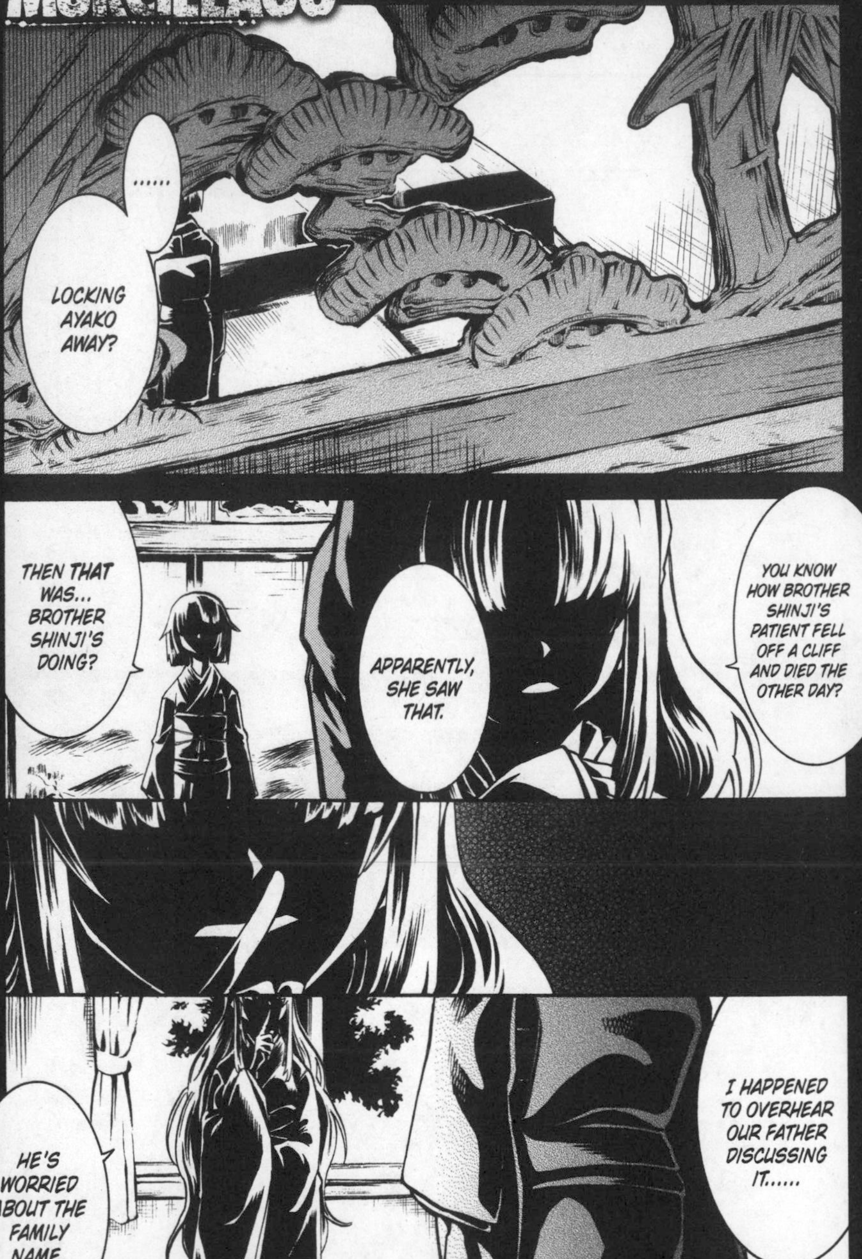
......
LOCKING AYAKO AWAY?
YOU KNOW HOW BROTHER SHINJI'S PATIENT FELL OFF A CLIFF AND DIED THE OTHER DAY?
APPARENTLY, SHE SAW THAT.
THEN THAT WAS... BROTHER SHINJI'S DOING?
I HAPPENED TO OVERHEAR OUR FATHER DISCUSSING IT......
HE'S WORRIED ABOUT THE FAMILY NAME.

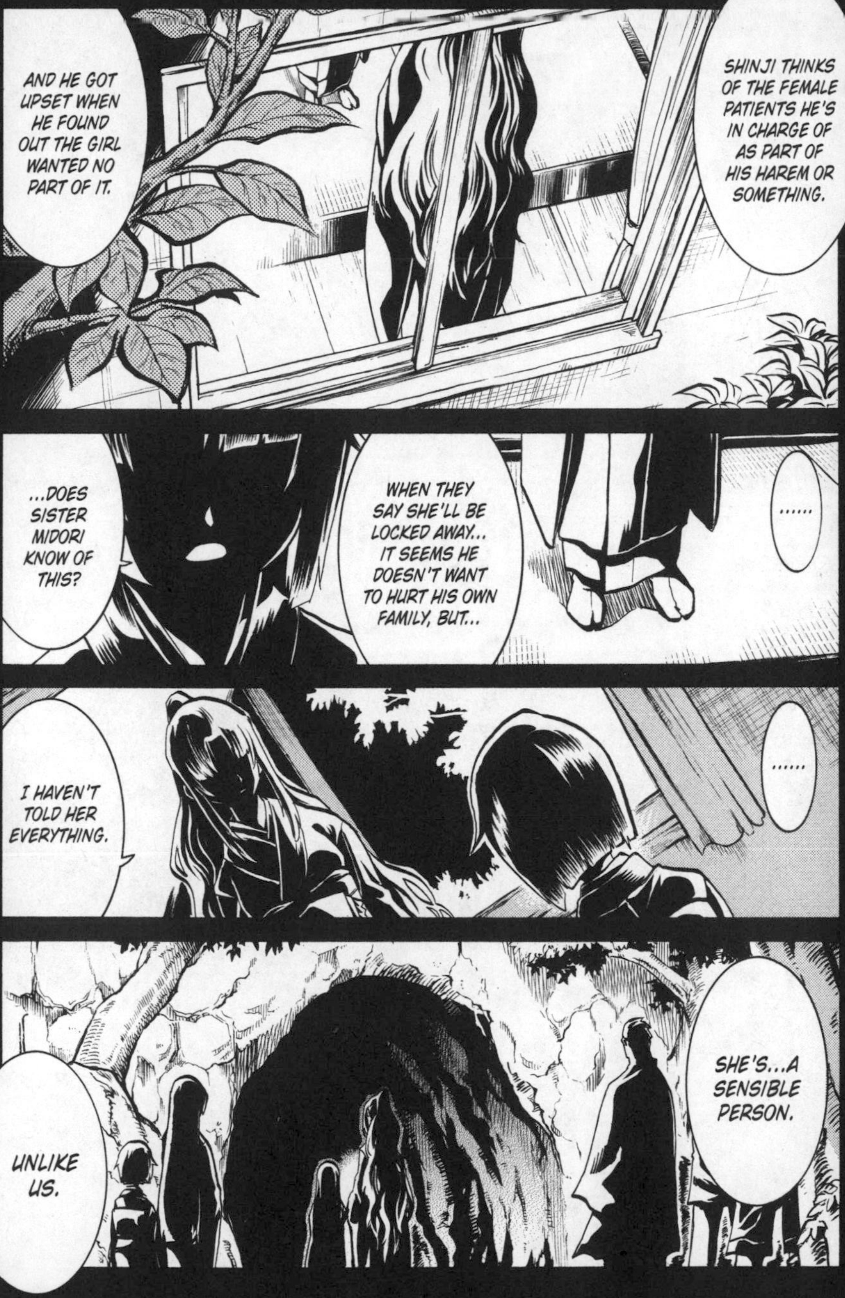
SHINJI THINKS OF THE FEMALE PATIENTS HE'S IN CHARGE OF AS PART OF HIS HAREM OR SOMETHING.
AND HE GOT UPSET WHEN HE FOUND OUT THE GIRL WANTED NO PART OF IT.
......
WHEN THEY SAY SHE'LL BE LOCKED AWAY... IT SEEMS HE DOESN'T WANT TO HURT HIS OWN FAMILY, BUT...
...DOES SISTER MIDORI KNOW OF THIS?
......
I HAVEN'T TOLD HER EVERYTHING.
SHE'S...A SENSIBLE PERSON.
UNLIKE US.

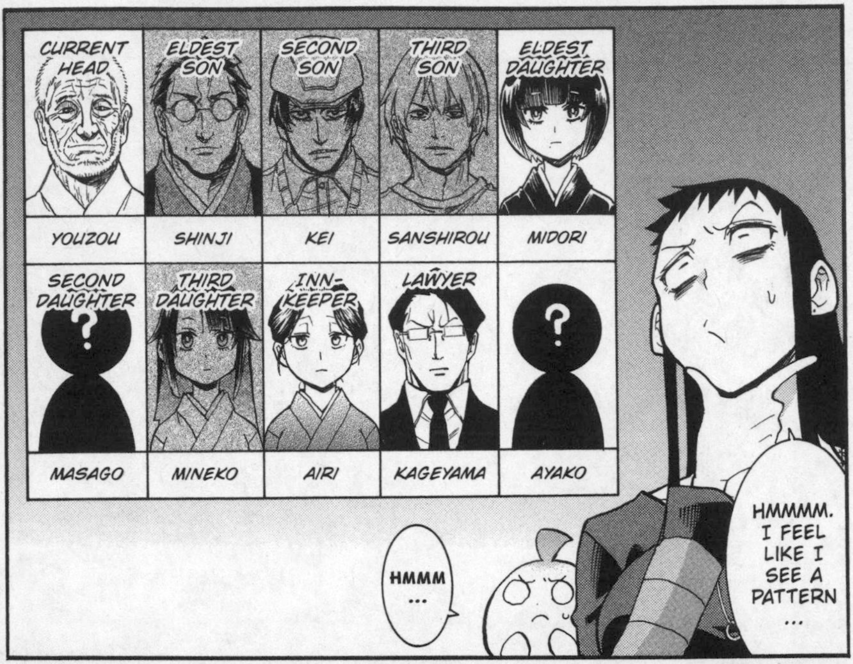
CURRENT HEAD
YOUZOU
ELDEST SON
SHINJI
SECOND SON
KEI
THIRD SON
SANSHIROU
ELDEST DAUGHTER
MIDORI
SECOND DAUGHTER
?
MASAGO
THIRD DAUGHTER
MINEKO
INN-KEEPER
AIRI
LAWYER
KAGEYAMA
?
AYAKO
HMMMM. I FEEL LIKE I SEE A PATTERN ...
HMMM ...

MURCIÉLAGO

Yoshimurakana

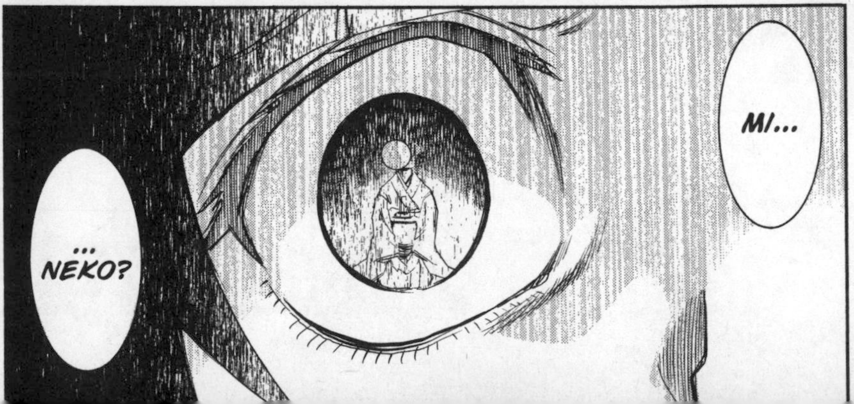
MI...
... NEKO?

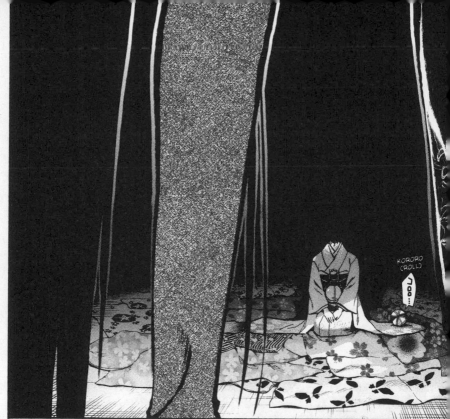

KORORO
(ROLL)

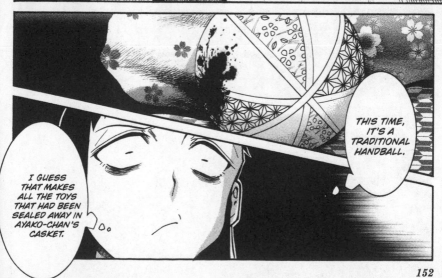

THIS TIME, IT'S A TRADITIONAL HANDBALL.

I GUESS THAT MAKES ALL THE TOYS THAT HAD BEEN SEALED AWAY IN AYAKO-CHAN'S CASKET.

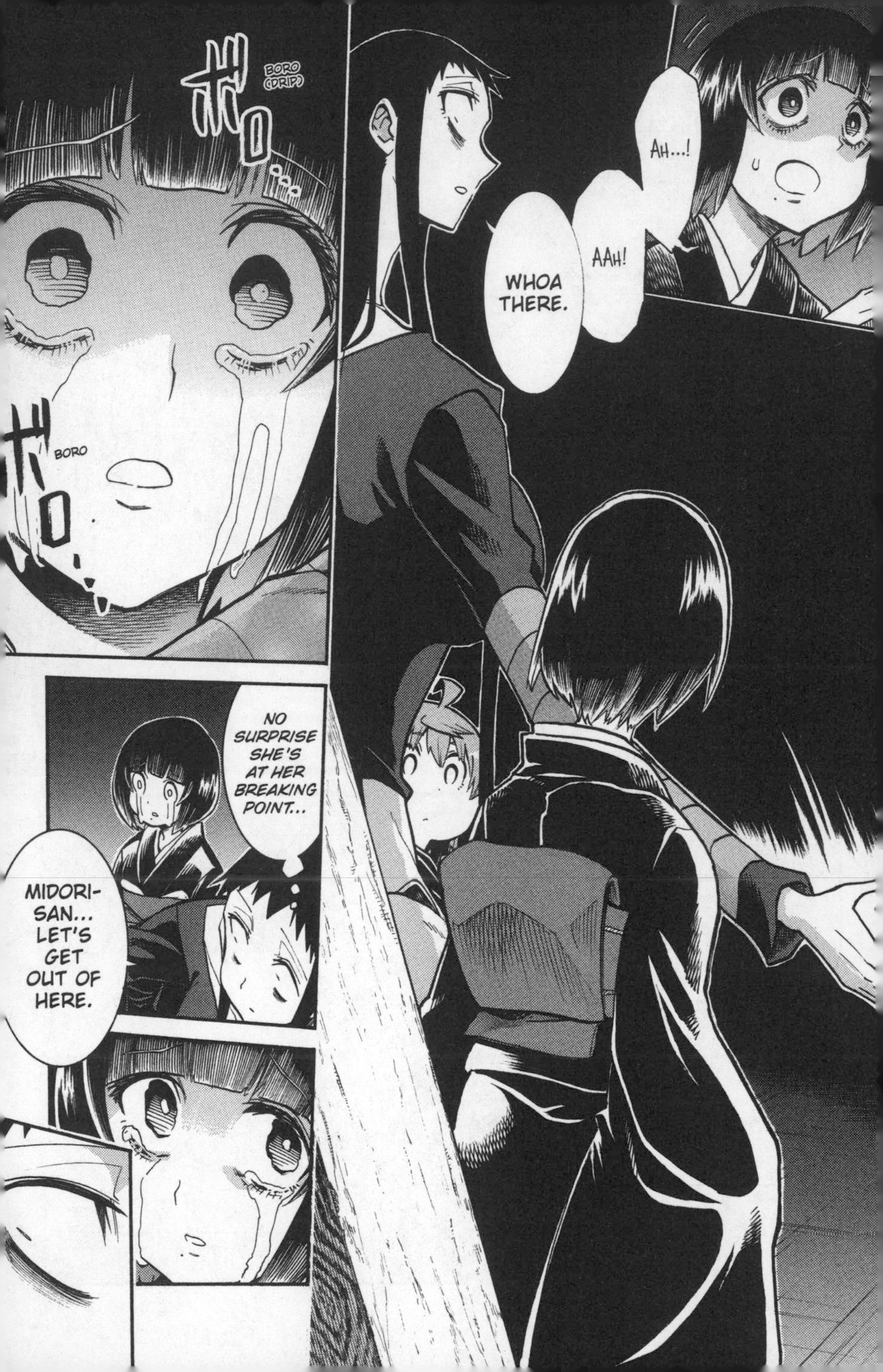
AH...!
AAH!
WHOA THERE.
BORO (DRIP)
BORO
NO SURPRISE SHE'S AT HER BREAKING POINT...
MIDORI-SAN... LET'S GET OUT OF HERE.

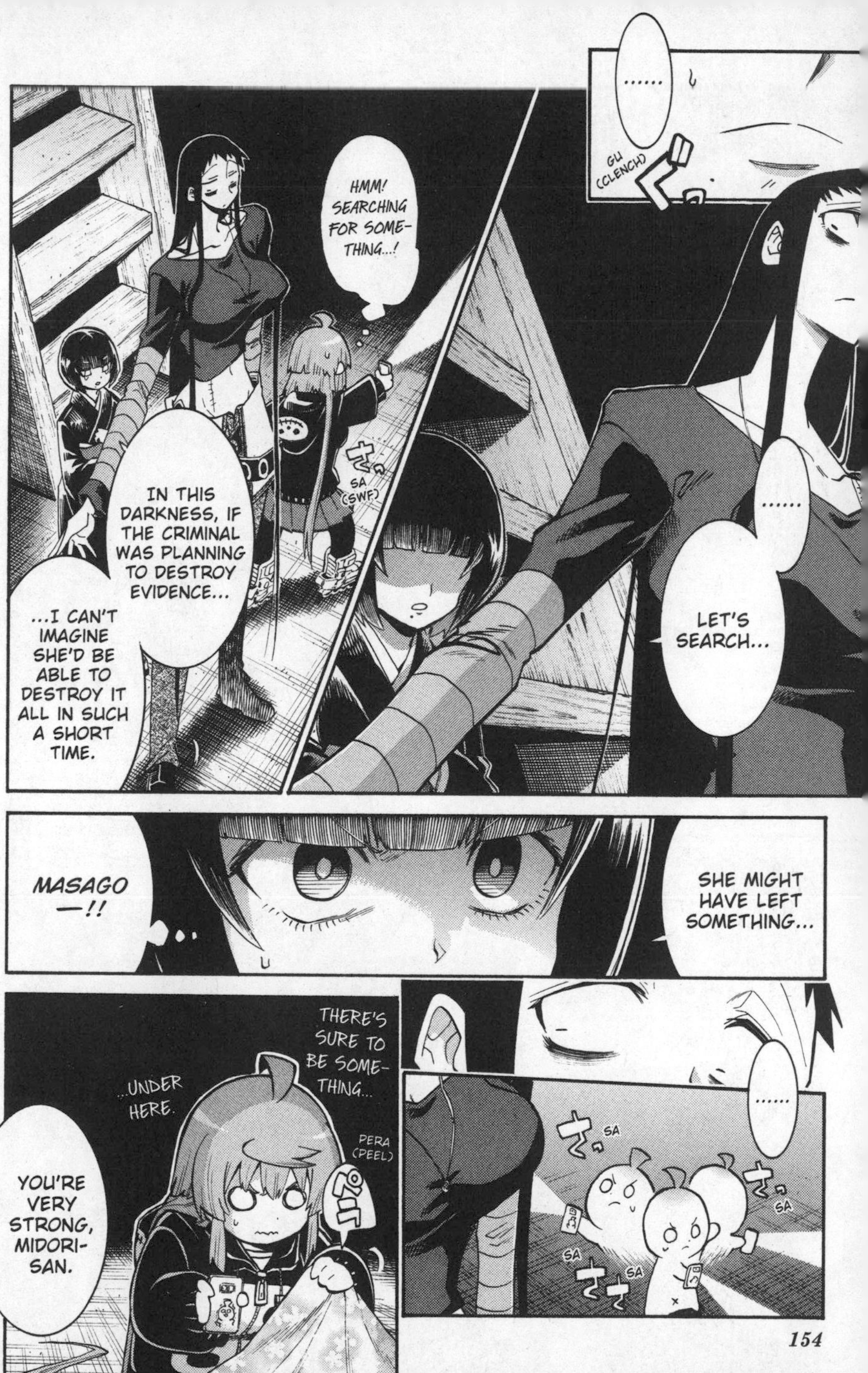
......
GU (CLENCH)
......
LET'S SEARCH...
HMM! SEARCHING FOR SOME-THING...!
SA (SWF)
IN THIS DARKNESS, IF THE CRIMINAL WAS PLANNING TO DESTROY EVIDENCE...
...I CAN'T IMAGINE SHE'D BE ABLE TO DESTROY IT ALL IN SUCH A SHORT TIME.
SHE MIGHT HAVE LEFT SOMETHING...
MASAGO—!!
......
SA
SA
SA
SA
THERE'S SURE TO BE SOME-THING...
...UNDER HERE.
PERA (PEEL)
YOU'RE VERY STRONG, MIDORI-SAN.

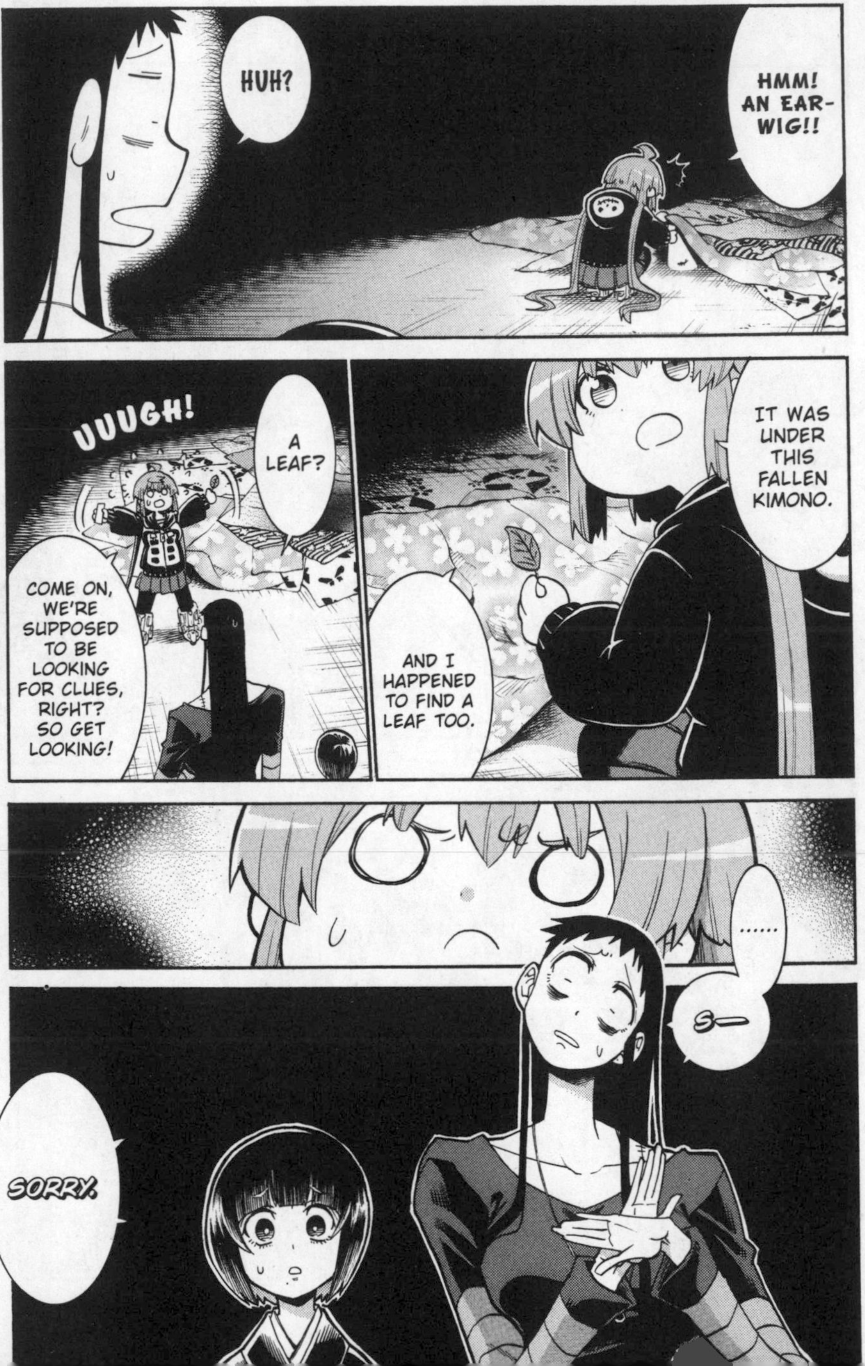
HMM! AN EAR-WIG!!
HUH?
IT WAS UNDER THIS FALLEN KIMONO.
AND I HAPPENED TO FIND A LEAF TOO.
A LEAF?
UUUGH!
COME ON, WE'RE SUPPOSED TO BE LOOKING FOR CLUES, RIGHT? SO GET LOOKING!
......
S—
SORRY.

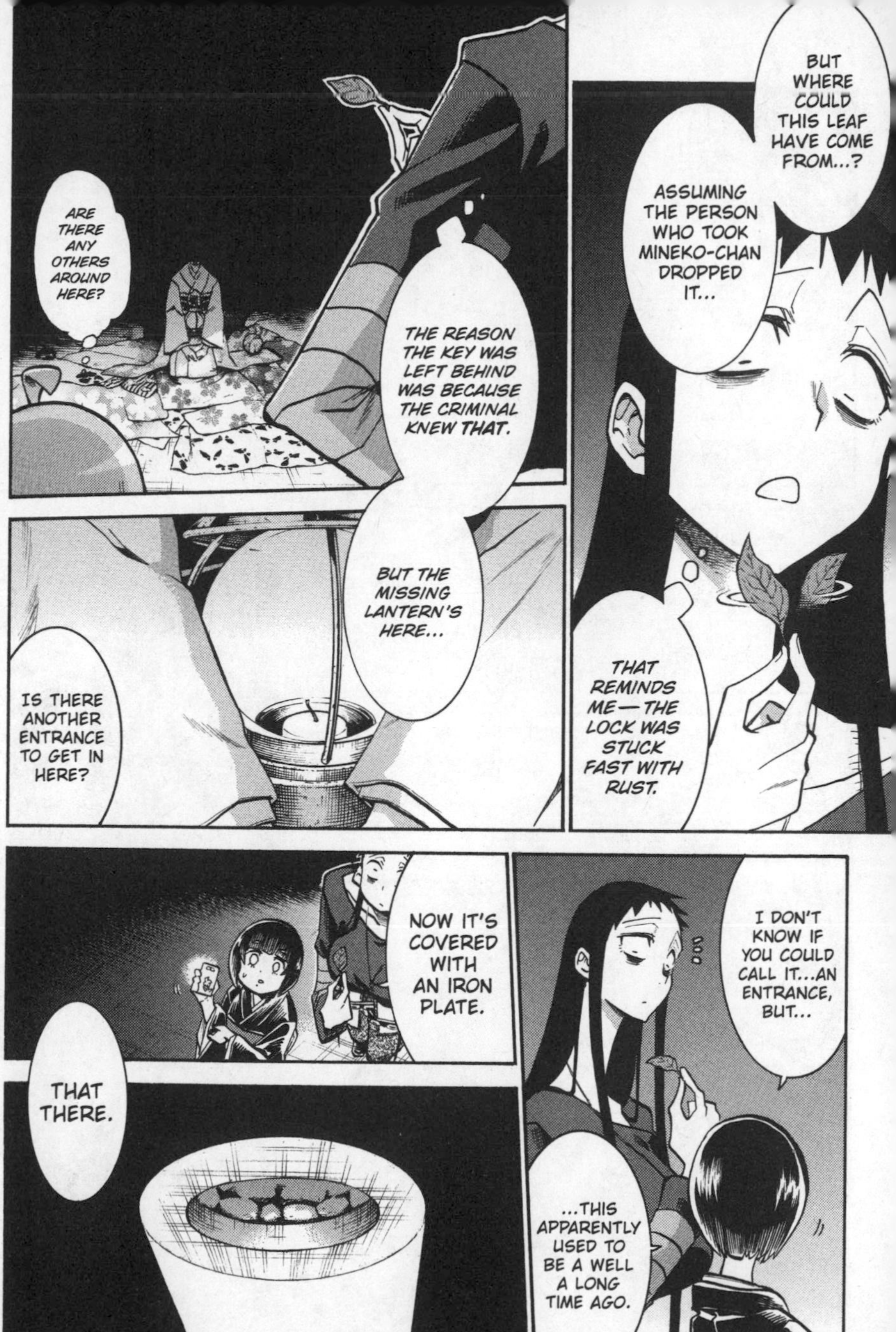
BUT WHERE COULD THIS LEAF HAVE COME FROM...?
ASSUMING THE PERSON WHO TOOK MINEKO-CHAN DROPPED IT...
THAT REMINDS ME—THE LOCK WAS STUCK FAST WITH RUST.
THE REASON THE KEY WAS LEFT BEHIND WAS BECAUSE THE CRIMINAL KNEW THAT.
ARE THERE ANY OTHERS AROUND HERE?
BUT THE MISSING LANTERN'S HERE...
IS THERE ANOTHER ENTRANCE TO GET IN HERE?
I DON'T KNOW IF YOU COULD CALL IT...AN ENTRANCE, BUT...
...THIS APPARENTLY USED TO BE A WELL A LONG TIME AGO.
NOW IT'S COVERED WITH AN IRON PLATE.
THAT THERE.

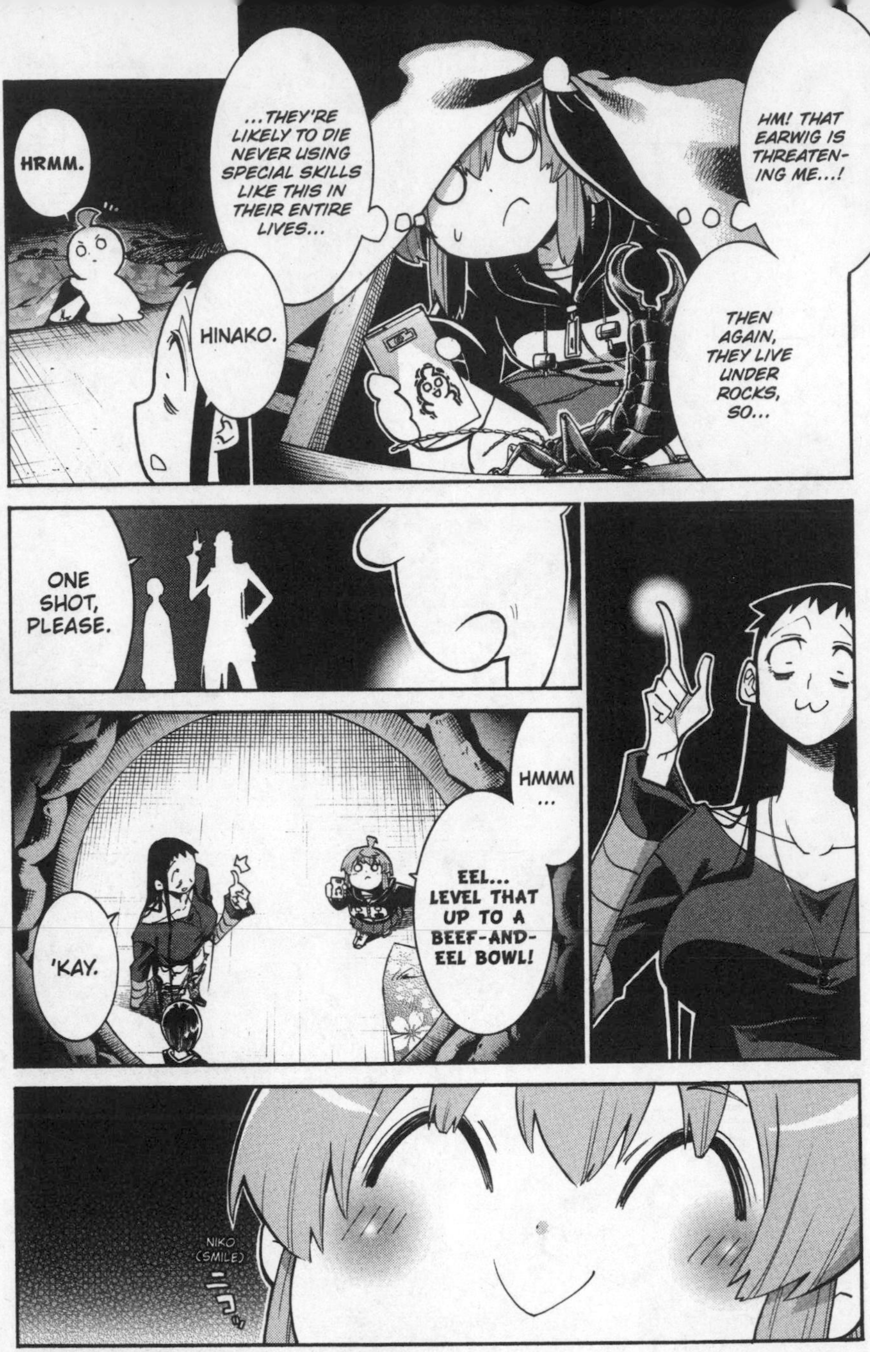
HM! THAT EARWIG IS THREATEN-ING ME...!
THEN AGAIN, THEY LIVE UNDER ROCKS, SO...
...THEY'RE LIKELY TO DIE NEVER USING SPECIAL SKILLS LIKE THIS IN THEIR ENTIRE LIVES...
HINAKO.
HRMM.
ONE SHOT, PLEASE.
HMMM...
EEL... LEVEL THAT UP TO A BEEF-AND-EEL BOWL!
'KAY.
NIKO (SMILE)

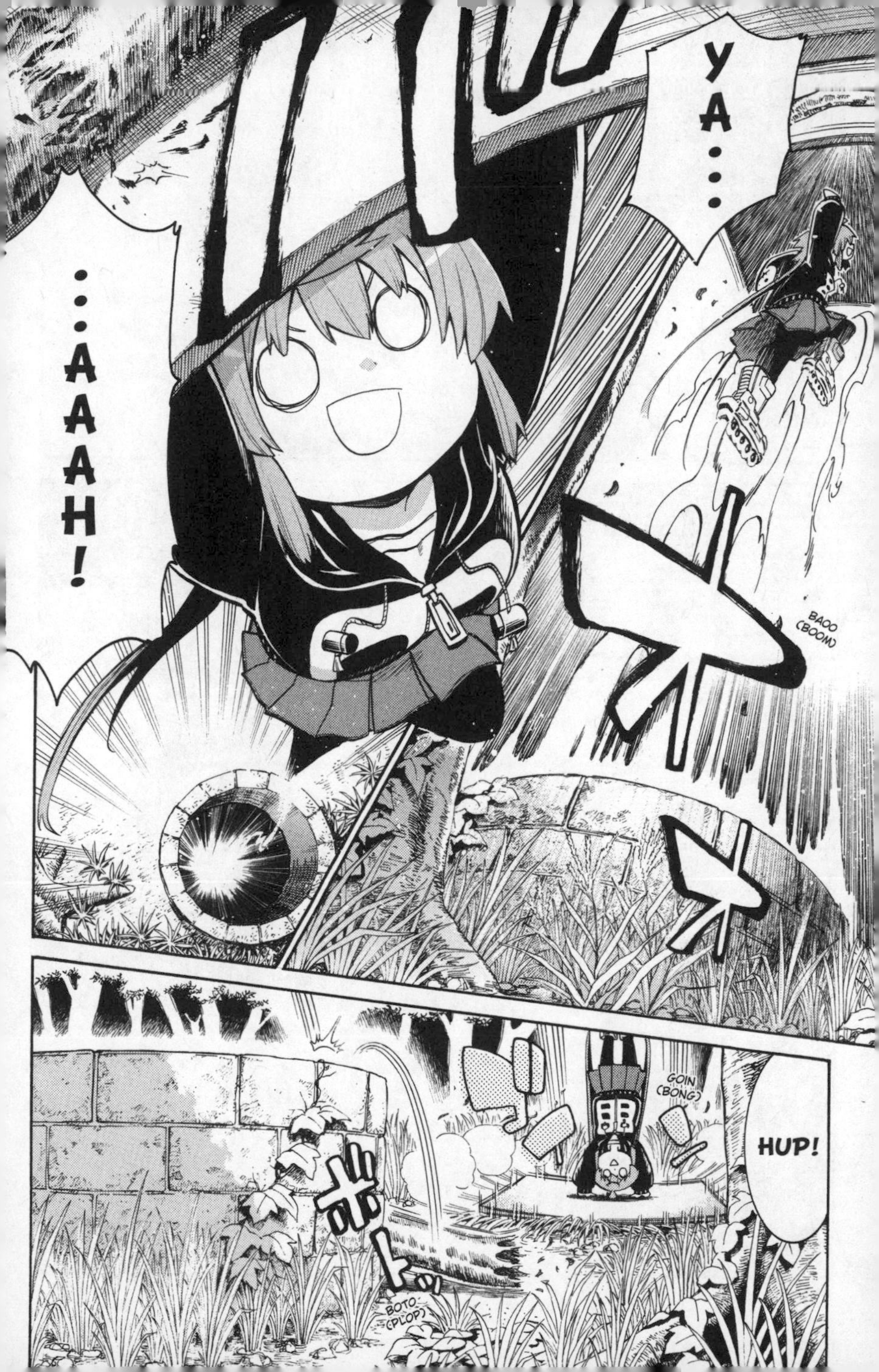
YA...
...AAAAH!
BAOO (BOOM)
HUP!
GOIN (BONG)
BOTO (PLOP)

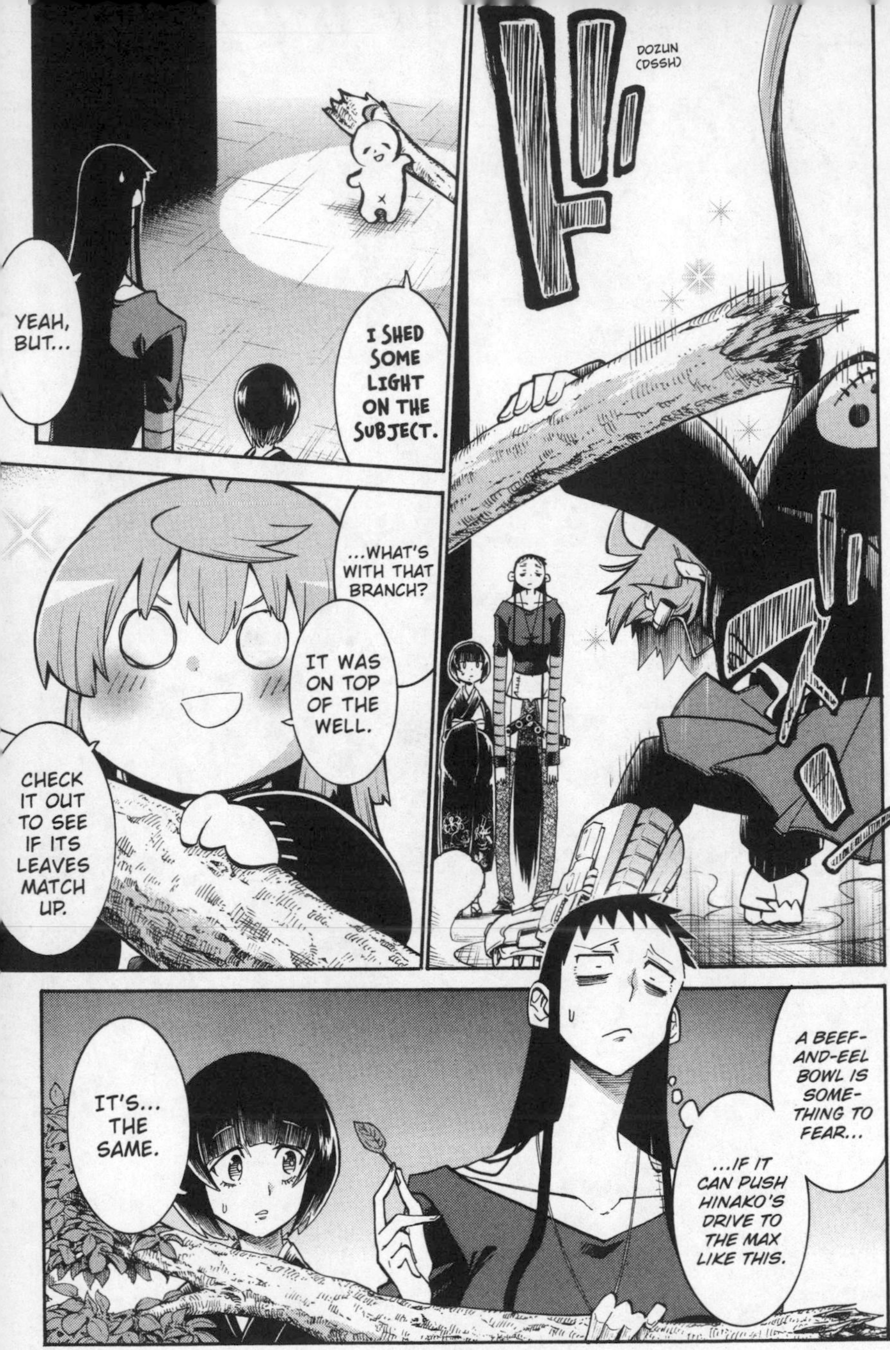
DOZUN (DSSH)
I SHED SOME LIGHT ON THE SUBJECT.
YEAH, BUT...
...WHAT'S WITH THAT BRANCH?
IT WAS ON TOP OF THE WELL.
CHECK IT OUT TO SEE IF ITS LEAVES MATCH UP.
A BEEF-AND-EEL BOWL IS SOMETHING TO FEAR...
...IF IT CAN PUSH HINAKO'S DRIVE TO THE MAX LIKE THIS.
IT'S... THE SAME.

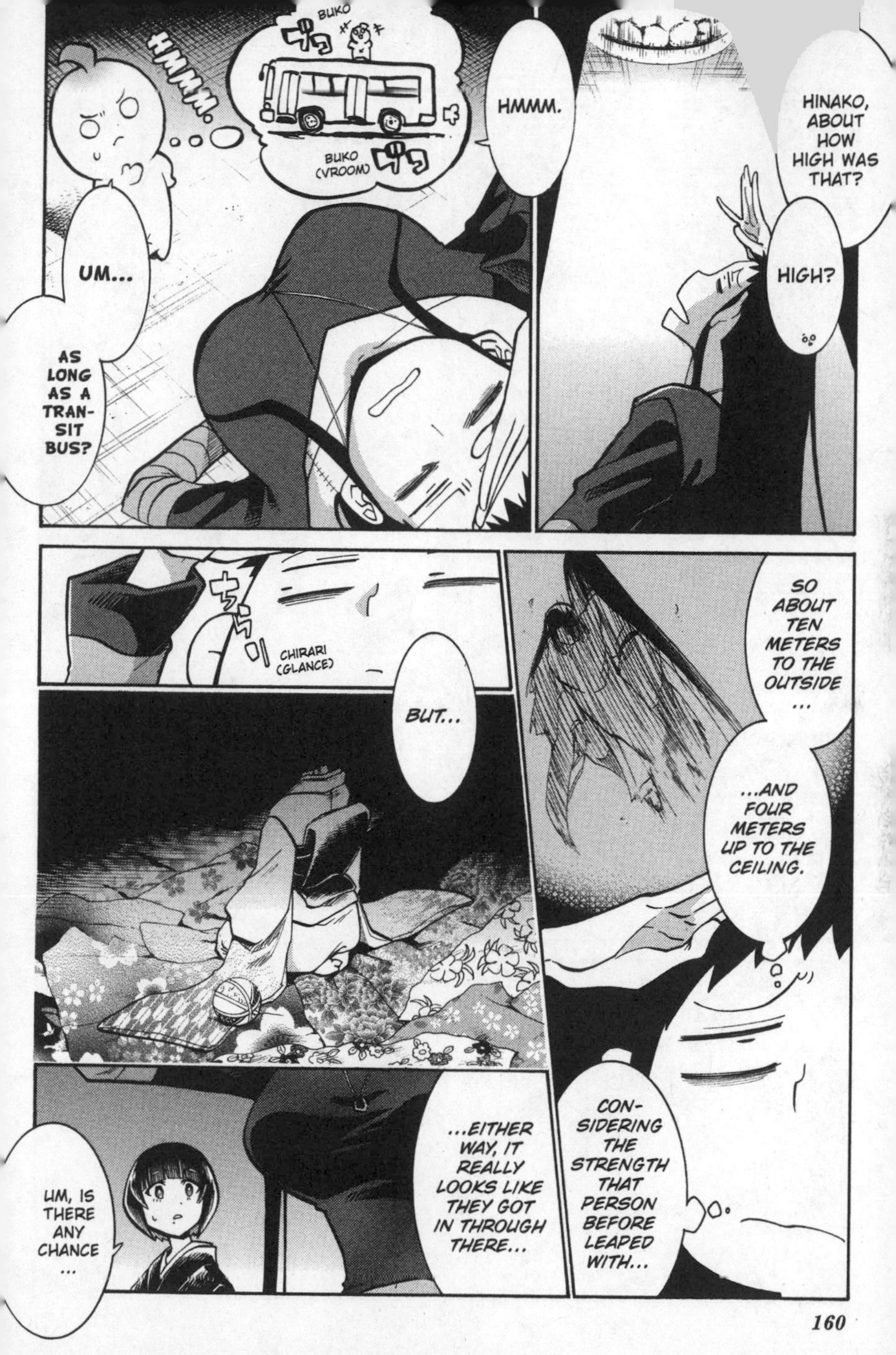
HINAKO, ABOUT HOW HIGH WAS THAT?
HIGH?
HMMM.
BUKO
BUKO (VROOM)
UM...
AS LONG AS A TRAN-SIT BUS?
SO ABOUT TEN METERS TO THE OUTSIDE...
...AND FOUR METERS UP TO THE CEILING.
CON-SIDERING THE STRENGTH THAT PERSON BEFORE LEAPED WITH...
CHIRARI (GLANCE)
BUT...
...EITHER WAY, IT REALLY LOOKS LIKE THEY GOT IN THROUGH THERE...
UM, IS THERE ANY CHANCE...

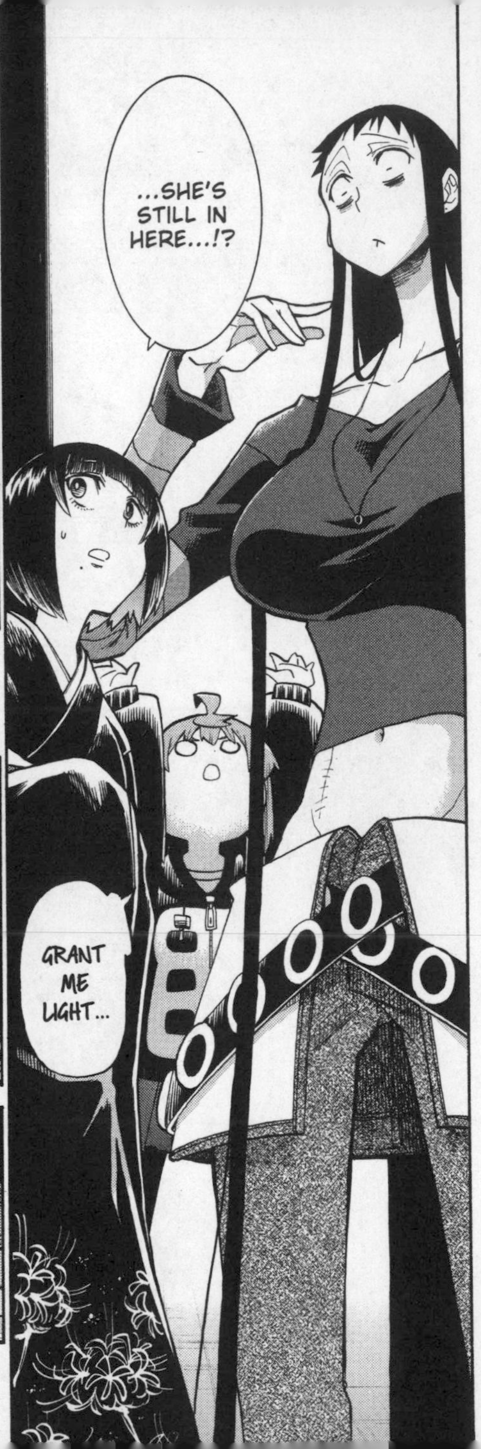
...SHE'S STILL IN HERE...!?
GRANT ME LIGHT...

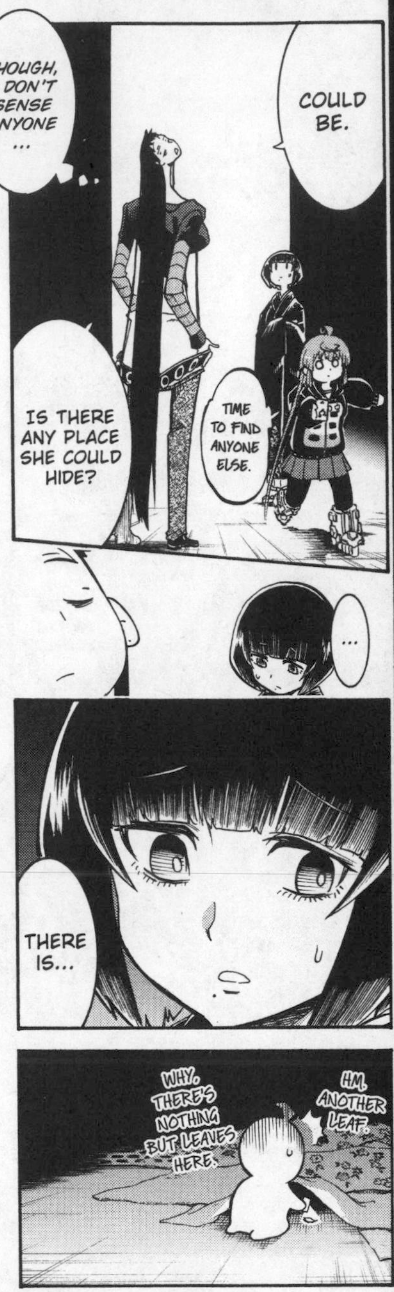
COULD BE.
THOUGH, I DON'T SENSE ANYONE ...
TIME TO FIND ANYONE ELSE.
IS THERE ANY PLACE SHE COULD HIDE?
...
THERE IS...
HM. ANOTHER LEAF.
WHY. THERE'S NOTHING BUT LEAVES HERE.

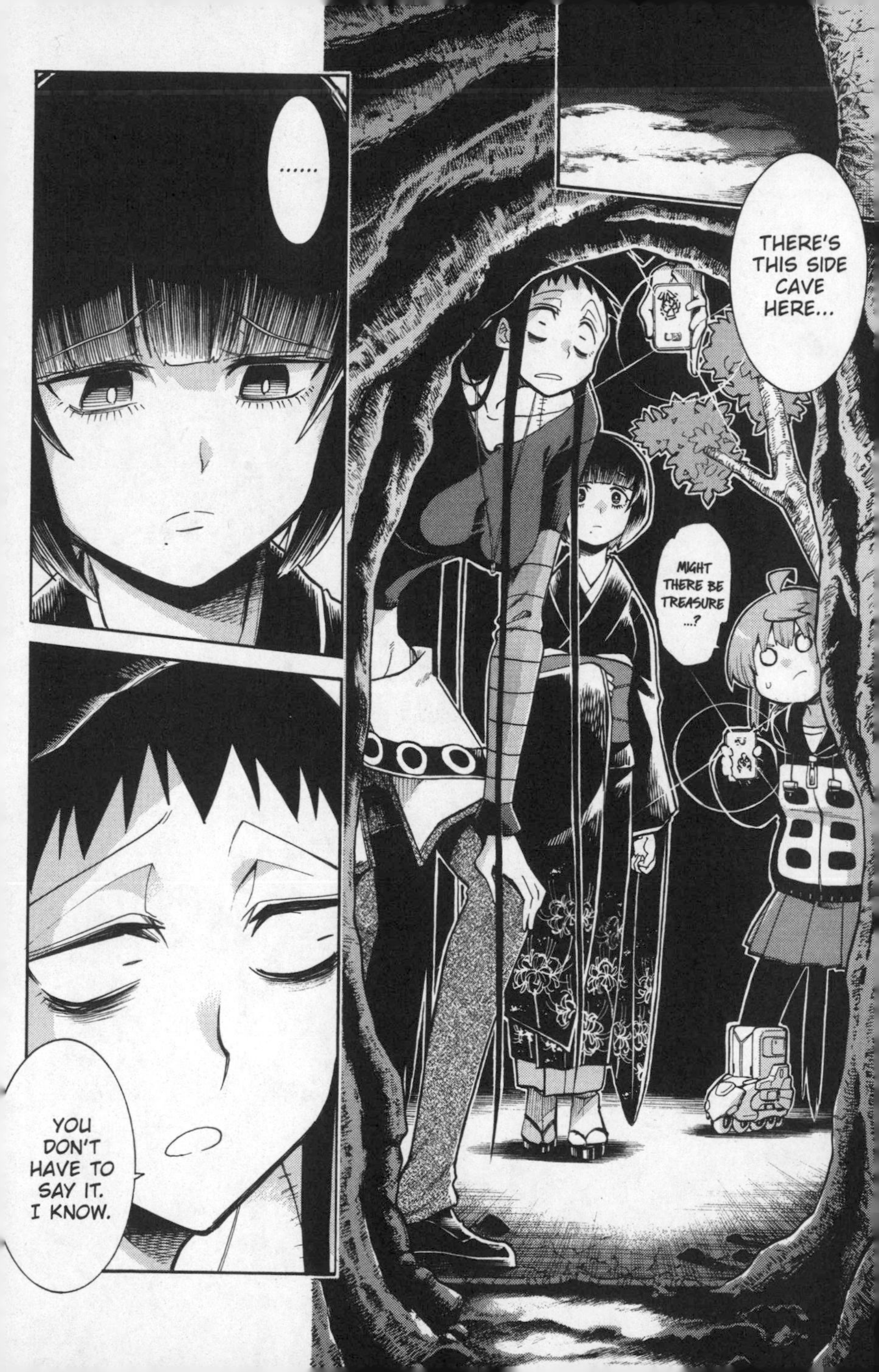
THERE'S THIS SIDE CAVE HERE...
MIGHT THERE BE TREASURE ...?
......
YOU DON'T HAVE TO SAY IT. I KNOW.

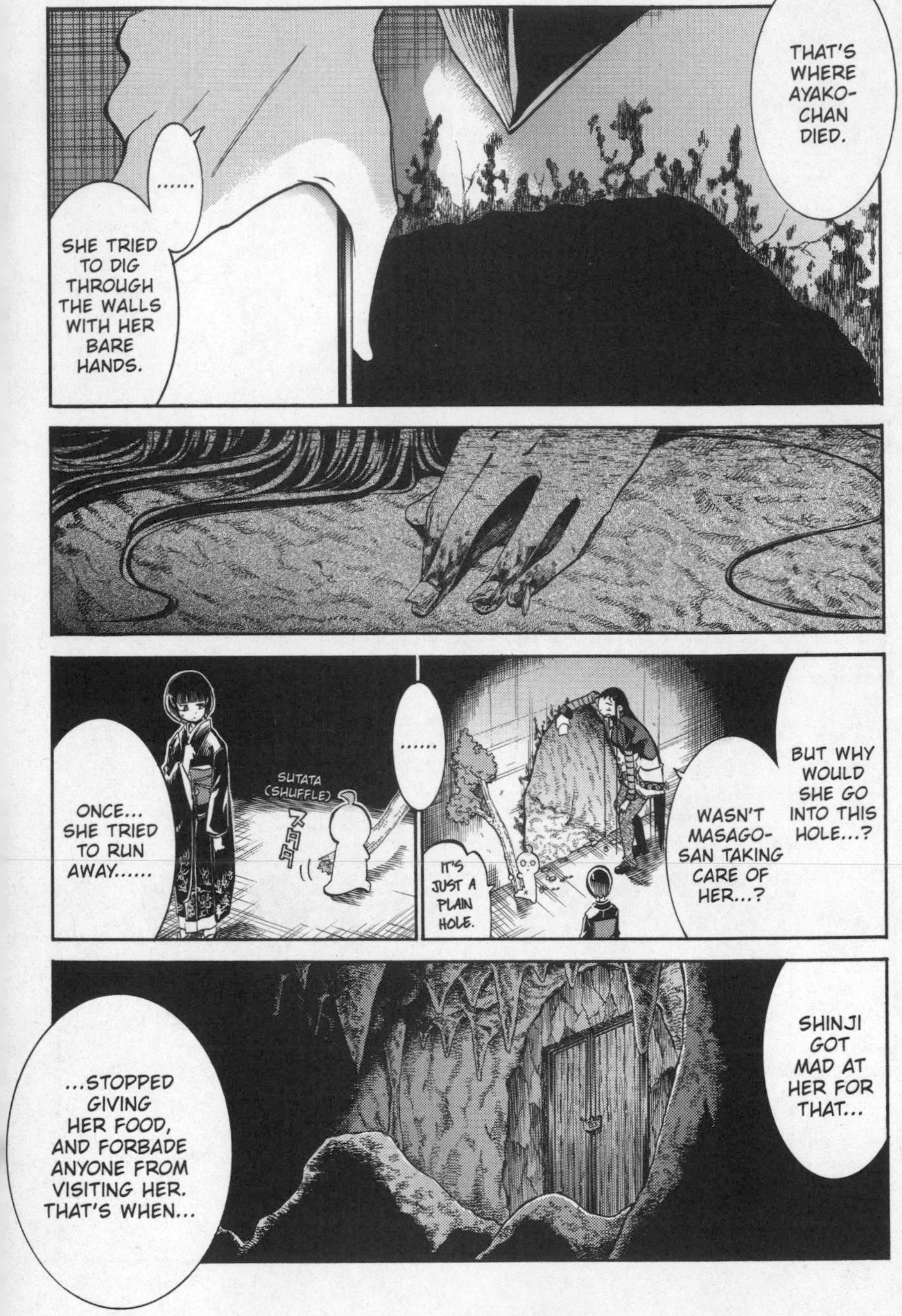
THAT'S WHERE AYAKO-CHAN DIED.
......
SHE TRIED TO DIG THROUGH THE WALLS WITH HER BARE HANDS.
BUT WHY WOULD SHE GO INTO THIS HOLE...?
WASN'T MASAGO-SAN TAKING CARE OF HER...?
IT'S JUST A PLAIN HOLE.
......
SUTATA (SHUFFLE)
スタタ
ONCE... SHE TRIED TO RUN AWAY......
SHINJI GOT MAD AT HER FOR THAT...
...STOPPED GIVING HER FOOD, AND FORBADE ANYONE FROM VISITING HER. THAT'S WHEN...

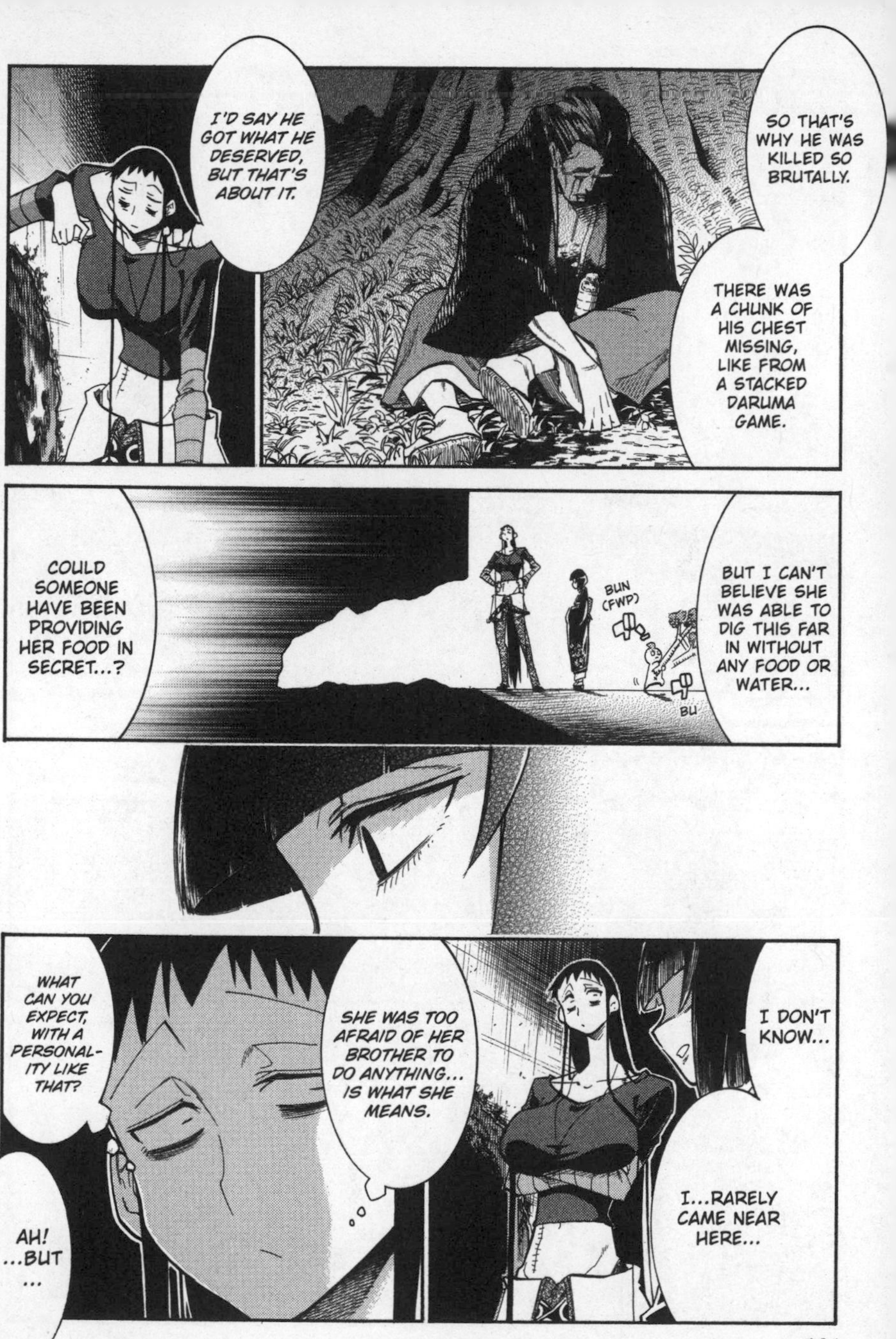
SO THAT'S WHY HE WAS KILLED SO BRUTALLY.
THERE WAS A CHUNK OF HIS CHEST MISSING, LIKE FROM A STACKED DARUMA GAME.
I'D SAY HE GOT WHAT HE DESERVED, BUT THAT'S ABOUT IT.
BUT I CAN'T BELIEVE SHE WAS ABLE TO DIG THIS FAR IN WITHOUT ANY FOOD OR WATER...
BUN (FWP)
BU
COULD SOMEONE HAVE BEEN PROVIDING HER FOOD IN SECRET...?
I DON'T KNOW...
I...RARELY CAME NEAR HERE...
SHE WAS TOO AFRAID OF HER BROTHER TO DO ANYTHING... IS WHAT SHE MEANS.
WHAT CAN YOU EXPECT, WITH A PERSONAL-ITY LIKE THAT?
AH! ...BUT ...

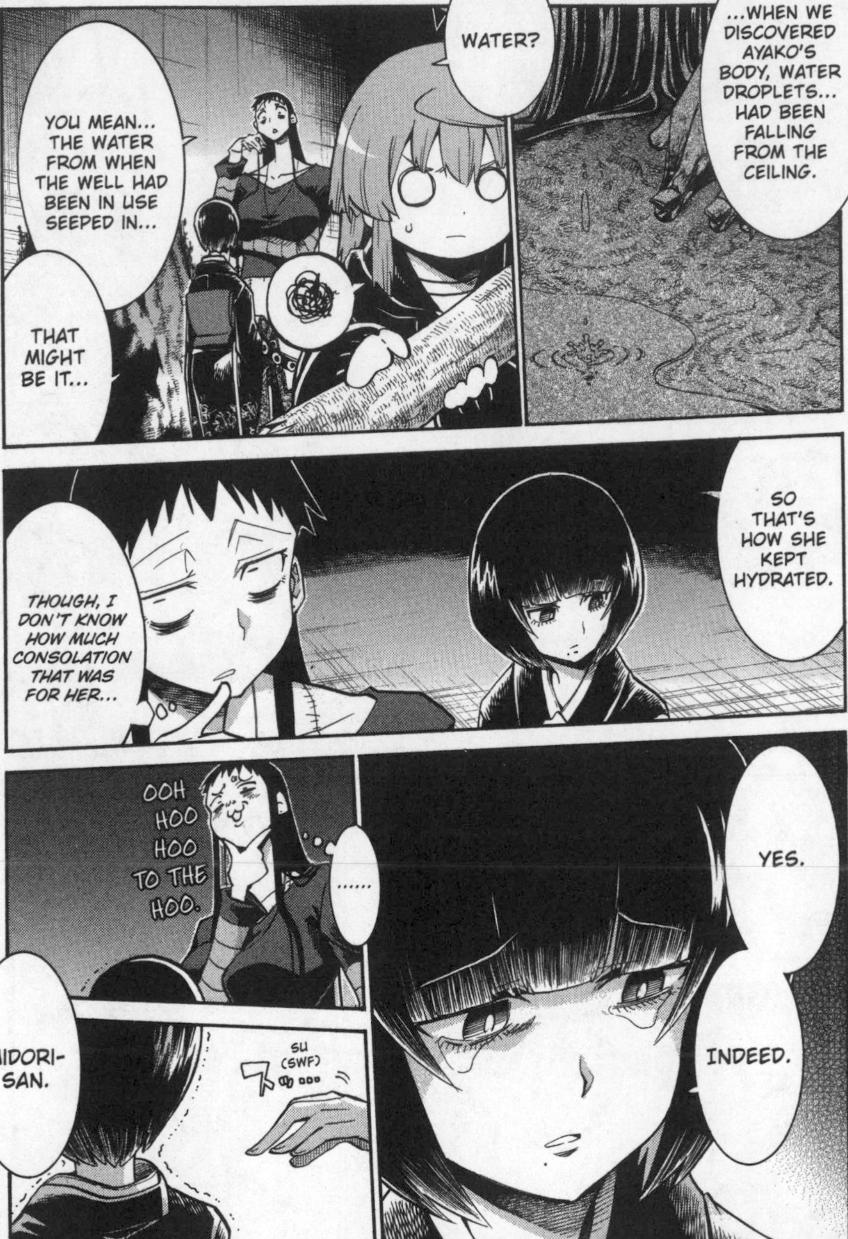
...WHEN WE DISCOVERED AYAKO'S BODY, WATER DROPLETS... HAD BEEN FALLING FROM THE CEILING.
WATER?
YOU MEAN... THE WATER FROM WHEN THE WELL HAD BEEN IN USE SEEPED IN...
THAT MIGHT BE IT...
SO THAT'S HOW SHE KEPT HYDRATED.
THOUGH, I DON'T KNOW HOW MUCH CONSOLATION THAT WAS FOR HER...
YES.
INDEED.
......
OOH HOO HOO TO THE HOO.
SU (SWF)
MIDORI-SAN.

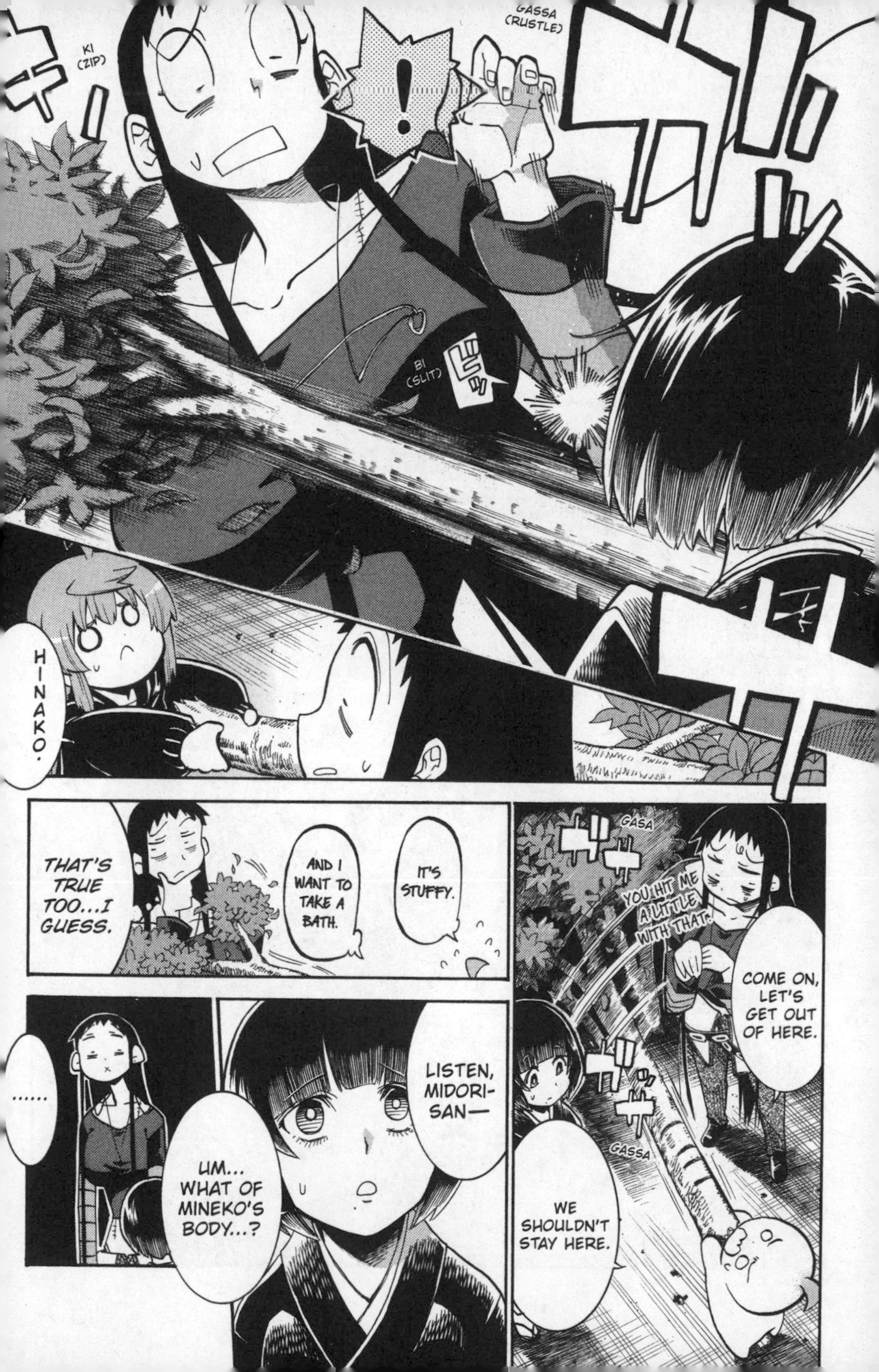
GASSA (RUSTLE)
KI (ZIP)
BI (SLIT)
HINAKO.
GASA
YOU HIT ME A LITTLE WITH THAT.
COME ON, LET'S GET OUT OF HERE.
GASSA
WE SHOULDN'T STAY HERE.
IT'S STUFFY.
AND I WANT TO TAKE A BATH.
THAT'S TRUE TOO...I GUESS.
LISTEN, MIDORI-SAN—
UM... WHAT OF MINEKO'S BODY...?
......

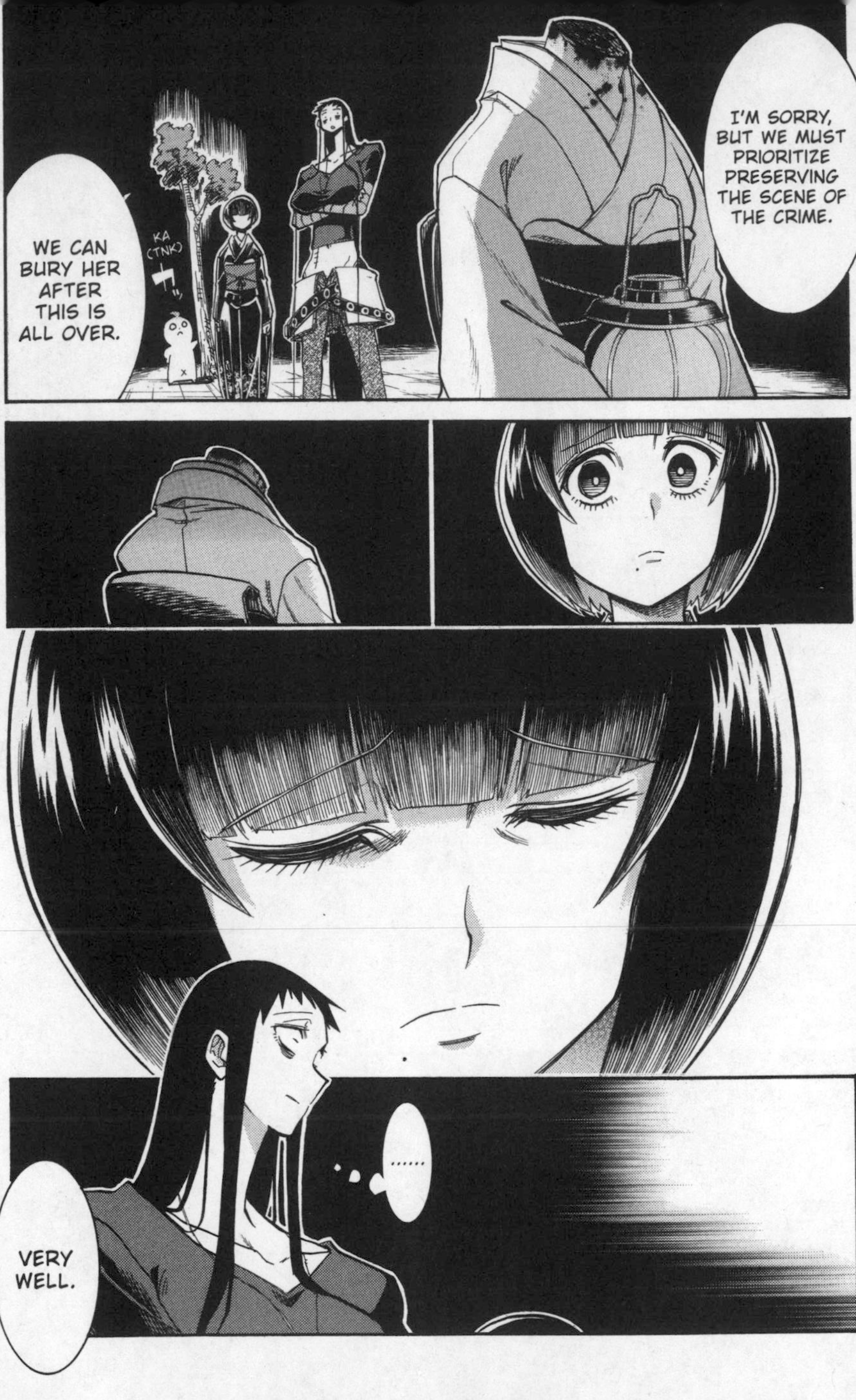
I'M SORRY, BUT WE MUST PRIORITIZE PRESERVING THE SCENE OF THE CRIME.
KA (TNK)
WE CAN BURY HER AFTER THIS IS ALL OVER.
......
VERY WELL.

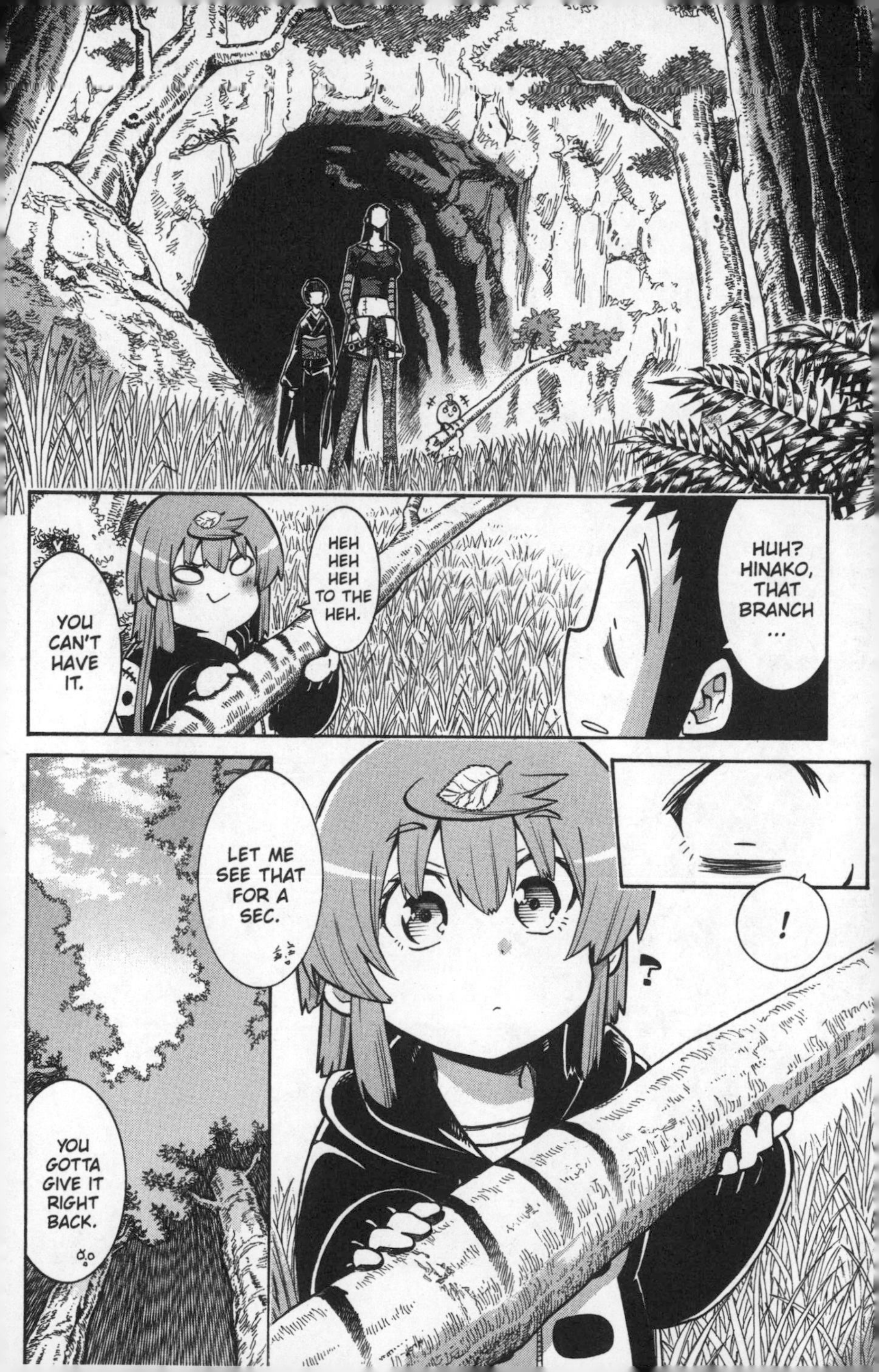
HUH? HINAKO, THAT BRANCH ...
HEH HEH HEH TO THE HEH.
YOU CAN'T HAVE IT.
!
LET ME SEE THAT FOR A SEC.
?
YOU GOTTA GIVE IT RIGHT BACK.

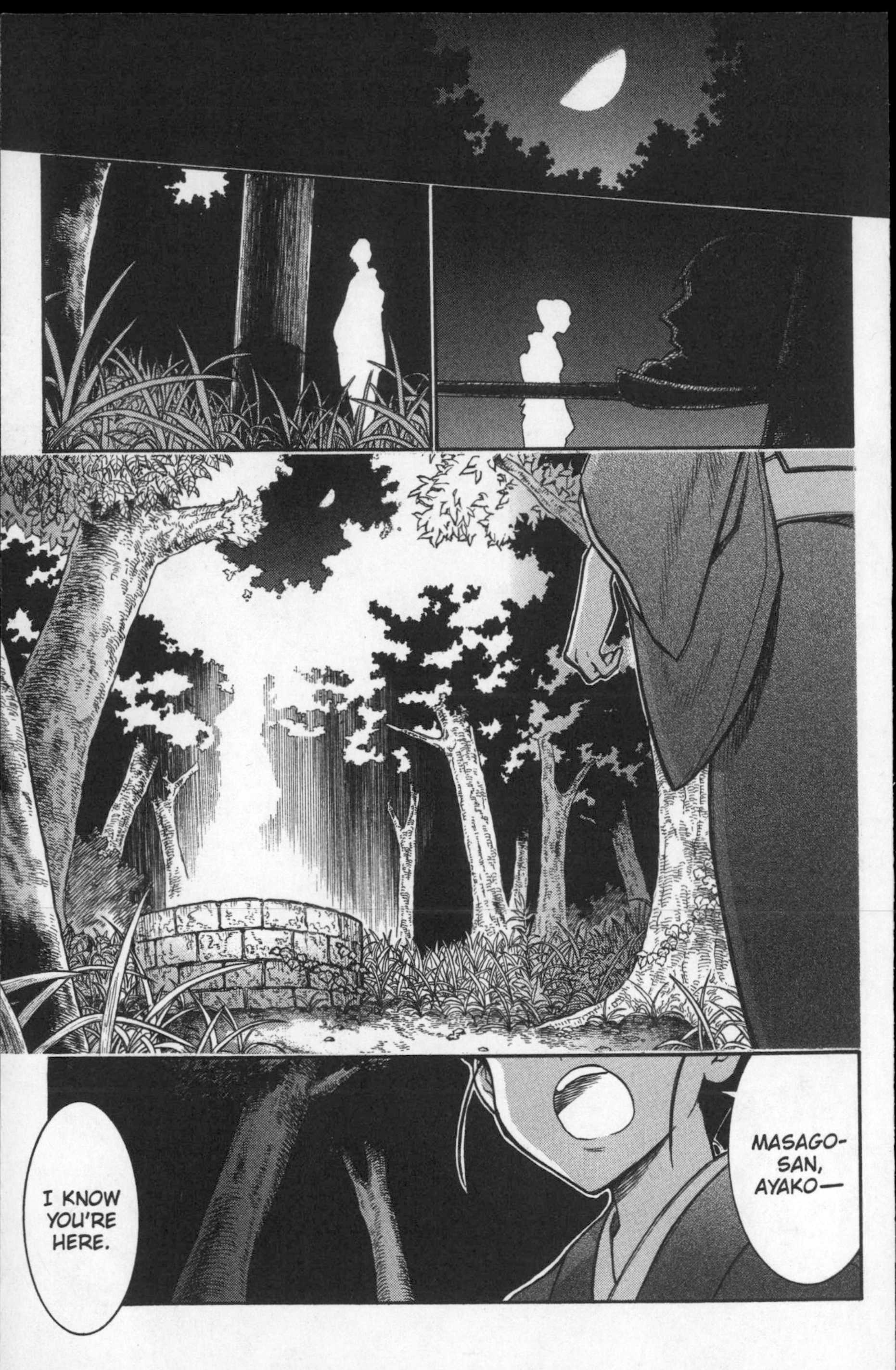
MASAGO-SAN, AYAKO—
I KNOW YOU'RE HERE.

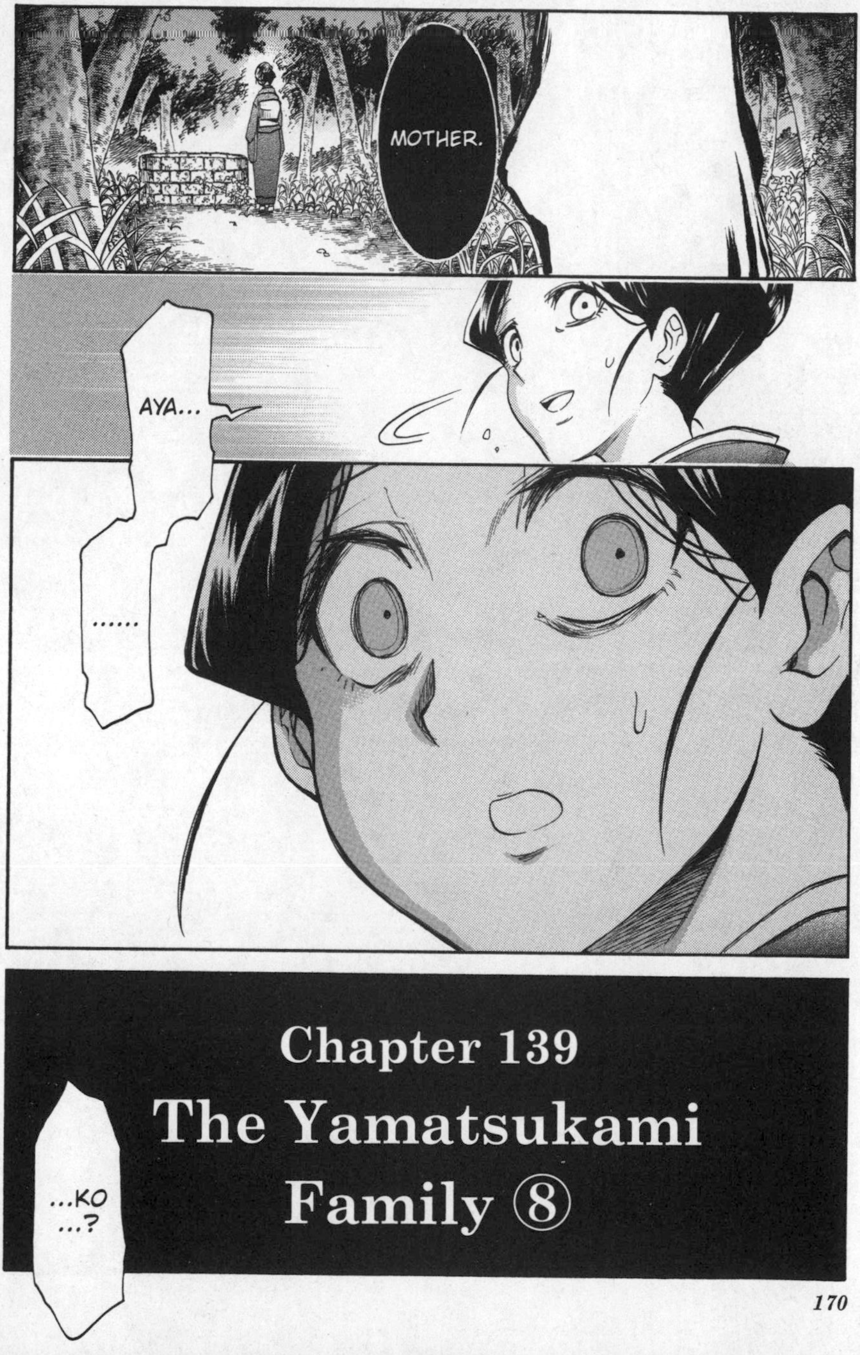
MOTHER.
AYA...
......
...KO ...?

Chapter 139

The Yamatsukami Family ⑧

MURCIÉLAGO

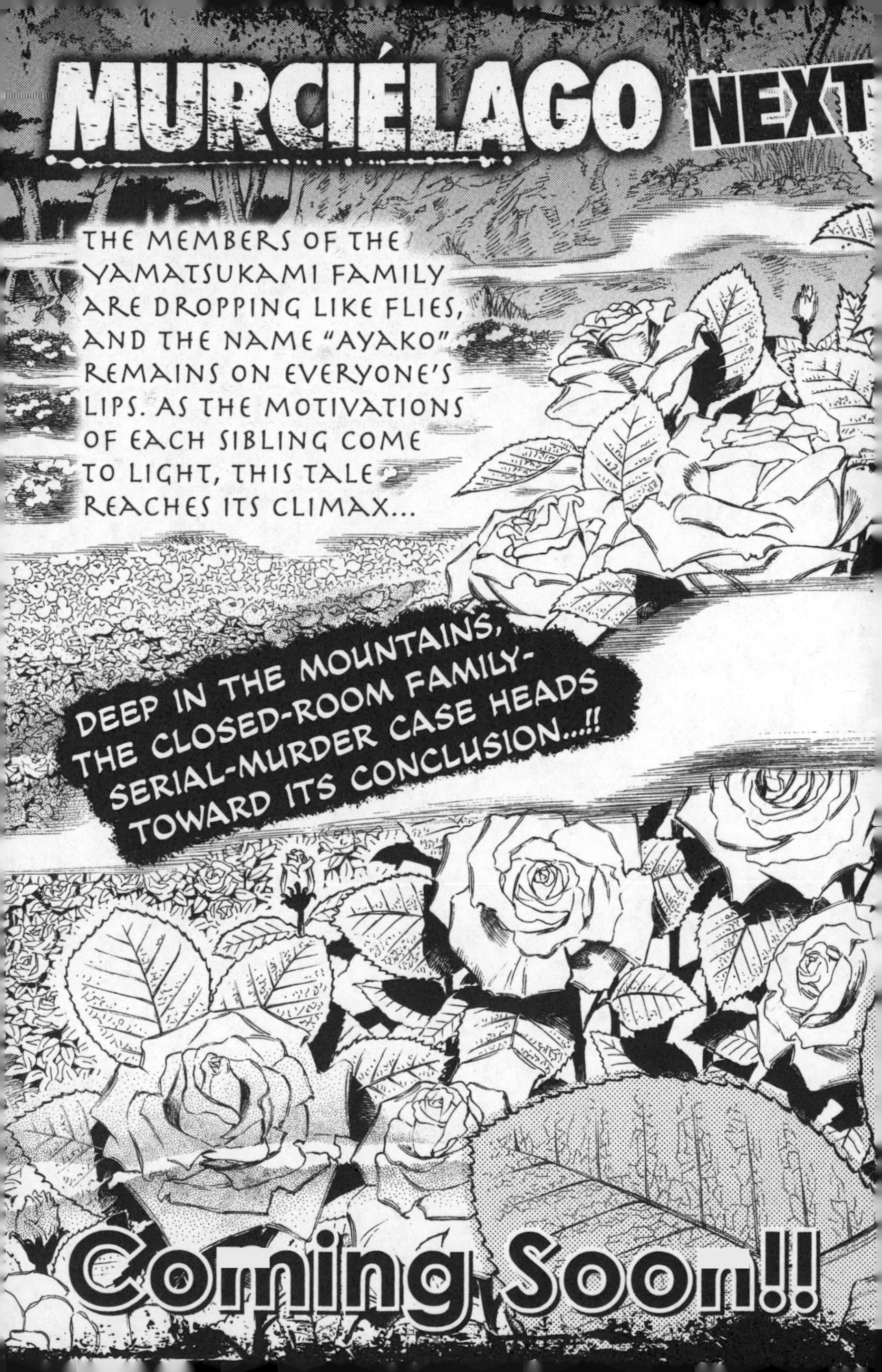
MURCIÉLAGO NEXT
THE MEMBERS OF THE YAMATSUKAMI FAMILY ARE DROPPING LIKE FLIES, AND THE NAME "AYAKO" REMAINS ON EVERYONE'S LIPS. AS THE MOTIVATIONS OF EACH SIBLING COME TO LIGHT, THIS TALE REACHES ITS CLIMAX...
DEEP IN THE MOUNTAINS, THE CLOSED-ROOM FAMILY-SERIAL-MURDER CASE HEADS TOWARD ITS CONCLUSION...!!
Coming Soon!!

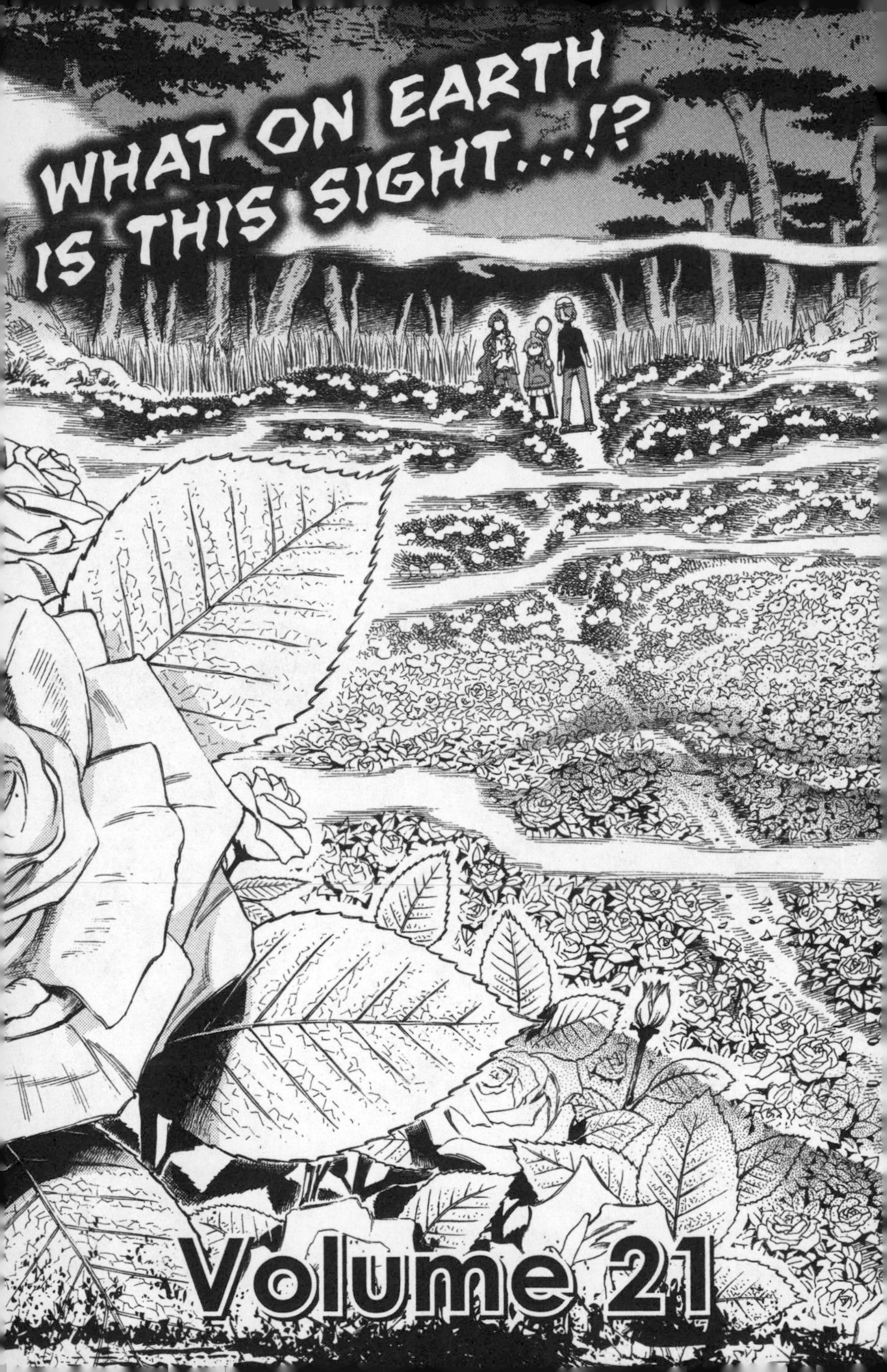
WHAT ON EARTH IS THIS SIGHT...!?
Volume 21

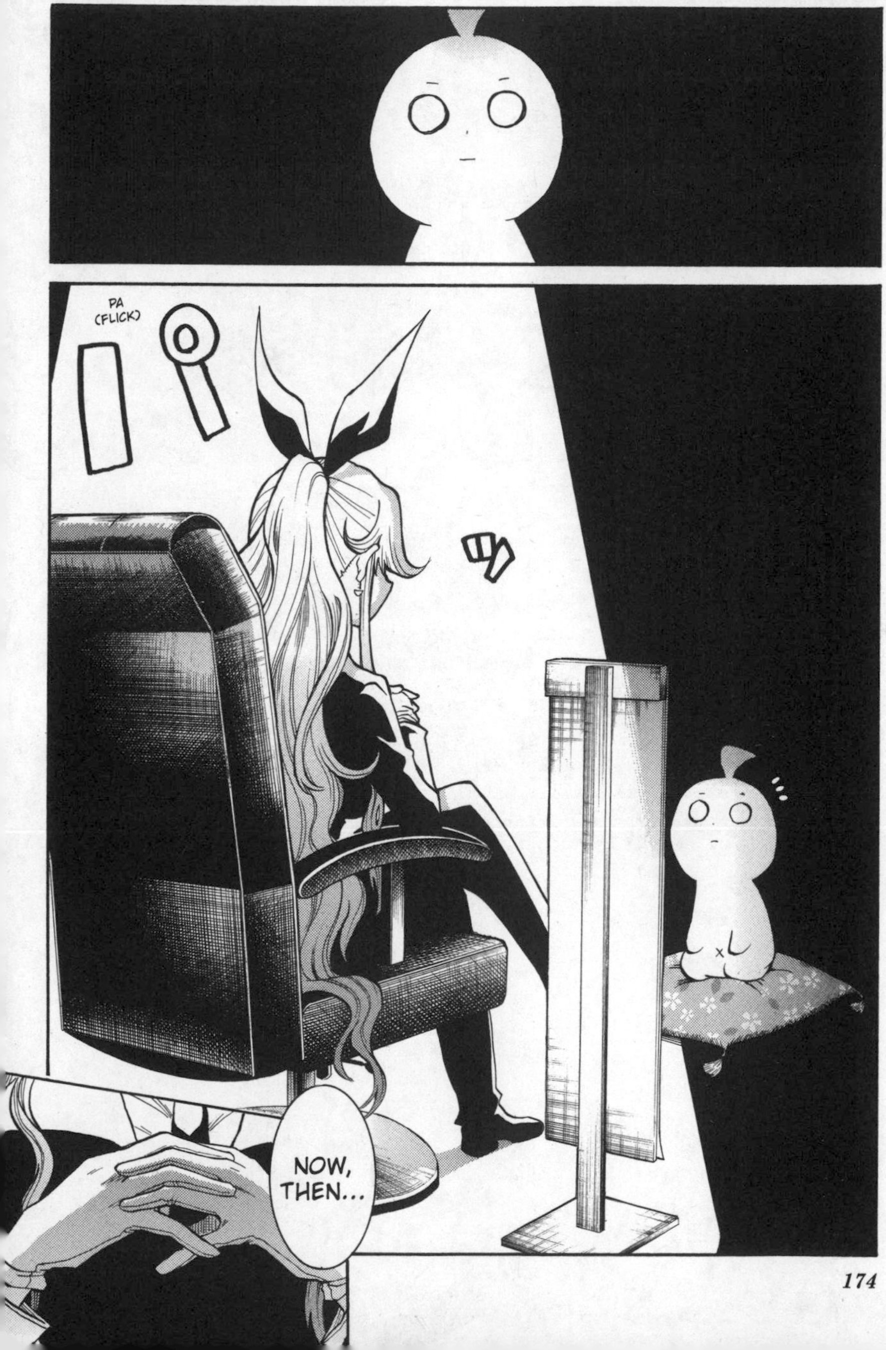
PA (FLICK)
NOW, THEN...

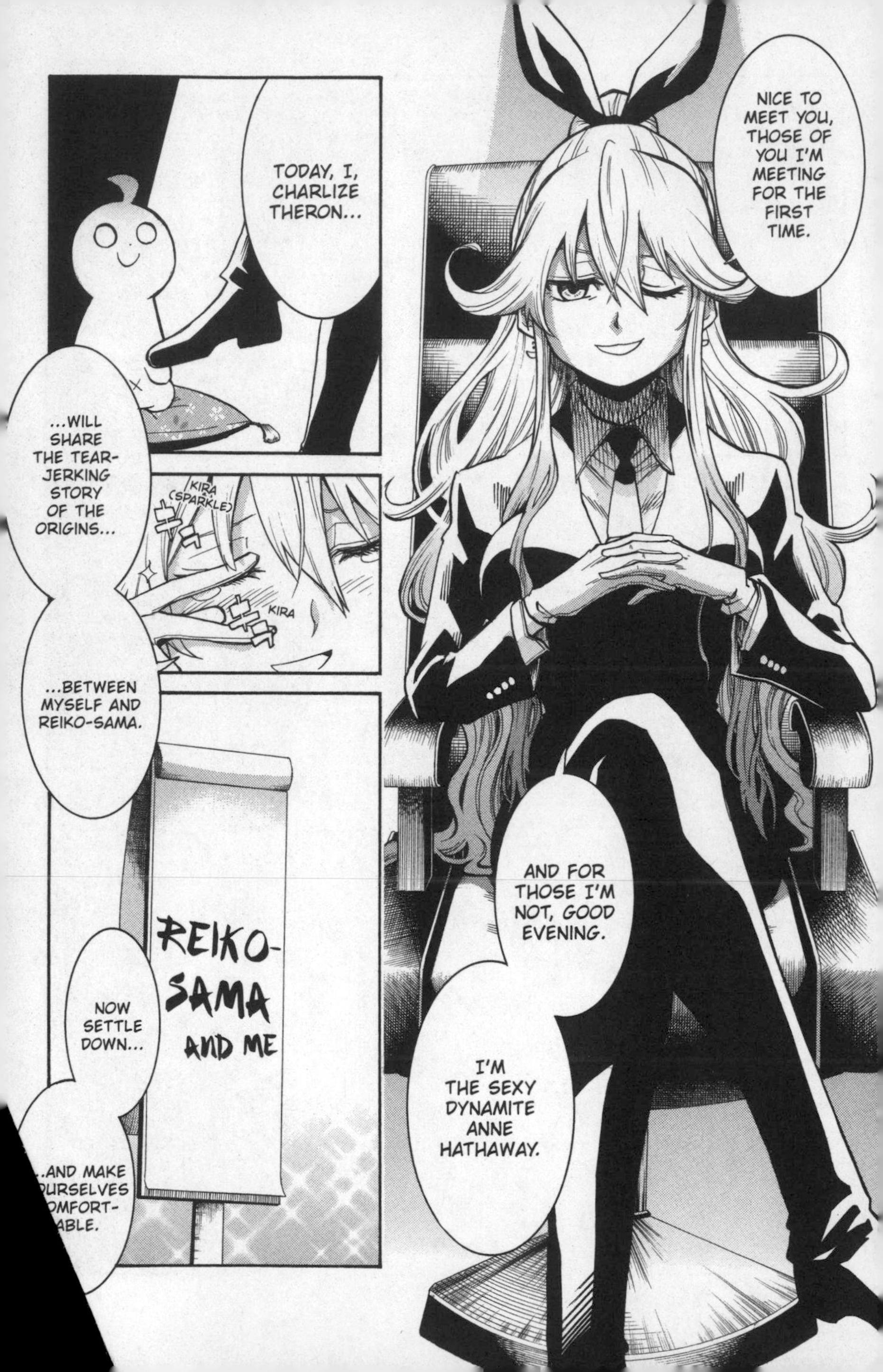
NICE TO MEET YOU, THOSE OF YOU I'M MEETING FOR THE FIRST TIME.
AND FOR THOSE I'M NOT, GOOD EVENING.
I'M THE SEXY DYNAMITE ANNE HATHAWAY.
TODAY, I, CHARLIZE THERON...
...WILL SHARE THE TEAR-JERKING STORY OF THE ORIGINS...
KIRA (SPARKLE)
KIRA
...BETWEEN MYSELF AND REIKO-SAMA.
REIKO-SAMA AND ME
NOW SETTLE DOWN...
..AND MAKE URSELVES OMFORT-ABLE.

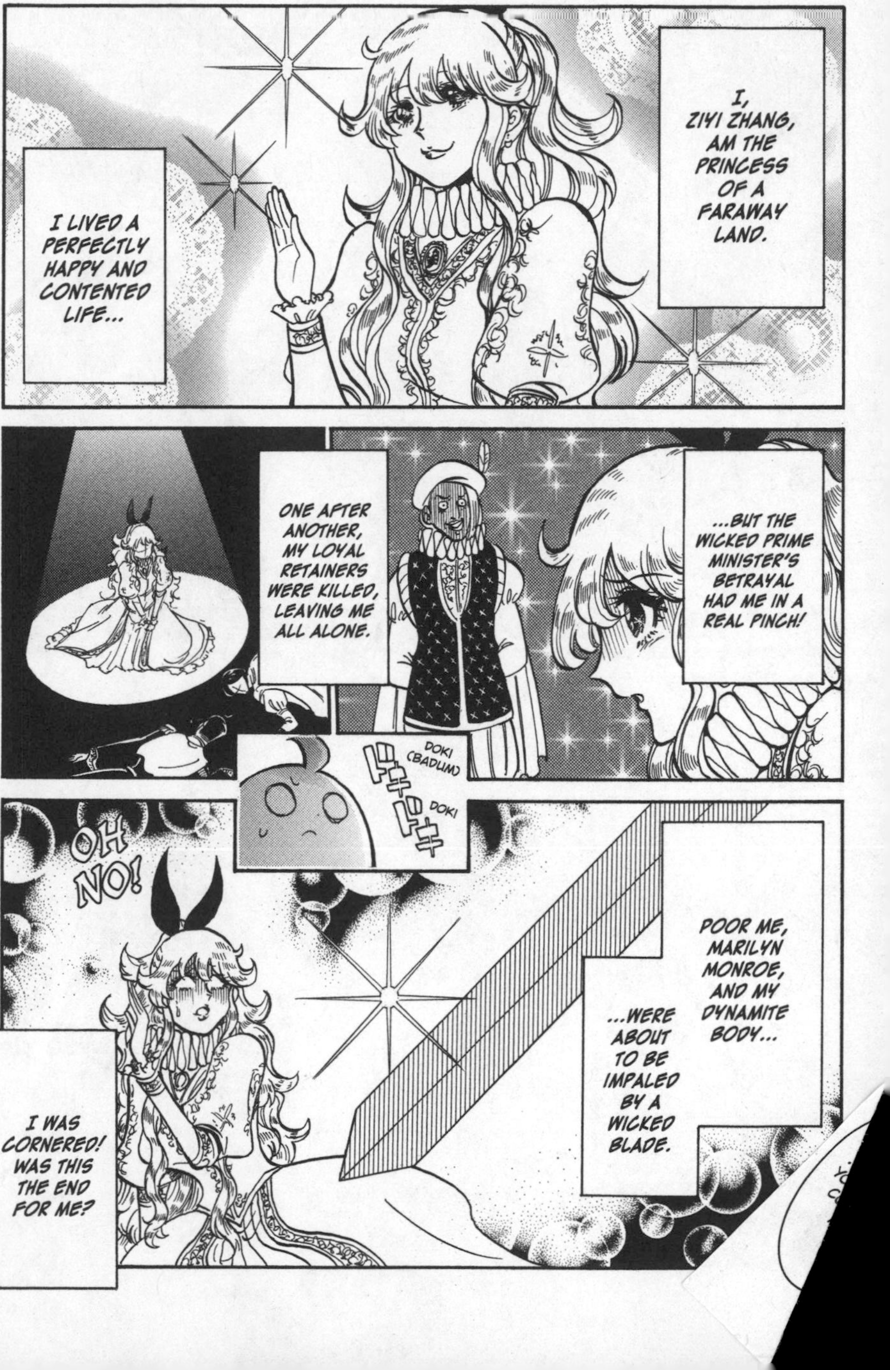
I, ZIYI ZHANG, AM THE PRINCESS OF A FARAWAY LAND.
I LIVED A PERFECTLY HAPPY AND CONTENTED LIFE...
...BUT THE WICKED PRIME MINISTER'S BETRAYAL HAD ME IN A REAL PINCH!
ONE AFTER ANOTHER, MY LOYAL RETAINERS WERE KILLED, LEAVING ME ALL ALONE.
DOKI (BADUM)
DOKI
POOR ME, MARILYN MONROE, AND MY DYNAMITE BODY...
...WERE ABOUT TO BE IMPALED BY A WICKED BLADE.
OH NO!
I WAS CORNERED! WAS THIS THE END FOR ME?

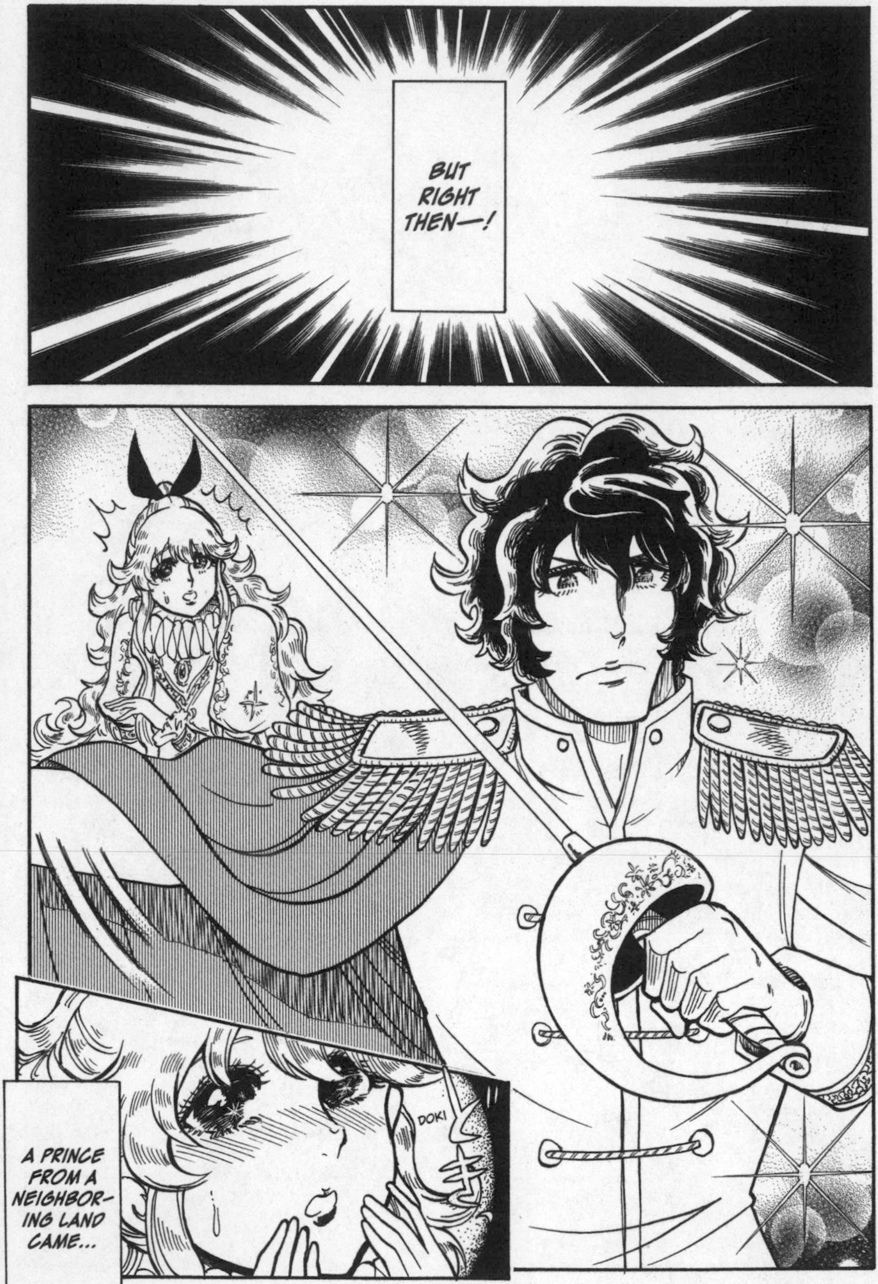
BUT RIGHT THEN—!
A PRINCE FROM A NEIGHBOR-ING LAND CAME...
DOKI

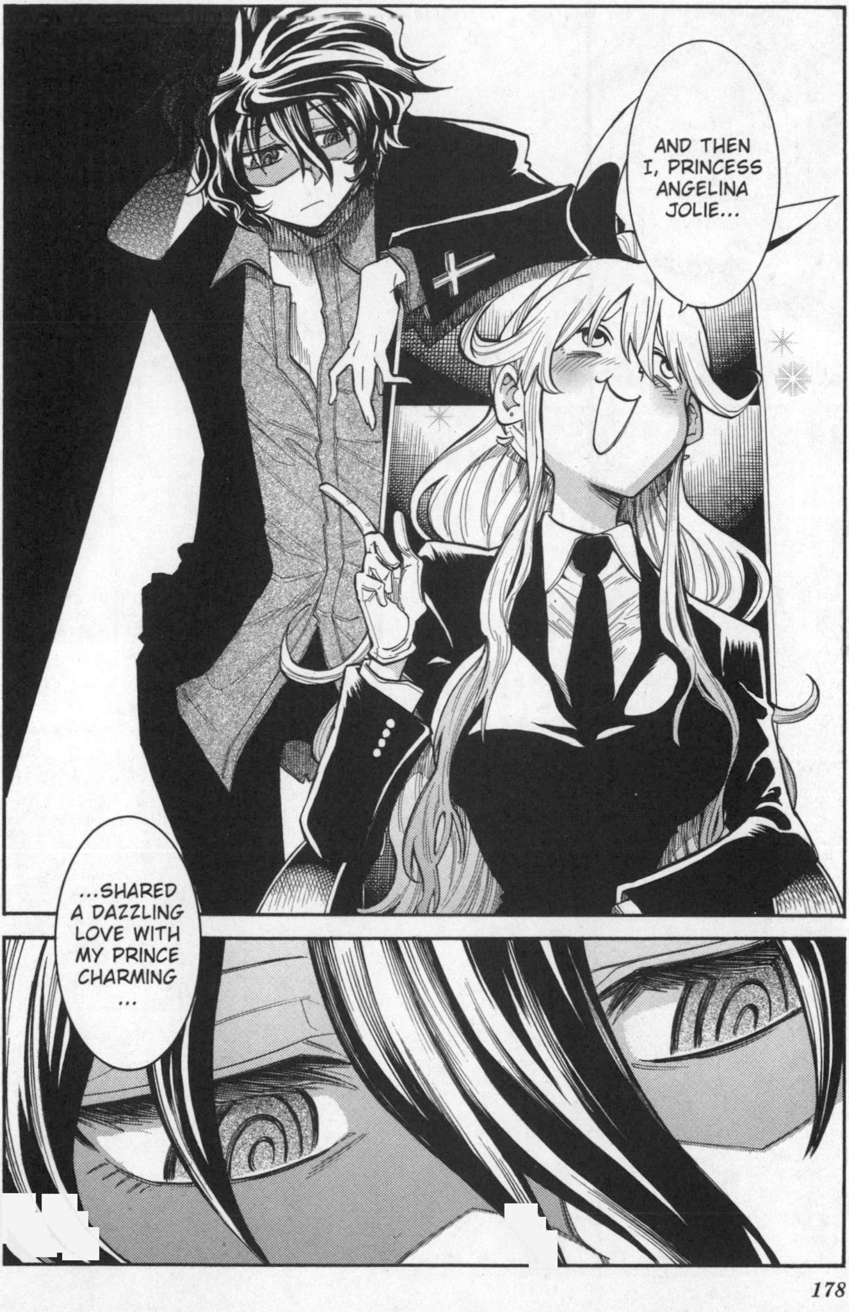
AND THEN I, PRINCESS ANGELINA JOLIE...
...SHARED A DAZZLING LOVE WITH MY PRINCE CHARMING ...

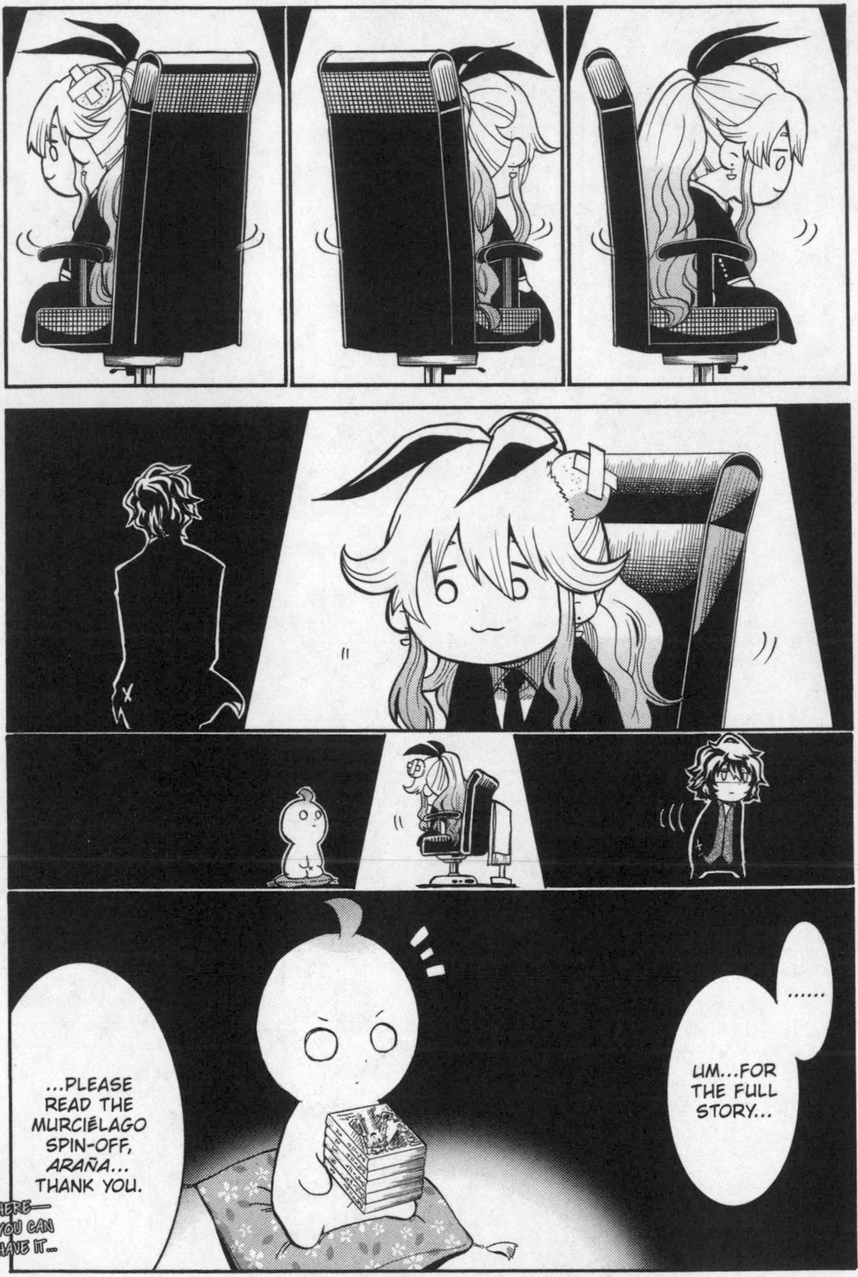
......
UM...FOR THE FULL STORY...
...PLEASE READ THE MURCIÉLAGO SPIN-OFF, *ARAÑA*... THANK YOU.
HERE— YOU CAN HAVE IT...

MURCIÉLAGO 20 THE END

Translation Notes

General

Murciélago is Spanish for "bat."

Suteki is Japanese for "lovely."

Kuroko means "black lake" in Japanese, and is a Cthulhu Mythos reference to the Lake of Hali, where the dark god Hastur dwells.

The city of **Ruruie** is a reference to R'lyeh, a fictional lost city in H. P. Lovecraft's "The Call of Cthulhu."

Page 3
Ohajiki is a traditional Japanese game mainly played by girls that involves flicking flattened pieces of glass, ceramic, or plastic and trying to hit a target.

Page 4
Yamatsukami, which here means "mountain harbor god" but can also be read as "mountain grabber," is a reference to H. P. Lovecraft's novella "At the Mountains of Madness" and the eldritch entity Shoggoth.

Page 46
Tranquilo is the catchphrase of pro wrestler Tetsuya Naito.

Page 118
Exemplary Answer is a reference to mobile-game phenomenon *Uma Musume: Pretty Derby*. The character Sakura Bakushin O gives answers to fan questions in order to help them with the game, and says, "Sakura Exemplary Answer!"

Page 133
Daruma dolls are traditional Japanese dolls rooted in Buddhism, and the stacked variant serves primarily as a game for kids. Players use a small wooden hammer to knock the blocks out from the bottom without toppling the tower itself.

Page 140
Hinako's pose is a reference to *Galileo*, a Japanese TV drama based on a series of novels by mystery writer Keigo Higashino. The main character, Manabu Yukawa, makes this pose after achieving a breakthrough.

Page 176
The art style depicted in this bonus manga is a not-so-subtle nod to *The Rose of Versailles*, a legendary *shoujo* manga set during the time of the French Revolution.

Page 179
Murciélago Araña is a spin-off series that focuses on Reiko Kuchiba. It ended its run at five volumes and is not currently available in English.

Pages 182-193
The volume counts noted for each manga featured are at the time of this volume's Japanese publication, which was in October 2021.

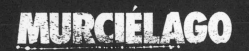

MURCIÉLAGO

Illustration Gallery

Celebrating Volume 20!

Manga creators/illustrators/animators who love
and respect series creator Yoshimurakana-sensei
have drawn original illustrations of *Murciélago*
in commemoration of the 20th volume! Please
enjoy each creator's character illustrations!!

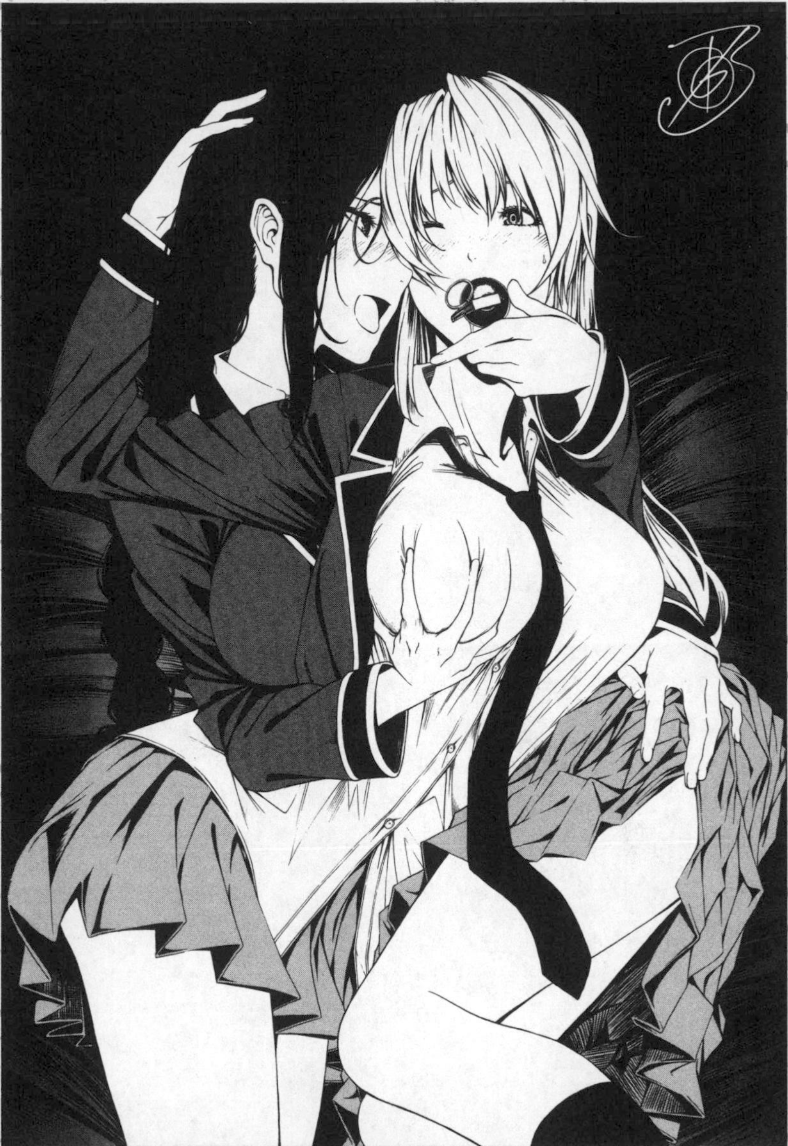

Jun Ogino

His series *Semelparous* is currently running in *Comic Yuri Hime*. To date, three volumes have been released in Japan.

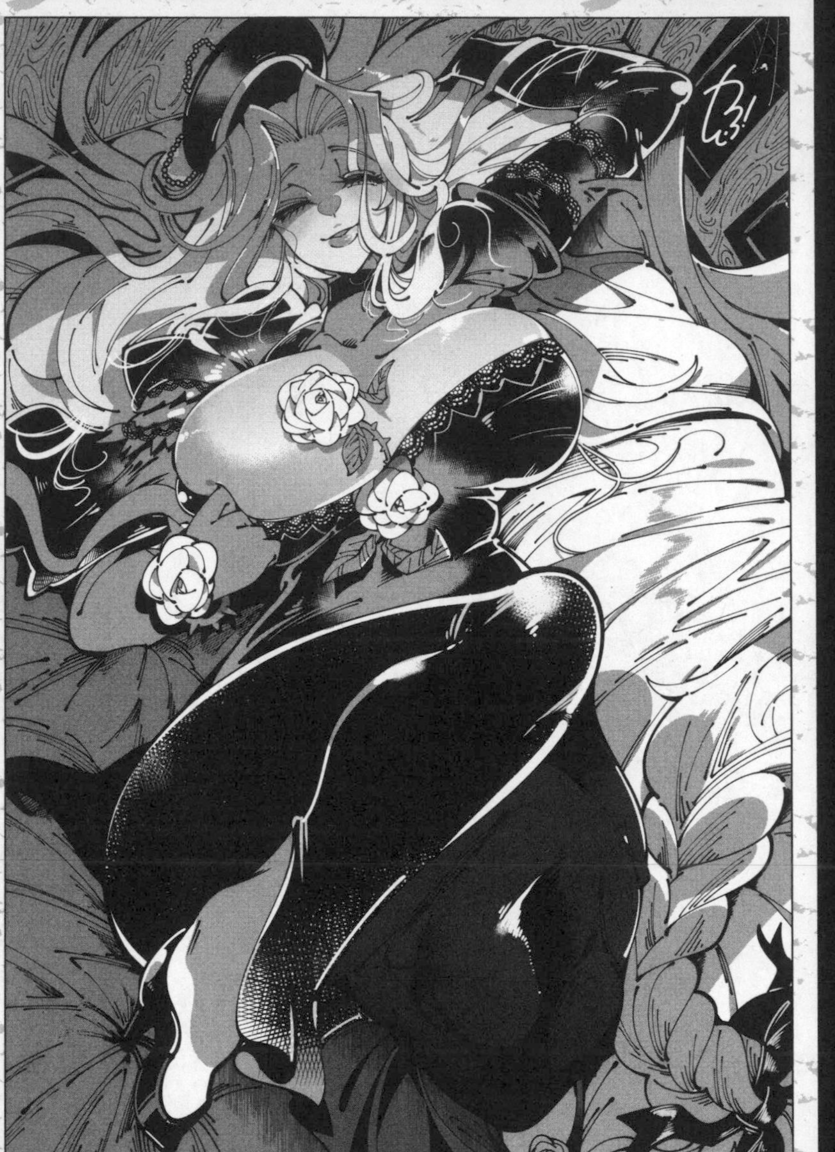

Kafun

Their manga *Kafun Mukashi Banashi*, *Shinsotsu Nana Fushigi*, and *Shinigami! Tahii-chan* are all in Japanese bookstores now.

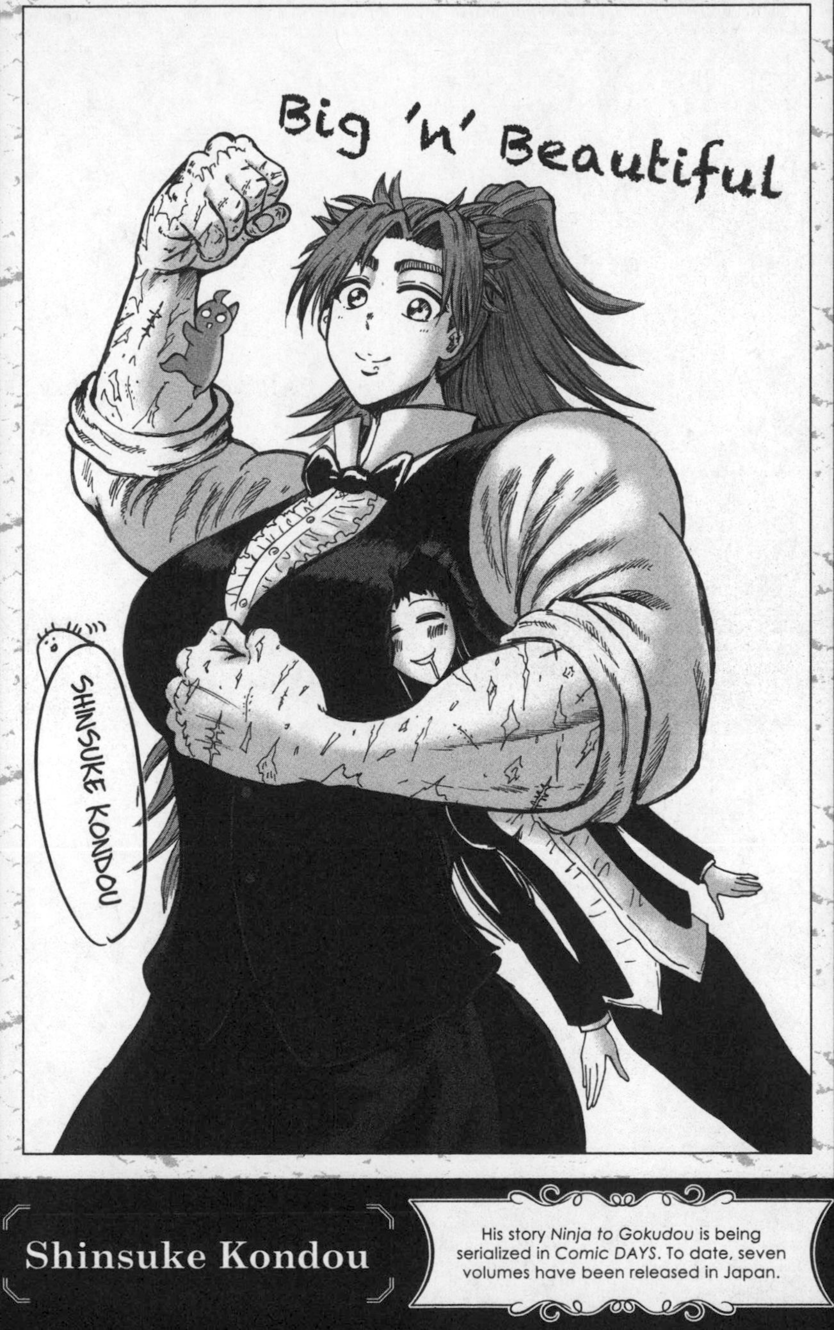
Big 'n' Beautiful
SHINSUKE KONDOU

Shinsuke Kondou

His story *Ninja to Gokudou* is being serialized in *Comic DAYS*. To date, seven volumes have been released in Japan.

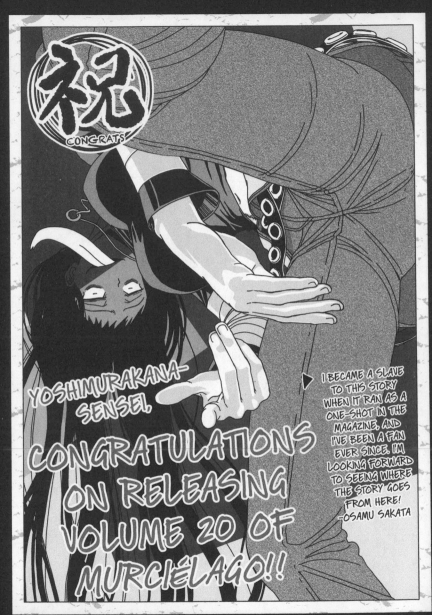

祝
CONGRATS
I BECAME A SLAVE TO THIS STORY WHEN IT RAN AS A ONE-SHOT IN THE MAGAZINE, AND I'VE BEEN A FAN EVER SINCE. I'M LOOKING FORWARD TO SEEING WHERE THE STORY GOES FROM HERE!
-OSAMU SAKATA
YOSHIMURAKANA-SENSEI,
CONGRATULATIONS ON RELEASING VOLUME 20 OF MURCIÉLAGO!!

Osamu Sakata

An animator who did the character design for and is chief animation director of the anime *Dog Days*.

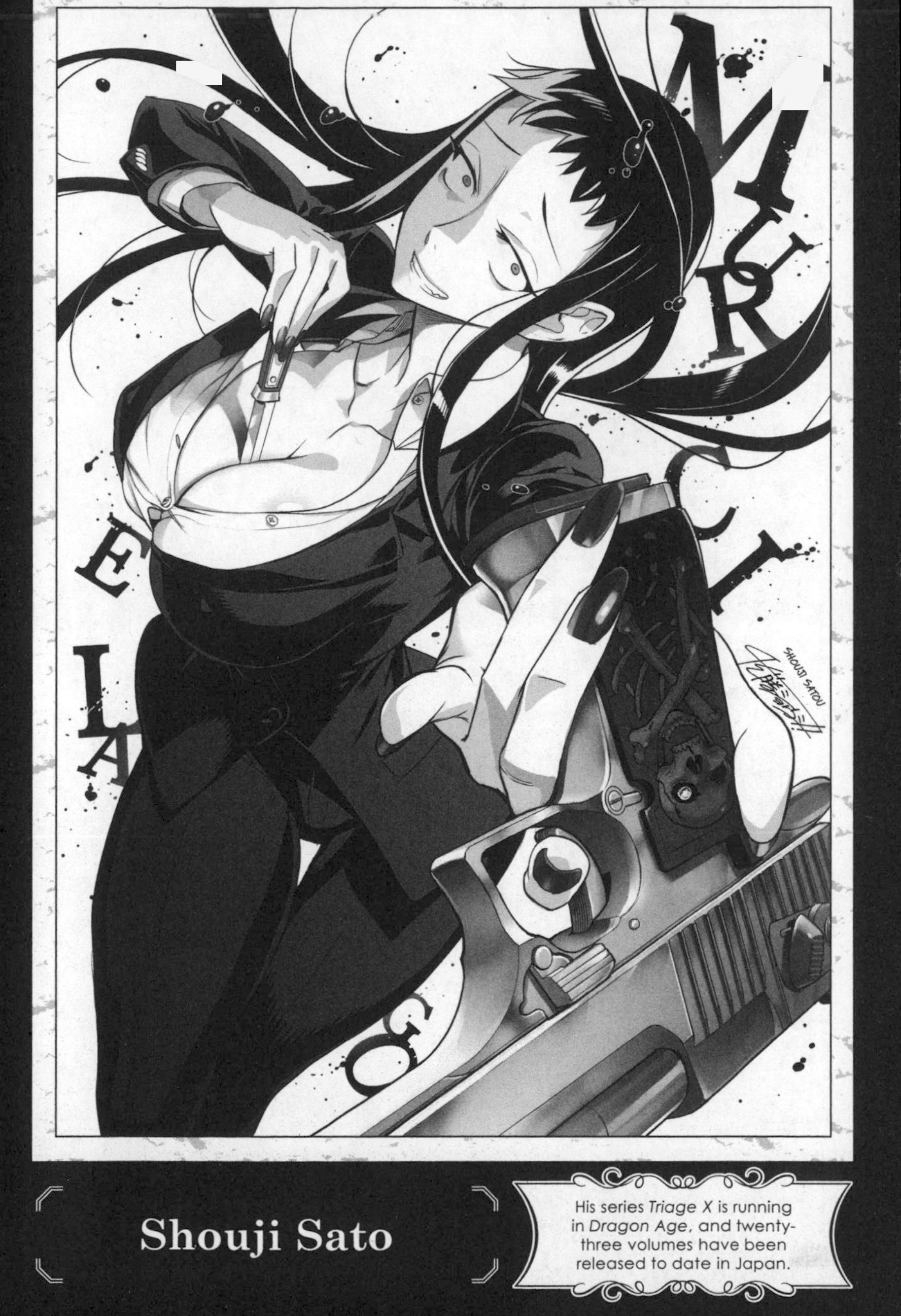
SHOUJI SATOU

Shouji Sato

His series *Triage X* is running in *Dragon Age*, and twenty-three volumes have been released to date in Japan.

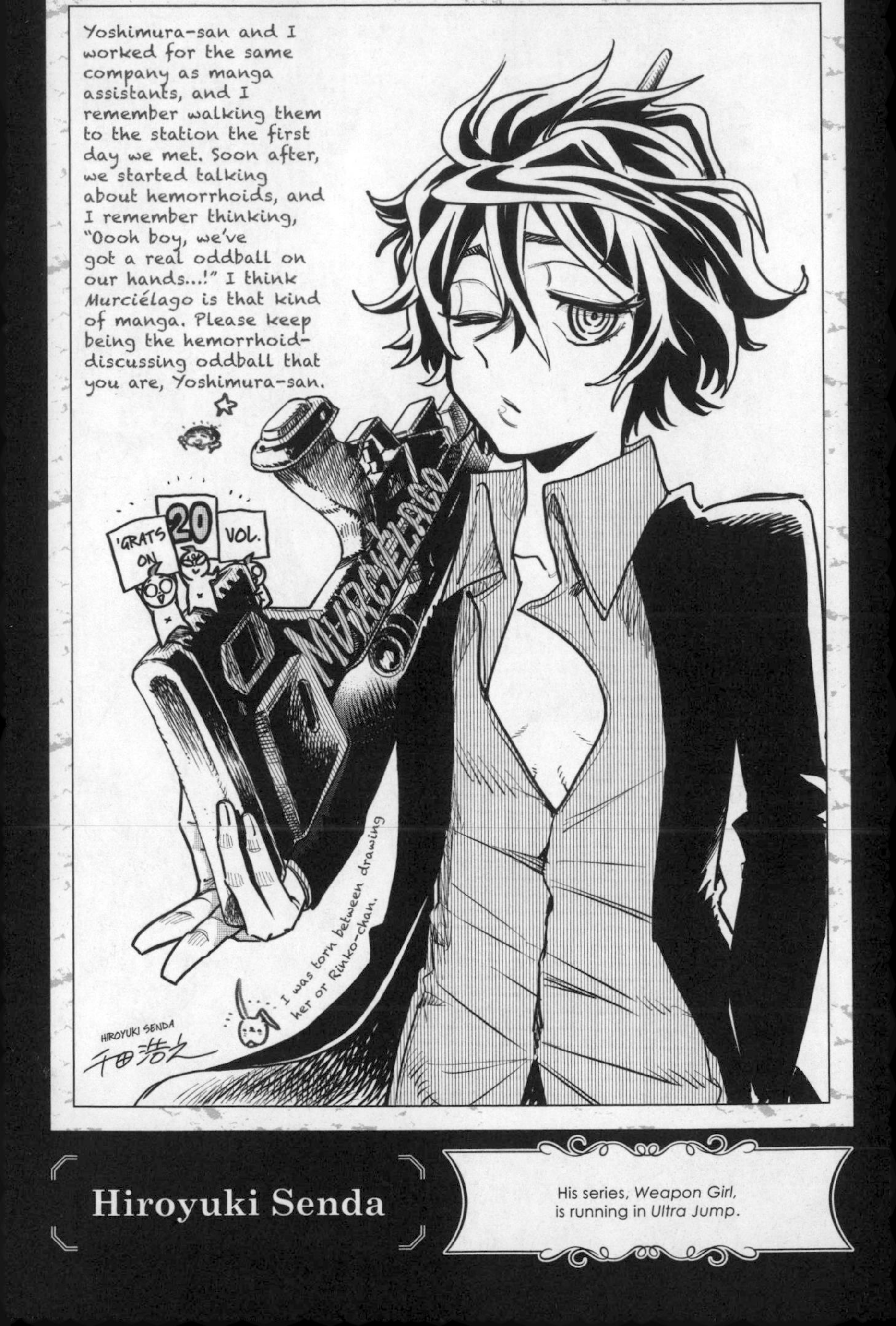
Yoshimura-san and I worked for the same company as manga assistants, and I remember walking them to the station the first day we met. Soon after, we started talking about hemorrhoids, and I remember thinking, "Oooh boy, we've got a real oddball on our hands...!" I think *Murciélago* is that kind of manga. Please keep being the hemorrhoid-discussing oddball that you are, Yoshimura-san.
'GRATS ON
20
VOL.
MURCIELAGO
I was torn between drawing her or Rinko-chan.
HIROYUKI SENDA
千田浩之

Hiroyuki Senda

His series, *Weapon Girl*, is running in *Ultra Jump*.

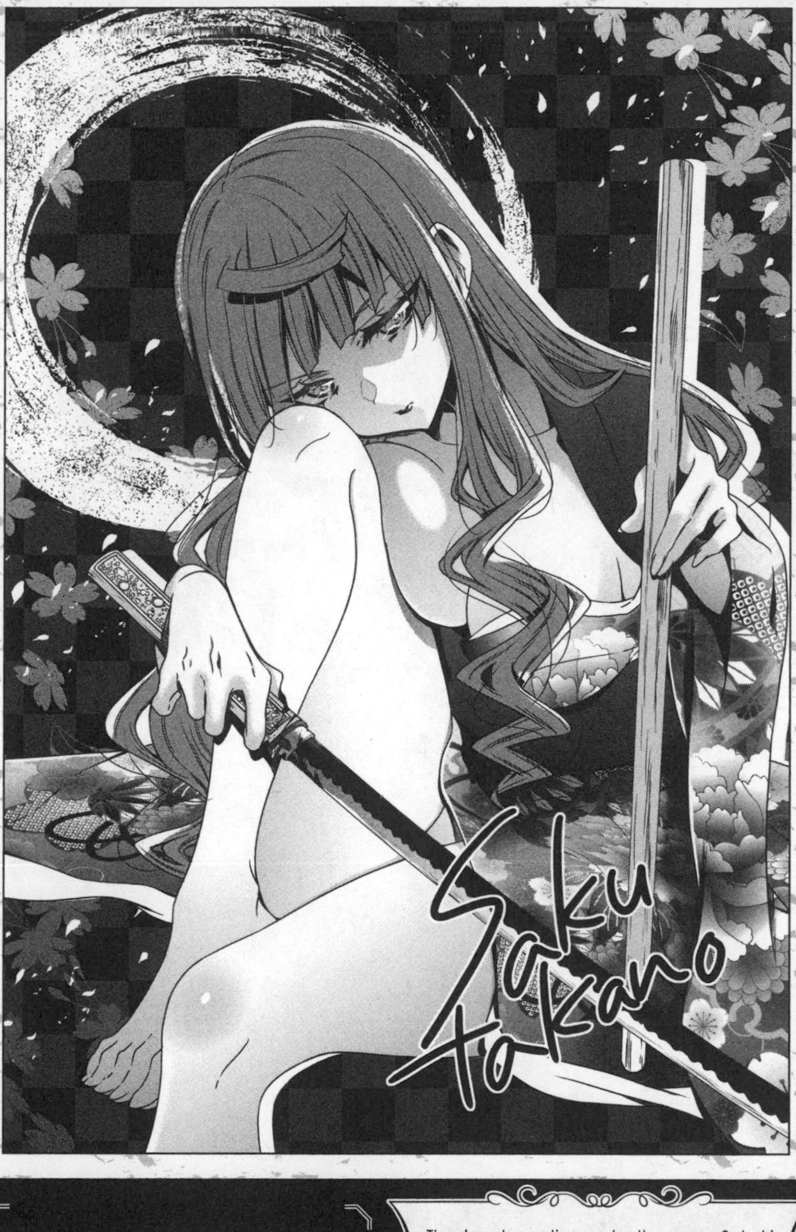
Saku Takano

Saku Takano

They're also active under the name Sakaki Yoshioka. Their manga *WIXOSS DIVA(A) LIVE TRY!!!* is available now in Japan.

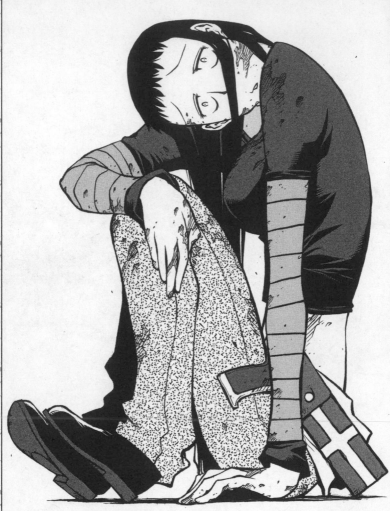

Yasuhiro Nightow

His series *Blood Blockade Battlefront Back 2 Back* is currently serialized in *Jump SQ.RISE*. Nine volumes have been released to date in Japan.

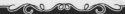

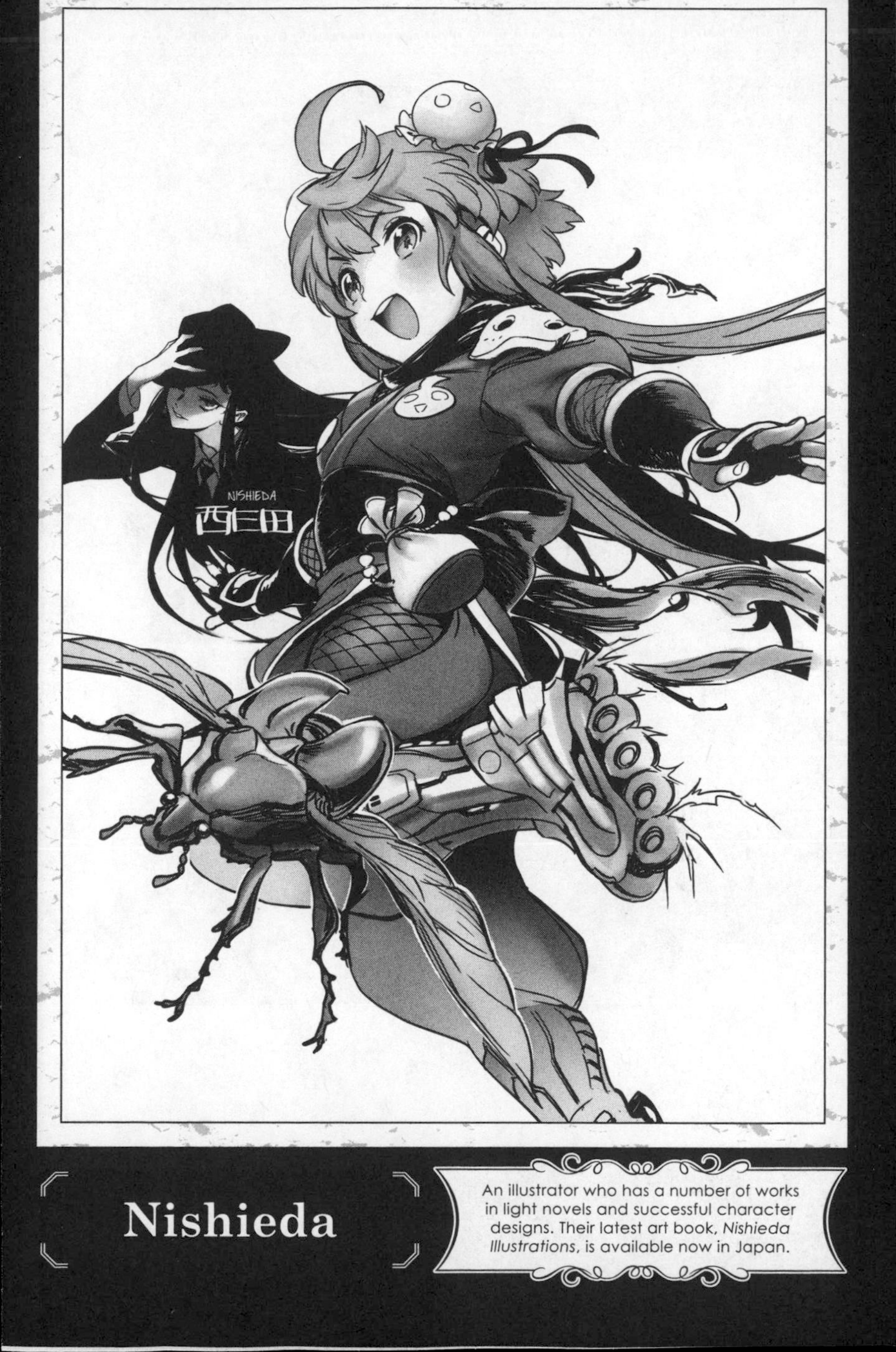
NISHIEDA
西E田

Nishieda

An illustrator who has a number of works in light novels and successful character designs. Their latest art book, *Nishieda Illustrations*, is available now in Japan.

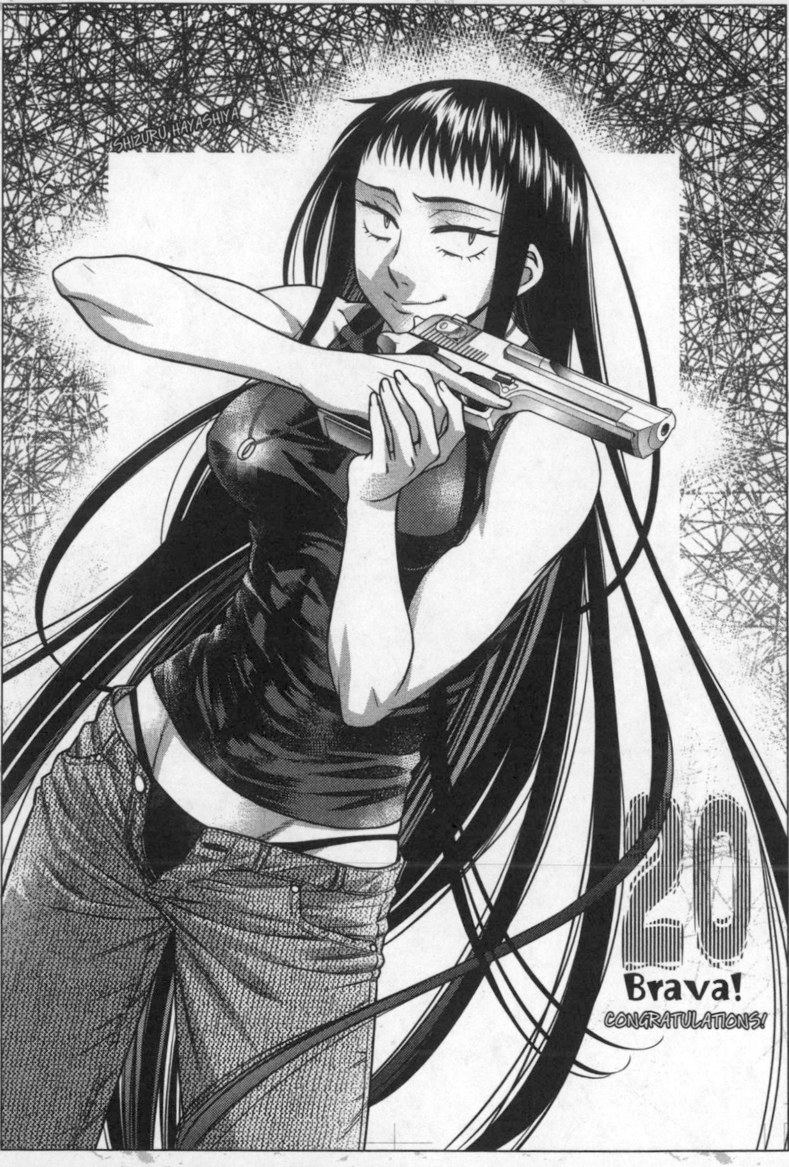
SHIZURU HAYASHIYA
20
Brava!
CONGRATULATIONS!

Shizuru Hayashiya

Her manga series *Hayate x Blade* completed at eighteen volumes, and *Strawberry Shake* and *Shishunki Seimeitai Vega* are also out in Japan.

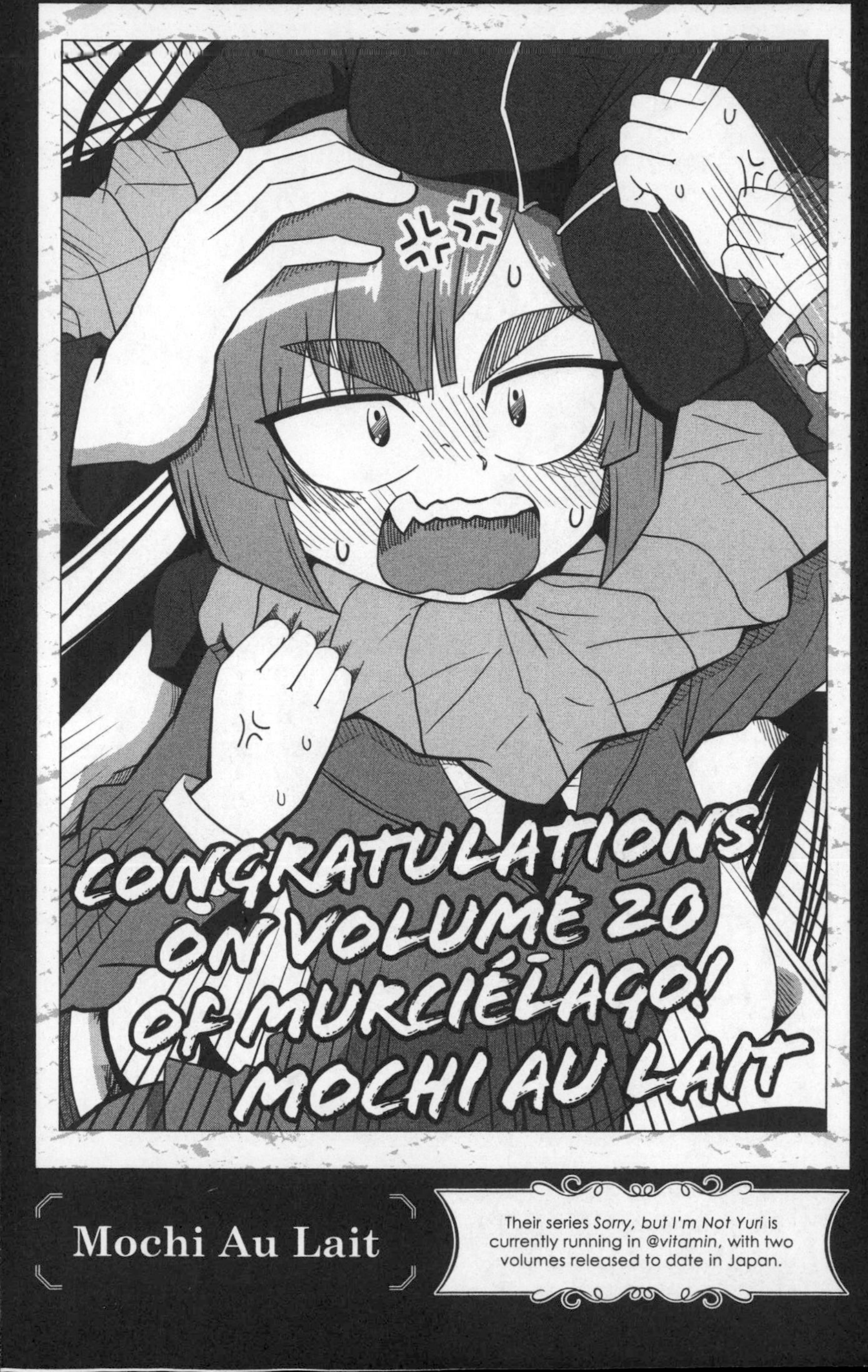
CONGRATULATIONS
ON VOLUME 20
OF MURCIÉLAGO!
MOCHI AU LAIT

Mochi Au Lait

Their series *Sorry, but I'm Not Yuri* is currently running in @vitamin, with two volumes released to date in Japan.

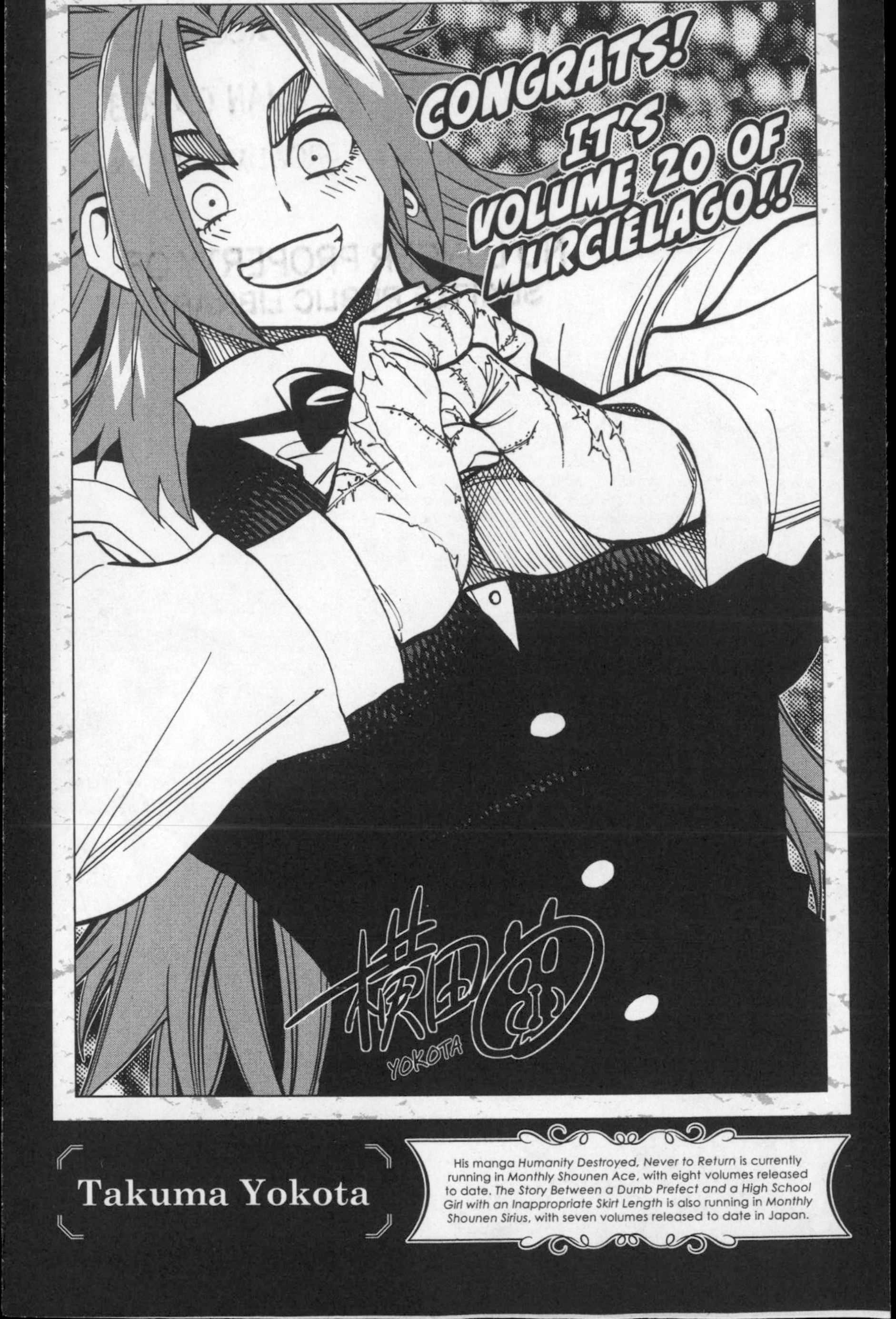
CONGRATS! IT'S VOLUME 20 OF MURCIÉLAGO!!
横田
YOKOTA

Takuma Yokota

His manga *Humanity Destroyed, Never to Return* is currently running in *Monthly Shounen Ace*, with eight volumes released to date. *The Story Between a Dumb Prefect and a High School Girl with an Inappropriate Skirt Length* is also running in *Monthly Shounen Sirius*, with seven volumes released to date in Japan.

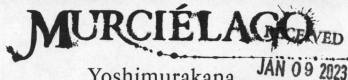

MURCIÉLAGO

Yoshimurakana

Translation: Christine Dashiell ✦ Lettering: Alexis Eckerman

© 2021 Yoshimurakana / SQUARE ENIX CO., LTD.
First published in Japan in 2021 by SQUARE ENIX CO., LTD.
English translation rights arranged with SQUARE ENIX CO., LTD. and Yen Press, LLC
through Tuttle-Mori Agency, Inc.

English translation © 2022 by SQUARE ENIX CO., LTD.

Yen Press
150 West 30th Street, 19th Floor
New York, NY 10001

Visit us at yenpress.com
facebook.com/yenpress
twitter.com/yenpress
yenpress.tumblr.com
instagram.com/yenpress

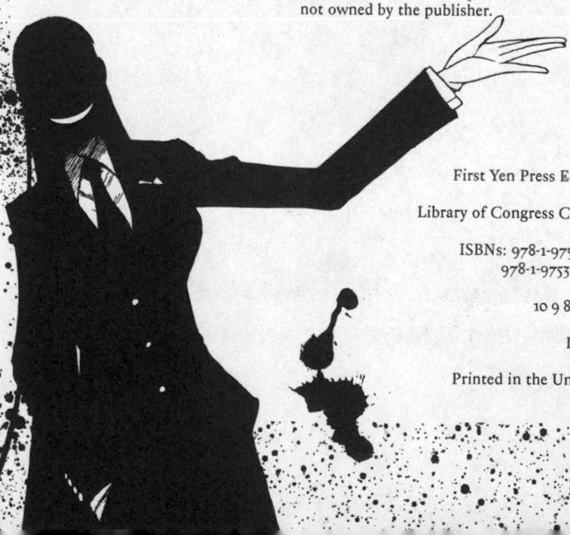

First Yen Press Edition: November 2022

Library of Congress Control Number: 2016958266

ISBNs: 978-1-9753-4970-7 (paperback)
978-1-9753-4971-4 (ebook)

10 9 8 7 6 5 4 3 2 1

LSC-C

Printed in the United States of America

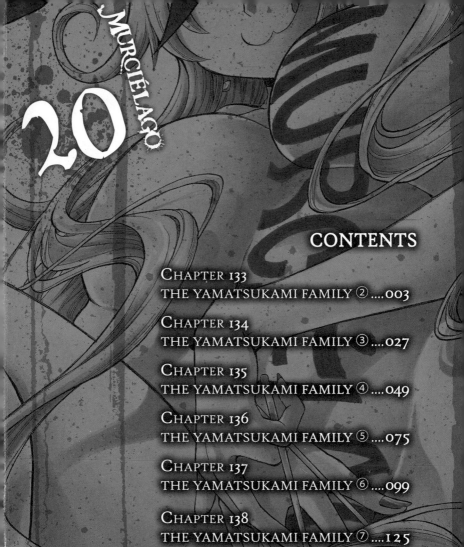

MURCIÉLAGO

20

CONTENTS

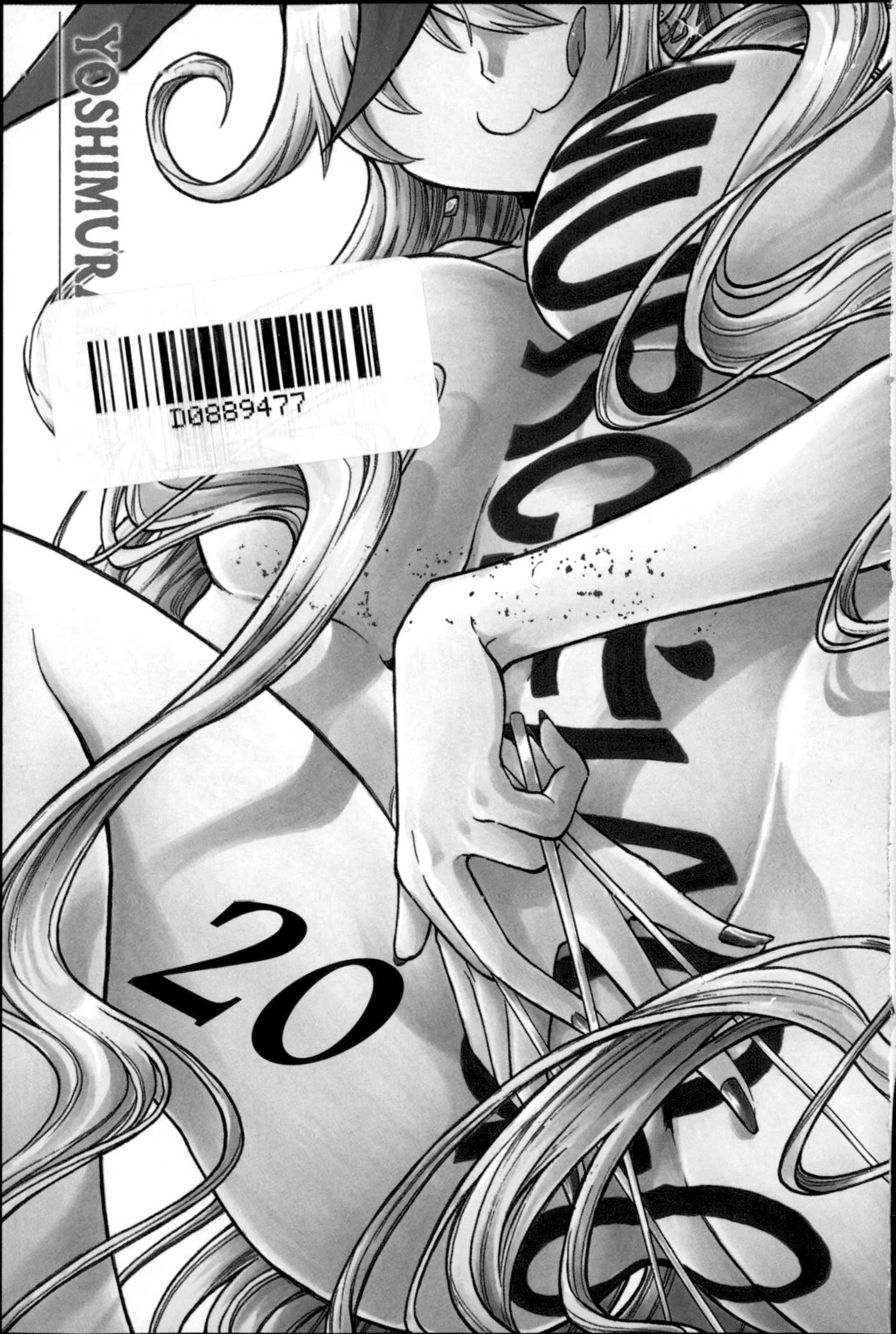
YOSHIMUR
20